María Félix with Rifle, 2002, pencil on two-ply museum board, 30" x 24". This work by Héctor Silva depicts
María Félix in a role as an extraordinarily effective female leader in the Mexican Revolution of 1910.

The Cisco Kid (right) and his rival, Sgt. Mickey Dunn, as played by Warner Baxter and Edmund Lowe in *The Cisco Kid* (1931)

The Cisco Kid

AMERICAN HERO, HISPANIC ROOTS

Bilingual Press/Editorial Bilingüe

Publisher
   Gary D. Keller

Executive Editor
   Karen S. Van Hooft

Associate Editors
   Adriana M. Brady
   Brian Ellis Cassity
   Amy K. Phillips
   Linda K. St. George

Project Team
   Jo Ann Briseño
   Brian Ellis Cassity
   Melanie Magisos
   Amy K. Phillips
   Linda K. St. George
   Karen S. Van Hooft

Additional Project Staff
   Alexis R. Cabrera
   Derrick J. Cohan
   Armando Espinoza, Jr.
   Jovan Espinoza
   Jordan M. Lake
   Daniel Martínez
   Raúl A. Martínez
   Brandon M. Ortega
   Julie Wagoner
   Amber Workman

Address
   Bilingual Press
   Hispanic Research Center
   Arizona State University
   PO Box 875303
   Tempe, Arizona 85287-5303
   (480) 965-3867

The Cisco Kid

AMERICAN HERO, HISPANIC ROOTS

FRANCIS M. NEVINS

&

GARY D. KELLER

PHOTOGRAPHERS

CRAIG SMITH • TOM STORY • MARILYN SZABO

Bilingual Press/Editorial Bilingüe

TEMPE, ARIZONA

Library of Congress Cataloging-in-Publication Data

Nevins, Francis M.
    The Cisco Kid : American hero, Hispanic roots / Francis M. Nevins and Gary D. Keller ; Craig Smith, Tom Story, and Marilyn Szabo, photographers.
        p. cm.
    Rev. ed. of: The films of the Cisco Kid . 1998.
    Includes filmography and index.
    ISBN-13: 978-1-931010-48-1 (hardcover : alk. paper)
    ISBN-10: 1-931010-48-X (hardcover : alk. paper)
    ISBN-13: 978-1-931010-49-8 (softcover : alk. paper)
    ISBN-10: 1-931010-49-8 (softcover : alk. paper)
1. Cisco Kid films—History and criticism.   2. Cisco Kid (Television program)—History and criticism.   I. Keller, Gary D.   II. Nevins, Francis M. Films of the Cisco Kid . 1998.   III. Title.
    PN1995.9.C5125N48 2008
    791.43'651—dc22
                                                    2007029884

Printed in China by Everbest Printing Co. through Four Colour Imports, Ltd.

Cover and interior design by John Wincek, Aerocraft Charter Art Service
Front cover art: Joe Ray, El Cisco Kid 2, *2000*

From your good amigo
Duncan Renaldo
Cisco Kid

Autographed publicity photo of Duncan Renaldo as the Cisco Kid

Best wishes from "Pancho" Leo Carrillo

Publicity photo autographed by Leo Carrillo, who played opposite Duncan Renaldo as the Cisco Kid's sidekick Pancho

CONTENTS

INTRODUCTIONS

The Cisco Kid: American Hero, Hispanic Roots XI

The Films of the Cisco Kid (1998) XIII

1 THE CISCO KID IN CONTEXT 1

2 O. HENRY, FATHER OF ALL CISCOS 21

3 CISCO IN THE SILENTS 29

4 CISCO TALKS: WARNER BAXTER 35

5 LOS OTROS CABALLEROS: A PANORAMA
OF LATIN-THEMED WESTERNS 57

6 CISCO OLD AND NEW: WARNER BAXTER AND CÉSAR ROMERO 69

7 DUNCAN RENALDO ENTERS 107

8 RIDE, AMIGOS, RIDE: GILBERT ROLAND TAKES OVER 127

9 DUNCAN RENALDO RETURNS 145

10 LEZWENT! CISCO ON THE SMALL SCREEN 169

11 CISCO DISCOVERS HIS ETHNIC SELF: JIMMY SMITS 185

12 THE CISCO KID FROM BAD GRINGO TO U.S. HISPANIC HERO 191

THE CISCO KID FEATURE AND TV FILMOGRAPHY

I Feature Films 229

II The Cisco Kid TV Series 237

Index 254

Bibliography: see http://noblebandits.asu.edu/ciscobook

Warner Baxter as the Cisco Kid in *The Return of the Cisco Kid* (1939)

THE CISCO KID: AMERICAN HERO, HISPANIC ROOTS

In 1998 Francis M. Nevins published a unique and enduring book, *The Films of The Cisco Kid*. Nevins's work is a thorough, chronologically ordered study of the filmic Cisco Kid cycle, and it provides us with in-depth information about the Cisco phenomenon. All of this information has been retained in the current book.

This 2007 version of the book expands the level of understanding of the Cisco Kid to include dimensions of its content that speak to the bilingual-bicultural person who is knowledgeable about Hispanic culture. This version is newly titled *The Cisco Kid: American Hero, Hispanic Roots*. The new title adds a Hispanic orientation to the history of the character in U.S. film and directs our attention to the fact that, despite the Cisco Kid's initial creation outside the Hispanic world by such mainstream writers and filmmakers as O. Henry and Webster Cullison (director of *The Caballero's Way*, Éclair, 1914), by 1929 with the first Cisco sound film, *In Old Arizona*, this fictional character was endowed with a Latino persona that it has invariably retained both in mainstream American culture and Hispanic culture within the United States and elsewhere.

The Cisco Kid is not the only example of Anglo-Mexican/other Latino cross-cultural hybridization in the character development of Hispanic fictional characters, historical figures, pseudo-historical figures, or composites. A host of both fictional personages and actual historically traceable figures with a range of grounding in fact have been elaborated creatively in this American-Mexican or other Latin manner, even by the Chilean Nobel laureate Pablo Neruda in his play *Joaquín Murrieta*. In the domain of fiction, film, and folklore, examples include Zorro, Don Q, the Arizona Kid, and Don Daredevil, as well as their female counterparts Daughter of Don Q, Lasca of the Rio Grande, Lady Robinhood, and Anita Delgado, the Avenging Arrow. With respect to historical, pseudo-historical, and composite figures, there are, to name a few, Joaquín Murrieta, Tiburcio Vásquez, Gregorio Cortez, Francisco "Pancho" Villa, and Emiliano Zapata along with their female counterparts Teresita Urrea, Coronela María de la Luz Espinosa Barrera, Margarita Neri, Margarita Ortega, and Beatriz González Ortega. In fact, intrigued by our review of personages including the Cisco Kid, Zorro, and Joaquín Murrieta, the Hispanic Research Center of Arizona State University has conceptualized and announced a major long-term multimedia project entitled Bold Caballeros and Noble Bandidas: The Good, the Bad, the Beautiful. We have invited collaborators to work with us on all aspects of the project.

BRIEF PROJECT OVERVIEW

This project focuses on Latina/o noble bandits in Iberoamerican culture (Spain, Latin America, the United States, and elsewhere), but it does so in a broad and generous way and thus provides, to a lesser degree, textual and visual information on banditry in antiquity and in other nations and cultures, including the Far East, the Middle East, Oceania, Africa, Europe, and elsewhere. We expect the project to run for decades and to undergo extensive development by a national and worldwide community interested in noble bandits in popular culture as well as in the related social science construct of "social banditry."

Project Initiatives and Product Development

This open-ended project is expected to produce the following initiatives and products:

- Web site. The Web site recently went online. It is still in its initial stages, but with the help of many participants it will continue to develop over months and years. The site is at http://noblebandits.asu.edu. It includes an introduction that interested collaborators will find useful, as well as a chronology of noble bandits/social bandits, numerous specific entries, and dozens of clips of relevant films.

- See the following URL for the bibliography of this book, Francis M. Nevins and Gary D.

Keller, *The Cisco Kid: American Hero, Hispanic Roots:* http://noble bandits.asu.edu/ciscobook.

■ A full-color, large-format book with the provisional title *Bold Caballeros and Noble Bandidas: The Good, the Bad, the Beautiful.* The project is committed to producing an outstanding and exceptionally attractive book. A few sample pages have been designed, which can be seen at http://noblebandit.asu.edu/Pages/.

■ A second full-color, large-format book scheduled for publication in 2010 to commemorate the centenary of the Mexican Revolution of 1910. The tentative title of this book is *The Mexican Revolution of 1910 and Its Cultural Legacy.* Visit http://latinoartcommunity.org/community/Gallery/1910/index/html for an exhibition being developed on this subject.

■ A DVD-ROM that will augment the Bold Caballeros book. The book itself will privilege images (photographs, artwork, posters, film stills, etc.). The DVD-ROM, scheduled for release in early 2009, will contain numerous essays, shorter entries, and thousands of additional images that could not possibly fit in a book on the general topic of noble and base bandits and particularly those from the Latina/o community worldwide.

■ One or more video DVDs that will anthologize films relevant to the project that are either in the public domain or for which permissions are available at reasonable costs. This will include films or film clips of the Cisco Kid.

Contacting and/or Obtaining Information About the Project

We invite interested individuals to participate in the project in one or more ways. Please contact us (information is below) with your ideas and interests. The easiest way to do this, if convenient for you, would be through e-mail. Additionally, the project uses the following membership groups: http://groups.google.com/group/bold-caballeros, and http://groups.yahoo.com/group/boldcab.

If you are interested in collaborating on this project contact:

Gary D. Keller, Regents' Professor
Hispanic Research Center
Arizona State University
PO Box 875303
Tempe, AZ 85287-5303

E-mail: gary.keller@asu.edu
Fax: 480-965-0315
General HRC telephone: 480-965-3990
Web site: http://www.asu.edu/clas/hrc/

Editorial Note

Film scholarship on Hispanic-related topics presents a special challenge with respect to the spelling of film professionals' names and the use of accents and other diacritical marks on Spanish proper nouns in general. Common U.S. practice has been to eliminate all diacritical marks in the titles of films and the names of actors and others, and little attention has been paid to consistency of spelling. This has resulted in profound variations in the spelling of Spanish names and other terms, and many of these variations were sanctioned or even initiated by the individuals themselves. Thus, in film materials, including scholarly works, the reader will find the name Soledad Jiménez spelled "Soledad Jiminez," "Solidad Jimines," "Saledad Jeminez," and numerous other variants. "Raúl Juliá," the standard spelling of the actor's name and the one normally used in Puerto Rico, was abandoned in U.S. usage—even by the actor himself—in favor of "Raul Julia."

Following this practice would violate the standards that the Bilingual Press/Editorial Bilingüe has maintained in the publication of all its previous books. Thus our practice in this book is to spell and use accents according to standard Spanish usage where feasible unless the individual has requested or is known to prefer otherwise, and we restore the accents in those cases where it is no longer possible to determine the wishes of the person in question.

A case in point: the editors have rectified misspellings of Joaquín Murrieta, which have included such variations as "Murieta" and "Murietta," wherever practical (the latter includes a consonant combination [tt] that is nonexistent in Spanish), but we have not changed the name in titles of films or other works.

Similarly, U.S. film scholarship related to Hispanic topics utilizes a number of mock Spanish terms that do not conform to the morphology of that language. The most notable examples are *federale* and *bandito* (the latter does happen to be standard Italian). Where feasible we have changed these to standard Spanish *federal* (pl. *federales*) and *bandido/a* (pl. *bandidos/as*). See chapter 12 for more discussion of mock Spanish.

THE FILMS OF THE CISCO KID (1998)

On the East Coast in the early 1950s when I was growing up, we had seven channels' worth of television programming to choose from and precious little on any of them except Westerns. If I had a dollar today for every hour of my childhood and early teens that I spent hunched in front of the 12½-inch screen soaking up old 60-minute B Western features and new 30-minute TV series in the same vein—well, I'd have a nice pile of dollars. Books have been written about lots of those pictures but none until now about the screen adventures of the Cisco Kid, so I decided it was time.

The Films of the Cisco Kid follows more or less the same format as my earlier book *The Films of Hopalong Cassidy* (1988), but there are some differences. Both the Cassidy character and the Cisco character first came to life in short stories written only a few years after the beginning of the twentieth century. But Clarence E. Mulford continued writing stories and novels about Cassidy until 1941: so many stories and novels, with such complex interconnections, that it took me a whole separate book to do justice to them. (That book, *Bar-20: The Life of Clarence E. Mulford, Creator of Hopalong Cassidy*, was published by McFarland & Co. in 1993.) The Cisco Kid, on the other hand, appeared in just one story, O. Henry's "The Caballero's Way" (1907), which I've included in chapter 2 of this book. The transformation of Cisco from his original incarnation into the hero of movies and TV was even more radical than the transformation of Mulford's Cas-

sidy character. Mulford lived long enough to make a sort of retirement hobby out of ridiculing what the Hollywood types had done to his knight of the frontier. O. Henry died young and never saw his creation on the screen, but I doubt he would have been pleased if he had.

Hopalong Cassidy was the hero of movies and TV episodes for exactly twenty years, from 1935 through 1954, during which he was portrayed by one man, William Boyd. The Cisco character showed up on large and small screens for just over eighty years, from 1914 through 1994, and was played by either seven or eight actors (depending on how you classify the 1917 feature *Betrayed*, which we'll discuss in chapter 3). Not only was each portrayal different from the others, but the best known of the screen Ciscos played the role in three different ways. If *The Films of the Cisco Kid* seems to be a looser, less unified book than *The Films of Hopalong Cassidy*, this is the reason why. But I hope it's just as enjoyable and informative as the Cassidy book and, knowing the publishers as I do, I'm sure it will be just as stunning visually.

I owe deep thanks to many people who helped but especially to Maris Allen, Pamela Boyer, Robert E. Briney, Bill Catching, Mary Dougherty, the late William K. Everson, Will Hutchins, Paul Landres, John Langellier, Boyd Magers, the late Troy Melton, William Nadel, Milton and Sharon Obrock, Mark Rudman, Sondra Schol, Anthony Tollin, Jon Tuska, and Nick Williams. ¡Muchas gracias, amigas y amigos!

Francis M. Nevins

ST. LOUIS, MISSOURI
SEPTEMBER 1996

Paul Landres (1912-2001), who directed many of the best episodes of the Cisco Kid TV series, shown here with Stanley Clements (back to camera) and a camera crew on the set of *Army Bound* (Monogram, 1952)

Bill Catching (1926–2007, pictured here) and Paul Landres were important to the Cisco Kid cycle. Catching was a stunt double and also played some minor roles.

Landres (on ladder) with Clint Walker and some of the cast and crew of the *Cheyenne* episode "Cross Purpose." Photo taken May 18, 1961

ONE, TWO . . .
MANY NOBLE BANDITS

It is interesting to evaluate the Cisco Kid—and other noble and ignoble bandits identified by the Arizona State University multimedia project—along the axis of good and evil. The overall project performs this sort of taxonomy of the bandits, especially the fictional ones and even the historical ones to the extent (and it has been a great extent) that they have been fictionalized. We have found that these larger-than-life figures can be categorized, for heuristic purposes, as taxa in a matrix ranging from simply and awesomely good through various gradations of good-bad to simply and irredeemably bad. Some examples follow that are covered in depth in the larger project.

The conventional American Western was straightforward in its depiction of good and bad. The good cowboys wore white hats, shot straight, and practiced a sort of gallantry that in a different and "fallen" Spanish seventeenth century (fallen with respect to chivalric standards) Don Quixote attempted to recover. The bad cowboys wore black hats, were lousy shots, and were cheats—often shrewd, lewd, and cynical ones. Nevertheless, there was always a subgenre of the Western that amalgamated the good and the bad within the same cowboy and occasionally cowgirl, and in both the literary and historical interpretation of noncowboy bandits who struggled against authority, good-bad has been the gold standard. Even Robin Hood, often the good-good exception, has partaken of the

good-bad lode, as in *Robin and Marian* (1976, starring Sean Connery), in which Robin's wanderlust drives Maid Marian first to desperation, then to a nunnery, and finally to mercy killing. It would appear that in popular culture, depictions of struggles by outsiders against the authority of the state reflect an important paradoxical phenomenon, which St. Augustine succinctly summarized in his *De civitate Dei* (*City of God*, 4.4):

> Take away justice, then, and what are governments but great bandit bands? And after all, what are bands of bandits but small states? The gang itself consists of men, it is directed by the authority of the chief, it is bound together by a pact of mutual support, and the loot is divided in accordance with an agreed law. If, as a result of the recruitment of desperadoes, this evil grows to such an extent that it takes control of a territory, establishes bases, occupies cities and subjugates peoples, then it assumes the name of a government, the more openly because this is now plainly applicable: not because the robbers have renounced their rapacity, but because they are no longer at risk of punishment.

St. Augustine goes on to illustrate this paradox with the reply that a captured pirate made to Alexander the Great, which St. Augustine considered apposite and legitimate. When the ruler asked the man how he could justify making the sea a dangerous place, he answered with defiant outspokenness,

1

The characters in *The Wild Bunch* (1969) ranged from irredeemably evil through various gradations of good-bad. This image features Jaime Sánchez (second from left), Ernest Borgnine, William Holden, Ben Johnson, Rayford Barnes, and Warren Oates in the foreground.

"In exactly the way that you justify doing the same to the whole world. But because I do it with a single paltry ship, I am called a robber; while you do it with a large navy, and are called an emperor."

The Cisco Kid during different periods of his depiction has been alternately bad, good, and good-bad. He was bad with just a touch of Latin redeeming generosity in his portrayal by Warner Baxter in *In Old Arizona*. He was good in a manner evoking a highly effective, virile protector of the oppressed, respectful of señoritas in the manner of Don Quixote, during the Duncan Renaldo and Leo Carrillo period. He was a good-bad do-gooder during the Gilbert Roland cycle.

With respect to the first Cisco Kid talkie, the character is far from good in any conventional sense. He has a certain Latin sense of honor (the origin story of Cisco in the Warner Baxter and César Romero era is that his father was Portuguese and his mother was born in San Luis Obispo), since he refuses to steal the passengers' money when he holds up a stagecoach and takes its strongbox. That's about all on the good side of the ledger. He steals cattle, kills other evildoers who are out to steal his ill-gotten money, has plenty of sex with Tonia, and fulfills the denouement of O. Henry's story "The Caballero's Way" by successfully conspiring to have her Anglo lover, Sergeant Dunn, kill her when the latter mistakes her for Cisco.

Cisco as played by Duncan Renaldo is a lighthearted, clean-cut hero who is frequently mistaken for a bandit but is instead a carefree adventurer whose exploits generally center on his ardor for beautiful señoritas. Despite this key motivation, in seven films

Renaldo's Cisco kisses a woman only once, in *The Daring Adventurer*, as his gentlemanly code of conduct means that he habitually restricts himself to courtly praise of female beauty. One line specifically is repeated throughout the films: "You are the most beautiful señorita in all the world. On my heart, I swear it." The films are fast-paced and comedic, with Pancho, Cisco's sidekick, providing much of the humor. As Professor Nevins points out in his chapters dedicated to Duncan Renaldo, both he and Leo Carrillo make a conscious effort to emulate the characters of Don Quixote and Sancho Panza, but without the feebleness and without most of the human frailties.

Gilbert Roland's Cisco is a much earthier character. In contrast to Renaldo's perfectly turned out, pure, and gentlemanly character, Roland's Cisco is more in the mold of a traditional Western gunslinger. He is undoubtedly a bandit, albeit a Robin Hood whose motives are above reproach, and he constantly smokes and drinks tequila. He is also far less proper in his advances toward women, whom he courts far more directly than his predecessor. Renaldo's oft-repeated flirtation is mirrored in this Cisco's penchant for presenting the ladies he admires with necklaces. Moreover, this series is far removed from the "buddy" style model of the Renaldo series. Although this Cisco does have a sidekick, they are seldom together on-screen, and they both travel with a large group of men. Let us then put the Ciscos into the matrix along with other characters.

GOOD

The Cisco Kid as played by Duncan Renaldo

Zorro as played by Douglas Fairbanks, Sr.

Lady Robinhood (1925) as played by Evelyn Brent

Anita Delgado, the Avenging Arrow, as played by Ruth Roland in a Pathé serial in 1921

Don José as played by Chano Urueta in *The Wild Bunch* (1969, director Sam Peckinpah)

GOOD-BAD

(ranked in suggested order of goodness)

The Cisco Kid as played by Gilbert Roland

Ángel as played by Jaime Sánchez in *The Wild Bunch*

The character Passin' Through as played by Douglas Fairbanks in *The Good Bad Man* (1916, director Allan Dwan)

Characters played by Charles Bickford, Raymond Hatton, Fred Kohler, and Joe de la Cruz in *Hell's Heroes* (1930, director William Wyler)

Characters played by William Holden, Ernest Borgnine, and others in *The Wild Bunch*

BAD

The Cisco Kid as played by Warner Baxter in *In Old Arizona* (1929)

General Mapache as played by Emilio "El Indio" Fernández in *The Wild Bunch*

Gold Hat as played by Alfonso Bedoya in *Treasure of the Sierra Madre* (1948, director John Huston)

Sam Peckinpah's *The Wild Bunch* provides an additional wide spectrum of characters useful for validating this matrix. At the top of the heap is Don José, played by Mexican director Chano Urueta, known for a host of films including a number of Blue Demon wrestling movies. Don José and the other villagers, dressed in white campesino clothes, are deserving and brave, but oppressed and without weapons to arm themselves. When they obtain these weapons, they use them for good purposes. The best of the good-bad men is Ángel. Fulfilling his name, Ángel is a fallen angel trying to reform himself, especially in his efforts to help the villagers where he was born, but he is a victim of Latino passions, particularly involving the opposite sex. The characters played by William Holden and Ernest

Jaime Sánchez plays Ángel in a scene from *The Wild Bunch*.

Alfonso Bedoya (left) as the Mexican bandit Gold Hat in *The Treasure of the Sierra Madre*, also starring Humphrey Bogart (right)

Borgnine, respectively Pike Bishop and Dutch Engstrom, are very bad hombres. But in one final paroxysm of fury, they cleanse and redeem themselves by aiding the villagers, killing Mapache, and routing the *federales* who are in the service of Mexican national traitor General Victoriano Huerta. At the bottom of the heap is General Mapache, played by world-renowned director and occasional actor Emilio "El Indio" Fernández. He is totally, irredeemably bad—a drunk, sadist, murderer, and lecher. Mapache, to use a category borrowed from Dungeons and Dragons, incarnates lawful evil while Alfonso Bedoya as Gold Hat represents chaotic evil.

The Cisco Kid, who we know has been one of the most enduring bandits of the Wild West and who has been, alternately, bad, good, and good-bad, is paradigmatic for this overall multimedia project, which represents a broad and extended commitment to the study of Latina/o noble bandits, and for that matter, for the purposes of contrast, base bandits as well. The story of how the book that is before you came into existence is worth telling, and doing so brings into perspective the sustained commitment of our project in the form of publication, outreach, instruction, and the fostering of further research on noble bandidas and bandidos that we will pursue for years and decades to come. How this book—and ultimately, project—came to be needs to be described, on the one hand, from the perspectives of both the thematic and topical development, and, on the other, chronologically, over the course of an invigorating decade.

HISTORY MEETS THE STUDY OF POPULAR CULTURE

The sustained, overall project that we have committed to, an example of which, of course, is *The Cisco Kid: American Hero, Hispanic Roots* by Francis M. Nevins and Gary D. Keller, is grounded in and marks the convergence of three separate strands of academic research or popularization of culture:

(1) the general body of work as it pertains to the Iberoamerican studies of Eric Hobsbawm, who coined and elaborated the term "social bandits," and those of his successors, who con-

tinued, modified, or critiqued that research or who applied it to the study of popular culture;

(2) the sustained attention in the form of Anglo-centric books, documentary films, radio programs, and the like on the part of either researchers of mainstream popular culture or active popularizers of mainstream culture whose goal has been explaining, either for an academic readership or for a readership of aficionados, the noble bandits with Latina/o personas;

(3) researchers and popularizers of the cultures of the various Iberoamerican communities who have specialized in the study of both bad bandits and noble bandits in the Iberoamerican world but who rarely have recognized Latina/o noble bandits who emerged from the non-Latino community, even as many of these same Latino popularizers have inadvertently adapted those figures to their culture.

The Work of Eric Hobsbawm and the Line of Research That He Initiated

In 1959 Eric Hobsbawm published an essay, "The Social Bandit," in his book *Primitive Rebels: Studies in Archaic Forms of Social Movement in the 19th and 20th Centuries*. In it he explored "the curious fact that exactly the same stories and myths were told about certain types of bandits as bringers of justice and social redistributors all over Europe; indeed, as became increasingly clear, all over the globe" (*Bandits*, 2000, ix). Ten years later, on the basis of further studies (particularly in Latin America), Hobsbawm expanded the 1959 essay into a book, *Bandits* (1969), that has been revised several times and translated into various languages.

The notion of social bandits has proved to be both controversial and enduring, as has Hobsbawm himself, partly because he is Britain's best-known Marxist historian, and partly because his work is conceived and executed on a grand scale. In a time when historians have been characterized as specialists, he has been an extraordinary generalist. Hobsbawm observes about *Bandits* that it "formed the starting-point of the rapidly growing contemporary study of bandit history, much of which . . . has not accepted the 'social banditry' thesis, at least in its original form" (*Bandits*, 2000, ix).

Controversial as the concept has been, it has launched a great deal of research about various figures around the world in numerous cultures and over vast periods. *Bandits* inspired a whole new field of historical study and brought its author popular acclaim. In Hobsbawm's analysis, social bandits transcend the label of "criminals"; they are robbers and outlaws elevated to the status of avengers and champions of social justice. Some, such as Robin Hood, Rob Roy, Jesse James, and Francisco "Pancho" Villa, are famous throughout the world, the stuff of story and myth. Others, from Balkan *haiduks* and Indian *dacoits* to Brazilian *cangaçeiros*, are known only to their own countries' people.

The broad Bold Caballeros and Noble Bandidas project owes an intellectual debt of gratitude to Hobsbawm and the legion of social science researchers whose work has been launched around social bandits. At the same time, the project, of which this Cisco Kid book is a telling example, makes a decided departure from conventional social bandit research. At the heart of the controversy that Hobsbawm initiated was the issue of the historical accuracy or legitimacy of specific social bandits. Thus, much historical and anthropological work has been devoted to whether a certain figure, for example Jesse James (1847-82) or Pancho Villa (1878-1923), was legitimately a social bandit from the perspective of social science, or whether, by dint of the aggrandizing effects of popular culture, that figure had undergone a certain positive transformation or even a transmogrification.

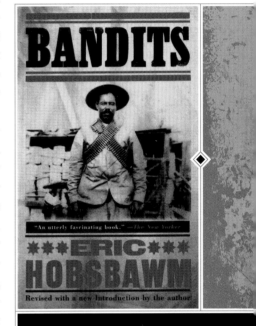

The multimedia Bold Caballeros and Noble Bandidas project primarily uses the tools of popular culture research. While we incorporate a great deal of historical information about the figures to whom our research is directed, our mission is not centered in history. A key distinguishing point between the study of "social" bandits from a historical and anthropological point of view and the study of "noble" bandits from the field of popular culture is that in the latter discipline the historical veracity of a specific bandit is secondary or, in the case of fictional personages, not an issue at all, whereas in the former disciplines it is central to the research. Moreover, we are just as concerned with pseudohistorical figures; one of these is Joaquín Murrieta, whose flesh-and-blood reality is a subject of some speculation and who may have existed as one person or may be a composite—although we know assuredly that he was not (if he was at all flesh and blood) an oppressed Chilean, as Pablo Neruda ardently asserted. Additionally, we are equally concerned with figures that are manifestly fictional such as the Cisco Kid, the Bandit Queen, Zorro, or Anita Delgado, the Avenging Arrow. Thus, our emphasis is on the dynamics of popular culture and its almost limitless ability to create noble bandits, whether from real-life models, the collective consciousness of a people (such as Robin Hood), or the pens of authors such as O. Henry, whose fictional character quickly assumed a cultural life of his own and a new Hispanic ethnicity to go with it.

Our project is also deeply attentive to the myth-making energies of popular culture and how they have played out in various forms of media as these forms have evolved over time and as a result of technological innovations. Thus, while the models in the living social reality of the Cisco Kid, Zorro, the Avenging Arrow, or the Bandit Queen are a secondary consideration given the particular research niche of this project, what is definitely of primary importance is the history of how these personages of popular culture have manifested themselves and evolved in various forms of communication, ranging from the media of oral tradition (ballads, tales, legends, drama, accounts, and so on), through the media of nineteenth-century publication (including posters, half-dime and then dime novels, literary fiction, newspaper serials, short stories, and poems), to the kinetic media of film and television. The project even includes radio, records, comic books, puzzles, and all manner of subsidiary spin-offs such as dolls, costumes, party favors, mugs, and the like.

Anglocentric Academic and Popular Works on Noble Bandidos/as

These works have been produced by a group of academic and popular writers who are not specialists in Iberoamerican studies. With respect to the Zorro phenomenon, Sandra R. Curtis, *Zorro Unmasked: The Official History*, published in 1998 to coincide with the release of *The Mask of Zorro* (1998, TriStar, director Martin Campbell, starring Antonio Banderas, Anthony Hopkins, and Catherine Zeta-Jones) is illustrative of the Anglocentric vein, but it is so only for the previous millennium. The current millennium is very different, as we will see below.

Curtis has an academic background, including a PhD (field not specified) as mentioned in her book, but she describes herself primarily as the vice president and creative director of Zorro Productions and as having an "extensive background in the develop-

ment of books, software, toys, screen and stage productions . . . [and] seven Zorro novels for the juvenile market" (1998, inside back cover). Her useful book even has an appendix that lists foreign films, but the book has no real Hispanic presence in interpretation or research except for a quotation from "J. A. Burciago," who almost certainly is José Antonio Burciaga, head of Zapata House at Stanford University for many years and creator of the "Drink Cultura" slogan and related art that is famous in the Chicano world.

By 2005, Curtis and Zorro Productions' contribution to Hispanic popular culture had taken a quantum leap. Isabel Allende credits Curtis as the person who inspired her to write her stirring novel *Zorro*. Of course, with the innovative development of the Zorro character beginning in 1998 with prominent Latina/o actors Antonio Banderas and Catherine Zeta-Jones in *The Mask of Zorro* (1998), *The Legend of Zorro* (2005), and even *Shrek 2* (2004, with the voices of Antonio Banderas and Cameron Díaz), this leap was a natural consequence. Our Bold Caballeros and Noble Bandidas Web site contains a paper by National University of Ireland, Maynooth professor Catherine Leen (http://noblebandits.asu.edu/Text/CLeen01.html). This research, "The Caballero Revisited: Postmodernity in *The Cisco Kid*, *The Mask of Zorro*, and *Shrek II*," breaks new ground by interrelating Cisco, Zorro, and Puss in Boots along the axis of postmodernity. The ogre and the itinerant good-bad feline-errant formula have been successful. In 2007 *Shrek the Third* appeared in the same animated-feature mold, again with the voices of Antonio Banderas and Cameron Díaz.

Additional examples of academic or aficionado research on figures with a Hispanic persona but without analysis or bibliographic control of the work by Hispanics themselves are Gerry Dooley's *The Zorro Television Companion* (2005) and Francis M. Nevins's first Cisco book, *The Films of The Cisco Kid* (1998). Mike Nevins's openness and willingness to work with this project has provided us with a splendid opportunity to enrich Cisco, and by extension Zorro, Joaquín Murrieta, and related research, with the outlook of Hispanic academicians and popularizers of culture alike.

The final chapter of this book, "The Cisco Kid from Bad Gringo to U.S. Hispanic Hero," written by Keller, reviews those aspects of the Cisco Kid filmic output upon which a scholar who is a specialist in Latino studies can shed light. Let us provide one example from Nevins's first Cisco Kid book of how an analysis from an informed Hispanic perspective can provide a more complete picture of the

Cisco character over 100 years. In *The Films of The Cisco Kid* the title of chapter 9 is "Lezwent! Cisco on the Small Screen." Similarly, Nevins concludes the narrative of his 1998 book with the rousing word "lezwent," which functions both to punctuate his book and also to evoke what in the television series functioned as a sort of motto equivalent to the Lone Ranger's cry, "Hi-yo, Silver, awaaaay!"

In 1998, Nevins thought of "lezwent!" as a humorous malaprop, a Panchoism that the character Leo Carrillo played was known for. Of course, it is that, but it is much more! Bilingualism and biculturalism are deeply embedded in the motto. When Carrillo's Pancho says to Renaldo's Cisco, "lezwent," he is not just mouthing a malaprop and displaying a less-than-native control of English verbal tenses. In fact, while the monolingual Anglo may have no alternative other than to interpret "lezwent" in this way, the phrase causes a totally different response in the fully equipped Spanish-English bilingual and bicultural viewer.

The reality is that Leo Carrillo was a man of considerable cultural achievement whose heritage went back to the early Californios and who wrote an engaging book that revealed him to be highly knowledgeable about the bicultural past, *The California I Love* (1961). With "lezwent!" Carrillo knew what he was doing, and he was at the top of his comic game. Carrillo's ingenious artifice is in fact a bilingual word game that only a Spanish-English bilingual would fully comprehend. "Lezwent" is what linguists call a "calque," a semantic transfer from Spanish to English of the Mexican regionalism "fuímonos." In standard Spanish, "let's go" is either "vamos," the origin of the English "vamoose," or, using the reflexive, "vámonos," as in the title of the well-known novel of the Mexican Revolution of 1910, *Vámonos con Pancho Villa* by Rafael F. Muñoz (1931). In nonstandard Spanish, especially in Mexico, "fuímonos" is used either in the countryside by less formally educated Mexicans, or more commonly by anyone irrespective of education as a humorous substitute for "vámonos." When used in this colloquial way, it embraces both the past and the imperative. In fact, it is remarkably similar to the contemporary English "I'm out of here," which implies that the speaker is already gone even though he or she hasn't left yet.

The Spanish-speaking and most especially Mexican *enterado* understands "lezwent" and finds it amusing at a level incomprehensible to an English-speaking monolingual. Linguistically, but for a different literary and cultural purpose, something similar occurs in some of Ernest Hemingway's most

Leo Carrillo had a rich repertoire of roles ranging from leads such as Pancho Villa through various sorts of bad guys to his most famous character, Pancho, Cisco's sidekick.

famous novels. In *For Whom the Bell Tolls* (1940) we encounter the following phrases:

1. . . . the blond one with the rare name . . .
2. "Very rare, yes," Pablo said. "Very rare and very drunk . . ."
3. Thou wert much horse.
4. Thou art much woman.
5. He went much with gypsies . . .
6. Four Fingers, a cobbler, who was much with Pablo then . . .

The use of "rare" and "much" by Hemingway in the examples above is analogous to the "lezwent" locution by Carrillo's Pancho. In both cases we experience the esthetic novelty of a character expressing himself in nonstandard English filtered through a clarifying and resonating grid of underlying Spanish. In the case of Carrillo, it is the Mexicanism "fuímonos." In the case of, say, "thou

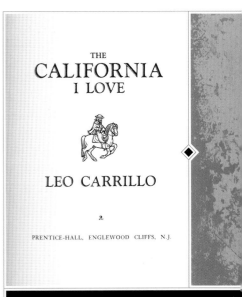

THE
CALIFORNIA
I LOVE

LEO CARRILLO

PRENTICE-HALL, ENGLEWOOD CLIFFS, N.J.

Etching by Gustave Doré depicting the adventures of Don Quixote and Sancho Panza, written by Miguel de Cervantes in the Spanish Golden Age. Don Quixote and Sancho Panza are the archetype for Cisco and Pancho and other heroes and sidekicks.

If a clod be washed away by the sea, Europe is the less, as well as if a promontory were, as well as if a manor of thy friends or of thine own were: any man's death diminishes me, because I am involved in Mankind; And therefore never send to know for whom the bell tolls; It tolls for thee.

In the case of the Cisco Kid, the goal is comedy and a certain parody of Hispanic articulation. For a monolingual Anglo speaker, it is something like a douse of bracing and chilly water on a hot, dusty Southwestern day.

Moreover, Carrillo and Renaldo certainly had humor in their agenda with the cry "lezwent!" but it was not entirely humor of the buffoonish, goofy kind. Encapsulated in the phrase was the Spanish language and a Mexican/Latino culture that cast attention upon itself to the bilingual-bicultural viewer and upon Pancho as a character who was *netamente latino*.

That Duncan Renaldo was attuned to establishing an affiliation between Cisco and Pancho and venerable Hispanic characters of comic-tragic bent is documentable. As Nevins points out, Jon Tuska (1976) quotes Renaldo to this effect. When Renaldo agreed to replace César Romero as the Cisco Kid, it was only if he could set the Kid in an entirely different cast. Renaldo's Cisco emerged during the Good Neighbor period when the United States was making a conscious effort to enlist the support of Latin America against the Axis, and Renaldo told Phil Krasne "how much trouble Romero had caused in Latin America playing the Kid as a vicious bandit." (See p. 109 for an evaluation of the accuracy of this comment.) Renaldo went on to suggest, "Why not base the character on the greatest book in all Spanish literature, *Don Quixote de la Mancha*? Cisco is a modern knight; Pancho is his Sancho Panza, a delicate comedy character—not a buffoon—who always gets his partner in trouble when they try to help people" (441).

The Work of Specialists in and Popularizers of Iberoamerican Culture

T he third strand that we deploy on behalf of *The Cisco Kid: American Hero, Hispanic Roots* and the broader project is the work of researchers and popularizers of culture from various Iberoamerican communities who have specialized in the study of both bad and noble bandits in the Iberoamerican world. This is my principal mission with respect to the book before you, and the component that describes Cisco appears principally in this first and in the concluding chapter.

wert much horse," it is the colloquial Spanish "tú eras mucho caballo." The English surface is readily recognizable, albeit strange or even nonsensical, but since it is "bounced off" Spanish, it becomes endowed with more than one meaning. Here again, the monolingual readers' recognition of the contextual implications of the words in the Hemingway examples and the bilingual viewers' experience of Sancho's motto cause the realization in both audiences that their task of understanding what has been communicated has been extended, that the writer in the one case and the actor in the other are expressing themselves in a dual code. In all of these cases, not one Spanish word is manifestly used, yet the articulation is in the esthetically novel medium of both English and Spanish. This is a medium that is manifest nonstandard English and latent standard Spanish (see Keller 1976a and 1976b for further analysis of this phenomenon).

Finally, in Hemingway the goal includes solemnity and gravity. In fact, "thou wert" and similar constructions tie the Spanish second person singular "tú" with its archaic analog in Elizabethan English, "thou," and with the John Donne epigraph from whence comes the title of the novel:

Coverage of the Cisco Kid can be found in numerous works by specialists in Iberoamerican studies, both in Spanish and English. First and foremost is the work of Emilio García Riera, whose *México visto por el cine extranjero* is a six-volume comprehensive review and analysis of Mexico as seen in foreign film for the years 1894-1988 inclusive and which covers principally, but not exclusively, U.S. film. Three of the volumes consist of filmographies. Essentially the work of a lifetime by Mexico's leading critic and researcher during the 1980s and into the 1990s (he died in 2002), García Riera's massive and seminal work provides information and analysis that is invaluable and that cannot be obtained anywhere else. An understanding of the Cisco Kid is not complete without integrating García Riera's research.

García Riera does not always get everything right, for he states that O. Henry's Cisco was a Mexican—"ese joven mexicano despiadado, astuto, mañoso y asesino por gusto" (Vol. 1, 147)—but in a field that is information-intensive he provides analysis on Cisco in relationship to the political climate and protests about Hollywood stereotyping in Mexico from the 1920s through the 1940s; on issues of broken English (el inglés chapurrado); on bad bandits and good-bad bandits; on the reception of Cisco, Zorro, and other bandits by the Mexican public; and on many other dimensions of American film from a Hispanic point of view. Moreover, no one has devoted as much attention, with such positive results, to the mishmash of music, lyrics, accents, cultures, costumes, sets, and choreography that American cinema blithely brought forward in its Mexican-focused films. These are themes that we will provide further attention to in the concluding chapter.

The vision from outside of Mexico in *México visto por el cine extranjero* is complemented by García Riera's opus magnum, the eighteen-volume *Historia documental del cine mexicano*. There is much Cisco Kid, Zorro, Joaquín Murrieta, and other noble bandit and bad bandit material to complement the story from the Mexican side. For example, in *El tigre de Yautepec* (1933), a good-bad bandit returns to the goodness of his birth origins, before he was kidnapped by a bandit gang, and gives up his life in admirable fashion. *Corazón bandolero* (1934) portrays a bandit hero during the struggle between Benito Juárez and Emperor Maximilian, and in the same year *Cruz Diablo* features a masked swashbuckler who robs the rich in order to help the poor and, in a convention echoing the Zorro analog, always places a cross on his victims' foreheads. In 1935, *Vámonos con Pancho Villa*, adapted from the novel, features

both the social banditry and the bandit atrocities of the Mexican Revolution of 1910. In 1940, *El Zorro de Jalisco* was produced to take advantage of Hollywood's *The Mark of Zorro* and featured a plot comparable and complementary to that Tyrone Power vehicle, but set in the Mexican state of Jalisco.

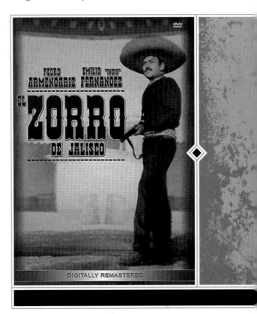

Additional research in Spanish includes Norma Iglesias, *Entre yerba, polvo y plomo: Lo fronterizo visto por el cine mexicano* (1991), which provides a good overview of the border as depicted in Mexican cinema. David Maciel reviews bandit stereotypes and contrasts them with others such as *mojados, alambristas,* and *pochos* in his *El bandolero, el pocho y la raza: Imágenes cinematográficas del chicano* (1994). Some of the essays in Gary D. Keller, ed., *Cine chicano* (1988) treat these stereotypes as well.

General treatments that have some coverage of interest to researchers of the noble and ignoble filmic bandit phenomenon can be found in works by Jorge Ayala Blanco, Aurelio de los Reyes, and Alejandro Galindo.

For the non-Spanish speaker interested in Mexican cinema, Carl J. Mora's *Mexican Cinema: Reflections of a Society, 1896-2004* (2005), now in its third edition, provides a quick overview, a listing of films by a handful of Mexican directors, and a list of useful film-related addresses in Mexico that is not available in García Riera's *Historia documental del cine mexicano*.

As one would expect, Cisco, Zorro, and others have been the object of considerable study in English from the Chicano/Latino point of view, both by academic researchers and popular interpreters. Clara E. Rodríguez, *Heroes, Lovers, and Others: The Story of Latinos in Hollywood* (2004), covers Cisco, Zorro, and other good and bad bandits from a biographical and chronological perspective. Gary D. Keller, *Hispanics and United States Film: An Overview and Handbook* (Tempe, AZ: Bilingual Press, 1994), and its companion book, Gary D. Keller, *A Biographical Handbook of Hispanics and United States Film* (1997), review film from the vantage points of topic and category, chronology, and individuals in the film industry, including numerous works treating good and bad bandits. Charles Ramírez Berg, *Latino Images in Film: Stereotypes, Subversion, and Resistance* (2002), distinguishes between Latina/o stereotypes and stock characters in a number of categories including the bandido, the Latin lover, and the buffoon. Christine List, *Chicano Images: Refiguring Ethnicity in Mainstream Film* (1996), treats the issue of stereotypes as well, as do several essays in Gary D. Keller (ed.), *Chicano Cinema: Research, Reviews & Resources* (1985).

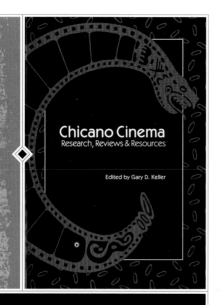

Keller and Keller, "The Depiction of Hispanics and Other Races and Ethnicities in United States Film, 1895-1920" (1998), cover the silent film period in the United States. Gary D. Keller also covers border-running films in "Running the United States-Mexico Border: 1909 through the Present" (2001).

More general treatments of Chicanos/Latinos as depicted in mainstream as well as Chicano/Latino film can be found in various works by Rosa Linda Fregoso, Ana López, and Chon Noriega.

For a pedagogical perspective see Gary D. Keller and others, eds., *Curriculum Resources in Chicano Studies* (1989), and Keller, "Chicanos and Film" (1989), as well as Carlos E. Cortés (1980, 1981, 1983, 1989, and 1992).

Luis Reyes and Peter Rubie, *Hispanics in Hollywood: An Encyclopedia of Film and Television* (1994), is a general reference book with an anecdotal quality written primarily by Reyes, an industry insider in his role as an agent of long standing. The book provides extensive coverage from a Hispanic point of view of the Cisco Kid films as well as of other noble and ignoble bandits, including Gregorio Cortez. An entire chapter is devoted to Cisco and Zorro. In a similar vein, George Hadley-García's book, *Hispanic Hollywood: The Latins in Motion Pictures* (1990), simultaneously published in a Spanish-language version, provides coverage on Cisco, Zorro, the figures of the 1910 revolution, and the social bandits of the nineteenth century such as Joaquín Murrieta and others, this time from a Hispanic aficionado's point of view.

DEVELOPMENT OF THE PROJECT OVER THE COURSE OF A DECADE

We have introduced both the book *The Cisco Kid: American Hero, Hispanic Roots* and the larger multimedia project from the perspective of both thematic and top-ical development. Let us turn now to its unfolding in the ten years since its inception.

In 1999-2000, the Publishing and Product Development (PPD) unit of the HRC, having been previously engaged over several years in an extensive process of research and the acquisition of thousands of items of textual and visual information on noble bandits, began to conceive a major scholarly publishing and educational outreach project, one that has grown and acquired additional dimensions over the last several years. The project was first conceived in response to the forthcoming centenary of the Mexican Revolution of 1910, about which the HRC has produced a virtual exhibition, with the following URL: http://latinoartcommunity.org/community/Gallery/1910/index.html.

We anticipate bringing forth, in stages beginning on or just before 2010, a full-color large-format book, a video DVD, a DVD-ROM, and possibly one or more Internet-based courses of instruction on the Mexican Revolution of 1910 and its cultural legacy in the United States, particularly as it affected (1) the visual and plastic arts; (2) film, television, video, and new media; and (3) the performing arts (see the introduction to this book). We also will be enhancing the coverage and depth of our existing Web site on the legacy of the Mexican Revolution. That project in turn will contain a significant component dedicated to noble bandits in popular culture and social bandits in the parlance of history and anthropology, although significant attention will not be paid therein to the Cisco Kid or Zorro because they are not characters directly pertinent to the subject matter.

As our intellectual understanding of and information resources on the noble/social bandit phenomenon have increased over the first years of the new millennium, the HRC has aspired to make a scholarly contribution *before* 2010 focusing on the Cisco Kid and Zorro as fictional noble bandits who, while cultural phenomena in their own right, we judged to bear a distinct temporal relationship to the iconic, culturally canonical revolutionaries of the Mexican Revolution of 1910, Francisco "Pancho" Villa and Emiliano Zapata.

There was something in the water, the earth, and the air in the 1910-1920 decade, and both the fiery ardor of war and the emergence of national mass media on wheels were at the heart of that quiddity. For one thing, the decade was the occasion of spectacular gains for cinema, both in the form of documentaries and feature films.

The documentaries developed significantly in their techniques through their coverage first of the

Image from D. W. Griffith's film *Intolerance: Love's Struggle Throughout the Ages* (1916).
The scene vividly highlights the epic scale of this film.

Mexican Revolution of 1910 and then of "The Great War." The feature films, the "seventh art," as it were, developed apace. Through the first decade of the twentieth century, the standard length of a film remained one reel, or about ten to fifteen minutes, partly based on producers' assumptions about the attention spans of their still largely working-class audiences. In the second decade, both in Europe and in the United States, multiple-reel extravaganzas began to push the envelope of film length. With international box office successes like *Queen Elizabeth* (France, 1912), *Custer's Last Fight* (U.S., Francis Ford, 1912), *Quo Vadis?* (Italy, 1913), Cecil B. DeMille's *The Squaw Man* (U.S., 1914) and *Cabiria* (Italy, 1914), the multi-reel or "feature" film was replacing the short as the cinema's central form. By mid-decade, the American director D. W. Griffith, with his historical epics *The Birth of a Nation* (1915) and *Intolerance* (1916), had produced films unprecedented in scale, status (*Birth* premiered in opera houses and with full orchestras), and sophistication in establishing techniques for film editing and visual storytelling. The former film was also notable as the first to inspire widespread national racial controversy so profound that it spilled over into the White House during the Wilson presidency.

The establishment of nationally and internationally distributed epic and historical feature films was strongly supported by the national print media outlets that had arisen after the Civil War, hugely aided by the creation of a transnational web of railroads for such distribution (Keller and Keller, 1998). The Union Pacific Railroad created its transnational line with a commemorative ceremony at Promontory Summit on May 10, 1869, a historical event that was the subject of the notable John Ford film *The Iron Horse* (1924). This and other events leading to the creation of a web of railroads forged a new technology of distribution of national newspapers, pulp fiction magazines, and half-dime and later dime novels that made their influence felt on American culture. The distribution of print media was conducted quite often in tandem with films, and each of these forms supported the other in various

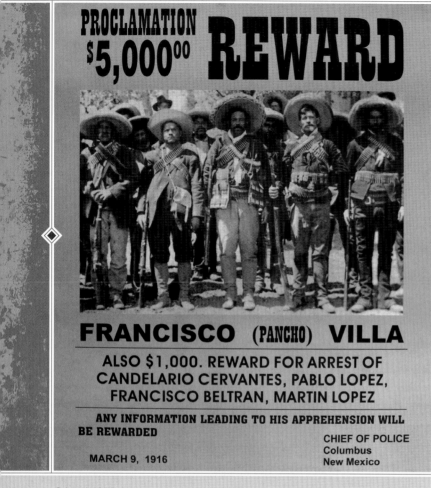

Original 1916 reward poster for Pancho Villa and associates

In this book we have reproduced in facsimile the story as it appeared in the edition of *Heart of the West* that was published as volume 4 of *The Complete Writings of O. Henry* (Doubleday Page, 1917). The attentive reader will notice that the text of the story, like thousands of other texts in English, incorporates some Spanish mistakes, which is particularly noticeable in the omission of most accents and other diacritical marks. This should not surprise us, as U.S. publishers have routinely ignored such features of the Spanish language.

O. Henry was the progenitor of Cisco, but he went no further in developing the protagonist than this one solitary story in his vast oeuvre. Devotees of the Hispanic Cisco surely thank the powers of providence for this liberation, for reasons that we will see subsequently in this book. The nondevelopment of Cisco is likely because, ill with both diabetes and cirrhosis of the liver, O. Henry expired in 1910, freeing Cisco, who from the beginning had deep Hispanic roots, to assume an actual Hispanic persona beginning in 1914 with the film *The Caballero's Way* (Éclair). It is a persona that the character has never shed since and from which he has never been deterred. That Hispanic persona has been alternately bad, good-bad, and good, depending on various factors, including the production company, the scriptwriter, the director, the actors depicting the character, and the changing social norms over the past 100 years.

Francisco "Pancho" Villa touched the American consciousness beginning in 1910, initially as a hero of Mexico's revolutionary enterprise. It is worth noting that Pancho is an *apodo* or nickname for Francisco, as is Cisco. This semantic fact links the Cisco and Pancho duo with Pancho Villa, and curiously enough, although to my knowledge this is never acknowledged, it endows both the Cisco Kid and Pancho with the same root name. Cisco Systems, the intrepid high-technology corporation with its logo of the Golden Gate Bridge, is also derived from the same root, but in this case the link is with the City of San Francisco. Nevertheless, and not surprisingly, John Chambers, the most prominent chief executive officer of Cisco Systems in its history and steward of the company's phenomenal growth, is frequently called the Cisco Kid, sometimes in tandem with such phrases as "riding off into the sunset" and "loco about Cisco."

On March 9, 1916, the Mexican revolutionary general Pancho Villa assumed the character of offensive malefactor when he conducted the first and only invasion of the United States by foreign military forces since the War of 1812. At the head of a contingent of 250 *dorados* immortalized by

ways, including advertising, reviews, adaptation of print narratives, narrativization of films, and so on.

Cisco, Villa, Zapata, and Zorro

Each of these four cultural icons, two of whom were flesh and blood and who have been mythologized and even apotheosized and two of whom were most definitely fictional, have generated a monumental cultural cycle of work manifesting itself in the literary, filmic, theatrical, and visual arts. It is no coincidence that all of these icons emerged around the same time, their personae cast large by the national mass media, both visual and print. They, along with other personages, were forged in the crucibles of the dream factory, and they, not just the subsequent *Maltese Falcon* (1941), became "the stuff that dreams are made of."

The Cisco Kid was struck from the *agridulce* and *amorodio* keyboard of William Sydney Porter (1862-1910), also known as O. Henry, in the form of a short story, "The Caballero's Way," first published in *Everybody's Magazine* for July 1907 and included in the collection *Heart of the West* (McClure, 1907).

Mexican popular culture, he entered the dusty little town of Columbus, New Mexico, population 300, thus providing the occasion for the town's entry into the realm of myth, history, and film.

The March 1916 Columbus attack greatly embarrassed President Woodrow Wilson. He dispatched a "punitive expedition" under the command of Brigadier General John J. "Black Jack" Pershing, who led 4,800 U.S. soldiers into Mexico six days later to find Villa. The operation failed, and in fact the *dorados* of the "Centauro del Norte" hit two small Texas towns on May 5, while in Mexico the punitive expedition was searching fruitlessly for the elusive Pancho Villa. The Pershing expedition did, however, expose George S. Patton Jr. to national public recognition. This was Patton's first real exposure to battle. In 1915 he was sent to Fort Bliss along the Mexican border, where he led routine cavalry patrols. A year later, he accompanied Pershing as an aide on his expedition against Villa. Patton gained recognition from the press for his attacks on several of Villa's men. Impressed by Patton's determination, Pershing promoted him to captain and asked him to command his headquarters troop upon their return from Mexico.

At the onset of World War I in 1914, tanks were not being widely used. In 1917, however, Patton became the first member and then commander of the newly established United States Tank Corps. Along with the British tankers, he and his men achieved victory at Cambrai, France, during the world's first major tank battle in 1917. The rest is both history and filmic history, and with the smash hit *Patton* (1970), the title character became another piece of "the stuff that dreams are made of," even, according to the rumor, to the extent that viewing the film helped motivate Richard Milhous Nixon to order the bombing of Cambodia. ¡Quién sabe!

Meanwhile, back on the border and in the Mexican hinterland, one person's *bandido muy malo* is another's spiritual intercessor. Pancho the man, the revolutionary, who was by turns the cross-cultural, transcultural, bicultural, and transgressive icon of both mainstream U.S. and mainstream Mexican culture and, straddling the two, an Amerexican or Mexamerican culture, has been the persona who has launched a thousand works of art, polemic, vituperation, and even hagiography. People pray to Pancho and publish in newspapers their gratitude for his intercessions.

Villa may have been the "Centauro del Norte," but Zapata was the "Atila del Sur." Emiliano Zapata, who also entered the American and Amerexican consciousness as a result of 1910, has had a *trans-*

curso más suave than Pancho, *más dulce,* more sustained in the heroic and tragic cast, but one also covered with glory, as it were. On some occasions his heroism has been associated with anarchism, and in fact, one of the main intellectuals with Zapata's army was anarchist Antonio Díaz Soto y Gama. Ricardo Flores Magón, also associated with anarchism, coined the slogan *Tierra y Libertad,* which was subsequently adopted by the Zapatistas.

At one film-historical moment, the years of intense controversy initiated by the oppressive hearings of the U.S. House Un-American Activities Committee (HUAC) affected the character development of the Mexican leader in the canonical film *Viva Zapata!* (1952, directed by Elia Kazan, screenplay by John Steinbeck, and starring Marlon Brando). In this film Zapata was depicted as a Camus-like, leftist populist "rebel," who stands in stark contrast to Fernando in the same film, the doctrinaire "revolutionary" motivated to betray his erstwhile allies in the name of an abstract cause (see Keller, 1985, 35-37; Morsberger, 1975, xi and 104-105).

Then there is Zorro, who emerged from the pop cultural mind of Johnston McCulley (1883-1958), an author who primed the personage like a pump, writing no less than sixty-four separate Zorro narratives during the course of his career, almost all of them subsequent to and as a result of the Fairbanks smash hit of 1920. Zorro first appears in the McCulley serial "The Curse of Capistrano," published in five installments in the pulp-fiction magazine *All-Story Weekly* beginning with the issue of August 9, 1919. Douglas Fairbanks and Mary

G. M. Anderson, best known for his role as Broncho Billy, here plays a sympathetic Mexican in *The Mexican's Faith*. In the background are Chick Morrison and Jack O'Brien.

second part of the novel was published in 1615, ten years after the 1605 publication of the first part and as a result of its enormous popularity. Cervantes tells us, in the voice of the character Sansón Carrasco: "Los niños la manosean, los mozos la leen, los hombres la entienden y los viejos la celebran" (Children paw it, lads read it, men understand it, and elders celebrate it).

I met "Mike" Nevins, my colleague in this Cisco Kid enterprise, at a fall 2002 conference of the Film and History Society in Kansas City, where I was giving a paper on the cinematic record of the Mexican Revolution of 1910 both in the form of documentaries contemporaneous with the event and feature films during and after the Revolution.

That conference and the conversations that grew out of it were the beginning of the Cisco Kid component of the grand project on noble and ignoble *bandidos y bandidas*. At first it did not occur to the PPD of the HRC to link Cisco with the *caudillos* and *generalas* and *coronelas* of the Mexican Revolution, the centenary of which was approaching. However, after some months, that became our plan. Mike Nevins has been a huge asset to the overarching project with respect to his contributions to the study of the Cisco Kid and, far beyond that, due to his vast knowledge of the popular culture of both Anglo and Hispanic bandits of the great binational American and Mexican West.

Mike Nevins brought into the project Boyd Magers, editor of *Western Clippings*. Boyd is the author of several important and relevant books including *Best of the Badmen* (2005, with Bob Nareau and Bobby Copeland) and *Westerns Women* (1999, with Michael G. Fitzgerald). He has been extremely helpful by making available to the project, from his own collection, films difficult to obtain, including *Broncho Billy and the Greaser* (1914) and several other *Broncho Billy* one-reelers; *Don Daredevil Rides Again* (1951, Republic Serial); *Hell's Heroes* (director William Wyler, in both silent and sound [1930] versions); *In Old Arizona* (1929, director Raoul Walsh); *The Irish Gringo* (1936), a cult classic as a movie so awful it is good camp *avant la lettre*; *Ramona* (1936, director Henry King, starring Loretta Young and Don Ameche, the fourth film to be shot in the "perfected" three-strip color process); *Three Bad Men* (1926, director John Ford, starring George O'Brien) and other notable films. Boyd permitted us to make 4" x 5" color transparencies of scores of lobby cards of the Cisco Kid films in his personal collection and also provided us with laser prints of many additional lobby cards.

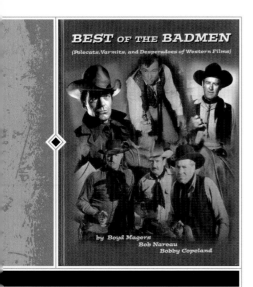

Pickford, joining forces personally and professionally, created United Artists with Charlie Chaplin and others and obtained the rights to the story, adapting it into the enormously popular *The Mark of Zorro* (1920).

Today Zorro, Cisco and Pancho, Emiliano Zapata and his brother Eufemio, and Pancho Villa are still going strong. Moreover, their strength lies in their popularity across age groups and generations. In the second part of his novel *Don Quixote*, Cervantes evokes the social function of the novel and its titular character as well as its popularity across age groups, and he predicts, based on a decade of outstanding popularity, its staying power for all time. The

Mike Nevins was also able to put us into contact with Bill Catching, who figures prominently in this book as Leo Carrillo's double, and we interviewed Bill on his ranch in the Yuma, Arizona area. Excerpts of the digital video interviews of both Bill Catching and Mike Nevins will appear in the grand project's forthcoming video DVD.

Our plan is, on the one hand, to do a new version of Nevins's 1998 Cisco book that brings into the original exposition a bilingual, bicultural, binational point of view, and on the other, for the PPD to create the overarching, expansive Bold Caballeros and Noble Bandidas project in the form of a book, a video DVD, a DVD-ROM with research and additional images, a Web site, and one or more Internet-based courses.

Female Counterparts

By the winter of 2003-2004 our plans had become sufficiently ambitious for us to develop the two projects. One would be on Cisco and Zorro, to be completed within two years, and the other was scheduled for around 2010 on the two caudillos, Pancho Villa and Emiliano Zapata, set in the rich context of the Mexican Revolution with its *coronelas* and *generalas* and *rieleras* and *soldaderas*, as well as a host of relatively or hugely underrecognized figures, both heroic and nonheroic, ranging from Francisco and Gustavo Madero to Félix Díaz, Pascual Orozco, Victoriano Huerta, Venustiano Carranza, Álvaro Obregón, Benjamín Argumedo, and Felipe Ángeles.

The rich lode of information got the better of those initial plans, however. After conducting additional research and acquiring even more items of information, the weight of that data set suggested to us that our project was only half-baked *y parcialmente cuajado*. We had one gender identity, but we were missing the other.

Heroic women played important roles in the Mexican Revolution of 1910 both on the battlefield and in other areas of the public arena, and in recent decades the pace of research on this topic has been dynamic and expanding prodigiously. These women represented the peasantry, the working poor, and intellectuals from the middle or upper classes. Moreover, the heroic women appear in considerable number both in history and in popular culture, and they fall into the same categories that we have reviewed in U.S. popular culture, ranging from historical figures, more or less expanded in the magnitude of their actions and personalities, to pseudo-historical, composite, and outright fictional personages.

La Cucaracha. MARIA FELIX DOLORES del RIO EMILIO FERNANDEZ ANTONIO AGUILAR y PEDRO ARMENDARIZ

The heroic women who have been identified by our research and that of many others generally have been notable either for their violent and "sinful" ways, comparable to those of their male counterparts, or for feminist activities, especially among the *clases letradas* but occasionally among the less educated. Let us first review some tough *hembras*.

Coronela María de la Luz Espinosa Barrera was one of the very few revolutionaries who received a pension as a veteran of the Mexican Revolution, having served with much distinction. However, she had survived all those battles only to find herself and her lifestyle socially unacceptable in peacetime. For one who "smoked, drank, gambled and feared no man" to revert to the timid submissiveness expected of women was unthinkable. Like many veterans, María found conformity impossible and spent the rest of her life as "a restless soul," an itinerant peddler still dressed as a man and carrying a pistol.

In 1910 Margarita Neri led a force of over 1,000, sweeping through Tabasco and Chiapas looting, burning, and killing. These were hardly unusual events in wartime, except for the fact that this particular group's commander, brandishing a bloody machete and vowing to decapitate Díaz, was a woman. Margarita Neri earned such a reputation for ruthless slaughter that the governor of Guerrero, on hearing of her approach, hid in a crate and was sneaked out of town. Some say that she served as an officer under Zapata. Others insist that, although Zapata admired and sent men to

Armed female revolutionary, Mexican Revolution of 1910, state of Sinaloa

tinguish between *federales* and *villistas* despite being whipped and threatened with death. Villa eventually treated González with respect, and her courage and humanity are honored by the numerous primary schools, nursing schools, streets, and villages that bear her name.

Many of the armed women of the Revolution were unnamed except by their *apodos*, often because they were outlaws and leaders of bandit gangs before and during the Revolution or because they had killed to avenge their dead men. These include La Coronela, La Chata, La Güera Carrasco, La Corredora, and La Valentina. In turn, these anonymous women or composites of different figures were brought into popular culture by way of the songs of the period and films that treat the Revolution. Examples of films that will be examined later include *La Adelita, La Cucaracha, La Valentina* (1940, starring Jorge Negrete and Esperanza Baur) and *La Soldadera*. Other armed women appear in films such as *Los de abajo* and *La Negra Angustias*; these are composite fictional characters modeled on actual tough *hembras*.

The period leading up to the Revolution beginning around the turn of the century, as well as the Revolution of 1910 itself and its aftermath, witnessed the creation of feminist organizations and journals. The latter included *La Mujer Mexicana* and *Mujer Moderna*, and among the organizations were La Liga Femenina Anti-reeleccionista "Josefa Ortiz de Domínguez" and the Hijas de Cuauhtémoc. In some of the surviving information about these women we find overt indications of the mythologizing tendencies that have also operated on the better-known Pancho Villa and Emiliano Zapata.

Choosing pen and petition over knife and gun eventually made Flores de Andrade, a member of the Hijas de Cuauhtémoc, an ally of Francisco I. Madero, but she was no less the rebel. When her grandparents died, leaving her a good inheritance, she displeased her family by immediately giving "absolute liberty" to all the peasants who had worked on the estate and supplying them with tools and animals to continue to work the land as long as they wished. She was an ardent member of a secret society whose aim was to overthrow Díaz and achieve freedom for *all* Mexicans. To this end, she marched and petitioned so successfully that she aroused both Díaz and the U.S. officials who supported him. Hunted by both, she sought refuge in the north but was eventually captured and sentenced to death. A presumably apocryphal "tall tale" about her is that facing the firing squad, she allegedly grabbed the commander's rifle, forced his men to

recruit her, they so offended her that she cut off their ears to emphasize her refusal. Whatever the truth, she seems to have deserved the accolade of "a superb guerilla commander."

A weapons expert, crack shot, and nurse, Margarita Ortega teamed with her daughter, Rosaura Gortari, to serve as couriers and spies. However, they fought on the losing side against Madero. Captured by the Maderistas, they were force-marched into the desert and left without food or water. They survived the ordeal, but Rosaura died soon after reaching refuge in Phoenix. Margarita did not long outlive her daughter. Sent on another mission into Sonora, she was recaptured. Forced to stand in a cage, poked, prodded, and savagely beaten, she still refused to betray her comrades and after four days of torture was summarily executed.

A different sort of bravery was exhibited by the heroic nurse of the *dorados*, Beatriz González Ortega, who refused when treating the wounded to disput down their weapons and held out until President Taft ordered her release! However improbable, she *did* survive to tell the tale. Her oral history, as recounted to Mexican anthropologist Manuel Gamio, has provided insight into the political activism of women among Mexican political refugees in Texas in the early twentieth century.

Elisa Acuña y Roseta (1887-1946) was an associate of anarchist Antonio Díaz Soto y Gama, one of the primary intellectual spokespersons for Emiliano Zapata and *zapatismo*. She cofounded, with the feminist, political radical, and iconoclast Juana Belén Gutiérrez de Mendoza (1875-1942), the journal *Vésper, Justicia y Libertad*, often praised by Flores Magón's journal, *Regeneración*, which on one occasion described it in partially masculine terms as "un haz de viriles energías. Las columnas del apreciable colega están nutridas de ideas avanzadas." Both Acuña and Belén Gutiérrez were imprisoned by the Díaz regime, and from jail they edited the socialist newspaper *Fiat Lux*. After the Victoriano Huerta coup, Acuña wrote propaganda for *La Voz de Juárez, Sinfonía*, and *Combate y Anáhuac* until Obregón's triumphant entry into Mexico City in August 1914, at which time she joined the *zapatistas* and served as a liaison between them and the *carrancistas* and as the head of propaganda in Puebla. In the 1920s she participated in the Consejo Feminista Mexicano and the Liga Panamericana de Mujeres.

An additional associate of Acuña and Belén Gutiérrez was Mexican American poet and political figure Sara Estela Ramírez (1881-1910), who, despite dying of unknown causes after an illness at the age of 29, was a leader of the Partido Liberal Mexicano, a member of the feminist organization Regeneración y Concordia, and the publisher of two newspapers, *La Corregidora* and *Aurora*. In addition to her political activities, she wrote poetry that evoked the bicultural nature of Tejano life along the border.

Hermila Galindo de Topete (1896-1954) was cofounder and editor of the feminist and pro-Carranza journal *Mujer Moderna* and one of Carranza's most energetic and visible collaborators and propagandists. She eventually wrote his biography in addition to at least five other books. Galindo was an early supporter of many (then) radical feminist issues such as sex education in the schools, women's suffrage, and divorce. She was one of the first feminists to state bluntly that the Catholic Church was the main obstacle to the advancement of feminism in Mexico.

Dolores Jiménez y Muro (1848-1925) was a member of the editorial staff of the feminist journal *La Mujer Mexicana*, a leader in the Liga Femenina Anti-reeleccionista "Josefa Ortiz de Domínguez," and

the president of the Hijas de Cuauhtémoc. Both groups were actively anti-Díaz, and the Hijas were arrested in September 1910 during a large but peaceful march in Mexico City protesting Díaz's policies. Their manifesto called for the political enfranchisement of Mexican women in their "economic, physical, intellectual and moral struggles." In 1911, Jiménez founded the group Regeneración y Concordia from her prison cell. The group's purpose was to "improve the lot of indigenous races, *campesinos, obreros*, unify revolutionary forces, and elevate women economically, morally and intellectually." In March 1911, Jiménez put together the Political and Social Plan to bring Madero to power by a rebellion near Mexico City. Her plan was unusual because it outlined the need for extensive social and economic reforms rather than simply expressing the desire for political change at the top. She specifically recognized in the plan that the daily wages of both men and women in urban and rural areas needed to be increased, as women made up more of the "economically active" population than was acknowledged by the official census. Emiliano Zapata was very enthusiastic about Jiménez's plan, particularly the part calling for the restitution of usurped village lands, and invited her to join his cause in Morelos. She did so after the death of Madero in 1913 and remained there until Zapata's assassination in 1919, well after her seventieth birthday.

We have provided a number of *semblanzas* of heroic women from the history of the Mexican Revolution of 1910, some of them clearly mythologized. Of course, the overall project will profile many others, including those active during time frames before and after that all-important historical event.

Let us turn now to providing a sampling of the fictional characters on the female side of the ledger in order to broaden our framework. Out of the same cauldron of 1910 we have the smoking, drinking, fighting, and remorseless killing of the personage La Pintada in Mariano Azuela's *Los de abajo* (1915), who is treated like a man by the other soldiers in the novel and who contrasts mightily with the other main female character, Camila, a more conventional "victim." The novel was adapted into a film, *Los de abajo* (1940, director Chano Urueta). The film *Enamorada* (1946, director Emilio "El Indio" Fernández, cinematography Gabriel Figueroa, starring María Félix and Pedro Armendáriz), somewhat akin to Shakespeare's *Taming of the Shrew*, features Beatriz, the daughter of an *hacendado* who despises *pelados* and *revolucionarios* alike. She is "tamed" by José Juan, a revolutionary commander who comes into the region and defends the poor because they are humble and true. For José Juan, conquering Beatriz is a challenge not unlike winning a battle in the Revolution, and he is willing to suffer the slaps and injuries to his macho persona with the filmic certainty that eventually he will tame this wild mare. The film ends with the proud Beatriz repudiating her class, leaving her family and fiancé behind (a kind of goofy gringo, no less!), and going with her man on foot, at the side of his horse, as a *soldadera*, a type that she formerly held in contempt. Is this a film about a noble bandida? Well, yes and no. Mostly no, with the attenuating circumstance that despite her subjugation by "love" to male authority, Beatriz is moved by the impetus for social justice revealed by the Revolution to spurn the values and comfort of the *hacendado* class that formerly had her allegiance.

In 1944, Francisco Rojas González published what has been billed as the first novel of the Mexican Revolution that has as its main protagonist a woman, Coronela Angustias Farrera. The novel, *La Negra Angustias*, has an ingenious title. "Negra" here indicates a woman of dark complexion (in the Mexican sense, which is possibly mulatto) with the name Angustias, and the double entendre that results is either "dark Angustias" or "acute anguish." The novel was adapted into a film in 1949 with the same title, directed by the notable female director Matilde Landeta and starring María Elena Marqués as Angustias and Agustín Isunza as her friend, el Huitlacoche. The film features the young and attractive Angustias, daughter of the *generoso bandido* Antón Farrera, who is marginalized because she lives with the witch Cresencia and because she

shuns the predatory males in her midst. Upon knifing to death a *charro* who attempts to violate her, she flees and becomes a Zapatista soldier, rising to *coronela* and following the noble teachings of her father, giving justice to women and *campesinos* alike.

The film *La Negra Angustias* is notable for its attention to the roles that are culturally assigned to the sexes. In other films of the same period that are superficially similar (*Enamorada, La Soldadera*), the female characters rarely get beyond lamenting their female condition. La Negra Angustias, however, takes the initiative with respect to male domination. When Angustias apprehends El Picado, who years earlier had forced himself on her, she orders that he be castrated in the name of the other *viejas* whom he had taken advantage of—Piedad, Rosa, Lupe from Agua Fría—"because only then are men less evil." In another scene, she orders the execution of a prisoner, but his fiancée pleads "woman to woman" for him to be freed. Angustias is undeterred, but when the girl tells her she is pregnant and that her child will become an orphan before he or she is born, this softens Angustias, and she frees the man.

La Cucaracha (1958, director Ismael Rodríguez, cinematography Gabriel Figueroa, starring María Félix, Dolores del Río, Emilio "El Indio" Fernández, Antonio Aguilar, Pedro Armendáriz, and Ignacio López Tarso) depicts the relationship that is established between the hard-fighting, rifle-wielding, drinking, cursing, and promiscuous Cucaracha (María Félix), who dresses like a man and is committed to the Revolution even unto death, and Colonel Zeta, a committed, traditional male revolutionary. The widow Isabel (Dolores del Río), dressed in black, a "good" woman who cries and cries, ends up taking colonel Zeta from the "hembra bravía," la Cucaracha.

La Soldadera (1966, director José Bolaños, cinematography Alex Phillips, starring Silvia Pinal and Narciso Busquets) is an emphatically traditional film in its roles for females, although for a time, Lázara (Silvia Pinal), whose husband is killed by the *villistas*, takes up arms with them before she comes under the authority of a new *villista*, who disarms her and forces her into a conventional role.

La Adelita occupies a fluid, ambiguous place between fiction and history. The most famous song of the Mexican Revolution of 1910 was "La Adelita," some of which follows:

En lo alto de la abrupta serranía,
acampado se encontraba un regimiento,
y una moza que valiente lo seguía
locamente enamorada del sargento.
Popular entre la tropa era Adelita,

The film *Enamorada* (1946), directed by Emilio Fernández, benefits from the visual artistry of cinematographer Gabriel Figueroa.

la mujer que el sargento idolatraba,
porque a más de ser valiente era bonita,
que hasta el mismo coronel la respetaba.

Y se oía que decía
aquel que tanto la quería:
Y si Adelita se fuera con otro,
la seguiría por tierra y por mar;
si por mar en un buque de guerra,
si por tierra en un tren militar.

There are differing accounts regarding La Adelita in popular culture. Some had her as a shy fourteen-year-old nurse, others as a vicious twenty-one-year-old killer. She was variously a harlot, a saint, the sweetheart of the regiment, or Pancho Villa's private paramour.

Although there is a photograph identified as Adelita, there is no proof that this most famous of *soldaderas* actually existed. Certainly, the glamorous heroine of song and story never did. Many of her purported exploits happened, but to other women who remain faceless and unsung. In time, the name came to denote any female soldier, so in a sense, the revolutionary Everywoman Adelita not only existed but, according to another song, "Adelita never dies!"

In 1948 the Adelita mythos and of course the *corrido* were the basis of a film, *Si Adelita se fuera con otro* (director Chano Urueta, starring Jorge Negrete and Gloria Marín), of the *comedia ranchera* genre. Here Adelita is a rich girl (shades of *Enamorada*, starring María Félix) who leaves home to follow her husband (Negrete), disappears, but at the end comes back to a rousing chorus of "Adelita," and she and her husband are reunited.

Five Continents and Seven Seas

At the same time that our research was uncovering a significant number of heroic and bad *bandidas* in both Mexican history and Mexican popular culture, we were in the process of recovering the female counterparts of the Hispanic bandits that had been developed in mainstream American popular culture. In the domains of pulp fiction, film and television, and legend and folklore, we traced the careers of good, good-bad, and bad female bandits that have sprung from American culture, including Anita Delgado (the Avenging Arrow), Lady Robinhood, Lasca of the Rio Grande, the Daughter of Don Q, the Bandit Queen, and others in the bandit firmament who are analogous to male characters (Cisco, Zorro, Billy the Kid, Don Q, the Arizona Kid, Don Daredevil, and others). It is worth noting that *Daughter of Don Q* (1946; Republic serial starring Adrian Booth) is a sequel to the Douglas Fairbanks Sr. film *Don Q, Son*

of Zorro (1925), thus making the daughter of Don Q the original fictional Zorro's granddaughter.

Responding to the prodigious information base that we have generated, one that calls for interpretation in new and counterintuitive ways, we have developed the general project. This endeavor will keep us intensely busy with the publication of large-format, full-color books on bold caballeros and noble bandidas and on the cultural legacy of the Mexican Revolution of 1910, the centenary of which is clearly in sight. Through the project we will generate original, new research with the aid of scholars worldwide, publish DVD-ROMs of a scholarly sort in addition to books, produce video DVDs, organize conferences around the noble bandit theme, and establish other events in support of the general community's enthusiasm for the noble bandit in popular culture.

Similar to Pancho Villa, La Adelita has had numerous interpretations in popular culture.

The project, in addition to tracing the media cycles generated by the fictional Zorro and Cisco and the mytho-historic Villa and Zapata, dedicates itself to female bandits, both noble and ignoble, as well as a host of other less recognized figures. This project spans the entire twentieth century, covering—or more accurately, recovering—a host of female and male counterparts to Cisco and Zorro as well as Joaquín Murrieta and analogous bandits whose presence has been obscured or lost. Some examples include the Anita Delgado character (played by Ruth Roland) in the serial *The Avenging Arrow* (1921); the *Bandit Queen* (1950), featuring a Zorroesque female avenger played by Barbara Britton; *Daughter of Don Q* (1946), starring Adrian Booth as the wily heiress; the serial *Don Daredevil Rides Again* (1951), with a Zorro character sans the name of Zorro because of intellectual property issues; the Disney TV series (*The Nine Lives of Elfego Baca*, 1958) and film (*Elfego Baca: Six Gun Law*, 1962) on Mexican American noble bandit Elfego Baca; *Lady Robinhood* (1925), starring Evelyn Brent, who takes on Cabraza (Boris Karloff), the evil grey eminence of Spanish old California; *Murieta* (1965), a contribution to the Joaquín Murrieta cycle, starring Jeffrey Hunter; *Robin Hood of El Dorado* (1936), with Warner Baxter as noble bandit Joaquín Murrieta; *Scarlet Days* (1919, director D. W. Griffith), with Richard Barthelmess playing a

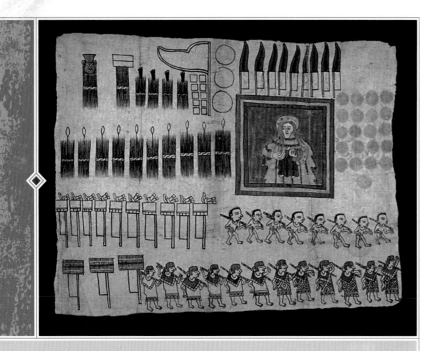

Image from the 1531 Huexotzinco codex, a document on *amatl* (a pre-Columbian paper made from the inner bark of the fig tree) written ten years after the Spanish Conquest in 1521. Huexotzinco was one of Hernán Cortés's staunchest allies against the Aztec Empire, and this codex is a legal document in support of grievances by this indigenous community against the Crown, grievances that were settled to their satisfaction by Carlos V in 1538. Facsimile, U.S. Library of Congress.

wars of independence in Latin America; the plentiful novels, poems, and works of art by such artists as Goya; and films. Among the latter are *Agustina de Aragón* (1929, director Florián Rey; remade in 1950, director Juan de Orduña, starring Aurora Bautista and Fernando Rey) and *The Pride and the Passion* (1957, director Stanley Kramer, starring Cary Grant, Frank Sinatra, and Sophia Loren), depicting the heroism of people caught up in the taking of Ávila from Napoleon's troops by a people's army.

The project also reviews the bandit-heroes of *Outlaws of the Marsh,* one of the four most famous works of classical Chinese literature, as well as Pearl S. Buck's discussion of the novel in her Nobel Prize lecture (December 12, 1938). It finds evidence of banditry and criminal circumstances in the relationship of the Triple Alliance (Tenochtitlan, Texcoco, and Tlacopan), generally known as the Aztec Empire, to other city-states such as Tlaxcala and Huexotzinco.

Additionally, the project covers the careers of twentieth-century bandit heroes Salvatore Guiliano (Sicily), Pablo Escobar (Colombia), and Jesús Malverde (both the original bandit killed in 1909 and the contemporary hip-hop phenomenon) and postmodern and often postmillennial and postfeminist films on the order of *El Mariachi* (1992, director Robert Rodríguez, starring Salma Hayek and Antonio Banderas); *Desperado* (1995, director Robert Rodríguez, starring Salma Hayek and Antonio Banderas); *From Dusk Till Dawn* (1996, director Robert Rodríguez, starring Harvey Keitel, Salma Hayek, George Clooney, and Cheech Marín); *Once Upon a Time in Mexico* (2003, director Robert Rodríguez, starring Antonio Banderas, Johnny Depp, and Salma Hayek); *And Starring Pancho Villa as Himself* (2003, director Bruce Beresford, starring Antonio Banderas); *Kill Bill Volume I* (2003, director Quentin Tarantino, starring Uma Thurman and Lucy Liu); *Kill Bill Volume II* (2004, director Quentin Tarantino, starring Uma Thurman and David Carradine); and *Bandidas* (2006, directors Joachim Roenning and Espen Sandberg, starring Salma Hayek and Penélope Cruz).

This is a multilingual, multicultural project that spans the five continents and the seven seas and will run for the next few decades. This book, *The Cisco Kid: American Hero, Hispanic Roots,* and the accompanying Web site, Bold Caballeros and Noble Bandidas, http://noblebandits.asu.edu/ launch the project.

In that spirit we bid you lezwent! y también, ¡fuímonos!

Joaquín Murrieta type named Álvarez; *Zorro, the Gay Blade* (1981), starring George Hamilton, a Zorro film with a gay component; and *Zorro's Black Whip* (1944), starring Linda Stirling, who takes up the Zorro mantle with her signature whip. The project covers personages as varied as Elfego Baca, Broncho Billy, the Cactus Queen, Cattle Kate, Butch Cassidy, Gregorio Cortez, Juan Cortina, the Sundance Kid, Teresita Urrea, and Tiburcio Vásquez.

The project also delves into ancient worlds and far-flung lands, finding the roots of twentieth-century popular culture banditry as far back as the Code of Hammurabi, the ancient Greek city-states, the Roman Empire, the Old Testament and the New Testament—including, of course, the narrative of the good thief (Luke 23:33-43)—and the paradoxes of good-bad banditry as analyzed by St. Augustine in *De civitate Dei.*

We have researched bandit heroism during the Middle Ages, including the Robin Hood cycle and the ballads and tales of other bandit folk heroes. We review the War of Independence in Spain (the Peninsular War) and the guerrilla warfare of Juan Martín Díaz, El Empecinado; the heroism of Agustina de Aragón (1786-1857) in the defense of Zaragoza; the

O. HENRY, FATHER OF ALL CISCOS 2

ere's adventure! Here's romance! Here's O. Henry's famous Robin Hood of the Old West—the Cisco Kid!"

When Duncan Renaldo and Leo Carrillo (or their doubles) came thundering across the desert to the tune of vaguely Latin-flavored agitato music, we grammar school kids of the 1950s sitting entranced in front of our parents' 12-inch TV screens knew next to nothing about what we were watching. Those of us who were too young to have seen any of the Cisco movies in theaters had never heard of the character before. We didn't know that the 30-minute telefilms we were seeing in black and white had been shot in color, or that the music score beneath the front and end titles had been composed by a never-credited Albert Glasser. Few of us had ever heard of O. Henry except as a candy bar.

Later, when we took American literature in high school and had to read "The Ransom of Red Chief" and "The Gift of the Magi," most of us learned a little about who O. Henry was. In those days nobody would dare ask a teacher about the connection between O. Henry and the Cisco Kid, and frankly, not many teachers would have known the answer.

So who was O. Henry?

He was probably the most popular American short story writer in the first half of this century. In ten years' time he wrote close to three hundred tales that, according to the entry on him in Volume 19 of *Twentieth-Century Literary Criticism* (1986), featured "familiar, conversational openings, circumlocutory dialogue, plots hinging on improbable coincidence, and variations on the surprise or twist ending. . . ." For twenty-odd years after his death his stories were studied in colleges as marvelous examples of short fiction. Then opinion shifted and his tales were dismissed as clever commercial concoctions. Nevertheless, some recent critics are finding links between his stories and the work of various avant-garde writers who haven't the slightest interest in well-constructed plots. The pendulum of opinion may well take several more swings as the twenty-first century lurches forward.

O. Henry, of course, is not the name he was born with. William Sydney Porter was born in Greensboro, North Carolina, on September 11, 1862, to Dr. Algernon Porter and his wife, who died of pneumonia when her second son was three. The doctor and his children moved in with his mother. Raised by his grandmother and an aunt, William Sydney left school at

William Sydney Porter (O. Henry) not long before his death

William Sydney Porter as a young bachelor in Austin

age 15 and went to work in his uncle Clarke Porter's drugstore, earning a pharmacist's license in 1881. Throughout his adolescence he was terrified of catching the pneumonia that had killed his mother. When he developed a persistent cough he moved to southwest Texas and worked for two years on a cattle ranch managed by the sons of the doctor who had taken over Algernon's practice. One of these sons was Lee "Red" Hall, a Texas Ranger who helped run down Sam Bass and other legendary outlaws. Around 1884, resettling in the state capital at Austin, Porter worked as a clerk and bookkeeper, as a draftsman in a state land office, and finally as a teller at the First National Bank. He married his first wife, the former Athol Estes, in July 1887.

In 1894 Porter bought a defunct weekly humor magazine for $250, retitled it *The Rolling Stone*, and tried to put it on its feet with the simple strategy of writing almost every word that appeared in it. The magazine failed and he began submitting humorous stories and sketches to other periodicals. Meanwhile, he'd been fired from his bank job when shortages were discovered in his accounts, and in 1895, believing he was about to be arrested and charged with embezzlement, he left his wife and spent a year on the run, holing up in Houston and New Orleans, then crossing the border and taking cover in Honduras and Mexico, traveling part of the time with the fugitive American outlaw Al Jennings. In 1897, when word reached Porter that his wife was seriously ill, he went back to Austin and surrendered. She died later that year.

Porter was convicted of embezzlement—whether rightly or wrongly is still disputed by his biographers—and sentenced to five years in the federal ward of the Ohio state pen. He worked the midnight shift in the prison pharmacy and spent his days

Orrin Henry, captain of the guard in the Ohio Penitentiary. He is probably the source of the pseudonym "O. Henry."

writing stories that he submitted to magazines using his in-laws' Pittsburgh address and the pseudonym of O. Henry, which apparently came from Orrin Henry, one of the prison guards. In July 1901, after serving three years and three months, he was released. After a brief stay with his late wife's parents, he relocated to New York City in the spring of 1902 at the urging of the *Ainslee's Magazine* editors who'd bought some material from him.

From then on he wrote like a demon, turning out hundreds of stories before the end of the century's first decade. The *New York World*, a paper with a readership of half a million, paid him a staggering $100 a week to write a story for each of its Sunday issues. He turned out copy at white heat, spent money lavishly, gave huge tips to waiters and generous handouts to derelicts, whiled away hours in bars and restaurants ad-libbing stories about the people around him, and drank two quarts of whisky a day. Somehow he found time to get married again—in November 1907, to the former Sara Coleman—but the marriage was quickly wrecked by his philandering and alcoholism. His greatest fear during his time as a literary superstar was that someone would go public with the hidden years of his life, so he falsified his biography to hide the fact that he'd been in prison. He died on June 5, 1910, of a combination of diabetes and cirrhosis of the liver, literally in the middle of his latest story, which was published incomplete in *Cosmopolitan* a few months later.

What was the secret of his success? At his best he was an astonishingly vivid writer. According to critic Hyder E. Rollins's essay "O. Henry" (*Sewanee Review*, Spring 1914), "No other writer has excelled him in the use of suggestive description." Perhaps more important was the care and skill with which he constructed his stories. Rollins described everything in an O. Henry tale as "a careful preparation for the denouement, even if the most searching reader can seldom detect it. . . ." Or, as Vachel Lindsay put it in his 1912 poem "The Knight in Disguise":

> He always worked a triple-hinged surprise
> To end the scene and make one rub his eyes.

"Twist ending" is the catchphrase that has remained associated with O. Henry's name from the beginning of the twentieth century to the present.

Tastes have changed over the course of the last hundred years, and much of what made O. Henry what he was isn't fashionable anymore. The out-

O. Henry referred to the lead female in the short story "The Caballero's Way" as "half Carmen, half Madonna."

landish coincidences that fuel his plots tend to make us either laugh or groan. The grandiose circumlocutions he loved not wisely but too well—like having A tell B to get off his mule by saying "Segregate yourself from your pseudo-equine quadruped"—strike today's readers as the prose equivalents of lead balloons. On the other hand, his realistic yet sympathetic portraits of con men, Western outlaws, and rogues of every description, sent blasts of critical heat his way while he was alive but today would be counted among his abiding strengths.

Most of his tales are set in the places he knew best: South America, the area around the Texas-Mexico border, the Appalachians, turn-of-the-century New York, and prison cells. He probably wrote "The Caballero's Way" in the Caledonia Hotel, which still exists in New York City today as an apartment house. The story was first published in *Everybody's Magazine* for July 1907 and included later that year in the O. Henry story collection *Heart of the West*. With its vivid description of Cisco's ride through the pear flat, its identification with a vicious protagonist, its occasional heavy-handed circumlocutions, its central ethical prob-

lem—how can a cold-blooded killer whose code forbids violence to any woman get even with the woman who betrayed him?—the tale demonstrates just about every element that critics have discovered in O. Henry's work.

It also, of course, gave birth to the film saga that we'll explore in this book, but the Cisco of movies and TV has nothing in common with O. Henry's Cisco except a name. The character as Porter conceived him was not at all a Robin Hood of the Old West, indeed not even a Mexican, but a murderous little Anglo probably modeled on Billy the Kid, while Cisco's nemesis Sandridge—at least in the opinion of William Nadel, a fan and distant relative of Porter—was based on Texas Ranger "Red" Hall. But O. Henry's tale was the original if remote starting point for 23 theatrical films, 156 half-hour TV films, a feature-length TV movie, a radio series, comic books, tons of tie-in items, and even a rock 'n' roll song.

The story follows in facsimile form, reproduced from *The Complete Writings of O. Henry*, Vol. IV, *Heart of the West* (Garden City, NY: Doubleday, Page and Company, 1917), 191-208.

XI

THE CABALLERO'S WAY

THE Cisco Kid had killed six men in more or less fair scrimmages, had murdered twice as many (mostly Mexicans), and had winged a larger number whom he modestly forbore to count. Therefore a woman loved him.

The Kid was twenty-five, looked twenty; and a careful insurance company would have estimated the probable time of his demise at, say, twenty-six. His habitat was anywhere between the Frio and the Rio Grande. He killed for the love of it—because he was quick-tempered—to avoid arrest—for his own amusement—any reason that came to his mind would suffice. He had escaped capture because he could shoot five-sixths of a second sooner than any sheriff or ranger in the service, and because he rode a speckled roan horse that knew every cow-path in the mesquite and pear thickets from San Antonio to Matamoras.

Tonia Perez, the girl who loved the Cisco Kid, was half Carmen, half Madonna, and the rest—oh, yes, a woman who is half Carmen and half Madonna can always be something more—the rest, let us say, was humming-bird. She lived in a grass-roofed *jacal*

191

HEART OF THE WEST

near a little Mexican settlement at the Lone Wolf Crossing of the Frio. With her lived a father or grandfather, a lineal Aztec, somewhat less than a thousand years old, who herded a hundred goats and lived in a continuous drunken dream from drinking *mescal*. Back of the *jacal* a tremendous forest of bristling pear, twenty feet high at its worst, crowded almost to its door. It was along the bewildering maze of this spinous thicket that the speckled roan would bring the Kid to see his girl. And once, clinging like a lizard to the ridge-pole, high up under the peaked grass roof, he had heard Tonia, with her Madonna face and Carmen beauty and humming-bird soul, parley with the sheriff's posse, denying knowledge of her man in her soft *mélange* of Spanish and English.

One day the adjutant-general of the State, who is, *ex officio*, commander of the ranger forces, wrote some sarcastic lines to Captain Duval of Company X, stationed at Laredo, relative to the serene and undisturbed existence led by murderers and desperadoes in the said captain's territory.

The captain turned the colour of brick dust under his tan, and forwarded the letter, after adding a few comments, per ranger Private Bill Adamson, to ranger Lieutenant Sandridge, camped at a water hole on the Nueces with a squad of five men in preservation of law and order.

Lieutenant Sandridge turned a beautiful *couleur de rose* through his ordinary strawberry complexion,

192

THE CABALLERO'S WAY

tucked the letter in his hip pocket, and chewed off the ends of his gamboge moustache.

The next morning he saddled his horse and rode alone to the Mexican settlement at the Lone Wolf Crossing of the Frio, twenty miles away.

Six feet two, blond as a Viking, quiet as a deacon, dangerous as a machine gun, Sandridge moved among the *Jacales*, patiently seeking news of the Cisco Kid.

Far more than the law, the Mexicans dreaded the cold and certain vengeance of the lone rider that the ranger sought. It had been one of the Kid's pastimes to shoot Mexicans "to see them kick": if he demanded from them moribund Terpsichorean feats, simply that he might be entertained, what terrible and extreme penalties would be certain to follow should they anger him! One and all they lounged with upturned palms and shrugging shoulders, filling the air with "*quien sabes*" and denials of the Kid's acquaintance.

But there was a man named Fink who kept a store at the Crossing—a man of many nationalities, tongues, interests, and ways of thinking.

"No use to ask them Mexicans," he said to Sandridge. "They're afraid to tell. This *hombre* they call the Kid—Goodall is his name, ain't it?—he's been in my store once or twice. I have an idea you might run across him at—but I guess I don't keer to say, myself. I'm two seconds later in pulling a gun than I used to be, and the difference is worth thinking about. But this Kid's got a half-Mexican

193

HEART OF THE WEST

girl at the Crossing that he comes to see. She lives in that *jacal* a hundred yards down the arroyo at the edge of the pear. Maybe she—no, I don't suppose she would, but that *jacal* would be a good place to watch, anyway."

Sandridge rode down to the *jacal* of Perez. The sun was low, and the broad shade of the great pear thicket already covered the grass-thatched hut. The goats were enclosed for the night in a brush corral near by. A few kids walked the top of it, nibbling the chaparral leaves. The old Mexican lay upon a blanket on the grass, already in a stupor from his mescal, and dreaming, perhaps, of the nights when he and Pizarro touched glasses to their New World fortunes —so old his wrinkled face seemed to proclaim him to be. And in the door of the *jacal* stood Tonia. And Lieutenant Sandridge sat in his saddle staring at her like a gannet agape at a sailorman.

The Cisco Kid was a vain person, as all eminent and successful assassins are, and his bosom would have been ruffled had he known that at a simple exchange of glances two persons, in whose minds he had been looming large, suddenly abandoned (at least for the time) all thought of him.

Never before had Tonia seen such a man as this. He seemed to be made of sunshine and blood-red tissue and clear weather. He seemed to illuminate the shadow of the pear when he smiled, as though the sun were rising again. The men she had known had been small and dark. Even the Kid, in spite of his

194

THE CABALLERO'S WAY

achievements, was a stripling no larger than herself, with black, straight hair and a cold, marble face that chilled the noonday.

As for Tonia, though she sends description to the poorhouse, let her make a millionaire of your fancy. Her blue-black hair, smoothly divided in the middle and bound close to her head, and her large eyes full of the Latin melancholy, gave her the Madonna touch. Her motions and air spoke of the concealed fire and the desire to charm that she had inherited from the *gitanas* of the Basque province. As for the humming-bird part of her, that dwelt in her heart; you could not perceive it unless her bright red skirt and dark blue blouse gave you a symbolic hint of the vagarious bird.

The newly lighted sun-god asked for a drink of water. Tonia brought it from the red jar hanging under the brush shelter. Sandridge considered it necessary to dismount so as to lessen the trouble of her ministrations.

I play no spy; nor do I assume to master the thoughts of any human heart; but I assert, by the chronicler's right, that before a quarter of an hour had sped, Sandridge was teaching her how to plait a six-strand raw-hide stake-rope, and Tonia had explained to him that were it not for her little English book that the peripatetic *padre* had given her and the little crippled *chivo*, that she fed from a bottle, she would be very, very lonely indeed.

Which leads to a suspicion that the Kid's fences

195

HEART OF THE WEST

needed repairing, and that the adjutant-general's sarcasm had fallen upon unproductive soil.

In his camp by the water hole Lieutenant Sandridge announced and reiterated his intention of either causing the Cisco Kid to nibble the black loam of the Frio country prairies or of haling him before a judge and jury. That sounded business-like. Twice a week he rode over to the Lone Wolf Crossing of the Frio, and directed Tonia's slim, slightly lemon-tinted fingers among the intricacies of the slowly growing lariata. A six-strand plait is hard to learn and easy to teach.

The ranger knew that he might find the Kid there at any visit. He kept his armament ready, and had a frequent eye for the pear thicket at the rear of the *jacal*. Thus he might bring down the kite and the humming-bird with one stone.

While the sunny-haired ornithologist was pursuing his studies the Cisco Kid was also attending to his professional duties. He moodily shot up a saloon in a small cow village on Quintana Creek, killed the town marshal (plugging him neatly in the centre of his tin badge), and then rode away, morose and unsatisfied. No true artist is uplifted by shooting an aged man carrying an old-style .38 bulldog.

On his way the Kid suddenly experienced the yearning that all men feel when wrong-doing loses its keen edge of delight. He yearned for the woman he loved to reassure him that she was his in spite of it. He wanted her to call his bloodthirstiness bravery

196

THE CABALLERO'S WAY

and his cruelty devotion. He wanted Tonia to bring him water from the red jar under the brush shelter, and tell him how the *chivo* was thriving on the bottle.

The Kid turned the speckled roan's head up the ten-mile pear flat that stretches along the Arroyo Hondo until it ends at the Lone Wolf Crossing of the Frio. The roan whickered; for he had a sense of locality and direction equal to that of a belt-line street-car horse; and he knew he would soon be nibbling the rich mesquite grass at the end of a forty-foot stake-rope while Ulysses rested his head in Circe's straw-roofed hut.

More weird and lonesome than the journey of an Amazonian explorer is the ride of one through a Texas pear flat. With dismal monotony and startling variety the uncanny and multiform shapes of the cacti lift their twisted trunks, and fat, bristly hands to encumber the way. The demon plant, appearing to live without soil or rain, seems to taunt the parched traveller with its lush gray greenness. It warps itself a thousand times about what look to be open and inviting paths, only to lure the rider into blind and impassable spine-defended "bottoms of the bag," leaving him to retreat, if he can, with the points of the compass whirling in his head.

To be lost in the pear is to die almost the death of the thief on the cross, pierced by nails and with grotesque shapes of all the fiends hovering about.

But it was not so with the Kid and his mount. Winding, twisting, circling, tracing the most fan-

197

HEART OF THE WEST

tastic and bewildering trail ever picked out, the good roan lessened the distance to the Lone Wolf Crossing with every coil and turn that he made.

While they fared the Kid sang. He knew but one tune and sang it, as he knew but one code and lived it, and but one girl and loved her. He was a single-minded man of conventional ideas. He had a voice like a coyote with bronchitis, but whenever he chose to sing his song he sang it. It was a conventional song of the camps and trail, running at its beginning as near as may be to these words:

> Don't you monkey with my Lulu girl
> Or I'll tell you what I'll do—

and so on. The roan was inured to it, and did not mind.

But even the poorest singer will, after a certain time, gain his own consent to refrain from contributing to the world's noises. So the Kid by the time he was within a mile or two of Tonia's *jacal*, had reluctantly allowed his song to die away—not because his vocal performance had become less charming to his own ears, but because his laryngeal muscles were aweary.

As though he were in a circus ring the speckled roan wheeled and danced through the labyrinth of pear until at length his rider knew by certain landmarks that the Lone Wolf Crossing was close at hand. Then, where the pear was thinner, he caught sight of the grass roof of the *jacal* and the hackberry

198

THE CABALLERO'S WAY

tree on the edge of the arroyo. A few yards farther the Kid stopped the roan and gazed intently through the prickly openings. Then he dismounted, dropped the roan's reins, and proceeded on foot, stooping and silent, like an Indian. The roan, knowing his part, stood still, making no sound.

The Kid crept noiselessly to the very edge of the pear thicket and reconnoitred between the leaves of a clump of cactus.

Ten yards from his hiding-place, in the shade of the *jacal*, sat his Tonia calmly plaiting a rawhide lariat. So far she might surely escape condemnation; women have been known, from time to time, to engage in more mischievous occupations. But if all must be told, there is to be added that her head reposed against the broad and comfortable chest of a tall red-and-yellow man, and that his arm was about her, guiding her nimble small fingers that required so many lessons at the intricate six-strand plait.

Sandridge glanced quickly at the dark mass of pear when he heard a slight squeaking sound that was not altogether unfamiliar. A gun-scabbard will make that sound when one grasps the handle of a six-shooter suddenly. But the sound was not repeated; and Tonia's fingers needed close attention.

And then, in the shadow of death, they began to talk of their love; and in the still July afternoon every word they uttered reached the ears of the Kid.

"Remember, then," said Tonia, "you must not

199

HEART OF THE WEST

come again until I send for you. Soon he will be here. A *vaquero* at the *tienda* said to-day he saw him on the Guadalupe three days ago. When he is that near he always comes. If he comes and finds you here he will kill you. So, for my sake, you must come no more until I send you the word."

"All right," said the ranger. "And then what?"

"And then," said the girl, "you must bring your men here and kill him. If not, he will kill you."

"He ain't a man to surrender, that's sure," said Sandridge. "It's kill or be killed for the officer that goes up against Mr. Cisco Kid."

"He must die," said the girl. "Otherwise there will not be any peace in the world for thee and me. He has killed many. Let him so die. Bring your men, and give him no chance to escape."

"You used to think right much of him," said Sandridge.

Tonia dropped the lariat, twisted herself around, and curved a lemon-tinted arm over the ranger's shoulder.

"But then," she murmured in liquid Spanish, "I had not beheld thee, thou great, red mountain of a man! And thou art kind and good, as well as strong. Could one choose him, knowing thee? Let him die; for then I will not be filled with fear by day and night lest he hurt thee or me."

"How can I know when he comes?" asked Sandridge.

"When he comes," said Tonia, "he remains two

200

THE CABALLERO'S WAY

days, sometimes three. Gregorio, the small son of old Luisa, the *lavandera*, has a swift pony. I will write a letter to thee and send it by him, saying how it will be best to come upon him. By Gregorio will the letter come. And bring many men with thee, and have much care, oh, dear red one, for the rattlesnake is not quicker to strike than is 'El chivato,' as they call him, to send a ball from his *pistola*."

"The Kid's handy with his gun, sure enough," admitted Sandridge, "but when I come for him I shall come alone. I'll get him by myself or not at all. The Cap wrote one or two things to me that make me want to do the trick without any help. You let me know when Mr. Kid arrives, and I'll do the rest."

"I will send you the message by the boy Gregorio," said the girl. "I knew you were braver than that small slayer of men who never smiles. How could I ever have thought I cared for him?"

It was time for the ranger to ride back to his camp on the water hole. Before he mounted his horse he raised the slight form of Tonia with one arm high from the earth for a parting salute. The drowsy stillness of the torpid summer air still lay thick upon the dreaming afternoon. The smoke from the fire in the *jacal*, where the *frijoles* blubbered in the iron pot, rose straight as a plumb-line above the clay-daubed chimney. No sound or movement disturbed the serenity of the dense pear thicket ten yards away.

When the form of Sandridge had disappeared, loping his big dun down the steep banks of the Frio

201

HEART OF THE WEST

crossing, the Kid crept back to his own horse, mounted him, and rode back along the tortuous trail he had come.

But not far. He stopped and waited in the silent depths of the pear until half an hour had passed. And then Tonia heard the high, untrue notes of his unmusical singing coming nearer and nearer; and she ran to the edge of the pear to meet him.

The Kid seldom smiled; but he smiled and waved his hat when he saw her. He dismounted, and his girl sprang into his arms. The Kid looked at her fondly. His thick, black hair clung to his head like a wrinkled mat. The meeting brought a slight ripple of some undercurrent of feeling to his smooth, dark face that was usually as motionless as a clay mask.

"How's my girl?" he asked, holding her close.

"Sick of waiting so long for you, dear one," she answered. "My eyes are dim with always gazing into that devil's pincushion through which you come. And I can see into it such a little way, too. But you are here, beloved one, and I will not scold. *Que mal muchacho !* not to come to see your *alma* more often. Go in and rest, and let me water your horse and stake him with the long rope. There is cool water in the jar for you."

The Kid kissed her affectionately.

"Not if the court knows itself do I let a lady stake my horse for me," said he. "But if you'll run in, *chica*, and throw a pot of coffee together while I attend to the *caballo*, I'll be a good deal obliged."

202

THE CABALLERO'S WAY

Besides his marksmanship the Kid had another attribute for which he admired himself greatly. He was *muy caballero*, as the Mexicans express it, where the ladies were concerned. For them he had always gentle words and consideration. He could not have spoken a harsh word to a woman. He might ruthlessly slay their husbands and brothers, but he could not have laid the weight of a finger in anger upon a woman. Wherefore many of that interesting division of humanity who had come under the spell of his politeness declared their disbelief in the stories circulated about Mr. Kid. One shouldn't believe everything one heard, they said. When confronted by their indignant men folk with proof of the *caballero's* deeds of infamy, they said maybe he had been driven to it, and that he knew how to treat a lady, anyhow.

Considering this extremely courteous idiosyncrasy of the Kid and the pride that he took in it, one can perceive that the solution of the problem that was presented to him by what he saw and heard from his hiding-place in the pear that afternoon (at least as to one of the actors) must have been obscured by difficulties. And yet one could not think of the Kid overlooking little matters of that kind.

At the end of the short twilight they gathered around a supper of *frijoles*, goat steaks, canned peaches, and coffee, by the light of a lantern in the *jacal*. Afterward, the ancestor, his flock corralled, smoked a cigarette and became a mummy in a gray

203

HEART OF THE WEST

blanket. Tonia washed the few dishes while the Kid dried them with the flour-sacking towel. Her eyes shone; she chatted volubly of the inconsequent happenings of her small world since the Kid's last visit; it was as all his other home-comings had been.

Then outside Tonia swung in a grass hammock with her guitar and sang sad *canciones de amor*.

"Do you love me just the same, old girl?" asked the Kid, hunting for his cigarette papers.

"Always the same, little one," said Tonia, her dark eyes lingering upon him.

"I must go over to Fink's," said the Kid, rising, "for some tobacco. I thought I had another sack in my coat. I'll be back in a quarter of an hour."

"Hasten," said Tonia, "and tell me—how long shall I call you my own this time? Will you be gone again to-morrow, leaving me to grieve, or will you be longer with your Tonia?"

"Oh, I might stay two or three days this trip," said the Kid, yawning. "I've been on the lodge for a month, and I'd like to rest up."

He was gone half an hour for his tobacco. When he returned Tonia was still lying in the hammock.

"It's funny," said the Kid, "how I feel. I feel like there was somebody lying behind every bush and tree waiting to shoot me. I never had mullygrubs like them before. Maybe it's one of them presumptions. I've got half a notion to light out in the morning before day. The Guadalupe country is burning up about that old Dutchman I plugged down there."

204

THE CABALLERO'S WAY

"You are not afraid—no one could make my brave little one fear."

"Well, I haven't been usually regarded as a jack-rabbit when it comes to scrapping; but I don't want a posse smoking me out when I'm in your *jacal*. Somebody might get hurt that oughtn't to."

"Remain with your Tonia; no one will find you here."

The Kid looked keenly into the shadows up and down the arroyo and toward the dim lights of the Mexican village.

"I'll see how it looks later on," was his decision.

At midnight a horseman rode into the rangers' camp, blazing his way by noisy "halloes" to indicate a pacific mission. Sandridge and one or two others turned out to investigate the row. The rider announced himself to be Domingo Sales, from the Lone Wolf Crossing. He bore a letter for Señor Sandridge. Old Luisa, the *lavandera*, had persuaded him to bring it, he said, her son Gregorio being too ill of a fever to ride.

Sandridge lighted the camp lantern and read the letter. These were its words:

DEAR ONE: He has come. Hardly had you ridden away when he came out of the pear. When he first talked he said he would stay three days or more. Then as it grew later he was like a wolf or a fox, and walked about without rest, looking and listening. Soon he said he must leave before daylight when it is dark and stillest. And then he seemed to suspect that I be not true

205

HEART OF THE WEST

to him. He looked at me so strange that I am frightened. I swear to him that I love him, his own Tonia. Last of all he said I must prove to him I am true. He thinks that even now men are waiting to kill him as he rides from my house. To escape he says he will dress in my clothes, my red skirt and the blue waist I wear and the brown mantilla over the head, and thus ride away. But before that he says that I must put on his clothes, his *pantalones* and *camisa* and hat, and ride away on his horse from the *jacal* as far as the big road beyond the crossing and back again. This before he goes, so he can tell if I am true and if men are hidden to shoot him. It is a terrible thing. An hour before daybreak this is to be. Come, my dear one, and kill this man and take me for your Tonia. Do not try to take hold of him alive, but kill him quickly. Knowing all, you should do that. You must come long before the time and hide yourself in the little shed near the *jacal* where the wagon and saddles are kept. It is dark in there. He will wear my red skirt and blue waist and brown mantilla. I send you a hundred kisses. Come surely and shoot quickly and straight.

THINE OWN TONIA.

Sandridge quickly explained to his men the official part of the missive. The rangers protested against his going alone.

"I'll get him easy enough," said the lieutenant. "The girl's got him trapped. And don't even think he'll get the drop on me."

Sandridge saddled his horse and rode to the Lone Wolf Crossing. He tied his big dun in a clump of brush on the arroyo, took his Winchester from its scabbard, and carefully approached the Perez *jacal*. There was only the half of a high moon drifted over by ragged, milk-white gulf clouds.

206

THE CABALLERO'S WAY

The wagon-shed was an excellent place for ambush; and the ranger got inside it safely. In the black shadow of the brush shelter in front of the *jacal* he could see a horse tied and hear him impatiently pawing the hard-trodden earth.

He waited almost an hour before two figures came out of the *jacal*. One, in man's clothes, quickly mounted the horse and galloped past the wagon-shed toward the crossing and village. And then the other figure, in skirt, waist, and mantilla over its head, stepped out into the faint moonlight, gazing after the rider. Sandridge thought he would take his chance then before Tonia rode back. He fancied she might not care to see it.

"Throw up your hands," he ordered loudly, stepping out of the wagon-shed with his Winchester at his shoulder.

There was a quick turn of the figure, but no movement to obey, so the ranger pumped in the bullets—one—two—three—and then twice more; for you never could be too sure of bringing down the Cisco Kid. There was no danger of missing at ten paces, even in that half moonlight.

The old ancestor, asleep on his blanket, was awakened by the shots. Listening further, he heard a great cry from some man in mortal distress or anguish, and rose up grumbling at the disturbing ways of moderns.

The tall, red ghost of a man burst into the *jacal*, reaching one hand, shaking like a *tule* reed, for the

207

HEART OF THE WEST

lantern hanging on its nail. The other spread a letter on the table.

"Look at this letter, Perez," cried the man. "Who wrote it?"

"*Ah, Dios!* it is Señor Sandridge," mumbled the old man, approaching. "*Pues, señor*, that letter was written by '*El chivato*,' as he is called—by the man of Tonia. They say he is a bad man; I do not know. While Tonia slept he wrote the letter and sent it by this old hand of mine to Domingo Sales to be brought to you. Is there anything wrong in the letter? I am very old; and I did not know. *Valgame Dios!* it is a very foolish world; and there is nothing in the house to drink—nothing to drink."

Just then all that Sandridge could think of to do was to go outside and throw himself face downward in the dust by the side of his humming-bird, of whom not a feather fluttered. He was not a *caballero* by instinct, and he could not understand the niceties of revenge.

A mile away the rider who had ridden past the wagon-shed struck up a harsh, untuneful song, the words of which began:

Don't you monkey with my Lulu girl
Or I'll tell you what I'll do—

208

How and when did the vicious Cisco of O. Henry's story, who wasn't even Mexican, evolve into the Latino Robin Hood of movies and TV? Everyone before now who has discussed the question says that the transformation took place in 1929 and credits Raoul Walsh, the original director and intended star of *In Old Arizona*. The truth is that a good deal of the process happened long before 1929, but Walsh still deserves much of the credit; more, in fact, than anyone has realized.

As of this writing Cisco's career on the screen has lasted for eighty years, beginning not long after O. Henry's death and extending through the time I worked on the first edition of this book. The saga began in March 1914 when the French-owned Éclair studio released *The Caballero's Way*, a three-reeler featuring J. W. Johnston as Sandridge, Herbert Stanley Dunn (whom reference books sometimes call Arthur Dunn or Herbert Stanley) as Cisco, and Edna Payne as Tonia. Dunn was born in Brooklyn, New York, on November 24, 1891, and died in Costa Mesa, California, on April 14, 1979. We would know nothing about his portrayal of Cisco beyond these bare facts except for a stroke of luck. Decades after his time in the movies and about a year before his death, Dunn was interviewed in his Costa Mesa home by reporter Don Cantrell. Apparently the interview was never published but Cantrell turned over his notes to John Langellier of the Gene Autry Western Heritage Museum, and thanks to

him we can hear Stan Dunn reminisce about his time as Cisco as if we were in his home with him.

Dunn's father was a ship captain of Irish descent and his mother an Algonquin Indian who, along with all four of her children, found work in early silent movies. (One of Stan's brothers, Eddie Dunn, wound up as a gag writer and bit player in Laurel & Hardy comedy shorts.) After appearing on the stage in various stock companies, thirteen-year-old Stan was hired by Vitagraph Films as a property boy in 1905. He moved to Biograph five years later and acted in countless one- and two-reelers. Then in 1913 or early 1914 he was hired by Société Française des Films et Cinématographes Éclair, a New York firm backed by French investors, and was sent to Tucson to be a prop man and actor in the company's Westerns. Some time after Stan arrived, Éclair director Webster Cullison (1880-1938) was preparing to make *The Caballero's Way*. Cullison was testing other actors for the part of Cisco, Dunn said, but "finally decided they were too old. He wanted a young kid. So he picked me."

The film proved such a hit that Éclair's front office wired Cullison to drop whatever else he was doing and make a series of Cisco shorts with Dunn in the lead. Whether O. Henry's estate was notified isn't known, but I suspect no one at Éclair thought it was necessary. Over the next year or so, until the pressures of World War I in Europe caused the studio's collapse, Dunn starred in a cycle of Cisco shorts that presumably were structured along the same general lines as the long-running Broncho Billy Anderson series. (How many were made is impossible to tell, but Dunn's estimate of 200 seems way too high.) Except for two days of filming in Tombstone and one junket to California, all the Éclair Ciscos were shot in the Tucson area. They have long since crumbled to dust and survive only in Stan Dunn's recollections almost sixty-five years later.

> After *The Caballero's Way* my wife Bertha and I wrote the rest of the scripts. I had the ideas and she wrote them out in longhand. She called herself Bert. A lot of people thought she was a man. She was a very pretty girl. She passed away in 1966, but we had a terrific life.
>
> We were the first ones [to make movies] in Tucson. . . . I was the first film cowboy to use two guns. [The fancy gloves he wore as Cisco] and the two-gun bit was Cullison's idea. I couldn't roll a cigarette or do much of anything while wearing that hot leather but I finally slit a few glove fingers and that worked out a little better. I couldn't ride a horse in the beginning or shoot a gun either but we were firing blanks so it really didn't matter.
>
> . . . They had ordered this leather costume from El Paso, Texas, and I had to get into it with a shoehorn, it was so tight. I never had to put my foot into a stirrup to mount a horse. I only grabbed hold of the pommel, started him off and threw myself into the saddle. I didn't have a mustache either but they made one up.
>
> My pay soon jumped from thirty-five to forty-five dollars a week, and that was big money in those days. You could buy a steak dinner in Tucson for twenty-five or thirty cents. We were paid in pieces of gold or silver since there was no paper money down there at that time.

Early in Dunn's stint as Cisco, a horse fell on him and broke his leg, leaving him with a limp for the rest of his life.

> I was lucky. There were no stunt men in those days. We did our own fistfighting and took our own falls. A lot of the actors suffered more serious injuries. Some were killed. The leg hurt me for quite a while . . . and I went through a lot of pain using it. I had to walk but I worked it out by using it. Trouble is, that same leg had been broken three times before. It wasn't so bad when I was younger but it's bothering me more and more as I get older.

> Another funny thing. I was riding into the San Xavier mission area from out in the hills. My horse was trotting along at a fast pace and he stepped in a hole. I went over his head and when I came to it was so funny. All these people, Papago Indians, were looking down at me. I must have hit my head, I went out of that saddle so fast. Then I got up and went back to my horse. The Indians thought that was great. The mothers and fathers were going: "That guy is great, he's going to do it again." They were hollering and cheering, even the kids.
>
> The people in Tucson accepted us very well. They took [moviemaking] as something new and fascinating. It excited them. . . . Downtown was about four blocks square then. There was about a hundred and fifty townspeople and there was a lot of consumptives, you know, tubercular cases. They had a sanitarium out there too but it was out to the east about twenty miles.
>
> Oh, it was beautiful country. It was still a little wild in 1913 but there was no hardship in finding local people to work in a picture. . . . We didn't use many but the ones we wanted we got: Mexicans, white men, white women. They all wanted to get in. These people worked for nothing, the extras I mean. They didn't get any money at all that I ever saw.
>
> As for fun, well, there was only one place there and that was the old Tucson Hotel. The restaurant closed around seven or eight o'clock. If you wanted a drink . . . Tucson was dry. There were no liquor stores or anything. I didn't see any bar. [But if] you ordered it, you got it. At the restaurant, I mean . . . you sort of got it under the table.
>
> There wasn't any free time to get away or ride off into the hills. We got enough of that during the week. We actually worked seven days a week. . . . We could get off if we had something to do but there was no place to go. We had horses to curry down and wash, and take care of the feeding. Each one of us had our own horses and we took care of them. There were no guys to take care of horses. Oh, there was so much to do.
>
> The location shooting was right around Tucson, all around the mountain areas there in different places. You see, in those days you could take a camera and move it all over and get a different location. We had no automobiles. All we had was horses and you couldn't run a horse too far, then work them all day and bring them back again. You wouldn't have a horse.
>
> Once we went up Sabino Canyon, that was fifteen miles from town. The trail goes up a mountainside, it goes up to a gold mine there. We passed a small stream and it was

very funny, because it had garnet stones. They're red stones, little bitty things. They're all over. When you first look at them they look like blood. It was fascinating to me because here I was a Brooklyn boy out on the prairie, and I knew nothing about those things. Sometimes we'd get so far out and the horses would get worked so hard that I'd just lie down there at night with my horse and go to sleep. I was used to sleeping on the ground.

The old studios were at Congress and Main Streets. Seems they were on the northwest corner. There was a house there, a two-story house, and in back of it was an adobe house but it was vacated. . . . We utilized that by putting a stage in there. [The property Éclair rented] was a couple of acres, and you had a corral in there for your horses, and you had a stable. We did quite a lot of the building. It took all the actors together because we had no carpenters but ourselves. . . .

Generally this is how we would work. In the mornings we would get out on the land, then in the afternoon we'd have the overhead lights in the studio. We had canvas over the rigging of the stage. That was to cut the sunlight down or diffuse it. We'd film along that whole range of mountains. There was the Santa Ritas, Catalina, and what they call the Big A today. . . . Then there was the saguaro forest. It was east of Congress Street and way out. There was a big bed of them there. . . . Some of those things must be a thousand years old.

We went down to Tombstone once. . . . And I said: "Gee, that's a long ride for a horse. What about the horses?" [Cullison or someone else replied:] "No, we got horses down there." So we went down there in a car. Very seldom I traveled in a car, very seldom. I don't remember much about Tombstone but Boot Hill wasn't filling up nearly as fast as it had back in the 1870s and 1880s. It was still pretty wild-looking to us New Yorkers, and it did give us a feeling of reality for the kind of shoot-em-ups we were filming. I remember the old Cochise County Court House and we filmed around there.

We went down to Nogales on our horses once because Pancho Villa had taken the town. They were fighting the Carranza forces. They were also fighting with American soldiers. . . .

One of the last photographs taken of Herbert Stanley Dunn in the den of his Costa Mesa, California, home a year before his death in mid-April 1979 at age 87. His den was covered with autographed stills from many of the stars he had worked with, including Jean Harlow, Clark Gable, Edward G. Robinson, Cary Grant, Nelson Eddy, and Leo Carrillo.

Herbert Stanley Dunn, the original Cisco Kid, confronts his adversaries in a scene from *The Caballero's Way,*
the first Cisco Kid movie, filmed in 1914 by Éclair Film Company in Tucson, Arizona.

The American soldiers told the Mexicans they better shoot the other way or they were going to dry them up. No bullets came our way because we were off at a distance. But I had the great pleasure of seeing Pancho Villa on a big white horse with a silver saddle and bridle. He had a white shirt on, a big brown sombrero and it looked to me like he had lots of pistol belts. . . . He was quite a showman anyway, you know.

Territorial days ended about a year before we came. I think Arizona became a state in 1912. The natives were talking about it. Yeah, they felt it was a great idea. It gave them a feeling of being something, of being more secure. Now they had the government behind them. They figured the government people would be coming in to take over the things they wanted, like running the water through. We had to rely on wells in those days. We had no electricity either, we used oil lamps.

The studio people stayed at the Tucson Hotel until they could find themselves a home to live in. They all went into private homes like I did. I lived in an old judge's home on Con-

gress Street. . . . He was my friend too. He was related to the rich people, the management. They all had nice homes. The people who had the space were glad to have us there. They loved the prestige. . . .

There was a movie house in Tucson. . . . I was in it once, the time they showed the first Cisco Kid picture. The company had sent it out for us to see it. We saw it first, then they let the local people see it. . . . Now they were seeing what they had worked in, so that made them feel big.

There was no dialogue in those days. We made it up as we went along. They inserted the words in New York when they put the picture together. Every day we had to send some cans in because it took three days to get there. . . . (Cantrell interview with Stan Dunn c. 1978)

After Éclair's collapse, Dunn acted off and on in both Hollywood and New York. Eventually Columbia Pictures hired him as a property master for $500 a week, much more than he'd ever earned as an actor. Twice during his subsequent career he was sent back to the area where in his early twenties he'd played Cisco: in 1940, to help construct Old Tucson for the filming of *Arizona* (Columbia, 1940, directed by Wesley Ruggles and starring William Holden and Jean Arthur), and in 1943, on loanout to Howard Hughes for *The Outlaw*. "Do I miss Arizona?" he was asked near the end of his life by Don Cantrell. "Yeah, I'd love to move back there. But I couldn't move from here if I wanted to. I can't walk!"

In 1935, Dunn remembered, he happened to meet Warner Baxter, who six years earlier had won an Oscar for his performance as Cisco in the first feature about the character, *In Old Arizona*. When Dunn claimed that he himself had been the first to play the part, Baxter wouldn't believe him until Stan showed some stills from the three-reel version of *The Caballero's Way* the next day. "They told me I was first!" an unhappy Baxter exclaimed. What is strongly suggested by this anecdote, and supported by Don Cantrell's 1975 photograph of Dunn wearing the original Cisco hat, is that the 1914 version of the character, like Baxter's of fifteen years later, was a Latino. So let's tip our own hats to that long-forgotten director Webster Cullison for transforming O. Henry's murderous Anglo into the ethnic rogue-hero who still survives in our new century's early years.

Everyone well versed in Western-film history knows that the first person to make a feature-length movie with O. Henry's character turned into a Latino was Raoul Walsh (1887-1980), whose Hollywood career endured for more than half a century. What no one has realized until now is that the movie in which he did it was not *In Old Arizona*.

Walsh was born in New York City on March 11, 1887. His mother's people were of Irish and Spanish descent and his father was an immigrant from Dublin who became a clothing cutter and later the co-owner of a prosperous wholesale garment business. Among the many celebrities of the late 19th century who frequently visited the Walsh home on East 48th Street was actor Edwin Booth, the brother of Lincoln's assassin.

Like every later movie hero with Irish-Spanish roots, Raoul had a zest for adventure. At sixteen he dropped out of school to sail to Cuba on a cargo schooner with his uncle. He went on from there to Mexico, learned riding and roping, joined the drovers pushing a trail herd north to Texas, then found work breaking remounts for the cavalry. Recuperating in San Antonio after a horse fall injured his leg, he was hired by a theatrical troupe to ride a cayuse across a treadmill in its production of *The Clansman*, the play based on Thomas Dixon's pro-Ku Klux Klan novel.

Herbert Stanley Dunn, wearing the original Cisco kid hat, and Mr. Marion Stoneking, an administrator with the North Orange County Community College District, in 1975. Cypress College had selected Dunn as an American Award winner (photographer: Don Cantrell).

In 1909, after he'd returned to New York, Walsh was signed by Pathé Frères as an actor in the one- and two-reel shorts that the studio was filming in the wilds of New Jersey. A chance meeting with Christy Cabanne, who was directing the same sort of pictures

Raoul Walsh is Pancho Villa in *The Life of General Villa* (1914).

Warner Baxter did not limit himself to playing Mexican roles. Here he appears as a Native American opposite Dolores del Río, a Latina, in one of the numerous films that are part of the Ramona cycle.

for the rival Biograph company, brought Walsh to the attention of Cabanne's mentor, the legendary D. W. Griffith. The result was that the young actor found himself not only a Griffith protégé in his own right, but a member of the group D. W. took with him to California when he launched his own production company. Before long Walsh was not only acting in but also scripting and directing two-reel action flicks.

Late in 1913 or early in 1914, Griffith sent Walsh back to the Rio Grande country to shoot footage of Pancho Villa and his rebel army as they fought battles across Mexico. On Walsh's return the studio expanded his material into a seven-reel feature, *The Life of General Villa* (Mutual, 1914), by splicing it together with fiction footage directed by Christy Cabanne and with Walsh himself decked out in Mexican garb (not for the last time in his career) as Pancho Villa. Walsh's best known screen performance came soon afterwards, in Griffith's 1915 classic *The Birth of a Nation*, based on the same Thomas Dixon novel in whose San Antonio stage version Walsh had appeared as a rider in the Ku Klux Klan. The role he played in Griffith's film was John Wilkes Booth, whose brother Edwin he had met years before in the Walsh home on East 48th Street.

Late in 1915 Walsh parted company with Griffith and joined the newly formed Fox studio as a writer-director. He spent the next five years making an incredible twenty full-length features, everything from exotic romances

starring Theda Bara to actioners with his younger brother George as the hero. It is the eighth of his early Fox pictures that concerns us here.

Betrayed (Fox, 1917), a five-reeler that Walsh both wrote and directed, is set along the Texas-Mexico border. Carmelita Carrito (Miriam Cooper), a lovely señorita engaged to Pepo Esperanza (Monte Blue), finds herself falling in love with Leopoldo Juárez (Hobart Bosworth), a bandit who takes refuge in her father's hacienda. When Leopoldo rides away, Carmelita stares out the window after him and eventually falls asleep. William Jerome (Wheeler Oakman), a U.S. Army officer also hunting for Leopoldo, comes to the hacienda, and Carmelita, infatuated once again, tells him that the bandido has made a date to meet her by a certain brook. At the climax Leopoldo discovers that he's been betrayed and makes Carmelita put on his coat and sombrero so that Jerome mistakes her for his quarry and shoots her down. This is when the señorita wakes from her siesta—that's right, the whole sequence lifted from "The Caballero's Way" has been a dream—and finds that Leopoldo is still hiding in the hacienda and that a squad of U.S. troopers led by none other than her fiancé Pepo are surrounding the house. The film ends with Pepo capturing the bandit, earning a nice reward, and reestablishing himself in Carmelita's affections.

O. Henry was still one of America's most widely read storytellers seven years after his death, and the reviewer for at least one trade paper pointed out that part of *Betrayed*'s plot was a rip-off. If O. Henry's estate took any legal action, then it was quickly settled and never led to a reported judicial opinion. Perhaps Walsh's decision twelve years later to direct and star in *In Old Arizona* was his way of making amends.

Between his two screen versions of the O. Henry tale came a long-forgotten two-reeler, *The Border Terror* (Universal, 1919), one of hundreds of shorts released late in the second decade of the twentieth century. Harry Harvey directed from a scenario by H. Tipton Steck which both the film's credits and Universal's copyright registration acknowledged as adapted from "The Caballero's Way." I presume this means that it was made with permission from O. Henry's estate. Cisco was played by Vester Pegg (1889-1951), a puncher who around the same time had small parts in some of the earliest films of John Ford. Tonia was portrayed by Yvette Mitchell. Whether the Cisco character had reverted to his Anglo origins in this twenty-minute version or was still presented as Latino is anyone's guess.

CISCO TALKS: WARNER BAXTER 4

or the lover of Westerns, moviegoing in the 1920s was cowboy heaven. Between 1917 and 1923 traditionalists could enjoy Paramount's cycle of features starring William S. Hart, which as often as not were written and directed by a man destined to play a meaty part in the Cisco saga later on: Lambert Hillyer. From 1918 through 1928 the Fox studio presented a series of slicker, more action-packed shoot-'em-ups with Tom Mix (three directed by Hillyer and two by the young John Ford) and, between 1920 and 1927, another popular series with Buck Jones (including two non-Westerns helmed by Ford, half a dozen by William Wellman, and a few late oaters by Hillyer). Universal's longest-running series (1921-30) show-cased the stunting and comedic skills of Hoot Gibson, who was directed twice by Ford but most often by action master B. Reeves Eason. Other Universal Western series featured stars like Jack Hoxie (1923-27) and Art Acord (1925-27). After Paramount's *The Covered Wagon* (1923, directed by James Cruze) and Fox's *The Iron Horse* (1924, directed by John Ford) created the frontier epic, MGM launched an elaborate cycle of Westerns with Tim McCoy and First National an equally well-made series with Ken Maynard, both running from 1926 through 1929. Paramount followed up *The Covered Wagon* with a set of generously budgeted pictures based (at least nominally) on novels by Zane Grey and usually starring Richard Dix or Jack Holt. Harry Carey, the

first actor groomed to stardom by John Ford, played the lead in dozens of Westerns at various studios through the twenties. FBO presented Tom Tyler (1925-29), Bob Steele (1927-29), and teenage Buzz Barton (1927-29) in three separate rangeland series. Lesser stars like Al Hoxie, Fred Humes, Buffalo Bill Jr., and Buddy Roosevelt hung their Stetsons at low-rent outfits like Action Pictures, Anchor, and Rayart. It seemed as if the cornucopia of Western fare would never go dry.

John Ford's *The Iron Horse* (1924) was an epic Western that used the construction of the first transcontinental railroad as a backdrop.

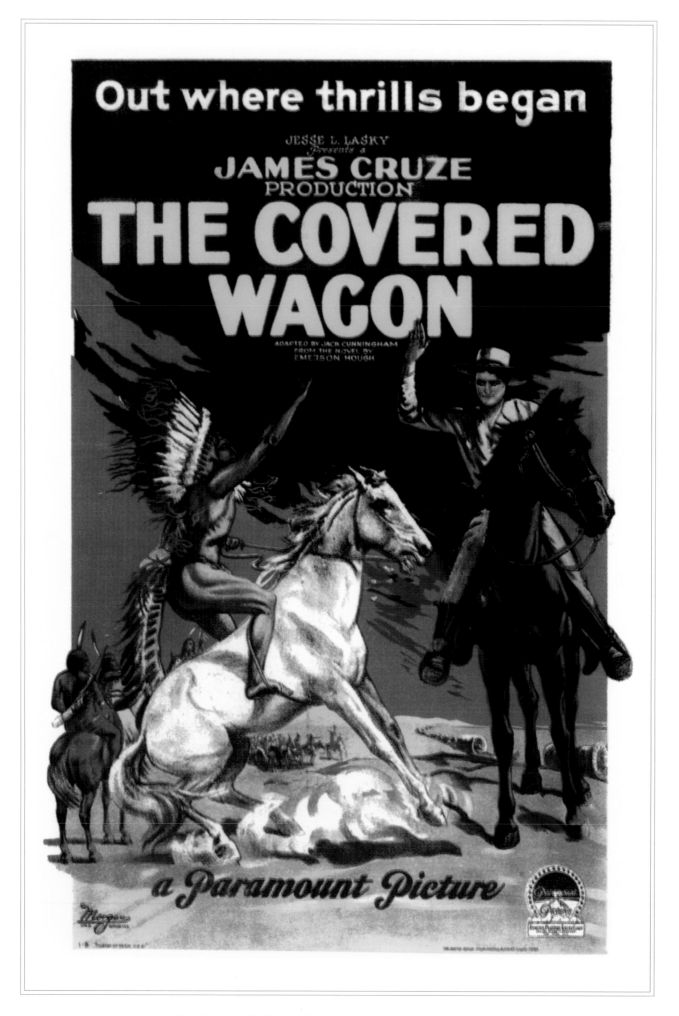

Based on a novel by Emerson Hough and provided with an ample budget,
Covered Wagon (1923) starred J. Warren Kerrigan, Lois Wilson, and Alan Hale.

Tiffany
presents
BOB STEELE

An All-Talking
PRODUCTION

This film poster
from the early
sound period
is a beautifully
rendered depiction
of a buckaroo.

And then almost overnight it did. Between the middle of 1926 and the end of 1929, the period chronicled in Alexander Walker's *The Shattered Silents* (Morrow, 1979), the printing of sound on film evolved from a technical novelty to a revolutionary development that brought one era of movie history to an end and gave birth to another. What seemed most drastically threatened by the coming of talking pictures was outdoor moviemaking in general and the Western in particular because Hollywood's new gurus, the sound technicians, insisted again and again that it was

impossible to record sound except indoors under tightly controlled conditions. Most of the studios resigned themselves to the death of the Western and ended their output of oaters.

John Ford, under contract to Fox at the time, was not convinced. As he told Peter Bogdanovich almost forty years later, "They said it couldn't be done, and I said, 'Why the hell *can't* it be done?' They said, 'Well, you can't because—' and they gave me a lot of master's degree talk. So I said, 'Well, let's try it'" (Walker 50). The result was *Napoleon's Barber* (1928), a twenty-two-minute short that Ford claimed to be "the first time anyone ever went outside with a sound system."

Raoul Walsh was directing at Fox then too. It was apparently in mid-1928 (although he doesn't give the date) when studio head Winfield Sheehan frantically summoned Walsh back from a Mexican vacation and sent him to the Beverly Theater to take in his first talking picture. "The triteness of the sets and the obvious nervousness of the female lead made me want to jump up and start shouting. Then a thought struck me. If the tedious dialogue could be supplemented and broken up by more action, the result might be thrilling instead of soporific" (219). As he was leaving the theater he heard "a burst of sound" from a Fox Movietone newsreel dealing with a dockworkers' strike, felt a rush of inspiration, and went back to Sheehan's office with the announcement: "I'm going to make the first outdoor sound feature." The film he made, or rather started to make as both director and leading man until a terrified jackrabbit entered his life, was *In Old Arizona* (1929), first and best known of the twenty-three full-length cinematic exploits of the Cisco Kid.

The source of the Beverly Theater anecdote is Walsh's autobiography, *Each Man in His Time* (Farrar, Straus and Giroux, 1974), prepared with the help of veteran screenwriter John Twist and published when the director was in his late eighties. It's a vividly written book but Walsh is hopelessly unreliable on facts and seems to have forgotten more than he remembered. In his recollection, neither he nor Sheehan knows anything about John Ford (who rates just three passing mentions in the entire Walsh memoir) having made or being about to make a short with full sound for Fox that same year. Walsh claims it was his idea to make the first full-length talkie and to call it *In Old Arizona;* he also

Raoul Walsh as the Cisco Kid in *In Old Arizona* before he injured his eye and was replaced by Warner Baxter

tells us three pages later that originally the "agreed length" of the film had been "two reels"—the same length as *Napoleon's Barber*—but that Sheehan liked the rushes of the first two days' shooting so much "that he demanded a five-reeler instead of the shorter footage" (222). You'd never know from Walsh's account that the finished picture ran almost ninety minutes. According to Walsh, the Cisco character as created by O. Henry "was a Mexican" (222). *Betrayed*, the 1917 feature in which the character had been turned into a Mexican by Walsh himself, gets dropped down the memory hole. In his autobiography Walsh also claims to have written the script for *In Old Arizona* himself. "Poor O. Henry. I hoped he would not turn over in his grave. After I finished with this version of his story, it would be a tossup who wrote what" (223). Whatever contributions were made by Tom Barry, who is credited on screen for adaptation and dialogue, are studiously ignored. Walsh describes shooting a scene for *In Old Arizona* with a stagecoach being chased by Indians. There's no such scene in the picture. He has Sheehan telling him: "Remember that scene where you fried the bacon? That goddamn sizzling was so real it made me hungry" (222). No bacon is fried in the movie, although Alexander Walker and countless other film commentators have described it vividly.

What is known for sure is that Walsh himself was playing Cisco in the picture, as witness the photograph of him in costume on horseback (see facing page), and that he was making the outdoor sequences in and around Bryce Canyon, Utah, with a Fox Movietone newsreel truck to capture naturalistic sound. When the truck was damaged beyond repair, Walsh shut down production, phoned Sheehan in Los Angeles, and made plans to finish the film on the Fox back lot. "I'll have to rewrite some of the end sequences to fit because there aren't any mountains. Build me some adobe house fronts, and I'll need one interior. Better get started right away because we're pulling out of here tonight" (224).

Walsh was in the front passenger seat of the lead car racing much too fast across the starlit Utah desert to the nearest Union Pacific rail link. "We missed outcrops and cattle and once scattered a herd of deer. The only thing we did not miss was a big jack rabbit. The headlights must have dazzled him, because he jumped at the windshield on my side and came crashing through it. There was no safety glass—Ford began to install it the next year—and the jack, dead from the impact, hit me squarely in the face, accompanied by a shower of glass splinters" (224-25). Walsh was hospitalized in Salt Lake City, where Tom Mix visited him with a bottle of five-star Hennessy cognac hidden under a basket of fruit. Eventually he was sent to a New York specialist to have his right eye removed. Fox contract director Irving Cummings took over *In Old Arizona*, with Warner Baxter and Dorothy Burgess cast as Cisco and his *enamorada*. "They were able to save all the long shots I had made, in which my face was not too distinguishable, and they used the same chase scenes through Bryce Canyon" (229). Walsh never comes out and says it, but what follows from his account is that every bit of *In Old Arizona* with Warner Baxter in front of the camera—in other words, the vast majority of the film we have today—was directed not by Walsh but by Irving Cummings, who must certainly be credited for Baxter's Oscar-winning performance.

Cummings was one of the countless directors who put in long years at his trade but never broke out from the pack to become either a household name like John Ford or a cult figure. Born in New York City on October 9, 1888, he started acting on the stage in his teens. One of his earliest parts was that of a man 70 years old. In September 1908, a month before his twentieth birthday, he was leading man opposite the legendary Lillian Russell in *Wildfire*. His first movie role was in *The Window*, a primitive one-reeler shot in New York. In one of his earliest feature-length pictures, *Uncle Tom's Cabin* (World, 1914), he donned blackface for the part of runaway slave George Harris. He had a minor role in one of the earliest cliffhanger serials, *The Million Dollar Mystery* (Thanhouser, 1914, twenty-three chapters), and played the male lead opposite Lottie Pickford in that thirty-chapter cinematic marathon *The Diamond from the Sky* (North American Film, 1915). By the end of the decade he'd been seen in more than

Warner Baxter in full costume as the Cisco Kid

forty silent features, usually under directors and alongside fellow actors who have been forgotten for generations but occasionally opposite an immortal like Ethel Barrymore, with whom he costarred in *An American Widow* (Metro, 1917).

Early in the twenties he cofounded the Cummings & Smith production company and made his debut as director in its first offering, *The Man from Hell's River* (1922), which he also starred in. The enterprise collapsed a year later but Cummings had no trouble getting work as a director at the established studios: first Universal, then First National, and finally Fox, which was to be his home for most of the next twenty years. His earliest Fox features were *The Johnstown Flood* (1926), starring George O'Brien and introducing Janet Gaynor, and *Rustling for Cupid* (1926), an O'Brien Western. Cummings was a solid, unpretentious craftsman who could be relied on to direct from two to five

films a year with minimal fuss. Most of his silents and early talkies were melodramas. Between 1935 and 1945 he specialized in musicals, directing four with Shirley Temple, three with Alice Faye and Don Ameche, and four starring Betty Grable, who headed the cast of *The Dolly Sisters* (1945), the last film of his long stay at what had become 20th Century-Fox. Near the end of his tenure, in 1943, he received a gold medal for outstanding achievement in the arts and sciences from the Thomas A. Edison Foundation. The last film he directed was the feeble *Double Dynamite* (RKO, 1951), starring Jane Russell, Frank Sinatra, and Groucho Marx and produced by his son, Irving Cummings Jr. He officially retired in 1954 and died in Cedars of Lebanon Hospital on April 18, 1959.

Except that he never became a director, Warner Baxter's career vaguely resembles that of the man under whom he earned an Oscar. He was

WILLIAM FOX
Presents
Peter B. Kyne's
RUSTLING FOR CUPID

Irving Cummings, who took over directing *In Old Arizona* (1929) when Raoul Walsh was hospitalized with an eye injury, directed *Rustling for Cupid* in 1926, starring George O'Brien and introducing Janet Gaynor.

Lobby card from *A Son of His Father* (1925)

born in Columbus, Ohio, on March 29, 1893, and, after graduating from high school, got a job selling farm implements. His first acting experience was in Louisville, Kentucky, when a stock company performer took sick and Baxter was more or less drafted to fill in. Four months later his mother found out young Warner was on the stage and made him come home. He went into the insurance business, became head of the Philadelphia office of Travelers, then decided to chuck it all and go west. In Oklahoma he invested his meager savings in a garage and lost every penny. In Dallas he joined a stock company at a salary of $30 a week. He spent the next several years acting all over the country and, in the fall of 1917, starred on Broadway in Frederic and Fanny Hatton's *Lombardi, Ltd*. Appearing in the Morosco Theatre production with the man who would be the talkies' first Cisco was the last and greatest of the Cisco sidekicks, Leo Carrillo.

Baxter's Hollywood career began in 1921 at the small Realart studio. He advanced quickly from featured player to male lead opposite stars like Constance Binney, Ethel Clayton, Madge Bellamy, Alice Calhoun, and Colleen Moore, hopping from studio to studio and from one director to another. (Lambert Hillyer, who directed him in the 1924 *Those Who Dance*, was to become a central figure in the Cisco saga long after Baxter left the role.) Late in 1924 he settled in at Famous Players-Lasky, which would eventually merge into Paramount, and stayed there, with occasional loanouts to other studios, until 1928. Perhaps his best role at Paramount was as the lead in *The Great Gatsby* (1926, directed by Herbert Brenon). Sandwiched among the pictures he played in at Paramount were two Westerns: *A Son of His Father* (1925, directed by Victor Fleming) and *Drums of the Desert* (1927, directed by John Waters). Near the end of his time at Paramount he was loaned out to play the romantic

In Old Arizona (1929) was the first sound film featuring the Cisco Kid.

D. W. Griffith's *Scarlet Days* (1919) was based on the popular culture interpretation of Joaquín Murrieta, who was depicted in this film as a noble Mexican and proto-Chicano bandit hero named Álvarez.

▪ WOMEN TAKE CHARGE ▪

In film and other popular culture genres (such as folklore, pulp fiction, radio and television, and others) the theme of the noble bandit has provided an extraordinary opportunity for the emergence of assertive, dynamic, and attractive female characters. The Hispanic characters in this cultural universe have not only been bandidos but also bandidas. One set of promotional pieces described these leading women as "athletic but feminine."

George Yepes, *Adelita*, 1991, serigraph, 38" x 25". This work by George Yepes, who has worked with Robert Rodríguez in designing film sets for his Westerns, evokes the figure of the assertive but feminine pistol-packing woman.

Edwina Booth played a white woman who sadistically ruled an African tribe in *Trader Horn* (1931). Harry Carey and Duncan Renaldo also appeared.

In *Zorro's Black Whip* (1944), Linda Stirling assumed the role of a Zorro-like character known as the Black Whip and fought corrupt politicians after her brother (the original Black Whip) was murdered.

María Félix appeared in *Juana Gallo* (1961, with brilliant cinematography by Gabriel Figueroa) as an assertive female leader.

THE BANDIT ENJOYS BEING WANTED

N oble bandit media have successfully used the convention of depicting the outlaw admiring his likeness on a wanted poster, relishing the attention and notoriety. Here are four such images.

PHILIP N. KRASNE presents

THE CISCO KID in "THE GAY AMIGO"

starring

Duncan RENALDO as CISCO   **Leo CARRILLO** as PANCHO   with **ARMIDA** and **JOE SAWYER**

Original Screenplay by Doris Schroeder   Based on CISCO KID character created by O. Henry   Produced by Philip N. Krasne   Directed by Wallace Fox

Above: Duncan Renaldo's Cisco Kid reads about crimes he is said to have committed in *The Gay Amigo* (1949).

Above right: In *The Texas Bad Man* (1932), Tom Logan (Tom Mix) is a Texas Ranger who infiltrates an outlaw gang. The Rangers planted "wanted" posters to throw off suspicion.

Left: This nineteenth-century newspaper cartoon depicts Joaquín Murrieta as being pleased with his renown.

Right: Warner Baxter's Cisco admires a similar poster in *In Old Arizona* (1929).

INSPIRATION PICTURES, INC. & EDWIN CAREWE PRESENT **DOLORES DEL RIO** IN "RAMONA"

HELEN HUNT JACKSON'S AMERICAN LOVE CLASSIC

AN EDWIN CAREWE PRODUCTION

UNITED ARTISTS PICTURE

SCREEN PLAY BY FINIS FOX

SUPPORTED BY WARNER BAXTER VERA LEWIS ROLAND DREW MICHAEL VISAROFF

The Ullman Mfg. Co., N. Y.   Made in U. S. A.

Ramona (1928), one of the numerous films based on Helen Hunt Jackson's 1884 novel of the same name, starred Dolores del Río as the part-Scottish, part-Native American orphan and Warner Baxter as the Native American shepherd who wins her heart.

Mexican Indian Alessandro opposite Dolores del Río in *Ramona* (Inspiration/United Artists, 1928). Before the end of that year he was at Fox, replacing Raoul Walsh in the role of the Cisco Kid, and would remain under contract to the studio till the end of 1939. His peak year during the talkie era was 1936, when he starred back-to-back in probably the finest films of his career—as Dr. Mudd in John Ford's *The Prisoner of Shark Island* and, at MGM, as Joaquín Murrieta in William Wellman's *The Robin Hood of El Dorado*—and was reportedly the highest paid actor in Hollywood.

But his time at the top soon ended. He suffered a nervous breakdown in the late thirties, went into psychoanalysis, and, looking considerably older and more ravaged, spent most of the forties at Columbia starring in a "B" detective series as Robert Ordway, The Crime Doctor. His medical problems kept getting worse and he gradually withdrew from Hollywood, moving to Malibu where he went into the real estate business and served a term as mayor. His arthritis became so severe he

had to retire from acting. The last film he appeared in was *State Penitentiary* (Columbia, 1950), a low-budget prison flick directed by Lew Landers, who a few years later would figure in the Cisco TV series. In April 1951 Baxter entered St. John's Hospital in Santa Monica for a partial lobotomy, which it was hoped would relieve his arthritis. He developed bronchial pneumonia and died three weeks later on May 7, survived by actress Winifred Bryson, his wife of thirty-three years.

Playing Baxter's *In Old Arizona* nemesis was Edmund Lowe, a native Californian born in San Jose on March 3, 1892. His father was a lawyer and judge while his Irish Catholic mother had no time for anything but motherhood, giving birth to a grand total of two daughters and twelve sons. The most famous of them was reportedly named for the hero of Dumas' *The Count of Monte Cristo*, but if so, his mother must have forgotten to check the book before filling out the paperwork because the Dumas protagonist spelled his name not with a U but the French way, Edmond, with an O. Lowe graduated from Santa Clara University, earned a master's degree in pedagogy, then began acting in Los Angeles stock companies and on Broadway beginning around 1912. His first movie appearances were in 1915. Three years later he began getting roles as featured player or male lead in a variety of silent melodramas and adventure films. As chance would have it, one of these (*Barbara Frietchie*, 1924) was directed by later Cisco stalwart Lambert Hillyer and another (*East of Suez*, 1925) by Raoul Walsh.

Lowe signed a long-term contract with Fox, where he enjoyed his best known silent role as Sergeant Flagg opposite Victor McLaglen's Captain Quirt in Walsh's ribald comedy about World War I, *What Price Glory* (1926). Before *In Old Arizona* his only work under Irving Cummings had been as star of the gangster flick *Dressed to Kill* (1928). He stayed at Fox till 1932, reprising his Sergeant Flagg role three more times—for Walsh in *The Cock-Eyed World* (1929) and *Women of All Nations* (1931) and for the undistinguished John Blystone in *Hot Pepper* (1933)—and playing Sergeant Mickey Dunn one more time for Cummings in *The Cisco Kid* (1931). During the thirties he bounced from studio to studio and, when not teamed with Victor McLaglen in other pictures about feuding friends in macho professions, was usually cast as either a suave detective in the Nick Charles manner or a tough sleuth in the tradition of Sam Spade. (Dashiell Hammett, creator of both characters, wrote the screen story that was adapted into one of Lowe's finest crime pictures, Universal's 1935 *Mister Dynamite*.)

As the thirties yielded to the forties and Lowe himself approached and then passed the half-century mark, the demand for his services fell off. By 1945, the last year in which he had any leading roles at all, he was relegated to Poverty Row outfits like Monogram, which by then had taken over the Cisco series, and PRC. Lowe tried to carve a niche for himself in early television as star of *Front Page Detective* (1951-52), whose production values made PRC look like MGM. In his sixties he did a few notable TV guest shots, for example as the villain in "War of the Silver Kings" (ABC, Sept. 22, 1957, directed by Budd Boetticher), the premiere episode of *Maverick*. His final appearance on the big screen was in *Heller in Pink Tights* (Paramount, 1960), directed by George Cukor and starring Sophia Loren and Anthony Quinn. His first and third wives had divorced him, his second (actress Lilyan Tashman) had died in 1934, and he had never had any children. Financially secure but alone and in poor health, he died in the Motion Picture Country Home on April 29, 1971.

The career of Dorothy Burgess proved less lucky than those of her male costars. She was born in 1907 and had never appeared in a feature before she was signed for *In Old Arizona*, in which she played the treacherous Tonia. After a few more roles in long-forgotten Fox pictures she was let go and began freelancing, usually in small parts at the major studios, once in a while as female lead in a Poverty Row quickie. Her big moment after *In Old Arizona* was as costar with Leo Carrillo and Johnny Mack Brown in *Lasca of the Rio Grande* (Universal, 1932), one of the many Latin-themed Westerns that poured out of Hollywood in the wake of the first Cisco feature's success. (Those films will be covered in the next chapter.) Burgess left the business in 1935 but came back five years later for tiny parts in half a dozen more pictures, the last of which was *Girls in Chains* (PRC, 1943), directed by the low-budget legend Edgar G. Ulmer. Then she dropped out of sight for keeps and died in 1961.

So much for the three stars and two directors who were responsible for *In Old Arizona*. Now let's take a look at the film.

The year, we learn from an offhand remark about the coming invasion of Cuba, is 1898. A stagecoach pulls into a nameless Arizona town and picks up a load of talkative passengers—including two Irish immigrants, an attractive young woman, and a ZaSu Pitts-like hag—while a Mexican street band makes music. The notorious Cisco Kid (Warner Baxter), on whose head there's a $5,000 reward, intercepts the coach in the desert (for no apparent reason dismounting from his black stallion Yaqui to do it), takes the Wells Fargo box, but refuses to steal anything from the passengers. "I never rob the individual," he declares, although he does make the pretty woman sell him the brooch she's wearing. The coach rolls on with the horses' harness gear jingling like sleighbells and the holdup is reported at the nearest army post to the background noise of a military barbershop quartet. The colonel (Roy Stewart) assigns Sergeant Mickey Dunn (Edmund Lowe), a homesick refugee from the sidewalks of "Noo Yawk," to take a squad, hunt Cisco down, and kill him.

In another distant Arizona town, the Italian barber (Henry Armetta) bewails having lost his $87 savings in the theft of the Wells Fargo box, and the citizens are forming a vigilante committee to go after the bandit. "I hate to see working man lose so much money," says the customer being shaved in the barber chair, who we discover is Cisco. (This sequence seems so much like the *Napoleon's Barber* two-reeler that I can't help wondering whether it was meant to tweak John Ford's nose.) Cisco, who is sprucing up for a visit to his *enamorada*, promises a generous tip if he can take a bath in the Italian's tub. While the barber is drawing hot water, a dust-caked Dunn arrives in town and stops off at the shop for a shave. Cisco and the sergeant trade macho banter in the manner of Walsh's Quirt & Flagg war-buddy movies, with an astonishing display of sexual innuendo as each man admires the size of the other's gun. After Cisco takes his bath he introduces himself to Dunn by the full name he will bear (with frequent variations that will be noted in due course) throughout the Fox series, Gonzalo Sebastiano Rodrigo Don Juan Chicuelo, and confides that women call him Conejito, which means "little rabbit." "Are you that fast?" Dunn asks in awe, and boasts that his own nickname among "goils" is Big Casino. As he promised, Cisco gives the barber a $100 tip. He and Dunn agree to meet in the local saloon for drinks at 3:00 P.M. Until then, Cisco says, he'll be with his girl. "I like lots of señoritas but I love only one." After he's ridden out of town, the blacksmith (James Marcus) who's been shoeing Dunn's horse tells the sergeant that the Latino he's befriended is the bandit he's been hunting. "Well, I'll be damned!" Dunn exclaims, while a jackass brays.

Whichever director is in charge brings us to the home of Tonia María (Dorothy Burgess) a little ahead of Cisco. "El Conejito is coming!" screeches the old lady (Soledad Jiménez) who keeps house for her, and Tonia hastily chases another man out of the way before Cisco arrives. "Someday he will catch you," the old lady warns, and then, she predicts, prefiguring the film's climax, "you will have a flower in your hand but you will not smell it."

There follows a long, drawn-out sequence of romantic byplay between Cisco and Tonia, spiced with vino and a plate of ham and eggs. (Walsh and countless commentators have misremembered the sizzling eggs on the soundtrack as the sound of bacon frying.) "You got something for me?" Tonia wheedles, and Cisco gives her the brooch he took from the stagecoach. After they unmistakably have sex, he sends her to town to break his date with Dunn and lies down for a no doubt well-earned nap.

Tonia finds the sergeant in the saloon and makes a play for him, but he snubs her and they exchange insults. "Don't get sore," he advises her. "Anybody can make a mistake. That's why they have rubbers on lead pencils." After she flounces out, Dunn discovers from another bar patron that he's been talking with Cisco's woman. Meanwhile, a refreshed Cisco is strumming a guitar for the old housekeeper and philosophizing. "Music, wine and love. I don't know which one I could give up if I have to. Maybe I would do without music and wine, but love I got to have always." Telling his Latino origin story for the first time, which will be repeated through the subsequent Cisco films with first Baxter and then César Romero as the lead, Cisco says that his father came from Portugal and his mother from San Luis Obispo. "I run away from Portugal when I was sixteen. I never see them no more. Now, well, I am sorry." "You are very mysterious," the old woman remarks. "Mysterious?" he says. "Life is full of mysterious. Yesterday and tomorrow. The rainbow's end and the moonbeam's kisses. Who knows?" Later he becomes even more reflective. "What is life after all? The warm breath of a few summers and the cold chill of a few winters, and then—by golly, I think I need a drink, huh?" And: "The most precious things in the world cannot be bought with gold. The tender touch of a little baby's fingers, the light in a woman's eyes, and the love in a woman's heart." When Tonia returns from town, he gives her a handful of gold and says he's going off to steal a cattle herd in Guadalupe. "Then," he promises, "we go far across the sea to Portugal." Or to any place else that appeals to her. "You got to be happy always. That is what I say to myself." In another line that anticipates the picture's climax, "I always like to see you wave to me when I ride away," he says.

Hardly is Cisco out of sight when Tonia starts bragging to the old lady about how Dunn at the saloon threw himself at her feet. At this precise moment the sergeant shows up, hunting either Cisco or sex or both, and in fact he does apologize to her until she invites him into her house. "I'm practically in," he chortles, then sings "There'll be a hot time in the old town tonight." The same overlong scene of romantic byplay she enjoyed with Cisco is now repeated with Dunn, culminating in her reading his fortune with cards and predicting that he'll fall madly in love with her. "You got much money, eh?" she asks. The sergeant offers to take her with him next month when he's reassigned to a New York post at Governor's Island and rhapsodizes about the Bowery, "finest street in the woild." Hoping to drum up more business with his squad, Tonia asks to be taken to his encampment. "Are there nice soldiers in the camp, eh?" "Yeah," he assures her. "Poifectly nice."

Now comes a sequence that, except for intercut close-ups of Baxter, was clearly shot by Walsh in

Utah before his accident. Cisco pockets $4,000 for the Guadalupe cattle he's stolen and is followed across the desert by three toughs (Frank Campeau, Tom Santschi, and Pat Hartigan) who plan to shoot him in the back, take the cattle money and collect the bounty on him too. In the film's single and all too brief action scene, Cisco plays dead, turns the tables on the hijackers, and kills two of them. "Hey! You coyote you!" he calls after the survivor. "Tell them you meet the Cisco Kid. These other two fellows don't talk no more."

Meanwhile at the squad's camp, while Dunn and two privates (James Bradbury Jr. and Jack Dillon) are belting out a hearty rendition of "The Bowery," Tonia searches the sergeant's tent and finds the reward poster offering $5,000 for Cisco. Knowing that Dunn wants Cisco and not her, she is still overcome by greed and offers a deal: if he'll give her all the reward money, she'll let him know when Cisco returns from Guadalupe so Dunn can kill him. "I'll get a promotion out of this," he tells her. "And a gal! That's enough for me, baby. You get the money." Elsewhere in camp the two privates are discussing how Dunn feels toward Tonia. "He's serious this time," insists the older. "This morning he asked me if I knew anything about buying furniture on the installment plan. Wanted to know how much it would cost to furnish a flat in Flatbush." The younger is unconvinced. "Say, listen, he buys wedding rings like you and me buy bananas. That is, if we bought bananas."

On his way back to Tonia, Cisco stops at a gypsy wagon to buy her a beautiful white mantilla but still returns earlier than expected. He finds Dunn's horse in front of her house, sees him leave after clearly having had sex with her, and overhears her betray herself: "I love no one but you. . . . the Cisco Kid? I never, never loved him, I swear to you. . . . He is a pig. I wish he was dead. . . . Will I get this reward money soon?" She promises to send Dunn a note by the housekeeper as soon as Cisco arrives. "I am not as good as I think I am," Cisco confides to his horse, "and maybe I never was."

He enters the house and engages Tonia in dialogue full of operatic irony. "I was afraid you might not come back," she says. "I would not disappoint you," he replies. "I know how anxious you have been for me to come back." He offers her a last chance to leave for Portugal with him that night but she puts him off till the next day. "You get ready for long, long journey," he tells her solemnly. While he's tending to Yaqui, Tonia writes her note to Dunn. Cisco intercepts the old woman in the stable yard

and reads the message, which ends very much like the note in O. Henry's story: "Do not fail, my love. Shoot quick and straight." He tears up the message and substitutes another to the effect that Cisco is terrified of being captured and will try to elude pursuit by leaving Tonia's place at 10:00 P.M. dressed in her clothes and wearing a white mantilla. When the note is delivered to Dunn, he rides off to kill Cisco as one of the privates reminds another that the sergeant is the best shot in the army.

Cisco is still with Tonia, waiting for the clock to strike ten. "You got something for me?" she demands. "The surprise of your life," he says, wrapping the mantilla around her. Then he pours wine and offers a toast. "To you, my faithful, loyal, constant sweetheart. To your eyes with their warm devotion, and to your lips with their warm kisses, and to the hearts of you and all the other girls in the world who—who are true, I drink." Hearing the hoofbeats of Dunn's horse outside, he prepares to leave. "Adiós, my beautiful angel. That is what you are and what you will be—an angel. When I ride away, you stand outside where I can see you, and wave goodbye to me. Then I know you love me. If it is to be the end, I want to know that you are thinking only of me." He mounts and rides away while Tonia stands outside and waves. We hear a shot and a scream and see the woman fall over but are left to imagine Dunn's reaction when he discovers whom he's killed. Bent over in the saddle, a grim, heartbroken look in his eyes, Cisco rides slowly into the night as the film's theme song, "My Tonia" by DeSylva, Brown, and Henderson, fills the sound track.

Seen from the perspective of generations later, *In Old Arizona* is something less than unanimously acclaimed. Jon Tuska in *The Filming of the West* (Doubleday, 1976) says that "Baxter invested his portrayal of Cisco with such complexity and lighthearted romance" that he richly earned the Oscar he won for the performance (440). William K. Everson in *The Hollywood Western* (Citadel Press, 1992) takes a negative view. "There are few exteriors in the film, and many of those take place at night, so they could as easily have been shot in the studio, and probably were. There's very little action, and so much talk that the film seems far longer than it is. . . . What probably caused the excitement . . . was the fact that Warner Baxter, a very staid and unexciting player in silents, here had a colorful role with a Mexican accent. That in itself probably provided the novelty that won Baxter the Academy Award . . . , though it was a routine piece of acting at best" (130-32).

My own opinion is somewhere between these poles. Baxter's Cisco projects a convincing philosophic sadness and his Latino accent is far superior to those of the other Anglo actors who played romantic bandido roles in the early thirties. The scenes that were clearly directed by Walsh in Utah are physically beautiful and, in an unself-conscious way lacking all trace of today's political correctness mania, reflect the multicultural ambience of the late nineteenth-century West, for example in the bits with the Russian immigrant waiting for the stagecoach and the Chinese in the crowd at the vigilantes' harangue. But the film is sadly deficient in action and betrays the story it's nominally based on by telegraphing O. Henry's surprise ending long before the climax. Some of the dialogue is rather poetic but there's far too much of it and at times it's drowned out by the orgy of background noises—everything from a saloon piano to a bawling baby to an ancient gramophone to the horses' jingling harness gear to the famous sizzling eggs—which constantly scream at us: "Listen! These are real sounds you're hearing!" In that sense *In Old Arizona* is the aural counterpart of those 3-D movies from the early fifties that bombarded audiences with chairs, flaming arrows, and anything else that could be hurled at a camera.

Whatever we think of the film today, the Fox executives in 1929 and their competitors at other studios knew very quickly that *In Old Arizona* was a winner. Over the next few years Hollywood launched a tidal wave of Latin-themed Westerns—including two more Fox features starring Warner Baxter, *Romance of the Rio Grande* (1929) and *The Arizona Kid* (1930)—which we will consider in chapter 5.

Baxter in his Cisco outfit also made a brief appearance—along with Wallace Beery, Gary Cooper, Joan Crawford, Richard Dix, Laurel and Hardy, Edward G. Robinson, and other early talkie stars—in *The Stolen Jools* (Paramount, 1931), a two-reeler made to raise funds for the Saranac Lake Tuberculosis Center, which today is the Will Rogers Hospital for Respiratory Diseases. Each major studio contributed its facilities to segments featuring its contract stars, with the Chesterfield cigarette company paying negative costs and technical fees.

Warner Baxter and Nora Lane in *The Cisco Kid* (1931), based on O. Henry's romantic bad man

Paramount distributed the picture free of charge to theaters, which collected donations from audiences.

Of course, before any more Cisco Kid features could be made, Fox had to negotiate a new arrangement with O. Henry's estate. Once that process was completed, work began on *The Cisco Kid* (1931), with Irving Cummings as both producer and director, and a screenplay by Alfred A. Cohn that picks up on and creatively varies the themes from *In Old Arizona*. Warner Baxter and Edmund Lowe of course were back as Cisco and Sergeant Dunn, and Cummings even rehired James Bradbury Jr. and Jack Dillon to reprise their roles as the two privates who try to help Dunn catch his man. This time Cisco had two love interests, the Latina played by Conchita Montenegro and the Angla by Nora Lane, and also two sidekicks. López was played by Charles Stevens, a grandson of Geronimo who enjoyed a long career in Hollywood playing Indians, Mexicans, South Sea witch doctors and other ethnic types, while the part of Gordito went to a grossly overweight actor who was to be involved with Cisco films for many years to come.

Ysabel Ponciana Chris-Pin Martin Píaz was born in Tucson in 1893 of a Yaqui father and a Mexican mother. In his teens he held menial jobs as a water boy and a barber's assistant until 1911, when he joined a troupe of Indians headed for Hollywood and movie work. He spent years as an extra or an unbilled bit player in countless silents and early talkies, most of them Westerns. At the time he appeared as Gordito in *The Cisco Kid* his screen name was Chris Martin, but he changed it to Chris-Pin Martin later in the thirties and, under his new byline, he continued to play Gordito as long as 20th Century-Fox released Cisco pictures and briefly came back in the part during Gilbert Roland's tenure as Cisco. In the spring of 1953, soon after returning from a personal appearance tour of Europe and the Middle East, he was hospitalized with a mild heart attack. He seemed to recover and was resuming his normal life when he collapsed with another heart seizure after addressing a meeting of the Montebello Moose Lodge. He died on June 27, 1953, at age 59, survived by a widow and five children and already thirty times a grandfather and twice a great-granddad.

The Cisco Kid opens on a bright morning during the administration of President McKinley when Sergeant Mickey Dunn (Edmund Lowe) and Privates Dixon and Bouse (James Bradbury Jr. and Jack Dillon) are sent out to capture Cisco, who's back in Arizona territory committing robberies despite the $5,000 price still on his head. Meanwhile, Cisco is running stolen cattle over the border with his compadres Gordito (Chris-Pin Martin) and López (Charles Stevens). Seeing the three troopers after him, Cisco has his pals shoot at him and pretend to be the owners of the cattle. The troopers chase Cisco to the accompaniment of agitato music, a genuine rarity in Westerns of the very early 1930s, but his black stallion Yaqui outdistances them and Cisco then heads for the town of Carrizo and the pleasures of women and wine.

In the local saloon, the sheriff (Frederick Burt) and banker Hankins (Willard Robertson) are at a balcony table, plotting to take over widowed Sally Benton's Star Bar ranch. Carmencita (Conchita Montenegro), with whom the sheriff is infatuated, performs a fiery Spanish dance for an appreciative audience including Cisco, who has a balcony seat across the saloon. Seeing romantic byplay between the dancer and the Mexican stranger, the jealous sheriff shoots across the room at Cisco. A gun battle breaks out and Carmencita keeps the sheriff from chasing after Cisco, then meets the stranger in a secluded spot for an interlude of *amor*. "When I look at jou," Cisco says, "then I drink from the fountain of joung. I love only the beauty and I trust no woman. No woman are faithful." This of course is a reference to his betrayal by Tonia María in *In Old Arizona*. "All women I hate," he declares just before taking Carmencita into his arms.

That same evening, Dunn and the two enlisted men ride into Carrizo. As soon as he steps inside the saloon, Dunn is mobbed by dance hall girls. Learning that his favorite, Carmencita, has gone off to dally with "the king of Mexico," Dunn suspects his rival is Cisco and sets out after them. One saloon girl slips away to warn Carmencita and Cisco. Racing out of town, Cisco is chased by the troopers and wounded. The next morning he falls off Yaqui in the front yard of the Star Bar ranch. Sally Benton (Nora Lane) and her children Billy and Ann (Douglas Haig and Marilyn Knowlden) nurse him back to health. Meanwhile in Carrizo, Dunn repeats his behavior with *In Old Arizona*'s Tonia by inviting Carmencita to return to his native New York City with him in three months when his hitch is up and he's collected the $5,000 on Cisco's head. More faithful than Tonia, the dancer sends him off on a wild goose chase by claiming Cisco told her he was headed for California.

During the next two weeks, while Dunn and the privates are hunting Cisco in all the wrong places, our romantic bandit is recovering at the Star Bar and befriending Sally and her children, who call him Tío (Spanish for uncle). Gordito and López show up at the ranch with a note to Cisco from Carmencita, explaining how she threw the troopers off the scent. Billy confides in his tío that banker Hankins will take over the ranch unless Sally can come up with the $5,000 her late husband had owed him. Sergeant Dunn happens to drop by the Star Bar, is invited by Sally to stay for supper, and soon learns that a wounded Mexican has been living there for the past two weeks. Luckily Cisco and his compadres have left the ranch that afternoon to visit Carrizo and take care of Sally's financial problem.

Before going into action, Cisco stops off at Carmencita's place for another romantic interlude. ("For one sweet kiss from jou, *mi adorada*, I would

spend a dozen years in purgatory.") Carmencita begs to be taken along when he returns to Mexico but, distrusting women as much as ever, he promises nothing. While Gordito and López stage a gun battle on the main street to distract the townspeople, Cisco steals $5,000 from the bank. Dunn rides in during the excitement just in time to see Carmencita apparently get shot by Hankins as he's firing at the fleeing Cisco, but this turns out to be another diversion so that the romantic rogue can get away.

Cisco returns to the Star Bar and gives Sally the $5,000 he claims he "withdrew" from the bank for her. Seeing Dunn riding up, he races off the property. But as Yaqui leaps a fence barrier where little Ann is standing, the child falls over. Cisco comes back to make sure she isn't hurt and Dunn arrests him. When the sergeant learns of his prisoner's good deeds for the Bentons, he abandons all hope of collecting the reward, pretends to Sally that he's convinced he had the wrong man, and allows Cisco to go back across the border.

Prints of *The Cisco Kid* are hard to come by, and no book on Westerns discusses it in any detail. In *Hollywood Corral* (Popular Library, 1976), by all odds the most knowledgeable volume ever written on the "B" Western, Don Miller dismisses the picture as "a throwaway production running a bare hour and [one that] made little impression" (182). The most extensive discussion I've seen comes from one of the program notes prepared by William K. Everson for his New School film series (May 1, 1981). Everson describes *The Cisco Kid* as

> by far the best of the early ones [i.e., the three Ciscos in which Baxter starred], partly because it is the shortest. There is no padding, no excess of dialogue, no novelty prolongation of Baxter's Spanish accent. True, there is not very much real action, but the story itself keeps on the move, and when there is some traditional action, it is punctuated both by music and first-class photography. The night chase near the beginning is beautifully done, and the short street shootout near the end is given added excitement by intelligent camera mobility. In fact the camera is mobile throughout, unusual both for the period and for the normally rather dull director. . . .

For whatever reason, Fox put no more Cisco exploits on its shooting schedules. But Westerns of the same general type as *In Old Arizona* and *The Cisco Kid* continued to pour out of other studios as the early thirties rolled on.

Newspaper advertisement from 1930 for *The Arizona Kid*

I n the golden decade of silent movies between the end of World War I and the coming of sound, Latino actors and characters figured prominently. The first superstar of the twenties was Rudolph Valentino, whom William K. Everson in *American Silent Film* (Oxford University Press, 1978) ranks with Clark Gable as "the most clear-cut romantic idol that the movies ever created" (166). Other studios hoping to match the success of the Valentino pictures concocted star vehicles for actors like Antonio Moreno, Ramón Novarro, and, down on Poverty Row, Don Alvarado. None of these men was identified with Westerns, although Valentino just missed starring in one. According to Richard Schickel's *D. W. Griffith: An American Life* (Simon & Schuster, 1984), Griffith had seriously considered the not yet famous Valentino for the male lead, loosely based on bandit Joaquín Murrieta, in his 1919 Western *Scarlet Days*, but had rejected him in favor of Richard Barthelmess, who played the dashing rogue Álvarez with "his hair plastered down and a goatee and a mustache plastered on . . ." (411). The period's best known Western with Hispanic motifs was *The Mark of Zorro* (Fairbanks/United Artists, 1920, directed by Fred Niblo), whose star Douglas Fairbanks was no more Latino than Barthelmess. Clearly by the time Warner Baxter was first cast as the Cisco Kid, the tradition of making Latin-themed Westerns with Anglo leads had been solid-

ly established. As silents gave way to talkies, that tradition continued.

About six months after *In Old Arizona*'s release, Fox followed it up with another romantic Western featuring a Latin ambience and Warner Baxter. *Romance of the Rio Grande* (Fox, 1929) was directed by Alfred Santell from a screenplay by Marion Orth based on Katharine Fullerton Gerould's 1923 novel *Conquistador*. Pablo Wharton Cameron (Warner Baxter), whose grandfather Don Fernando (Robert Edeson) disowned Pablo's mother years before for

Robert McKim and Douglas Fairbanks display excellent swordplay in *The Mark of Zorro* (1920).

marrying a gringo, is injured by bandits and brought to Don Fernando's hacienda to recover. There he falls in love with the Don's adopted daughter Manuelita (Mona Maris) and defeats the scheme of a fortune hunter (Antonio Moreno) to marry the young woman and take over the family estates. A dozen years later, as we'll see, an almost completely different adaptation of Gerould's novel became the basis for a Cisco picture with the same title as this film.

One of the earliest talkies to show a trace of *In Old Arizona*'s influence was a low-budget serial produced by Mascot Pictures, the Poverty Row outfit specializing in quickie cliffhangers that entrepreneur Nat Levine had founded in 1927. The company's first all-talking release, *The Lone Defender* (Mascot, 1930), was directed by Richard Thorpe and starred the legendary Rin-Tin-Tin. Silent serial hero Walter Miller played the human lead, a reputed outlaw by the name of Ramón Roberto who joins Rinty and a plucky teenager (Buzz Barton) to track down the killers of a Mexican prospector and recover the treasure map the dead man had concealed in his pocket watch. At the end of chapter 12 of the serial we discover that Ramón isn't a bandido at all but a special agent of the Justice Department!

The first of the larger studios to enter the Latino Robin Hood genre in Fox's footsteps was RKO, the new incarnation of what in the silent era had been known as FBO. *Beau Bandit* (RKO, 1930) was directed by Lambert Hillyer, who had turned out several of the William S. Hart features for Paramount during the twenties, and the screenplay was by Wallace Smith, based on his own magazine story "Strictly Business" (*Cosmopolitan*, April 1929). It's in this film that the idea of giving the Cisco figure a sidekick seems to have originated. The outlaw Montero (Rod LaRocque) and his deaf-mute partner Coloso (Mitchell Lewis) are being pursued by Sheriff Bobcat Manners (Walter Long) and a posse. Montero decides to replenish his funds by holding up a bank, but he changes his plans when the corrupt banker Perkins (Charles Middleton) offers him money to kill the fiancé (George Duryea, later and better known as Tom Keene) of music teacher Helen Wardell (Doris Kenyon), whom he wants for himself. Montero pretends to commit the murder, collects his blood money, then lets Perkins know he's been scammed and forces the banker, who happens also to be a justice of the peace, to unite the music teacher and her lover in wedlock. This is precisely the kind of story that in the late thirties and early forties would serve the Cisco series well. As luck would have it, Lambert Hillyer ended up directing one Cisco feature (after the series moved from 20th Century-Fox to Monogram) and dozens of thirty-minute Cisco TV films.

Meanwhile the people at Warners were treading on RKO's tail with *Under a Texas Moon* (Warner Bros., 1930), the first talkie in the Cisco mold to be shot in color. The screenplay was by Gordon Rigby, based on Stewart Edward White's short story "Two-Gun Man" (*Famous Story Magazine*, October 1925), and the director was Hungarian-born Michael Curtiz, who would stay longer at Warners and helm more of the studio's Golden Age classics (including *Captain Blood*, *The Charge of the Light Brigade*, *The Adventures of Robin Hood*, *Angels with Dirty Faces*, *Dodge City*, *The Sea Hawk*, *Casablanca*, and *Mildred Pierce*) than any other filmmaker. *Under a Texas Moon*, however, keeps far from the roster of Curtiz's greatest hits. While hunting some stolen Texas cattle whose recovery will net him a huge reward, that dashing caballero Don Carlos (Frank Fay) dallies with four separate and distinct señoritas (Armida, Raquel Torres, Mona Maris, and Myrna Loy) before stowing the bad guys in a food cooler and galloping back to Mexico with the luckiest of the quartet (Loy) by his side. Frank Fay's freckled Irish mug makes him hard to buy as a Hispanic.

Errol Flynn (as Robin Hood) versus Basil Rathbone (as Sir Guy of Gisbourne) in *The Adventures of Robin Hood* (1938)

Early in 1930 Fox began planning a sequel to *In Old Arizona* with Warner Baxter again cast as Cisco and Edmund Lowe as his adversary the cavalry sergeant, but just before shooting was to commence, the studio discovered that all it had ever purchased from O. Henry's estate was the right to make a single movie about the Cisco character. This is why *The Arizona Kid* (Fox, 1930), directed by Alfred Santell from a screenplay by Ralph Block, looks and feels like a second full-length Cisco exploit but in fact isn't: Baxter's character was renamed and Lowe's scrapped at the last minute. In the picture as released, the notorious Arizona Kid (Warner Baxter) poses as a wealthy Mexican mine owner and romances the beautiful Lorita (Mona Maris) while pursuing his career as a thief. Then he falls in love with Virginia Hoyt (Carole Lombard), an Eastern woman who's come west with her brother Nick (Theodor von Eltz). When bandits raid the mine that's supposed to be the source of his wealth and kill two of his compañeros, the Kid discovers that behind the murders are Virginia and Nick, who is not her brother but her husband. After the Kid takes appropriate revenge, he and Lorita make their getaway. "Considering the relative paucity of spectacular action," says William K. Everson, "*The Arizona Kid* does keep nicely on the move. The outdoor locations are excellent, the saloon and other interiors big and colorful, and full of busy extras. Scenes never run too long so that the stress on dialogue doesn't slow it down, and it does move steadily towards a good climax. It's a handsome film, and the only disappointing aspect is the miscasting of Carole Lombard, and her resulting rather pallid performance."

By this time other studios had come to believe they too might profit from romantic bandido movies and were rushing to put their own variations on the theme into release. Paramount weighed in with *The Texan* (Paramount, 1930), directed by John Cromwell from a screenplay by Daniel Nathan Rubin based on Oliver H. P. Garrett's adaptation of another O. Henry story, "A Double-Dyed Deceiver" (*Everybody's Magazine*, December 1905; collected in *Roads of Destiny*, 1909.) On the run after killing a gambler he'd caught cheating at poker, the Llano Kid (Gary Cooper) boards a train and is persuaded by fellow passenger Thacker (Oscar Apfel) that he's the perfect man to impersonate Enrique, the long-lost son of wealthy Señora Ibarra (Emma Dunn), and become her heir. At the Ibarra hacienda, however, the Kid falls in love with the Señora's niece Consuelo (Fay Wray) and learns that the genuine Enrique is none other than the man he killed over

John (later Johnny) Mack Brown as Billy in *Billy the Kid* (1930)

the poker game. The Kid breaks with Thacker, is framed for a robbery at the hacienda, and has to go on the run again with his old friend the Bible-quoting sheriff John Brown (James Marcus) in hot pursuit. After the Kid kills Thacker, the sheriff lets him go and identifies Thacker's body as that of the young fugitive. This may sound like a rip-off of the climax from King Vidor's *Billy the Kid* (MGM, 1930) where—in defiance of historical fact—Pat Garrett pretends to have killed Billy and lets him escape across the border, but *The Texan* actually came out several months earlier.

On almost anyone's list of Western stars who should never have been allowed to play Latinos, Ken Maynard would surely rank near the top. But that's precisely what he played in *Song of the Caballero* (Universal, 1930), directed by Harry Joe Brown. The adaptation of this picture was by Bennett Cohen, the dialogue by Lesley Mason, and the story by Kenneth

C. Beaton and Norman Sper. Juan (Ken Maynard), a bandit who preys only on the properties of the Madera family because of the way Don Pedro Madera (Francis Ford) mistreated Juan's mother, falls in love with Anita (Doris Hill), the fiancée of Don Pedro's worthless son José (Gino Corrado). After fighting a duel with José, Juan reveals that he's Don Pedro's nephew. William K. Everson in *The Holly- wood Western* describes this sixty-minute quickie as

about the most bizarre Western ever made. It looks for all the world like an imitation-Fairbanks swashbuckling script . . . [which was converted] into a Western with no changes other than that of transposing a (presumably) European locale into California. The most curi- ous aspect of it all, perhaps indicative of haste, is that all of the dialogue was taut and stilted, as though the players were limited to mouthing the original subtitles. There was an endearing quality to the bemused heroine . . . listening to Maynard's declarations of love, couched in phrases better suited to Valentino or Fairbanks, and which Maynard delivered as though read- ing them for the first and only time, which he probably was. Even casual expressions retained the flavor of a different locale and period; May- nard constantly refers to his pals as "com- rades," and the dusty trail is always "the king's highway." Fisticuffs are jettisoned in favor of rapiers, and in the climactic set-to, Maynard is leaping over balconies and dueling with a half dozen of the villain's cronies . . . Maynard's distinct- ly clumsy swordplay is far from convincing. (129-30)

It does not seem a great injus- tice that, except for Everson's discussion, *Song of the Caballero* remains unsung.

Next out of the cinematic tortilla press came the low-budget, low-action *Rogue of the Rio Grande* (SonoArt WorldWide, 1930), starring Argentine actor José Bohr as, to quote film historian Jon Tuska, "a glamorous road agent dressed in black and bedecked in tooled leather and silver, who steals from the rich and provides for the poor and who is finally reformed from his wayward life through the love of a beautiful señorita." The screen- play was by prolific B Western

A contemporaneous image of the quin- tessential good-bad Joaquín Murrieta, legendary bandit of the California Gold Rush. He has been one of the favorite heroes of the Mexican and Mexican- American/Chicano communities since the nineteenth century.

scripter Oliver Drake and the director was Spencer Gordon Bennet, at his best a maker of superb seri- als and Westerns but so often nowhere near his best. The notorious bandit El Malo (José Bohr) and his men rob the safe of Seth Landport (Gene Morgan), the mayor of Sierra Blanca. Sheriff Rankin (Walter Miller, who starred in several of Bennet's silent cliffhanger serials for Pathé) offers a reward for the thief. Later El Malo and his sidekick Pedro (Ray- mond Hatton) come back to town for romantic interludes with the cantina dancers Carmita (Myrna Loy) and Dolores (Carmelita Geraghty). Eventual- ly El Malo witnesses the mayor committing a stage- coach robbery, denounces Landport to the sheriff, escapes arrest himself by the skin of his teeth and, in company with Pedro and Carmita, heads for the border. In his essay on Spencer Bennet, reprinted in revised form in *A Variable Harvest* (McFarland, 1990), Tuska has little good to say about the film. "Bohr spoke in a labored, exaggerated accent and this only made the long, static indoor sequences move even more slowly. Myrna Loy sang a couple of songs . . . but they were ineptly staged and proved tedious" (128).

The title character in *Captain Thunder* (Warner Bros., 1930) was not a comicbook superhero as the name suggests but one more Latino rogue in the Cisco mold. Capitán Tronido (Victor Varconi), a romantic scoundrel being hunted by Comandante Ruiz (Charles Judels), becomes involved with beau- tiful Ynez Domínguez (Fay Wray) and her impov- erished lover Juan Sebastián (Don Alvarado). When Ynez is pressured by her father (John Sainpolis) to marry wealthy and corrupt rancher Pete Morgan (Robert Elliott), Juan vows to earn money and win his *enamorada* by collecting the price on Captain Thunder's head. The Captain has been smitten by Ynez himself and almost falls into the comandante's trap when he visits the señorita, but she hides him and helps him escape. Morgan, to whom Captain Thunder owes a favor, compels the bandido to make prisoners of Ynez and Juan as they're on their way to be married and then to force Ynez into marrying Morgan himself. Man of honor that he is, the Cap- tain keeps his word. As the film ends, Ynez hears a shot and Captain Thunder informs her that she's just become a widow. Alan Crosland directed from a screenplay by Gordon Rigby and dialogue by William K. Wells, based on Pierre Couderc and Hal Davitt's original story "The Gay Caballero." It's not clear whether the picture was meant to be funny.

The last of the year's bandido films and one of the most ambitious was *The Lash* (First National,

Captain Thunder (1930), starring Victor Varconi and Fay Wray, is a lighthearted film about a gallant bandit who always keeps his promise, whether to friend or foe.

1930), an attempt at a wide-screen epic along the lines of Fox's *The Big Trail* and MGM's *Billy the Kid*. Frank Lloyd directed from a screenplay by Bradley King based on Lanier and Virginia Stivers Bartlett's 1929 novel *Adios!* Don Francisco Delfino (Richard Barthelmess), whose father has been murdered by corrupt land commissioner Peter Harkness (Fred Kohler), creates the identity of the outlaw El Puma in his quest for revenge. Sheriff David Howard (James Rennie) falls in love with Francisco's sister Dolores (Marian Nixon) and, after Francisco has killed Harkness, allows him to escape and rejoin his sweetheart Rosita (Mary Astor). Everson, in *The Hollywood Western*, calls the picture "a pedestrian . . . Western in which only a fairly large cattle stampede sequence could in any way be said to justify big-screen treatment" (140). But this strange mix of elements from *Billy the Kid*, *In Old Arizona*, and *The Mark of Zorro* was by no means the poorest of the Ciscoesque early talkies.

After the deluge of such pictures that came out in 1930, it seems amazing that only three more joined the ranks in 1931. (Fox's *The Cisco Kid*, the first official sequel to *In Old Arizona*, was also a 1931 title but isn't being considered here.) Columbia's Western star Buck Jones played the lead in *The Avenger* (Columbia, 1931), directed by that fine visual stylist Roy William Neill from a screenplay by George Morgan based on an original story by Jack Townley. The time is 1849, and on the stagecoach taking him to visit his brother, Joaquín Murrieta (Buck Jones) strikes up a friendship with Helen Lake (Dorothy Revier), who is coming to California to teach school. Later in town, Joaquín gets into a fight with three vicious Anglo gold hunters led by Al Goss (Walter Percival). The trio follow Joaquín to the claim being worked by his younger brother Juan (Paul Fix), get the drop on the Murrietas, beat Joaquín brutally, tie him to a tree, and make him watch them hang Juan. Later they file on the Murrieta claim and take over the mine. Forging a

Zorroesque identity for himself as the Black Shadow, Joaquín attacks every stagecoach containing profits from the claim and secretly leaves placards in town, threatening Goss and his partners with death. Assigned to track down the Black Shadow is none other than Helen Lake's father (Edward Hearn), an army captain. Ultimately Joaquín manipulates events so that the three killers wind up dead but not by his hands, and on learning the facts Captain Lake agrees to let Joaquín go free and take Helen with him. Everson, in *The Hollywood Western,* describes *The Avenger* as "a grim little film played for tension rather than action, [with] superb lighting and camera work . . ." (161), while Tuska, in *The Filming of the West,* rhapsodizes about "one stunning shot when Buck, a black silhouette against a clouded horizon behind which the setting sun blazes, rides off into a diffused haze" (226). It's a shame that Roy William Neill (who is best known for Universal's Sherlock Holmes series starring Basil Rathbone and Nigel Bruce) never again directed a Western,

and even more of a shame that this stunningly made little film was spoiled by Buck Jones's ludicrous stabs at a Mexican accent.

In the fall of that year and about a month after the release of Fox's *The Cisco Kid,* Universal offered its second entry in the Latin Western sweepstakes, but, like most of the later 1930s Westerns with Latin protagonists or backgrounds, this one wasn't a romantic bandido picture and owed little to the Cisco films except *In Old Arizona*'s female lead, Dorothy Burgess. *Lasca of the Rio Grande* (Universal, 1931) was directed by Edward Laemmle from a screenplay by Randall Faye and a story by Tom Reed with roots in, of all unlikely things, a poem: "Lasca" by the English-born cowboy writer Frank Desprez. Both Texas Ranger José Santa Cruz (Leo Carrillo) and handsome young Miles Kincaid (Johnny Mack Brown) are in love with Lasca (Dorothy Burgess), a dance hall girl wanted for murder. At the end of this strange picture, Lasca saves Santa Cruz from having to choose between

A film loosely based on Joaquín Murrieta, *The Avenger* (1931) starred Buck Jones as a Mexican seeking vengeance for the death of his younger brother.

love and duty by diving into a herd of stampeding cattle and killing herself.

The next few salsa-flavored Westerns had even less of a Cisco connection than that one. In *Two Gun Caballero* (Imperial, 1931, directed by Jack Nelson), Robert Frazer starred in a dual role as an Anglo cowboy framed for murder and a Mexican who happens to be his identical double. The plot, of course, has Frazer returning to the States in Latino disguise to root out the real killer.

Hardly had a new year begun when the studio that had started the bandido cycle released *The Gay Caballero* (Fox, 1932), directed by Alfred Werker from a screenplay by Philip Klein and Barry Connors based on Tom Gill's 1931 novel *The Gay Bandit of the Border*. No matter how much this may sound like another unofficial sequel to *In Old Arizona*, it isn't, and Fox action star George O'Brien is cast as an Anglo. College football hero Ted Radcliffe (George O'Brien) comes West to inspect the inherited cattle ranch that's supporting him and falls in love with Adela Morales (Conchita Montenegro). The señorita's father Don Paco (C. Henry Gordon) and his henchman Jito (Weldon Heyburn) are behind the systematic looting of Ted's ranch. The mysterious outlaw El Coyote who's been fighting Don Paco's schemes to rule the territory turns out to be another Anglo, Don Bob Harkness (Victor McLaglen). Except for the title there's no similarity whatever between this film and 20th Century-Fox's 1940 Cisco feature of the same name.

The next entry in Columbia's Buck Jones series borrowed somewhat from *The Avenger*, with Buck not only playing another Mexican but again seeking vengeance for the death of a younger brother played by Paul Fix. This time, however, he stays on the side of the law all the way. *South of the Rio Grande* (Columbia, 1932) was directed by Lambert Hillyer (who had helmed *Beau Bandit* two years before) from a screenplay by Milton Krims and a story by Harold Shumate. Carlos Olivárez (Buck Jones), an officer in the Mexican *rurales*, pursues the cantina dancer Consuela (Mona Maris), who's responsible for the death of his brother Juan (Paul Fix). As coincidence would have it, Consuela's latest target is Carlos's best friend, Ramón Ruiz (George J. Lewis), whom she's trying to ruin so that her partner Clark (Philo McCullough) can take over the oil-rich Ruiz lands. "Buck Jones does a Warner Baxter in this one," *Variety* commented, "and gets away with it nicely."

Tom Mix half-heartedly worked the same territory in *The Texas Bad Man* (Universal, 1932), direct-

ed by Edward Laemmle, who had helmed *Lasca of the Rio Grande* the previous year. Mix plays a ranger posing as an outlaw to infiltrate the gang he's been assigned to break up, but about halfway through the picture and for no particular reason he dresses up as a Mexican and spends the next scenes inadvertently amusing us with his Pennsylvania Spanish accent. Maybe Mix's experience taught Buck Jones a lesson. In his next Western with Latin motifs, *The California Trail* (Columbia, 1933), directed by Lambert Hillyer from a screenplay by Jack Natteford, the setting is California prior to 1849; just about everyone else in the cast is supposed to be Latino, but Buck plays an Anglo scout, Santa Fe Stewart, who becomes a sort of Zorro figure to help free a province from the tyrannical rule of two brothers (Luis Alberni and George Humbert).

If a prize were offered for the most obscure oater of the thirties that owed a debt to the Cisco saga, one of the prime contenders would be *Call of the Coyote* (Imperial, 1934, directed by Patrick Carlyle). This fifty-minute hunk of junk, which Everson describes in *The Hollywood Western* as "memorably inept" (278), stars Kenneth Thomson as Don Adiós, a sombreroed Robin Hood who tries to save a hidden gold mine for its murdered owner's baby daughter. Our hero's sidekick, portrayed by Charles Stevens (Warner Baxter's compadre from *The Cisco Kid*), is called Pancho.

Another candidate for the prize, *The Pecos Dandy* (Security, 1934), starred George J. Lewis in the title role of a fancily garbed caballero who's framed as a horse thief by his rival for a woman's love. The screenplay, assuming there was one, seems to have been by L. V. Jefferson, and the director was either Victor Adamson (a grade-Z hack also known as Denver Dixon and Art Mix) or Horace B. Carpenter. A reviewer for England's *Kinematograph Weekly* (November 5, 1936) described the film as "so badly mutilated in the cutting that it is only with difficulty that the plot can be followed, while added to this there are players of little standing or ability, and dialogue that is more often than not out of sync . . . [S]o clumsily edited is the picture that it is impossible to know which [actor] plays the part of the villain." That George J. Lewis's character was Latino is an educated guess: he'd been born in Mexico and appeared mainly in Spanish-language features until he became established as a character actor in B Westerns. He had substantial roles opposite both Duncan Renaldo and Gilbert Roland in Monogram's Cisco films of the middle 1940s, and in

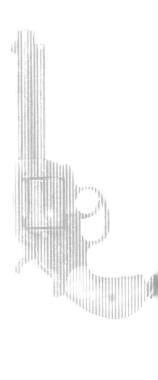

the late fifties he was seen regularly on the Disney *Zorro* teleseries as Guy Williams's father.

Among the Westerns from 1935 that deserve a moment of our attention are a pair of long-forgotten quickies that sound less like films in the Cisco tradition and more like romantic musicals with a Latin flavor. *Under the Pampas Moon* (Fox, 1935) gave Warner Baxter yet another chance to show off his accent as César Campo, who follows the trail of his stolen horse to Buenos Aires and a fling with singer Yvonne LaMarr (Ketti Gallian). James Tinling directed from a screenplay by Ernest Pascal and Bradley King, based on an original story by Gordon Morris, with additional dialogue by Henry Johnson. Featured in the cast of this tuneful trifle were Tito Guízar (who would play the Ciscoesque lead in *The Llano Kid* four years later) and future Cisco sidekick Chris-Pin Martin. In more or less the same vein was *Hi, Gaucho!* (RKO, 1935), directed by Tommy Atkins from a screenplay by Adele Buffington based on Atkins's original story. In his first starring role, John Carroll as the heroic Lucio sets out to save lovely but naive Inez (Steffi Duna) from an impostor posing as the man to whom she's been promised in marriage. The villain was portrayed by Rod LaRocque, who had played a spiritual cousin of Cisco five years before in the same studio's *Beau Bandit*.

Another strong contender for the Most Obscure Latin Oater award is *The Irish Gringo* (Keith, 1935), directed by veteran B-movie cinematographer William C. Thompson from a screenplay by "Patrick Petersalia," apparently a joint alias for Thompson himself and Patrick Carlyle, who also starred as Irish-Mexican adventurer Don O'Brien. (Did the makers of this atrocity think "Gringo" was another word for "Latino"?) While roaming the West with his pals Pancho and Buffalo, O'Brien is framed for the murder of old prospector Pop Wiley (William Farnum), who before his death had drawn a map showing the location of the Lost Dutchman mine in his little granddaughter's blouse. As if that weren't trouble enough, O'Brien has to contend with the jealousy of a girlfriend who mistakenly believes he's romancing another woman. In February 1936 the trade press reported that unpaid creditors had foreclosed on the negative of this picture. Small loss.

So little is known about *The Tia Juana Kid* (Sunset, 1936) that even the three-volume American Film Institute Catalog covering features of the thirties isn't much help. The picture was directed and written by Jack Nelson, who had also been responsi-ble for the 1931 *Two Gun Caballero*. The hero, a gallant bandido calling himself El Capitán, seems to have been played by Patrick Carlyle, who directed *Call of the Coyote* and starred in *The Irish Gringo*. The release date, or maybe I should say the date it escaped, was sometime in January 1936. I wouldn't want to bet money that anyone actually saw it.

Of all the decade's films with roots in the Cisco saga the best was *The Robin Hood of El Dorado* (MGM, 1936), directed by William A. Wellman from a screenplay by himself, Joseph Calleia, and Melvin Levy based on Walter Noble Burns's heavily fictionalized biography of Joaquín Murrieta, *The Robinhood of El Dorado* (1932). In perhaps the finest performance of his career, Warner Baxter starred as the honest farmer who turns revolutionary outlaw after his wife (Margo) is murdered by Anglos with designs on the Murrieta property. In *The Hollywood Western* Everson describes the film as a "romanticized but still very rugged" account of the historic character whom Buck Jones had played in *The Avenger* with much less conviction.

The actors most of us identify with the saga made separate if minor contributions to the pseudo-Cisco cycle later that year. In *Rebellion* (Crescent, 1936), directed by Lynn Shores from a screenplay and original story by John Thomas Neville that seems somewhat indebted to *The Robin Hood of El Dorado*, the setting is California in 1850. Sent to protect the new American territory's Mexicans from Anglo raiders, Captain John Carroll (Tom Keene) falls in love with Paula Castillo (Rita Cansino) and helps her brother Ricardo (Duncan Renaldo) and his guerrilla band defeat the oppressors. Cansino was to become better known as Rita Hayworth and Renaldo as the Cisco Kid. In release at around the same time was *The Gay Desperado* (Pickford-Lasky/United Artists, 1936), a musical comedy directed by Rouben Mamoulian in which a crooning Mexican theater usher (Nino Martini) is drafted into a post-Prohibition outlaw group whose leader Braganza (Leo Carrillo), taking his cue from American movie gangsters, has decided to specialize in kidnapping. The singing draftee falls in love with the ring's first victim (Ida Lupino) and the rest is romance and music. Thirteen years later Carrillo would join forces with Renaldo and inaugurate what (for my generation anyway) is the golden age of the Cisco legend.

One of the last Ciscoesque features to be released was actually one of the first to be shot. *The Phantom of Santa Fe* (Burroughs-Tarzan, 1936), directed by Jacques Jaccard from a scenario by

Charles Francis Royal, starred twenties matinee idol Norman Kerry as a sort of cross between Cisco and Zorro. By day he poses as the spineless idler Miguel Morago, but when romantic banditry beckons, he leaves a servant behind disguised as himself to furnish an alibi and rides out at the head of his caballeros, calling himself the Hawk, or sometimes the Phantom of Santa Fe. Both he and Anglo entrepreneur Steve Gant (Frank Mayo) are romancing Teresa Valarde (Nena Quartaro), daughter of the district's wealthiest ranchero, although Gant is also involved with Lola (Carmelita Geraghty), a cantina girl. Framed by his rival for the theft of priceless religious treasures from the local mission, Miguel enlists the jealous Lola to expose Gant's treachery. At the climax, as Gant pulls a gun and tries to escape from the Valarde hacienda, a padre cries out, "In the name of the Lord, stop!" and a crucifix magically drops from the wall to knock the pistol from the villain's hand. According to Everson in *The Hollywood Western*, the film was made at Universal around 1929, as a silent in Cinecolor, but was then shelved for several years before being sold to the short-lived Burroughs-Tarzan, which released the picture in 1936 as a talkie "with most of the key roles curiously redubbed by other actors" (140).

From late 1936 through 1940 the figure who dominated Latin-themed Westerns was not Cisco but Zorro. Republic Pictures resurrected the black-garbed swashbuckler in *The Bold Caballero* (1936), directed in color by Wells Root with Robert Livingston in the lead, and followed up that weak effort with two excellent twelve-chapter serials about the character: *Zorro Rides Again* (1937), starring John Carroll, and *Zorro's Fighting Legion* (1939), starring Reed Hadley. Both cliffhangers were directed by the action powerhouse team of William Witney and John English. Once 20th Century-Fox came back into the Cisco business, its moguls decided to corner the Latin Western market by presenting Tyrone Power in a big-budget remake of *The Mark of Zorro* (1940), directed by *The Gay Desperado*'s Rouben Mamoulian.

Over the next few years there appeared an occasional B Western with marginal ties to the Cisco films. In *Law and Lead* (Colony, 1937), directed by Robert F. Hill from a screenplay by Basil Dickey based on an original story by Hill under his writing pseudonym Rock Hawkey, Rex Bell starred as cattle detective Jimmy Sawyer, who helps reformed bandido Pancho Gonzales (Donald Reed) track down the people responsible for resur-

Tyrone Power in *The Mark of Zorro* (1940)

recting Pancho's old outlaw identity as the Juárez Kid. Tim McCoy took a hand in the game, playing ranger Tim Carson in *Two Gun Justice* (Monogram, 1938), directed by Alan James from a screenplay by Fred Myton. Posing as an infamous rogue who calls himself the Vulture, Carson joins the outlaw gang led by Bart Kane (John Merton) in order to destroy it. Later that year Tim again played a lawman posing as a Mexican in *Lightning Carson Rides Again* (Victory, 1938), directed by Sam Newfield from a screenplay by E. R. O'Dasi (a byline of veteran scripter Isadore Bernstein), this time passing himself off as gambler José Hernández while working to prove his vanished nephew (Robert Terry) innocent of a bank theft charge.

Tim McCoy played Lightning Bill Carson, a gunfighter who disguises himself as a Mexican to infiltrate a gang of robbers, in *Lightning Carson Rides Again* (1938).

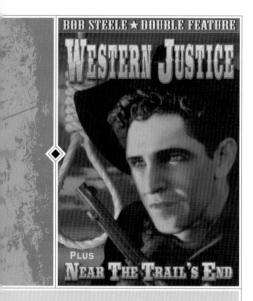

Western Justice (1935) starred Bob
Steele and was scripted and directed by
Steele's father, Robert North Bradbury.
In this film, Steele had a Latino sidekick
played by Julián Rivero.

During the years when
Zorro supplanted Cisco, the most
notable Hollywood feature with
ties to the Cisco tradition was
Thunder Trail (Paramount, 1937),
a superb entry in Paramount's
long cycle of films more or less
based on the works of Zane Grey.
This one was directed by Charles
Barton from a screenplay by
Robert Yost and Stuart Anthony
adapted from Grey's 1932 novel
Arizona Ames. The protagonist,
Arizona Dick Ames (Gilbert
Roland), was separated in childhood from his brother Bob (James
Craig) when villainous Lee Tate
(Charles Bickford) killed their
father and stole Bob to raise as
his own son. Fifteen years later,
Dick finds Tate transformed
from just plain robber into a rob-
ber baron, determined to drive Amy Morgan (Marsha Hunt) and her father from their gold mine.
Then Dick discovers that the man Amy loves is his
long-lost kid brother, who still believes himself to
be Tate's son. Everson, in *The Hollywood Western*,
calls this film one of the best of all Paramount's
Zane Grey adaptations. "[I]t ran a mere fifty-six
minutes, yet despite almost constant action, it found
time for good writing, subtle characterizations, a
modicum of romance and comedy, some superb
locations, an excellently staged runaway ore wagon
sequence, and a well-sustained action climax" (165).
If the storyline seems familiar to B Western fans it's
because the same Zane Grey novel was also
the uncredited inspiration for three first-rate
series shoot-'em-ups of the same decade:
Westward Ho (Republic, 1935, directed by
Robert N. Bradbury and starring John
Wayne), *Across the Plains* (Monogram, 1939,
directed by Spencer Bennet and starring Jack
Randall), and *Saga of Death Valley* (Republic,
1939, directed by Joseph Kane and starring
Roy Rogers). My only excuse for covering
Thunder Trail here is that its star,
Gilbert Roland, was a genuine Latino and a future Cisco. The Arizona Ames character, of
course, is not meant to be
Hispanic, but the filmmakers
account for his accent by hav-

ing him raised after his father's murder by a kindly
Mexican prospector (J. Carrol Naish).

Director Charles Barton shot *Thunder Trail* at
the same time and on the same locations with another Zane Grey-based feature, *Born to the West* (Paramount, 1937), starring John Wayne and Johnny
Mack Brown. When those pictures were finished,
Paramount handed over the production reins on the
last films in its Grey cycle to Harry Sherman, who
was also producing the classic Hopalong Cassidy
series for release by the studio. After 20th Century-
Fox revived the Cisco character in *The Return of
the Cisco Kid*, Sherman managed to squeeze into his
production schedule *The Llano Kid* (Paramount,
1939), a remake of Paramount's 1930 feature *The
Texan*. The director of the new version was Edward
D. Venturini (1888-1960), born in New Jersey of
Argentinian and Italian descent and a specialist in
making Spanish-language versions of Hollywood
films, whose only other English-language feature
was *In Old Mexico* (Paramount, 1938), a powerful
entry in the Cassidy series. The screenplay by Wanda
Tuchock was based, as *The Texan* had been, on O.
Henry's 1905 story "A Double-Dyed Deceiver."
Tito Guízar played the singing bandit who teams
up with scheming Lora Travers (Gale Sondergaard)
to bilk wealthy old Doña Teresa (Emma Dunn,
reprising her role in *The Texan*) by posing as her
long-lost son. After falling in love with the old
woman's adopted daughter Lupita (Jane Clayton),
he breaks with Lora and turns over a new leaf.

Once the flood of Cisco imitations from the
early thirties had subsided, Latino characters other
than Cisco himself and Zorro were rarely the
heroes of Westerns, but several of the decade's
oaters included a strong supporting role for a Latino who was either framed for crimes he didn't
commit or bent on avenging a loved one's murder.
Character actor Julián Rivero played such a part
opposite Bob Steele in *Western Justice* (Supreme,
1934, directed by Robert N. Bradbury), as did Ted
Adams opposite Jack Randall in *Gunsmoke Trail*
(Monogram, 1938, directed by Sam Newfield) and
Noah Beery opposite Gene Autry in *Mexicali Rose*
(Republic, 1939, directed by George Sherman).
Any B Western fan worth his salt can add others to
this list. No less surprising is the number of thirties
oaters in which the hero had a Hispanic sidekick.
When the part was serious, as it tended to be in the
decade's early and middle years, the man directors
usually signed was again Julián Rivero. When the
role was to be played for laughs, as was typical a few

years later, more often than not it went to Frank Yaconelli, who in the mid-1940s was to play the sidekick in four of the Monogram Ciscos with Gilbert Roland in the lead. During the late thirties the "straight" Mexican sidekick was confined to one studio, Republic, and one actor, future Cisco star Duncan Renaldo. For the fifteen-chapter serial *The Lone Ranger Rides Again* (1939), which owed much of its format to Republic's Three Mesquiteers series of trio Westerns, directors William Witney and John English signed Renaldo as Juan Vásquez to join Robert Livingston as the masked man and Chief Thundercloud as Tonto. Later the same year Renaldo joined the Mesquiteers series, playing Rico opposite Livingston as Stony Brooke and Raymond Hatton as Lullaby Joslin, and he kept the role throughout the 1939-40 season.

At the end of the decade, soon after 20th Century-Fox had brought back Warner Baxter in *The Return of the Cisco Kid*, Leo Carrillo played a vaguely Ciscoesque character in *The Girl and the Gambler* (RKO, 1939), directed by Lew Landers from a screenplay by Clarence Upson Young based on Willard Mack's 1925 stage play *The Dove*. Carrillo, as the bandit El Rayo, is smitten by cantina dancer Dolores Romero (Steffi Duna) and, in the guise of wealthy José María López y Tostado, attempts to win her heart, unaware that it has already been won by Johnny Powell (Tim Holt), a dealer at the cantina's card tables. At the climax our noble outlaw stifles his emotions and lets the lovers elope. In the silent movie *The Dove* (Schenck, 1928), based on the same stage play, the members of the triangle had been played by Norma Talmadge, Noah Beery, and future Cisco Gilbert Roland, while in the earlier talking remake, *Girl of the Rio* (RKO, 1932), the parts had gone respectively to Dolores del Río, Carrillo himself, and Norman Foster, who would later turn director and helm one of 20th Century-Fox's Cisco features with César Romero in the title role. Lew Landers, who helmed the 1939 movie version of Mack's play, was to direct Duncan Renaldo as Cisco and Carrillo as Pancho in some of their TV adventures of the fifties.

Once 20th Century-Fox resumed making Cisco films, many of the Latino actors who eventually would figure in the saga found work in trio Westerns. Perhaps the most generously budgeted picture of this sort was *Rangers of Fortune* (Paramount, 1940), directed by Sam Wood and starring Fred MacMurray, Albert Dekker, and, in the part of Sierra, Gilbert Roland. In *Road Agent* (Universal,

1941), directed on a more modest scale by Charles Lamont, the trio was played by Dick Foran, Leo Carrillo, and Andy Devine. It's a sober historical fact that Carrillo's character in this film was called Pancho. But when 20th Century-Fox dropped its Cisco series other studios lost interest in the Latin theme too. During the war years it resurfaced only in *Vengeance of the West* (Columbia, 1942, directed by Lambert Hillyer), a loose remake of *The Avenger* with Bill Elliott as Joaquín Murrieta and Tex Ritter as the ranger captain on his trail. By gifting this version of Murrieta with a Virginian mother, Hillyer relieved Elliott of the need to compete with Buck Jones for worst Mexican accent ever heard in a Western, but of course Elliott didn't sound Southern, either.

After the war, and while Gilbert Roland was at Monogram playing Cisco in a six-picture series that will be covered in chapter 8, there was a brief flurry of films in more or less the same vein, released by even smaller studios. *Don Ricardo Returns* (PRC, 1946) starred Fred Coby as a Spanish nobleman who comes to California to claim an inheritance only to find that his evil cousin has had him declared legally dead. Ricardo goes into hiding, poses as a peon, and, with help from the local padre, sets things to rights. Terry Morse directed from a screenplay by Jack DeWitt and Renault Duncan based on an original story by Zorro creator Johnston

Episode thirteen of *The Lone Ranger Rides Again* (1939), starring Robert Livingston as the Lone Ranger and Duncan Renaldo (left) as Juan Vásquez. Here, Renaldo stares down Ralph Dunn, who played the role of Bart Dolan.

McCulley. Renault Duncan was the byline on the quickie scripts ground out between acting jobs by—who else?—Duncan Renaldo.

Bells of San Fernando (Screen Guild, 1947) was also directed by Morse, scripted by DeWitt and Duncan, and set in early California. Despite these facts and its title, the film doesn't belong in a chapter on Cisco's rivals since the main character, portrayed by Donald Woods, isn't even Latin but an Irish seaman. A picture from the same period that definitely belongs is *The Adventures of Don Coyote* (Comet, 1947), directed by Reginald LeBorg from a screenplay by Bob Williams and Harold Tarshis. Don Coyote (Richard Martin) and his sidekick Sancho (Val Carlo) take jobs on a ranch and try to save its lovely owner (Frances Rafferty) from losing her property to schemers who know the railroad is coming through. Soon after wrapping up this forgettable oater, Richard Martin was signed by RKO to join its superb Western series starring Tim Holt. He continued to play Tim's impulsive sidekick Chito José Gonzales Bustamante Rafferty until five years later when the series ended.

While the Cisco TV series with Duncan Renaldo and Leo Carrillo was in its prime, one minor studio and two majors offered features which might have been vaguely inspired by the telefilms. *Bandit Queen* (Lippert, 1950), directed by William Berke from a screenplay by Victor West and Budd Lesser based on West's original story, seems, however, to owe much more to the screen's other great Latin hero figure. Lola (Barbara Britton) returns to her home in early California, finds her parents murdered, becomes a sort of female Zorro, and joins with our old friend Joaquín Murrieta (Philip Reed) in her quest for revenge against the men behind the local reign of terror (Willard Parker and Barton MacLane). *Branded* (Paramount, 1951) was directed by Rudolph Maté from a screenplay by Sydney Boehm and Cyril Hume based on *Montana Rides!*, a 1933 novel by Evan Evans, who is much better known as Max Brand. The outlaw Cholla (Alan Ladd) is hired to impersonate the long-lost son of a wealthy rancher (Charles Bickford) but falls in love with the rancher's daughter (Mona Freeman) and redeems himself by bringing back the genuine son from the stronghold of the Mexican bandit (Joseph Calleia) who raised him. Finally came *Apache War Smoke* (MGM, 1952), directed by Harold Kress from a screenplay by Jerry Davis very loosely based on the Ernest Haycox short story "Stage Station" (*Collier's*, April 22, 1939; collected in *Outlaw* [Little,

Brown, 1953]). In his last starring role in a U.S.-made Western feature, Gilbert Roland portrayed Peso, a legendary bandit pursued by Apaches who blame him for the murder of some fellow warriors. When he takes refuge at a way station run by his illegitimate son Tom Herrera (Robert Horton), the Apaches besiege the place and try to make the other trapped whites turn Peso over to them. This film was a remake of *Apache Trail* (MGM, 1942, directed by Richard Thorpe), but the central character of the first version had been an Anglo played by Lloyd Nolan.

The last film we consider here is also one of the strangest. *The Naked Dawn* (Universal, 1955) was set in contemporary Mexico and starred Arthur Kennedy as the bandit Santiago who, fleeing from the law after a botched train robbery, encounters a bewitching young woman (Betta St. John) and her dirt-poor but brutal and greed-racked husband (Eugene Iglesias). With all the philosophic and sometimes mystical dialogue that the script by Nina and Herman Schneider gives him, the role of Santiago would have been perfect for Gilbert Roland, but since he was working steadily in major pictures at the time, he almost certainly would have turned down the lead in this shoestring production. The main reason for the film's reputation is that it was directed by Edgar G. Ulmer (1904-1972), who helmed such cult classics as *The Black Cat* (Universal, 1934), *Bluebeard* (PRC, 1944), and *Detour* (PRC, 1945). Interviewed not long before his death by Peter Bogdanovich, Ulmer included *The Naked Dawn* as one of his favorites among the films he'd made. With a draggy pace, sparse action and all too many signs of its rock-bottom budget, this picture is unlikely to appeal to the hardcore shoot-'em-up fan as it did to Ulmer. But its bizarre storyline and characterizations make it a fitting film with which to bring this survey of a quarter century of Latin-themed Westerns to an end.

Before swimming back into the mainstream of the Cisco saga, I'd like to announce the winner of my Celluloid Serape award for the worst imitation-Cisco film ever made. But, faced with what seem to be four equally awful contestants—*Call of the Coyote, The Pecos Dandy, The Irish Gringo,* and *The Tia Juana Kid*—how can I make a single choice among them? Aha! Rather than giving the award to a picture, I shall present it to a man—to the man who somehow contrived to star in two of these four disasters and to direct a third. The serape is hereby awarded to—Patrick Carlyle. If he's still alive and I ever run into him I'll arrange for a ceremony.

Once the studio heads realized that talking Westerns were feasible in terms of both technology and economics, the genre flourished. During the first half of the thirties, Columbia offered a first-rate series starring Buck Jones (1930-34) and another with Tim McCoy (1931-35). Universal presented first a Tom Mix series (1932-33), then a Ken Maynard series (1933-34), and it began releasing an offtrail series with Buck Jones (1934-37) after that ace of the saddle had left Columbia. Warner Bros. briefly experimented with a John Wayne series (1932-33) and RKO with an excellent series starring Tom Keene (1930-33). Paramount remade most of its silent films based on Zane Grey novels into talkies, with the spectacular action footage from the silent versions recycled intact. Fox continued its silent-era practice of making a few Westerns a year, with George O'Brien in the leading role and Zane Grey novels or stories as the usual if nominal literary basis. Of the major studios, MGM alone never ventured into Western territory. And of course there were countless Poverty Row outfits that cranked out ultra-cheap oater series and somewhat more respectable and longer-lived studios that made heavy commitments to the genre. Between 1931 and 1935 Monogram, for example, released five different series respectively starring Bill Cody, Tom Tyler, Rex Bell, Bob Steele, and, last and best of all, John Wayne.

In 1935 the Fox corporation merged with another studio, but the new entity, 20th Century-Fox, showed little interest in Westerns. Elsewhere it was a watershed year for the genre. Paramount launched the classic Hopalong Cassidy series (1935-44) starring William Boyd. Republic Pictures, a new entity formed from Monogram and several other small studios, offered a short series with John Wayne (1935-36), a much longer series with singing cowboy Gene Autry (1935-42), and, a year later, the excellent Three Mesquiteers series (1936-43), not to mention the oaters with Johnny Mack Brown (1936-37) and Bob Steele (1936-38) that were released as Republic pictures but were actually made by a smaller outfit with lower standards. Monogram, split off from Republic and reconstituted as a separate entity in 1937, presented series with Jack Randall (1937-40), Tom Keene (1937-38), Tim McCoy (1938) and Tex Ritter (1938-41). Columbia launched the longest-lived Western series of them all with Charles Starrett in the lead (1935-52), plus less successful cycles with Ken Maynard (1935-36), Bob Allen (1936-37), and the unendurable Jack Luden (1938), plus an excellent series with Bill Elliott (1938-42). After losing Buck Jones, Universal began a series with Bob Baker (1937-39) and a fine action-packed brace of sagebrush sagas with Johnny Mack Brown (1939-42). Republic introduced Roy Rogers (1938-51) at around the same time RKO came back into the

Western fold with former Fox star George O'Brien (1938-40). These plus the many low-budget efforts from short-lived outfits like Ambassador and Grand National added up to a total of more than nine hundred feature-length Westerns put on the market between *In Old Arizona* and the beginning of 1939. No wonder the executives at 20th Century-Fox wanted to try the genre again!

The studio still owned rights to the Cisco Kid character and, in the last year of the decade, decided to reintroduce America's moviegoers to the romantic bandido. The problem they faced was that so many of the people who had worked on the first two Cisco features either weren't under contract or weren't interested. Edmund Lowe was freelancing at Paramount, Universal, and elsewhere. Raoul Walsh had left Fox in 1933 and was about to begin a long-term association with Warner Bros. that would lead to more than a decade's worth of classic films with Cagney, Flynn, and Bogart. Irving Cummings was still with 20th Century-Fox but by 1939 was specializing almost exclusively in biopics and musicals. Warner Baxter too was under contract but ill health had made him look much older than his forty-six years. Still, he was the only Cisco anyone knew, and in *The Return of the Cisco Kid* (1939) he took up the role one more time—but with some differences.

He had dominated *In Old Arizona* and, to a slightly lesser degree, *The Cisco Kid*. In his late forties he couldn't do that again but, thanks to the development of the trio Western concept in the thirties, he didn't have to try. His third and last outing as Cisco was structured roughly along the lines of the Hopalong Cassidy and Three Mesquiteers series: Cisco as the father or older brother figure, his henchman López from *The Cisco Kid* transformed into a wild young hothead along the lines of Jimmy Ellison from the Cassidys or Robert Livingston from the Mesquiteers films, and the Gordito character from the 1931 feature upgraded (if that's the right word) to traditional comic sidekick. Chris-Pin Martin was at least as fat as he'd been in 1931 and seemed perfect to reprise his role as Gordito, but who should be cast as the young blood López?

"I'm a Latin from Manhattan," César Romero liked to say of himself. His ancestry was Cuban and the island's revolutionary hero José Martí was his maternal grandfather, but he was born in New York City on February 15, 1907, and grew up on the East Coast. His first acting experience came at boarding school when he played four parts in Shakespeare's *The Merchant of Venice*. The family lost its fortune with the collapse of the sugar market early in the

Depression and César went to work in a Wall Street bank. He broke into show business by forming a dance team with a woman friend and soon was both dancing and acting on Broadway. His stage role in *Dinner at Eight* brought him to the attention of MGM, which purchased movie rights to the play but cast Romero in another classic picture, *The Thin Man* (1934), where he appeared as the wealthy, decadent Chris Jorgenson. (The movie of *Dinner at Eight* did happen to include former Cisco costar Edmund Lowe among its distinguished cast.)

For the next three years Romero found work at a variety of studios in more than a dozen featured parts, most notably opposite Marlene Dietrich in Josef von Sternberg's *The Devil Is a Woman* (Paramount, 1935). "They said I was going to be the next Valentino," he recalled in a 1984 interview, but usually he played either gigolos or gangsters. In 1937 he signed an exclusive contract with 20th Century-Fox and was cast by John Ford as an evil Hindu in the Shirley Temple vehicle *Wee Willie Winkie* (1937). Then, in one of those strange coincidences that make up film history, he was starred in *Dangerously Yours* (1937), a remake of a 1933 Fox feature whose leading man had been Warner Baxter. Two years later Romero and Baxter appeared together for the first time, opposite Loretta Young and Binnie Barnes, in the romantic comedy *Wife, Husband, and Friend* (1939). Shortly after that confection wrapped he was teamed with Baxter again, this time playing López to the older man's Cisco Kid. It was Romero's first experience in a Western and he came across as a hairy loudmouth with a vicious streak. Maybe the director had seen too many of his gangster pictures.

With Raoul Walsh gone from 20th Century-Fox and Irving Cummings occupied with lighter fare, a new director had to be found for *The Return of the Cisco Kid*. The man who wound up with the job was a former film editor still in his twenties with only a year's experience directing. Like most of the small army who made the thousands of movies Hollywood churned out during its golden age, Herbert I. Leeds came and went in modest anonymity, attracting little attention beyond the moment. Reference books will tell you that besides *The Return of the Cisco Kid* he directed three later Cisco features with Romero, plus entries in most other 20th Century-Fox series of the late thirties and early forties and a number of nonseries pictures. If you are extremely well informed you may know that he also directed two episodes of the Cisco TV series of the early fifties with Duncan Renaldo and Leo Carrillo. But whether you search high or low, you are unlike-

MARLENE DIETRICH

THE DEVIL IS A WOMAN

LIONEL
ATWILL
CESAR
ROMERO
Edward Everett
HORTON
ALISON SKIPWORTH
DON ALVARADO
Directed by
JOSEF VON
STERNBERG
A Paramount Picture

Marlene Dietrich (left) and César Romero in *The Devil Is a Woman* (1935)

ly to find a word about Leeds himself. Unless, that is, you are lucky enough to have discovered *Realm of Unknowing* (Wesleyan University Press, 1995), a collection by Leeds's nephew, the poet Mark Rudman, whose uncle is the subject of his title essay.

Herbert Levy was born in New York City around 1910 or 1911. His affluent family sent him overseas to be educated at La Villa Lozanne in Switzerland, where he learned to speak fluent French. Although accepted by Yale, he chose to attend Lehigh University in Pennsylvania so as to be near a favorite cousin. He became a gun enthusiast and often went hunting with his grandfather. Thanks to his family's friendship with Jack Warner, he landed a job at Warner Bros. as an assistant cutter and soon graduated to film editor. Still calling himself Herbert or Bert Levy, he earned his first screen credits as editor on Warners-First National pictures like *Week-end Marriage* (1932), *Dark Hazard* (1934), and *Side Streets* (1934). In 1936 he moved to 20th Century-Fox and edited *A Message to Garcia, Half Angel,* and *Dimples.*

Early in 1938 he changed his name to Leeds and began to direct. Among the four pictures he made that year were *Five of a Kind*, with the Dionne quintuplets, shot on location in Quebec, and the crime melodrama *Island in the Sky*, starring Gloria Stuart, Michael Whalen, and Paul Kelly, which is considered his finest film by most of those who know Leeds's work at all. In 1939 he turned out six pictures: a Mr. Moto with Peter Lorre, a Charlie Chan with Sidney Toler, the last of the Ciscos with Warner Baxter, the first with César Romero, and two Jane Withers "adorable child" flicks that costarred the last and greatest Cisco sidekick, Leo Carrillo. Interviewed in 1991 for Mark Rudman's essay on his uncle, Withers described Leeds as "loved by everybody that he worked with. The one word I'd choose to say what he was like is kindness." He sent Withers a doll for her huge collection every year for the rest of his life.

"My uncle took up a lot of room," Rudman writes. "He was thick-set, bulky, barrel-chested. He wore shades of brown: heavy tweeds. There was something suffocating about him." His sister

A Message to Garcia (1936) was the second filmic interpretation of Elbert Hubbard's 1899 essay of the same name that encouraged persistence and loyalty.

Marjorie, Rudman's mother, said he was known as "the man who never smiled." He had "brown velvet chocolate eyes" and "a reputation as a difficult man." When the script for one of his Cisco films called for the romantic rogue to pull a guitar from his saddlebag and start to sing, Leeds said the scene was impossible and flatly refused to shoot it.

"Bert always read the crime magazines," an old relative told Rudman. "He was always looking for stories." Apparently there were few he liked, for he directed just one low-budget feature in 1940, the last pair of Romero Ciscos and a Michael Shayne detective flick with Lloyd Nolan in 1941, and three more Shaynes plus a war film with Nolan in 1942. Although a trick knee exempted him from the draft, he volunteered for service and wound up in Europe with the OSS. According to his father, he was one of two Americans on the Remagen bridge across the Rhine when the Germans blew it up with mines. But in the best tradition of Cisco and other Western heroes, he escaped unhurt.

When Leeds returned to Hollywood at the end of the war there seemed no room for him in Westerns or detective films. He directed two comedies for 20th Century-Fox, one in 1946 and the other in 1948, but seems to have concentrated most of his energy on serving as secretary of the Directors Guild. During the 1949-50 season he migrated into the new medium of television and—along with Leslie Goodwins, who would later become the last director of Cisco TV episodes—cranked out segments of *The Life of Riley*, a short-lived sitcom on the ill-fated Dumont network, starring Jackie Gleason and Rosemary DeCamp. (The series fared much better a few years later when it moved to NBC with William Bendix in the lead.) In 1950 Leeds directed a quickie thriller for RKO and a final comedy feature for Monogram. Except for occasional second unit work on large-scale 20th Century-Fox features like *Broken Arrow* (1950) with Jimmy Stewart and *Diplomatic Courier* (1952) with Tyrone Power, that was the end of his studio career.

The Big Trail (1930), starring John Wayne and directed by Raoul Walsh, is considered the first epic Western of the "talkie" period.

The Avenger (1931) is a Joaquín Murrieta story pitting a Latino against three vicious Anglo gold-mine claim jumpers.
Third from left is Buck Jones as Joaquín. Raising the whip is Walter Percival; Paul Fix is the man about to be hanged.

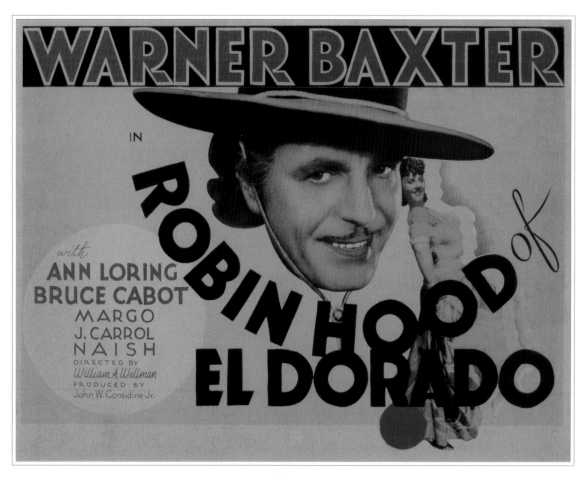

In *Robin Hood of El Dorado* (1936), Warner Baxter gave a stellar performance as Joaquín Murrieta,
who is both an avenger and a noble outlaw in the same vein as the Cisco Kid and Zorro.

Spanish-language poster for the U.S. film *Under the Pampas Moon* (1935), a vehicle in which Warner Baxter
played his trademark daring-Latino character, this time in the Argentine pampas

In *The California Trail* (1933), set in pre-Gold Rush California, Buck Jones played the conventional role of the Anglo hero who frees the Latino *pueblo* from the oppression of their Latino overseers.

In *The Gay Caballero* (1932), George O'Brien (hatless and wearing the reddish shirt) played Ted Radcliffe, a football player from the East who inherits a cattle ranch. The same title was used for a 1941 Cisco Kid film.

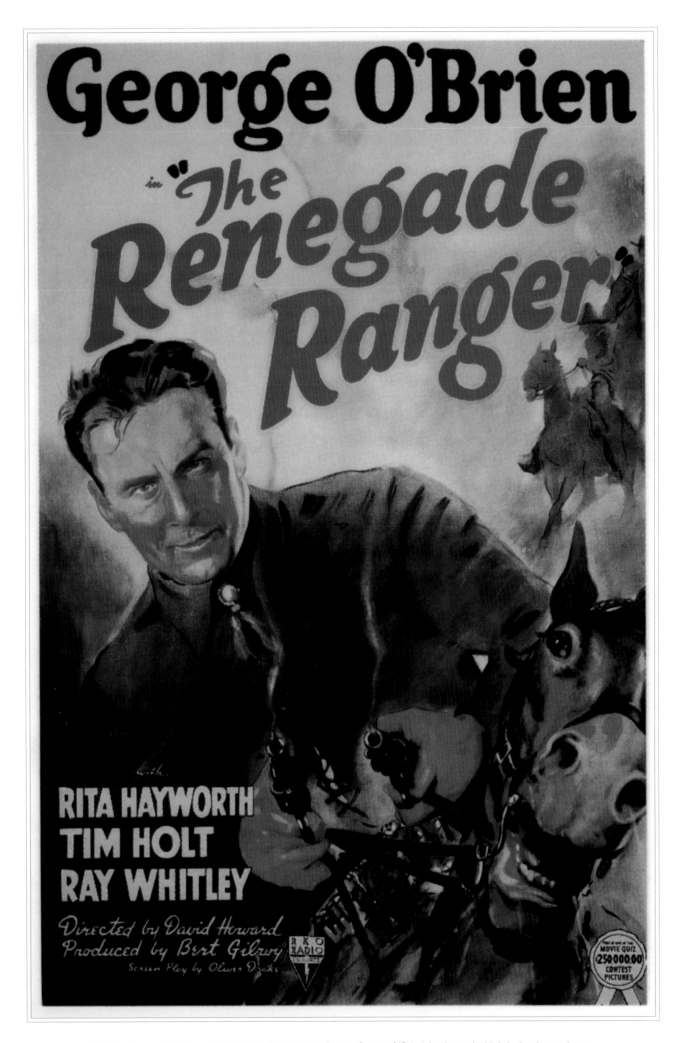

In *The Renegade Ranger* (1938), Texas Ranger Jack Steele (George O'Brien) is charged with bringing in murderess Judith Álvarez (Rita Hayworth), the leader of a gang waging war on crooked politicians who stole their land.

Leo Carrillo did not always play sidekick roles. In *Pancho Villa Returns* (1950), a Mexican film released for an American audience, he played the lead character, Pancho Villa.

Warner Baxter played his final role as the Cisco Kid in 20th Century-Fox's *The Return of the Cisco Kid* (1939). Plagued by ill health, Baxter portrayed Cisco as a father figure to a hotheaded youth instead of the daring bandit of earlier films.

Billy the Kid and the Cisco Kid were influential in popularizing "Kid" characters in a deluge of Westerns that incorporated the word in their titles. "Kid" films of the boxing genre also gained popularity.

King Vidor's *Billy the Kid* (1930), starring John (later Johnny) Mack Brown as Billy and Wallace Beery as Pat Garrett, influenced a number of subsequent good and good-bad bandit films.

The most decorated serviceman in World War II, Audie Murphy portrayed Billy the Kid in Universal-International's *The Kid from Texas* (1950).

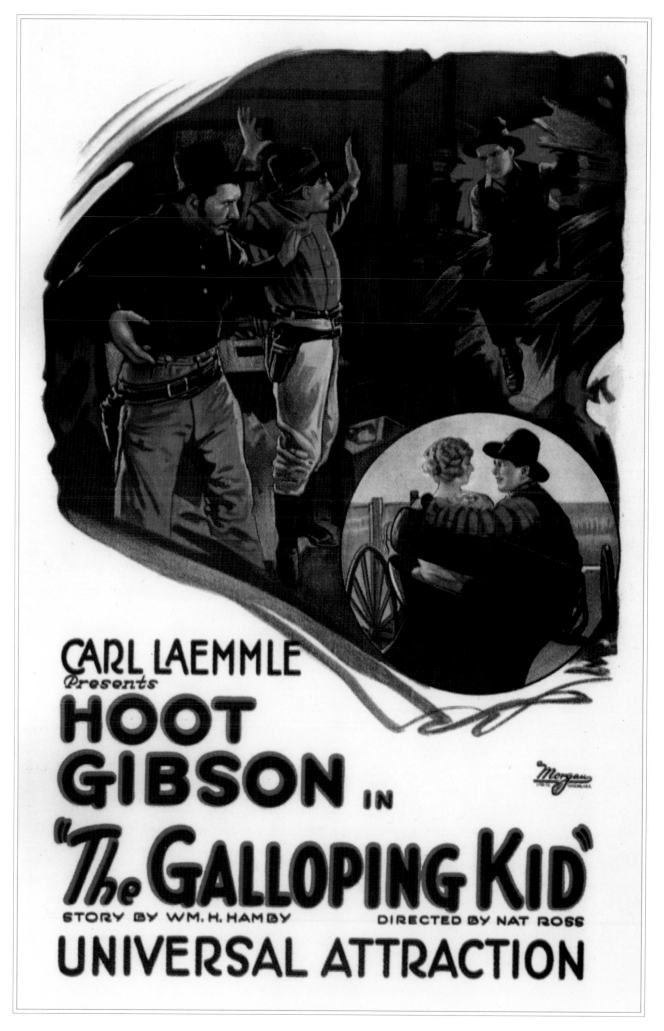

Hoot Gibson portrayed an easygoing bodyguard in the silent Western *The Galloping Kid* (1922), an example of an early "Kid" movie.

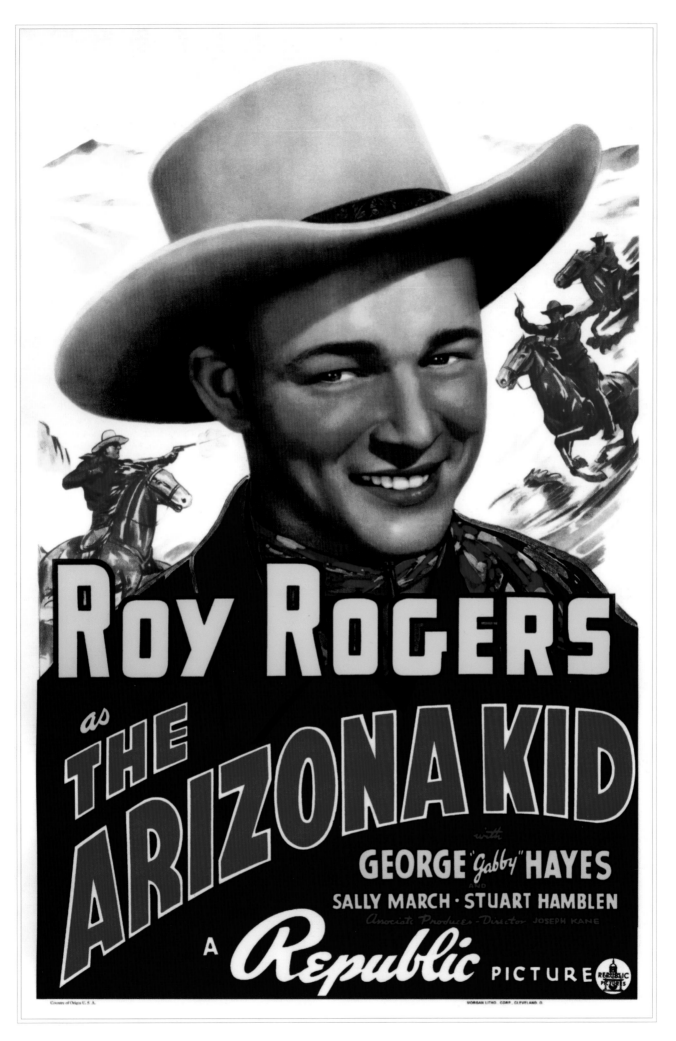

Roy Rogers portrayed a Confederate officer faced with ordering the execution of his friend, who had become a Confederate terrorist, in Republic's *The Arizona Kid* (1939).

James Cagney and Humphrey Bogart tackled the Western genre in *The Oklahoma Kid* (1939).

The Tonto Kid (1934) was one film in Resolute Pictures' trio-series featuring Rex Bell, Ruth Mix, and Buzz Barton.

Hoot Gibson (in the red shirt) and Bob Steele (just below Gibson) starred in Monogram's *The Utah Kid* (1944).

Roy Rogers played a cowboy who seeks vengeance for his brother's murder in *The Carson City Kid* (1940). Beside him is Pauline Moore.

T he masked outlaw character, whether noble or base, was not confined to such well-known figures as Zorro and the Lone Ranger. These characters were seen in a variety of films.

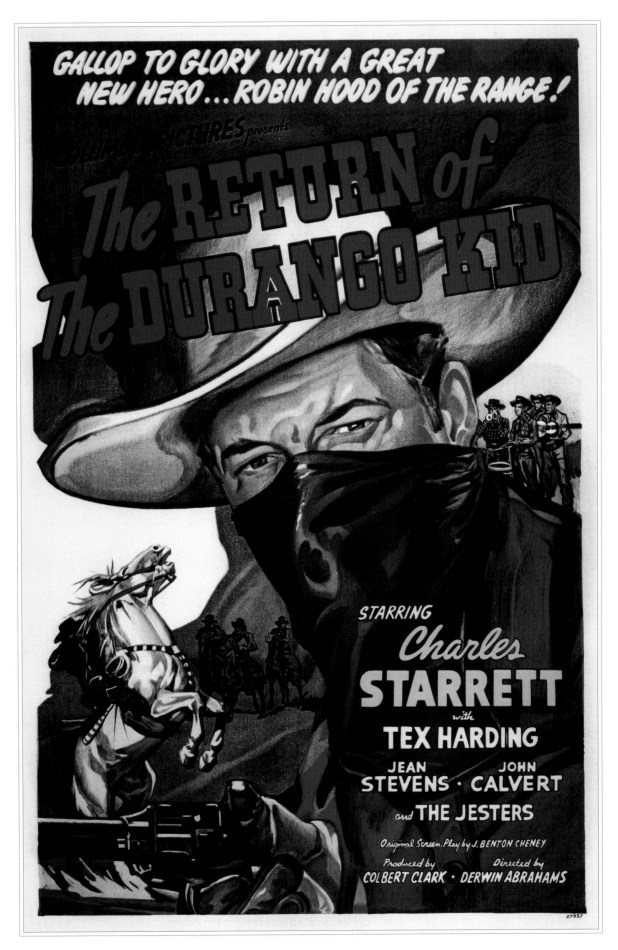

Charles Starrett reprised his heroic character from *The Durango Kid* (1940) in sixty-four subsequent films, beginning with *The Return of the Durango Kid* (1945).

After the success of Douglas Fairbanks's silent film *The Mark of Zorro* (1920), the character became quite popular. In the late thirties, Republic Pictures resurrected the character in a number of cliffhanger serials beginning with *Zorro Rides Again* (1937).

Duncan Renaldo and Leo Carrillo ended their silver-screen Cisco series with *The Girl from San Lorenzo* (1950). Here, they are held up by a masked bandit played by stuntman David Sharpe.

He went back to Manhattan and, says Rudman, began wandering around "in a fog of depression." The only other TV episodes he is known to have directed are the two thirty-minute *Cisco Kid* segments he made in 1953. Whatever stunted his career, it wasn't the blacklist, for according to Rudman his uncle was a "hysterical" anti-Communist. Whatever money he had saved, he spent all too quickly. "Even during his last days he had the newspaper delivered to his [hotel] room . . . , needing to tip the bellboy a buck, rather than go downstairs and get it for a nickel at a newsstand."

On April 1, 1954, Leeds moved out of the more expensive hotel where he'd been staying and into a $5-a-day room at the Wyndham between Fifth and Sixth Avenues on 58th Street. On May 15 he underlined a passage in the book he was reading and set the book down on his bathroom floor. "I'm so sorry to do what I'm doing. I'm so ashamed," the passage read. Then he loaded his 20-gauge shotgun with a single shell, sat on his hotel bed, held the gun with its stock in the air, and blew out his chest. Jane Withers had no idea that her favorite director had been dead almost forty years when Mark Rudman spoke with her but when told of his suicide she thought she

knew the reason. "He was much too kind and sensitive. He couldn't take the world he was living in."

The Return of the Cisco Kid was clearly influenced by the trio Western vogue but its three compadres were by no means equals. Romero is billed third, after Baxter and female lead Lynn Bari, with poor Chris-Pin Martin relegated to eighth place in the cast. Between Romero and Martin were three old reliables and one still young—Henry Hull, Kane Richmond, C. Henry Gordon, and an unusually hammy Robert Barrat—while future Western favorites Eddy Waller and Ward Bond wound up at or near the bottom of the credits. The screenplay by Milton Sperling keeps to the quasi-operatic mode of previous Cisco features, with romantic complications at every turn and action nowhere. Baxter looks like a dissipated old man and the way his little mustache turns up at the corners can give a modern viewer the giggles, but Leeds manages to make his star's appearance work for the picture: Baxter may be certain Lynn Bari loves him alone but it's clear to us in the audience that this beautiful young woman would never choose him over virile Kane Richmond. (That Cisco is Hispanic is never made an issue for a moment.) Baxter's Mexican accent had degenerated

Warner Baxter made his last appearance as the Cisco Kid in *The Return of the Cisco Kid* (1939), eleven years after he first played the role. Smoking the cigar is Robert Barrat.

badly since *In Old Arizona* and Leeds doesn't help by letting his dialogue be saturated with Y sounds for him to mangle. ("Why do jou think I get execute?" "When jou see the stagecoach come, jou know what to do.") But there are some lovely outdoor shots, and the philosophic sadness Baxter projects is not only consistent with his previous renditions of Cisco but eerily prophetic of the shape of what was left of his life.

The year is 1900 and we open outside the ruins of a fort in northern Mexico near the Arizona border with a Mexican captain (C. Henry Gordon) and a firing squad executing the Cisco Kid. As soon as the troops ride off, Cisco climbs out of his open grave and collects his pals López (César Romero) and Gordito (Chris-Pin Martin), who had replaced all the soldiers' bullets the night before with blanks. The three amigos ride north to launch a new wave of thievery with Baxter singing a Spanish love song in English and a flurry of close-ups of the trio riding sawhorses or something.

The first job they plan in Arizona is a stagecoach holdup with López and Gordito pulling the actual robbery while Cisco is inside the coach as a passenger. But his plans change when, at the wilder-

ness way station where he's to board the coach, Cisco encounters the alcoholic and slightly larcenous Colonel Joshua Bixby (Henry Hull) and his lovely granddaughter Ann Carver (Lynn Bari), by whom our romantic rogue is smitten on the spot. Cisco bails the colonel out of a financial embarrassment at the way station tavern by cashing a check for him, knowing that he'll shortly be getting his money back in the holdup. As in previous films in the series, Cisco introduces himself as Gonzalo Sebastiano Rodrigo Don Juan Chicuelo, whose father was Portuguese and whose mother came from San Luis Obispo. On the coach, Ann tells Cisco that she's inherited $5,000 and given it to a friend, Alan Davis (Kane Richmond), who is to buy a ranch with it for her and her grandfather outside the town of Fronteras, which is their destination. By the time López and Gordito hold up the stage, Cisco is so blindly befuddled by Ann's charms that, to their astonishment, he opens fire on them and chases them away.

When the coach reaches Fronteras, Cisco invites Ann to have dinner with him that evening, then finds his amigos and explains that he aborted the holdup because he's fallen in love and decided to stay dead and go straight. Meanwhile Ann and the colonel discover that Alan Davis not only didn't buy the ranch for them but has been in jail for the past week. Alan tells them from his cell that Sheriff McNally (Robert Barrat), who is also the mayor of Fronteras, the saloonkeeper, and the chief landowner in the area, simply confiscated the money and threw him into a cell. Cut to McNally's saloon where a local man (Ward Bond) is put on trial (for rustling cattle that McNally had stolen from him), beaten to a pulp by McNally, and kicked out of town. A few minutes later Ann and the colonel confront McNally in the saloon and get thrown in jail beside Alan Davis.

Meanwhile, Cisco has made elaborate preparations for his dinner date with Ann, including vintage wine, an orchestra, and special decorations. When she doesn't come and the hotel clerk finally tells him that she's been locked up, it's too late in the evening for him to visit her legally, so he starts a fire outside the general store that quickly spreads to a large part of town, including the jailhouse, and he has to break in and pistol-whip a deputy in order to save the three prisoners from the blaze he set. Seeing Ann and Davis embrace, he becomes insanely jealous. Davis is wounded as they all flee town, and we must imagine that Cisco takes a special pleasure in the next scene when, on the trail in the middle of the night, he cauterizes his rival's wound. Then he fakes an attack by McNally's men so that he has an excuse to ride off

Publicity photo of César Romero from *The Cisco Kid and the Lady* (1939)

alone with Ann and romance her in the light of "the most beautiful sunrise in the world." Taking her to the top of a mountain, he demonstrates the echo chamber effect of the place by shouting lines like "Jou are beautiful" and hearing them repeated over and over. Then he tells her of the dream he first told Tonia in *In Old Arizona*—of returning to the Portugal he hasn't seen since childhood with the love of his life—and her reply misleads him into thinking she loves him. Later the reunited group of six cross into Mexico to hide out at the house of old Mamá Soledad (Soledad Jiménez). After a hearty meal, Cisco, López and Gordito return north to get the ranch back from McNally, with Cisco still convinced that as soon as her grandfather is secure, Ann will go to Portugal with him.

Back in Fronteras, Cisco poses as a big cattleman from Sonora, offers to buy the property McNally stole from Alan Davis, and agrees to pay McNally's outrageous asking price of $100,000. They agree to close the deal the following Monday evening at McNally's ranch. McNally, of course, plans to con-

fiscate the money just as he had with Davis before, while Cisco's scheme is to get the money by stealing it from McNally's bank. The three amigos pull the job the next day. In the course of the robbery Cisco has to pistol-whip the teller. The deputy whom he'd pistol-whipped earlier in the fire scene happens to be in the bank and recognizes the technique from before. From this information McNally figures out that Cisco plans to keep his Monday night date to get the deed and sets a trap at his ranch. Meanwhile south of the border, Ann and Alan Davis fall in love.

On Monday night a still love-smitten Cisco sets out to exchange the stolen money for the deed. At the last minute McNally's trap is augmented by the arrival of the Mexican captain who had headed Cisco's firing squad. Cisco, of course, has slipped into the ranch house early and captures McNally and the captain, whose face drops at the sight of what he thinks is a ghost. A simple ruse enables Cisco, López, and Gordito to overpower the deputies

César Romero played his first role as Cisco in 20th Century-Fox's *The Cisco Kid and the Lady* (1939).
Pointing his gun at Romero is Robert Barrat, to whose right is Chris Pin-Martin.

who've surrounded the house. As Cisco is about to take off with the deed, McNally challenges him to a fistfight. "Oh, no," Cisco declares. "Thees impossible. No, I do not juse the fists. If I hurt the hand I cannot play the guitar, and if I cannot sing love song I cannot make love, and if I cannot make love, I die." This may have been intended as a dig at *Golden Boy* (1939) with its young boxer hero (William Holden) having to choose between the ring and a classical violinist's career, but its effect is to destroy any hope for action in a film that sorely needs it.

The three amigos return to Mexico just in time to abort the colonel's scheme to sell Mama Soledad some phony gold mine stock. When the colonel reveals that Ann and Alan are going to be married, he breaks Cisco's heart. Furious and bent on revenge, Cisco sends out Gordito to instruct Davis to ride alone in the dark through the pass where McNally's men are waiting in ambush, and meet Cisco on the other side. But at the last minute, when Ann tells Cisco that she and Alan have always been in love

and that she never loved Cisco at all, Cisco repents and he and Gordito race like the wind to save Alan's life. After a wild riding sequence intercut with more of those ugly close-ups of Baxter on a sawhorse, Cisco uses the mountain's echo chamber effect to fool McNally and his men into thinking they're surrounded. McNally ultimately agrees to leave the young couple alone if Cisco will stay out of the territory, and we close with the three amigos back in Mexico and Cisco dreaming of another girlfriend, a certain Carmencita. (Not, we hope, the señorita of that name from 1931's *The Cisco Kid*.) "But Carmencita have feet like a duck!" protests Gordito. "I do not have to look at her feet," Cisco tells him. This is the last line Warner Baxter was ever to speak in his role as Cisco. After two more undistinguished films, neither of them Westerns, his twelve-year stint at 20th Century-Fox limped to an end.

It isn't known whether Romero was tapped to replace him before or after *The Return of the Cisco Kid* was wrapped, but roughly six months after Baxter's

Cisco (César Romero) lets Gordito (Chris Pin-Martin) disarm Robert Barrat while he concentrates elsewhere.

adiós, the Latin from Manhattan took over in a six-film series, released between the end of 1939 and the spring of 1941, which Everson in *The Hollywood Western* describes collectively as "strong in casts and elaborate production values, but by their very nature mild in action content" (228). Herbert Leeds smoothed the transition by directing the first of the six, *The Cisco Kid and the Lady* (1939), which might better have been titled "The Cisco Kid and the Baby." Romero was transformed from a hairy lout to a foppishly dressed, boastful poseur with a somewhat mannered and hyper style but lacking the world-weariness and reflective edge that Baxter brought to the role. The screenplay for Romero's first outing as Cisco was by Frances Hyland from an original story by Stanley Rauh. With Marjorie Weaver and Virginia Field as the ladies in the bandido's life, young George Montgomery as Cisco's romantic rival, Robert Barrat reprising the sort of villain part in which Leeds had cast him in *The Return of the Cisco Kid*, and Ward Bond upgraded from his tiny role in the last Cisco film, one can appreciate Everson's remark about the strength of the cast. It's too bad the film itself was rather routine.

After an opening montage showing Cisco perpetrating a crime wave all over Arizona, we cut to our caballero crooning a Spanish love song and riding peacefully with Gordito across lovely barren country. They catch sight of a lone traveler crossing the desert in a covered wagon and decide to steal his horses, but before they can reach the man he's shot from ambush by Jim Harbison (Robert Barrat) and his henchman Stevens (John Beach), and the horses run away with the wagon. In a well-directed action sequence, Cisco stops the horses. Harbison rides up from behind and searches the dying man's pockets as Cisco and Gordito look into the wagon and find, cooing and googling in the rear of it, a baby boy (Gloria Ann White). The dying man, Drake (J. Anthony Hughes), tells Cisco, Gordito, and Harbison that he had discovered a gold mine and was on his way to record his claim—something Harbison was already well aware of—and offers the mine to all three men if they'll swear to give an equal share to the baby. His last act before dying is to tear his map of the mine into three pieces and give one to each man.

No sooner have they buried Drake than Stevens and the rest of Harbison's gang show up, draw their guns on Cisco and Gordito, and demand their portions of the map. Too late: Cisco has turned his scrap of paper into a cigarette and burned it up, and Gordito has eaten his. Harbison has to keep them alive if he ever wants to locate the mine. They set out with the dead man's wagon and, so they think, with the baby, but Gordito has stupidly left the infant back at its father's gravesite. The child crawls out to the middle of the road and, in a stunningly unfaked-looking shot, is almost run over by a passing stagecoach. When Cisco realizes that the baby isn't with them, he races back to their starting point with Harbison and his men in hot pursuit, then in another swift and well-directed action set-piece, chases after the stagecoach with the baby. They halt the coach and find the infant in the arms of Julie Lawson (Marjorie Weaver), the schoolteacher in the nearby town of Oro Grande. Cisco, as usual, falls for the woman in two seconds flat but claims the baby as "his."

In Oro Grande, Cisco, Gordito, and the baby take a room in Harbison's saloon-cum-hotel and the adult partners in the gold mine share tequila to bind their bargain. Walton (Ward Bond), the town drunk, gets into a loud squabble with dance-hall girl Billie Graham (Virginia Field) that brings Billie into Cisco's ken and sets off a new light of love in his heart. Harbison bribes Billie with a cameo locket to play up to Cisco and wheedle out of him the information on his piece of the map. Gordito amuses the baby by shooting off his pistol and Cisco gives the child a bath. Before the partners go off to hunt for the mine, Cisco spots Harbison sending his men out of town and suspects a double-cross. The baby is dropped off with Julie at the schoolhouse and the gold seekers leave town on the treasure hunt.

A stagecoach arrives in Oro Grande and disgorges Julie's fiancé, Tommy Bates (George Montgomery), on an unannounced visit to marry Julie and take her back to Kansas City. When he finds her caring for the baby, he comes instantly to the conclusion that she is, as they used to say, damaged goods, and he storms off to get drunk. Meanwhile, out on the trail, Cisco pretends to be lost, rides off alone to try to find landmarks, comes upon Harbison's men in ambush, uses the old rope-across-the-road gambit to get the drop on them, and makes Harbison and his gang march behind them for miles, trussed together and shouting, "Amigo! Amigo!"

Back in town, Cisco romances Julie (who doesn't bother to mention how "his" baby has cost her a fiancé), filches a photograph of her, drops into Harbison's saloon for a drink, happens to run into the sloshed Tommy Bates, and stumbles into his own comedy of errors when Tommy sees Julie's picture in Cisco's pocket and jumps to the conclusion that Cisco is Julie's seducer and the baby's dad. Tommy falls over drunk after taking a swing at Cisco, who puts the young man to bed in the room he's sharing with Gordito, then comes back downstairs for a romantic interlude with Billie.

Harbison trudges into town from his twenty-mile walk just in time to catch them dancing and smooching. Billie tells Cisco that she knows who he is but that she's too smitten with him to turn him over to the law and hints that she'll be only too happy to steal Harbison's portion of the map and form a partnership of her own with the romantic rogue. Cisco sneaks up to the balcony overlooking Harbison's room and watches her take the map from Harbison's pocket while he's taking a bath and hide it inside the locket Harbison had given her. It's the work of a few moments for Cisco to sneak into Billie's room, romance her in the dark, and snatch the locket from her pretty neck. When she finds the brooch gone, she goes back into partnership with Harbison and tells him that "Rodríguez Gonzales Sebastiano Don Juan Chicuelo" is really the Cisco Kid.

Back in his own room, Cisco finds a photo of Julie in the pocket of the passed-out Tommy Bates and understands why the drunken youth tried to punch him out. Before Cisco and Gordito can get out of town they're captured by Harbison and his gang and turned over to the sheriff, who wires the nearest military authorities to come pick them up. Tommy is locked up with them, for no better reason than that he was found drunk in their room. When everyone has left the hotel, Billie finds the locket on the floor where Cisco hid it—with the map still inside—and realizes that she made an awful mistake betraying him.

The next morning Julie visits Tommy in his cell and Cisco finally realizes that the two, despite the little misunderstanding over the baby, are in love. That evening Billie pays Cisco a secret visit to ask his forgiveness, which he gladly gives, and to slip him a gun, which he graciously accepts. Before he can use the pistol, Harbison drops by the cell and offers to break Cisco and Gordito out if they'll lead him to the mine. Cisco maneuvers Harbison into agreeing to dress up in a Cisco outfit and hold up that night's stage so that the sheriff will think he has the wrong men behind bars and let them loose. After Harbison has gone off to pull the robbery, Cisco and Gordito use Billie's pistol to break jail, kidnap the justice of the peace, and force him at gunpoint to make Tommy and Julie man and wife—even though they're still at each other's throats. This scene is supposed to be funny but would strike most viewers today as sick.

The last few minutes of the picture pack in a bewildering amount of story.

The military patrol sent to pick up Cisco and Gordito reach Oro Grande and find the prisoners gone. The night stage comes back into town and the driver reports a robbery attempt by the Cisco Kid. Harbison in his Cisco togs returns with his gang, they find Cisco's and Gordito's horses where Billie has left them, a gun battle breaks out when Cisco and Gordito come for their steeds, and Harbison winds up getting mistaken for Cisco by the burghers of Oro Grande and shot in the back. As dawn breaks, Cisco and Gordito show the location of the mine to the new husband and father Tommy Bates, and they ride off with Billie at their side to the strains of another Spanish love song.

The second of the Romero Ciscos was no more an action classic than the first, but it boasted an unusual storyline and director. Norman Foster, born Norman Hoeffer in Richmond, Virginia, on December 13, 1900, was acting on Broadway opposite his then wife, Claudette Colbert, when both of them were offered movie contracts at Paramount. His first screen role was in the newspaper melodrama *Gentlemen of the Press* (Paramount, 1929), starring Walter Huston, and he costarred with Colbert and newcomer Ginger Rogers in *Young Man of Manhattan* (Paramount, 1930). Later he divorced Colbert and married actress Sally Blane. Foster played the lead in many low-budget early talkies but eventually decided that directing was more to his taste and between 1937 and 1941 was under contract at 20th Century-Fox, where he worked mainly on whodunits in the studio's Charlie Chan and Mr. Moto series, with occasional ventures into new territory like a Cisco picture. His finest films—*Journey into Fear* (RKO, 1943) with Joseph Cotten, Dolores del Río, and Orson Welles, and *Kiss the Blood off My Hands* (Norma/Universal, 1948) with Joan Fontaine and Burt Lancaster—are classics of the noir thriller, so packed with visual bravura that Welles himself is sometimes credited with ghost-directing them. In the fifties he went to work for the Disney studio where, among other films, he helmed the Davy Crockett segments of *Disneyland* (1954-55) and thirteen episodes of the first season (1957-58) of the Disney TV series *Zorro*. Near the end of his career he left Disney to direct episodes of series like *The Loner* (1965-66), *The Monroes* (1966-67), and *The Green Hornet* (1966-67). He died in 1976.

The novelty of his single contribution to the Cisco saga, *Viva Cisco Kid* (1940), is the conception of the villain, who is clearly modeled on Charlie Chaplin's rendition of a buffoonish Hitler figure in the same year's *The Great Dictator*. Whether we

In *Lucky Cisco Kid* (1940), César Romero's Cisco smiles with Dana Andrews (left) as Joe Sawyer (right) holds a gun on him.

should credit this to Foster or the authors of the screenplay, Samuel G. Engel and Hal Long, is anyone's guess, but I'll lay my bet on Foster. Lovely Jean Rogers (the original Dale Arden in Universal's Flash Gordon serials) had the female lead, the usually unnotable Stanley Fields cut a fine figure as the frontier fuehrer, and B Western stalwarts like Leroy Mason, Bud Osborne, Tom London, Hank Worden, and Eddy Waller had unbilled bit parts.

This adventure begins with a sequence not the least connected with the plot as Cisco discovers that Gordito is about to get married—Foster mercifully never shows us what the woman looks like—and extracts his amigo from disaster by convincing the bride's wealthy brother Don Pancho (Charles Judels) that the dowry he's about to pay will be wasted because, all appearances to the contrary, Gordito is a walking corpse and will soon be dead. The partners ride away together and come upon a stagecoach holdup that went wrong because the $25,000 the bandits wanted had been in the form of $500 bills that the driver had hidden in a tiny envelope under his seat. The leader of the bandits is a masked Leroy Mason, whose name doesn't appear in the film's

credits. Coming upon this scene and chasing the thieves off, Cisco meets lovely Joan Allen (Jean Rogers), who has come from the east to live with her father, Jesse Allen (Minor Watson). As we follow Mason and his men back to the town of Towash, we discover that Jesse and saloonkeeper Hank Gunther (Harold Goodwin) are in with the robbers and that, along with countless other badmen in the region, they all take orders from a mysterious Professor Moriarty-like figure known only as the Boss.

After driving the stage into town, Cisco and Gordito escort Joan to her father's house in the countryside with Cisco singing a Spanish love song to help pass the time. He also sneaks in a bit of his philosophy. "All my life I have lived for freedom, adventure, laughter, and danger. It is the price I must pay for being a little niño." On the road they pass a crazy preacher called Moses (Nigel de Brulier), who is painting THE WAGES OF SIN IS DEATH on a huge rock. Jesse isn't home when they arrive, but they get to meet his Chinese servant Wang (Willie Fung) and Cisco makes a date with Joan for that night. This is the same night Gunther and Jesse plan to steal the $25,000 from the express office safe where it's being kept. Jesse goes home to find his daughter in residence but returns to town almost at once to take part in the robbery. Just as he's leaving, Moses the preacher drops by for a handout. Later when Cisco shows up for his date with Joan, he admits that he's a wanted man and says goodbye to her. "Don't change," she tells him. "Just keep on being a little niño."

Moses rides into town, happens to witness the express office break-in, recognizes one of the thieves as the man who had given him a handout earlier that evening (although, being new in the area, he doesn't know Jesse by name), and leads the sheriff and a posse to the Allen cabin. Catching sight of the posse on his trail, Jesse doesn't return home but goes into hiding. The sheriff and posse search the house for Jesse in vain. When they're gone, Jesse comes back home, arranges to meet Joan later in a shack outside the town of Grande, and takes off. Gunther and Leroy Mason meanwhile catch Moses alone and shoot him in the back so that he can never identify Jesse Allen.

On the way to Grande the next day, Joan is thrown from her horse and stumbles upon Cisco and Gordito again. Then all three stumble upon the sheriff, who arrests them for the express office robbery. The sheriff and posse find Moses's body along the trail and the three prisoners are accused of the murder. Cisco and Gordito break away and ride for their lives. Meanwhile Gunther and Leroy Mason grab Joan and set out to take her to the headquarters of the Boss so that Jesse will be forced to give them the stolen money to get her back. The excellent chase scene with Cisco and Gordito being pursued by the posse is the only real action sequence in the film.

The headquarters of the Boss is the Sugarloaf Mine, and we soon discover that this fearsome Moriarty of the frontier (Stanley Fields) is nothing but a loudmouthed buffoon who loves to play practical jokes on his underlings and everyone he meets. He locks Joan up in a secret underground room and sends out his men to hunt for Jesse. Meanwhile, Cisco and Gordito are captured at a country inn by its bearded proprietor (Francis Ford) but are saved by Jesse, who happened to have chosen the place for his rendezvous with Joan. Cisco, Gordito, and Jesse pick up Joan's trail where she was kidnapped and follow it to the Sugarloaf. Leaving Jesse in the rocks overlooking the mine, Cisco and Gordito take the stolen money into the oafish lion's den, identify themselves as the wanted men they in fact are, and ask to join the Boss's organization. The Boss indulges himself in a string of practical jokes like

exploding cigars and squirting rings at Gordito's expense while the gang's black chef (Mantan Moreland) prepares a lavish dinner—and drops a remark that reveals to Cisco that Joan is a prisoner beneath their feet. After another flurry of practical jokes on poor Gordito including a dripping whisky jigger, a water bucket over a door, and a rubber turkey, Gunther and Mason return to the Sugarloaf and tell the Boss that it was Cisco and Gordito who broke up their stagecoach robbery and became friends with Joan Allen. Cisco talks his way out of a tight spot by handing over the express money and claiming that he killed Jesse and now wants revenge on Joan. Gordito manages to pick the Boss's pocket and recover the money on the spot. The Boss takes Cisco to where Joan is being held but tells her the lie Cisco told him about having killed her father.

That night Cisco sneaks back to the underground room and explains everything to Joan, but meanwhile Gunther and Mason have captured Jesse alive and bring him to the Boss, whose men then capture Cisco, Gordito, and Joan just as they're about to escape. The four prisoners are taken to a special mine tunnel that the Boss has rigged like a terror trap in a cliffhanger serial so that when one beam is removed the whole tunnel will cave in. It turns out, however, that this trap is about as well designed as a trap in a Roadrunner cartoon. When the special beam is taken away, the entire mine collapses, killing the Boss and his gang in one fell swoop. The climax of the picture has Cisco desperately hunting for a way out of the tunnel before he, Gordito, and the Allens all suffocate. After a *conejito* (little rabbit) shows them the way to its hole, they manage to blast their way into daylight. Jesse goes back to Towash to settle his debt with the law and return the express money, while Cisco and Gordito ride off to new adventures.

Next in the series came a routine entry that has earned a tiny niche in film history as perhaps the only movie named for its director. *Lucky Cisco Kid* (1940) was helmed by H. Bruce Humberstone, a man of modest achievements whose career was well profiled in an essay by Jon Tuska included in his anthology *Close-Up: The Contract Director* (Scarecrow Press, 1976). Humberstone was born in Buffalo, New York, on November 18, 1903, and won his first movie job at the age of nineteen, as prop boy and assistant cameraman on a Universal silent Western starring Hoot Gibson and directed by the young John Ford. He worked his way up to assistant director, began directing films himself in 1932, and earned his nickname after he and the legendary action director B. Reeves

César Romero (left) as Cisco and Dana Andrews (center) as Sergeant Dunn in *Lucky Cisco Kid* (1940)

Eason got blind drunk together at a Hollywood Hills party. On the way home Eason, who was driving, lost control of the car. "We hit a culvert and the car rolled over three times. Breezy and I were thrown clear. When I reported for work the next day, everyone on the lot kept calling me Lucky . . ." (62). Perhaps the only truly distinguished picture in his career was *I Wake Up Screaming* (20th Century-Fox, 1941), an early film noir starring Betty Grable and Victor Mature, with Laird Cregar literally stealing the show as a psychotic cop clearly based on the doom-haunted noir suspense novelist Cornell Woolrich. Humberstone died in 1983.

The screenplay for his only contribution to the Cisco saga was by Robert Ellis and Helen Logan from an original story by Julian Johnson. Despite its title and fine cast—Mary Beth Hughes and Evelyn Venable as the love interests, young Dana Andrews in Edmund Lowe's old part as Sergeant Dunn, small parts for cinematic Westerners like Joe Sawyer, Francis Ford, and Frank Lackteen—*Lucky Cisco Kid* wasn't a particularly lucky film. Its main interest is in the number of motifs recycled from *In Old Arizona* (the bathtub and vigilante scenes) and *The Cisco Kid* (the widow and small boy trying to keep the economic exploiter played by Willard Robertson from taking over the family ranch) and in the ways this film's storyline is at odds with those of Fox's earliest entries in the series (the Sergeant Dunn of this one, for example, has clearly never laid eyes on Cisco before). This is hardly enough to recommend the film except for those who, like myself, are determined to follow the saga from A to Z with no letters skipped.

As the film opens, a horseless Cisco and Gordito are waiting to board a stagecoach for one leg of the journey to Chicago where—I'm not making this up—they have jobs awaiting them with Buffalo Bill's Wild West show. The coach turns out to be full of drunken miners who have struck it rich and are paying the driver (Dick Rich) a bonus for not taking on any other passengers. The miners harass the two Hispanics (without a single ethnic slur passing anyone's lips) and the coach rolls on. Cisco and Gordito decide to rent horses and exact some revenge. That we never see what they do is typical of the actionlessness of 20th Century-Fox's Cisco pictures.

Meanwhile, Sergeant Dunn (Dana Andrews), that familiar figure from the first two films in the series, is out on patrol with several troopers, vainly hunting Cisco, as usual. The soldiers come upon the miners along the trail, learn that the coach was hijacked by two Mexicans, and give chase. Cisco and Gordito elude the cavalrymen by leaping off the empty coach and walking to the next town.

Finding that Dunn and his men have reached the town first and are searching for them, the two split up. Cisco climbs to a hotel balcony, slips into a suite that is clearly a woman's, makes his way to the bathroom—complete with 1940s-style taps!—and treats himself to a hot tub while Gordito blunders into a temperance meeting and fools the soldiers by belting out anti-liquor songs alongside the ax-faced harridans. The suite where Cisco is scrubbing belongs to Lola (Mary Beth Hughes), a flirtatious dance hall girl and, as chance would have it, a special favorite of Sergeant Dunn, who barges into the room hunting for Cisco. It's clear from his dialogue with her that he and his quarry have never met, and if you know otherwise from *In Old Arizona* and *The Cisco Kid*, well, as the Brits say, hard cheese. Cisco ducks under the suds in the tub, comes out fully dressed after Dunn has left, and introduces himself by his nickname from previous films, "Conejito." "You got more nerve than a brass monkey," Lola tells him. Cisco gives her a ring and a gentle rebuke for being too mercenary. "Love is never cheap. It is more valuable than all the gold. Especially when it come from me!" A little later, when he overhears Judge McQuade (Willard Robertson) forming a vigilante committee to track him down, he realizes that an impostor has been using his name to commit crimes and decides to stay around for a while.

That night in the saloon, Cisco and Dunn almost come to blows over Lola's favors. The stage driver identifies Cisco as the man who hijacked his coach and Cisco and Gordito are about to be strung up when young Tommy Lawrence (Johnny Sheffield) comes racing into town with the news that "Cisco" and his gang are raiding his mother's ranch. Cisco and Gordito join the posse that rides to the rescue and actionlessly capture a gang member (Frank Lackteen) who is killed by his confederates before he can talk. Quickly smitten by Tommy's widowed mother, Emily Lawrence (Evelyn Venable), Cisco learns that she's in debt to Judge McQuade and that he's been pressuring her to sell the ranch to him. When the judge offers $5,000 for Cisco, Emily's

hands quit their jobs to join the hunt. Looking to catch the impostor and pocket the reward, Cisco and Gordito agree to help her run the ranch. When she tells of having had two solid years of hard luck, Cisco's reply is meant to explain the film's title. "I am very lucky fellow. I have horseshoes in both pockets."

The next morning Cisco finds out that the Lawrence ranch controls all the water in the area and concludes that McQuade is behind Emily's troubles. When he rides into town to order supplies for the ranch, storekeeper Ed Stokes (Otto Hoffman) claims that Emily already owes him $386 and refuses to extend more credit. Looking over the account book, Cisco discovers that the store belongs to McQuade and that Emily has been charged twice what anyone else pays for supplies. He distracts Stokes by tossing an apple at a mule on the street so the animal will run amok. Then he sneaks behind the counter, steals the money with which he's just paid Emily's past-due bill and, a few minutes later, buys fresh supplies for her with the same money.

Sergeant Dunn meanwhile is making sweet talk with Lola until McQuade cuts in and demands a military escort for the night stagecoach, which will be carrying a Wells Fargo strongbox. Cisco takes over the pleasant chore of romancing Lola as soon as Dunn is out of the way. While out buggy-riding with Cisco, she mentions that some of the jewelry she's wearing was given to her by local gunman Bill Stevens (Joseph Sawyer). Cisco jealously rips the jewels from her, cuts her finger in the process, and bandages it with one of his special handkerchiefs embroidered with a little rabbit figure.

In the saloon that night, Cisco and Dunn are again on the brink of a fight when Stevens and his men start shooting up the town. Swaggering into the saloon, Stevens sees Lola playing up to Cisco and forces him at gunpoint to down three glasses of tequila. Cisco pretends to have a giggling fit and gets the drop on Stevens. "You make big mistake when you give me tequila. I was raised on it," he boasts, and slaps Stevens's face before he and Gordito ride out of town.

Back at the ranch, Cisco romances Emily and, without revealing who he is, says that his mission in life is to arrange things "so the rich people don't have so much and the poor people have some more." This is as close to the Robin Hood theme as a 20th Century-Fox Cisco film will venture. Hoping that the impostor will try for the strongbox on the night coach, Cisco and Gordito hit the trail. But Dunn is also expecting the coach to be robbed, and both his troops and the vigilantes are waiting in ambush at

Big Rock Pass, the likeliest spot for an attack. Lola overhears this news and rides to the ranch to warn Cisco. We now learn what most of us long suspected, that the phony Cisco is Bill Stevens. (We are left to imagine what an Irish mug like Joe Sawyer would do with a Mexican accent.) The outlaws send the coach over a cliff but while taking the Wells Fargo box they're attacked by Gordito and Cisco, who catches a bullet in the shoulder during the fracas. When the troops and vigilantes ride up and a rabbit-embroidered handkerchief is found at the crime scene, Dunn realizes at last that the Hispanic who's stealing Lola from him is Cisco himself.

At the Lawrence ranch, the wounded Cisco admits his identity to Emily but convinces her he's been framed so that she will hide him in the attic when the troopers and vigilantes ride up. Just as a thorough search of the house begins, Lola, who's been spying from outside, dashes in and claims she just saw Cisco and Gordito riding away. "Cisco, women are the craziest people," marvels Gordito when the coast is clear. "That is why I love them so much," Cisco says.

The posse stays out all night, accompanied by Lola, who is eager to collect McQuade's reward. When everyone returns to town the next morning and Lola goes up to her hotel room, Cisco is waiting to thank her. This is when he learns that the only person who's been in her room since he gave her his special handkerchief was Stevens. The troops and vigilantes spot Cisco on Lola's balcony and a gun battle breaks out but ends in seconds as Cisco single-handedly gets the drop on McQuade, Stevens, and everyone else. He accuses Stevens of being the fake Cisco, and the Wells Fargo gold is found in the gunman's saddlebags.

This being the wild and woolly West, Stevens is immediately taken to the saloon, put on trial before Judge McQuade, and convicted on Cisco's and Lola's testimony. Meanwhile Gordito produces some mysterious paperwork he stole from McQuade's safe that proves the judge is behind the raiders. Pulling a gun on McQuade, Cisco makes him mark all Emily Lawrence's IOUs as paid and then forces him to hand over the $5,000 reward he offered. Slipping the cash to Lola, he and Gordito once again race out of town. As the film ends we discover that Gordito palmed half the money, so our heroes are not broke after all as they ride out of this rather lackluster adventure.

The fourth of Romero's half-dozen Cisco films introduced yet another director into the cycle. Born in Grand Rapids, Michigan, in 1895, Otto Brower cut his directorial teeth on seven consecutive late silents and early talkies in Paramount's series inspired by the novels of Zane Grey. During the pit of the Depression, from 1931 through 1935, he bounced from studio to studio on one-shot or short-term arrangements, directing four Hoot Gibson shoot-'em-ups for Allied, a Jack Hoxie for Majestic, the twelve-chapter cliffhanger serial *The Devil Horse* (1932, starring Harry Carey) for Mascot, two excellent Tom Keenes (*Scarlet River* and *Cross Fire*, both 1933) for RKO, and three Tim McCoys for Columbia, among other jobs. Near the end of the lean years he and B. Reeves Eason codirected two well-remembered Mascot serials: *Mystery Mountain* (1934, starring Ken Maynard) and *The Phantom Empire* (1935, starring Gene Autry). In 1936 Brower signed with 20th Century-Fox, and the next and last decade of his career paralleled Eason's at Warners as he alternated between directing B pictures on his own and helming elaborate action sequences for his studio's big-budget efforts like *Under Two Flags* (1936) and *Suez* (1938). He died in 1946.

The Gay Caballero (1940) is the only Western Brower made at 20th Century-Fox and the only one of that studio's Cisco features to be directed by an action professional. The difference shows. Despite a two month hiatus in mid-production when Romero (depending on which account you believe) either broke a leg or came down with paratyphoid, the picture came out so well that Don Miller in *Hollywood Corral* called it "the best Cisco in the series" and added: "There was nothing new about the plot . . . but the way Brower sent it humming through the course made it seem better" (183). The screenplay was by Albert Duffy and John Larkin, from an original story by Walter Bullock and Albert Duffy. The nice young couple Cisco brings together were played by rising stars Sheila Ryan and Robert Sterling, with sturdy reliables like C. Montague Shaw and Hooper Atchley in character parts. Since no prints or cassettes of this film seem to be available anywhere, I have no choice but to base my description on existing plot summaries.

If it actually begins as those summaries suggest, *The Gay Caballero* boasts the most dramatic opening of any picture in the series. Cisco and Gordito come upon a woman weeping beside a grave whose headstone reads: *Here Lies the Cisco Kid*. The woman is Carmelita (Jacqueline

Dalya), a servant working for rancher Kate Brewster (Janet Beecher). Questioned by an understandably curious Cisco, she explains that the grave holds her fiancé, Manuel, whom ranch foreman Joe Turner (Edmund MacDonald) accused of being the notorious Cisco Kid and shot down. A little while later Cisco and Gordito happen upon and chase away three outlaws trying to rob the passengers in a wagon and discover that the people they've saved are George Wetherby (C. Montague Shaw) and his daughter Susan (Sheila Ryan), who have come from England to purchase part of the Brewster ranch. Seeing a golden opportunity to find out why Turner falsely accused and shot Manuel, Cisco and Gordito accompany the Wetherbys on the final miles of their journey.

At the ranch, calling himself Rodríguez Gonzales Sebastiano Don Juan Chicuelo as usual in the 20th Century-Fox films, Cisco meets Kate and her nephew Billy (Robert Sterling), who has recently been appointed a deputy sheriff. That night at dinner Turner tells the Wetherbys that much of the property they intend to buy had been pillaged by the nefarious Cisco Kid before the foreman shot the outlaw down. George Wetherby announces that his life's savings, which he plans to invest in the Brewster ranch, will soon be arriving by stagecoach. At this point the three outlaws who had tried to rob the Wetherbys show up at the ranch. Over her other guests' protests Kate allows them to stay, declaring that her late husband's policy had been to offer sanctuary to any visitor. Later when everyone else has gone to bed and Kate berates Turner for sending the three badmen to the ranch, we learn that she and her foreman are plotting to steal the Wetherbys' money and then scare them away.

Eventually Cisco discovers the truth, but by then Kate has caught on that "Chicuelo" is the real Cisco Kid and sends for Sheriff McBride (Hooper Atchley) to arrest him. Cisco claims the same right of sanctuary the three robbers had invoked earlier, and somehow the sheriff lets him get away with it. George Wetherby and deputy Billy Brewster are convinced by now that Cisco is a vicious gunman but Susan defends him.

Kate and Turner launch a new plot: she will lure Cisco away from the ranch on a romantic pretext while the foreman dresses in an outfit like Cisco's and robs the coach bringing in the Wetherbys' money. The plan works and the sheriff arrests Cisco and Gordito. Cisco escapes but goes back to rescue his compañero and gets caught. He escapes again, rides back to the Brewster ranch for a showdown, and kills Turner in a shootout. Kate is crushed under

her wagon while trying to get away. As the sheriff's posse approaches, Cisco tells the Wetherbys not to let Billy learn the truth about his aunt and, with Gordito in tow, rides out of the frame.

Herbert Leeds was back in the director's chair for Romero's fifth outing as Cisco. The screenplay for *Romance of the Rio Grande* (1941) was written by Harold Buchman and Samuel G. Engel and nominally based on Katharine Fullerton Gerould's 1923 novel *Conquistador*, the same book that had been the nominal basis for the early Fox talkie *Romance of the Rio Grande* (1929), starring Warner Baxter but not, of course, as Cisco. Back in those days, when a studio bought movie rights to a book it had the power of God over the novelist's creation and could even make two or more worlds out of the author's one. Except for a few well-directed moments, there was little special about this second version, but the cast was fun to watch and, as usual, included both actors who were rarely in Westerns, like Patricia Morison and Ricardo Cortez, and people like Lynne Roberts, Raphael Bennett, Trevor Bardette, and Tom London, who were rarely in anything else.

During a fiesta at the sprawling Rancho Santa Margarita in the Arizona territory, we are rapidly introduced to Don Fernando de Vega (Pedro de Córdoba), his nephew Ricardo (Ricardo Cortez), his ward Rosita (Patricia Morison), and María Córdova (Lynne Roberts), the daughter of his best friend. Rustlers have been raiding the property and Ricardo is pressing his elderly uncle to turn over management of the rancho to a younger and more vigorous man like himself. But Don Fernando has sent to Spain for his estranged grandson Carlos Hernández (Joseph McDonald), his only direct descendant and his choice both to manage the rancho and to marry Rosita.

The coach bringing Carlos through Arizona is attacked by outlaws Carver (Raphael Bennett) and Manuel (Trevor Bardette), who shoot the driver and Carlos. Cisco and Gordito stop the runaway coach and are about to bury the two dead men in it—"It is better to be buried in the ground than in the stomach of a coyote"—when they discover that one of them, Carlos, is still alive, and an identical double of Cisco to boot. Cisco and Gordito take him to the country inn of Mamá López (Inez Palange) to recover. Reading the letters Carlos was carrying from Don Fernando, Cisco sees his chance to come to the rancho as Carlos and steal the de Vega family jewels. On their journey to Santa Margarita, Cisco and Gordito stop to shoot a bullet into the St. Christopher medal Carlos had been wearing.

In *Romance of the Rio Grande* (1941), Patricia Morison and Ricardo Cortez played a conniving couple intent on swindling Cortez's uncle out of his ranch.

Cisco makes his triumphal entry during a fiesta in Carlos's honor, is introduced to the lovely María and Rosita, displays the medal he says stopped the bullet the stagecoach bandits fired at him, and enjoys a Hollywood Latin-style production number with María singing "Ride On Vaquero," also the title of the next and last film in 20th Century-Fox's Cisco series. Ricardo becomes extremely jealous of the attention "Carlos" is paying to Rosita, who we learn is Ricardo's partner in planning both the rustler raids and the attack on the stagecoach, which they now believe to have been a failure.

Gordito, who supposedly rescued "Carlos" from the runaway coach, flirts with the cook Marta (Eva Puig) and learns where the family jewels are kept. Meanwhile, "Carlos" romances María—almost giving himself away when he mentions "our rich wine gardens in Portugal" where Cisco in his 20th Century-Fox incarnations was raised—and learns not only that the notorious Cisco Kid is

being blamed for the rustler raids but also that Ricardo claims to have shot at him during one of those raids and describes Cisco as short and "filthy as a pig." The information convinces him that he'll soon be Ricardo's target just as the real Carlos was.

Don Fernando shows "Carlos" around Santa Margarita and so impresses Cisco with his kindness and love that our good-hearted bandido decides not to steal his jewels after all. That night, in a sequence full of the kind of menacing shadows later identified with film noir, Ricardo shoots at "Carlos" in his room and, while escaping, clubs Don Fernando in the darkness. The blow turns out to be mortal. On his deathbed the patriarch tells his family that his will leaves the rancho to Carlos, but if Carlos should die without a son the property will pass to Ricardo. His final request is that "Carlos" should look after María. "Do you not know that the wish of a dying man is holy?" Cisco admonishes Gordito as he explains why he's now determined to save the rancho for the genuine Carlos. Later both Cisco and María overhear Ricardo and Rosita arguing over "Carlos." Rosita thinks she can get the property on her own by marrying him. "After tomorrow," Ricardo proclaims, "I will be the master of Santa Margarita." Cisco knows that another attempt on his life is imminent.

The next morning Ricardo claims that Cisco raided the ranch's herds again and persuades "Carlos" to join the hunt for the raiders. The group from Santa Margarita rides out to where Carver and his gang are waiting in ambush. Cisco gets the drop on Ricardo and Manuel and makes them ride ahead of the others into the trap, where Manuel is shot down and Ricardo escapes to join Carver and his men. Later, as bad luck would have it, Ricardo and Carver stop at the country inn of Mamá López for food and drink, find the real Carlos there restored to health, and realize that they've been dealing with an impostor.

Leaving Carver to stand guard over Carlos, Ricardo rides to the town of Río Oro, tells the marshal (Tom London) of the impersonation, and claims that the real Carlos is near death. Thanks to having a wanted poster on Cisco, the marshal identifies the impersonator at once. Meanwhile, Mamá López slips away from Carver, comes to Cisco at the ranch and warns him that the game's up. Just then Ricardo rides up with the marshal and a posse. Mamá López creates a diversion while Cisco and Gordito escape. The posse members chase them in a well-directed action sequence, climaxing when the fugitives trick their pursuers and leave them without guns or horses and miles from anywhere.

Cisco and Gordito reach the country inn and get the drop on Carver as he's about to kill Carlos. The identical doubles talk to each other for the first time and Cisco explains his impersonation. Then he returns to Santa Margarita, pretending to be the genuine Carlos and claiming that the marshal has Cisco in jail. This second impersonation works as well as the first.

That night María visits "Carlos" in his room and warns him of what she learned during the Ricardo-Rosita conversation she overheard with Cisco, namely that Ricardo's out to kill him. Cisco romances her without bothering to tell her who he is. Later, while Ricardo is eavesdropping in Rosita's room, "Carlos" drives a wedge between the conspirators by asking Rosita to marry him the next day. As soon as she agrees and he leaves her room, Ricardo comes out of hiding, gets into another fight with Rosita, and they wind up shooting each other to death. Softly singing "La Cucaracha," Cisco returns to his room. The next day he leaves the rancho and

sends the genuine Carlos back in his place and into María's arms. "When you're about to get married," he advises Gordito as they ride off, "don't."

Twentieth Century-Fox's involvement with Cisco came to an end with *Ride On Vaquero* (1941), directed by Leeds from a screenplay by Samuel G. Engel. Mary Beth Hughes and Lynne Roberts made their second appearances in a Cisco feature, each playing a different role than in her first, and the cast was rounded out by Robert Lowery, William Demarest, Paul Sutton, Don Costello, and a long-forgotten African American actor named Ben Carter who literally steals the picture in a small part as night watchman at the chief villain's bank. Let this be Herbert Leeds's epitaph: at a time when the deck was viciously stacked against people of color, he gave one black man his moment in the sun.

The film opens with the by now familiar sequence of Cisco being betrayed by a predatory señorita (Joan Woodbury) and locked up with Gordito by the *soldados americanos*. But Colonel Warren (Paul Harvey) has an ulterior motive for arresting Cisco: in a secret midnight meeting in his office, he explains that he wants Cisco, acting as an undercover agent, to go to the town of Las Tablas and break up a gang that specializes in holding people for ransom. The dialogue stresses what a dirty crime kidnapping is and shows how the snatching of the Lindbergh baby was still echoing in popular culture almost ten years after it happened. When the colonel reveals that the gang's latest victim is Carlos Martínez (Robert Lowery), son of the family that raised Cisco, an outraged Cisco agrees to take on the job. The colonel then gives Cisco his gun back and helps him and Gordito escape the stockade.

Cisco and Gordito arrive at the Martínez rancho and have a reunion with Carlos's wife Marguerita (Lynne Roberts), who knows her dashing guest only as Gonzales Sebastiano Rodríguez Don Juan de Chicuelo and has no idea that her childhood amigo has grown up to become the notorious Cisco Kid. And it's a good thing she hasn't because the ransom note that she received and now shows her guest, demanding $50,000 for Carlos's return, is signed by—you guessed it—the Cisco Kid himself. Somehow managing to keep his face on straight, Cisco argues that the note must have been written by an impostor because its language is idiomatic English and Cisco, as everyone knows, is Latino. (Is this a subtle insiders' joke for the few who might remember that Cisco as O. Henry created him was as purebred an Anglo as they come?) Marguerita

César Romero and Mary Beth Hughes in *Ride On Vaquero* (1941)

tells Cisco that in order to raise the ransom money she's had to mortgage the rancho to Las Tablas banker Dan Clark (Edwin Maxwell).

At this point Cisco and Gordito ride into Las Tablas and drop into the local saloon, where in one coincidence-packed scene the plot of this picture is sorted out for us. No sooner has Cisco downed a couple of tequilas than an aggressive dance-hall girl named Sally (Mary Beth Hughes) comes on to him and demands that he buy her a drink. Over wine at a corner table she tells him that she knows he's the infamous Cisco Kid. How can she be sure? Because he romanced her a few years before in another town and has forgotten the affair completely! (Could this be a sly dig at Hughes's role in *Lucky Cisco Kid* as virtually the same character she plays here but with a different name?) While they're talking, Sheriff Johnny Burge (Arthur Hohl) drops into the saloon, but Sally doesn't give Cisco away. Then some cavalry troopers hunting the escaped Cisco drop in for a whistle-wetter, but again Sally says nothing. The sheriff jokingly orders milk, gets a shock when that's exactly what he's served, and the brainless waiter

mumbles something about the milk having been obtained for some mysterious special guest of Redge (Don Costello), the saloon's owner.

Now comes the nightly ritual when Sally "raffles her bustle," which means she auctions off the chance to dance with her, while Redge's silent bouncer Sleepy (Paul Sutton) is posted on the saloon staircase with a shotgun in case the hands of Sally's partner get to wandering. Cisco makes the highest bid, whirls Sally around, and receives a whispered order from her to book a room for the night in the town hotel. Meanwhile, the banker Dan Clark drops in for a nightcap, and the conversation he has in private with Redge and the sheriff makes it clear to any movie-goer who might have been napping that these three are behind the kidnap gang and that Redge's mystery guest is Carlos Martínez. Clark tells the others about Marguerita's having mortgaged the rancho and instructs them to set up the swap whereby Carlos, who has refused to eat anything during his confinement and will drink nothing but milk, will be exchanged for the cash. Later that night Sally visits Cisco, whom she too believes to be behind the rash of kidnappings, and demands the release of Carlos, who also happens to have been a longtime friend of hers, in return for her not turning him in. The arrival of a messenger from the Martínez rancho with news that the instructions for Carlos's return have just been received convinces Sally that Cisco is innocent.

The instructions order Marguerita to go out into the countryside and put the ransom money in the bucket at the well on Turkey Creek, ride away, and come back later when she'll find a note in the bucket telling where her husband can be found. Cisco decides to drop off the money for her. En route he and Gordito purchase an old covered wagon, which they drive to the well. Cisco keeps his head covered with a serape as he drops off the money. Then he rides back to the covered wagon that Gordito is driving, hides inside, and watches Redge and the sheriff pick up the cash-filled strong-box. The note they leave in the bucket tells Cisco that Carlos can be found in a deserted cabin in San Luis Canyon. Cisco returns to Las Tablas and discovers the identity of the head of the kidnap gang when he sees Redge and the sheriff give the money to Clark to be put in the bank vault.

Meanwhile the muchacho of the peasant family from whom Cisco bought the wagon remembers that the last time he saw the buyer's face it was on a "wanted" poster and goes running to the law. That night, while Cisco is dancing with Sally in the saloon, the sheriff tries to arrest him. Cisco and Gordito shoot their way out of the place and race out of town with a posse at their heels, the only genuine action sequence in the picture, halfway decently directed but nothing special. Fleeing from the posse, Cisco and Gordito ride to San Luis Canyon and find Carlos tied up in a closet in the cabin, but before they can get away the posse lays siege to the cabin, sets it afire, and forces them to surrender. They are locked up in the local jail, and Cisco wrongly believes it was Sally who betrayed them, but when she makes a late-night visit and sweet-talks the idiot deputy into tangoing with her so that Cisco can reach his gun and make him set them free, Cisco knows he's misjudged her. He and Gordito break into the bank and surprise the gleefully larcenous watchman, Bullfinch (Ben Carter), who instantly sees what side his grits are buttered on and becomes Cisco's partner for what's left of the film, stealing the picture in the process. Cisco overpowers Clark, who lives above the bank, and makes him open the vault and disgorge the $50,000 in ransom money. Then with Bullfinch's help he tricks Redge and the sheriff into thinking Clark is about to take off with the loot. When they come to the bank, he gets the drop on them and makes them sign a confession. With the $1,500 Cisco has given him in his jeans, Bullfinch says goodbye and heads for Memphis, while Cisco and Gordito lock the evil trio in the bank vault and hit the trail for new adventures—which took four years to materialize.

Ride on Vaquero marked the end of Romero's tenure as Cisco but his acting career lasted for another half-century and more. He remained under contract to 20th Century-Fox and graced several of the studio's musical romances until mid-1943, when he left to serve in the Coast Guard. From late 1946 through 1950 he was back at 20th Century-Fox playing major roles in Henry King's *Captain from Castile* (1947), Ernst Lubitsch's *That Lady in Ermine* (1948), and other films. Throughout the fifties he free-lanced in movies and, to an ever greater extent as time went by, on TV. Two of his best roles during that decade were in Westerns. He appeared opposite Gary Cooper, Burt Lancaster, and Denise Darcel in *Vera Cruz* (Flora/United Artists, 1954, directed by Robert Aldrich), and in *The Americano* (Stillman/RKO, 1954), which starred Glenn Ford and Frank Lovejoy, he played a Latin Robin Hood character vaguely reminiscent of Cisco. Romero and the future Cisco star Gilbert Roland had major roles together in Henry Hathaway's *The Racers* (20th Century-Fox, 1955), starring Kirk Douglas and Bella Darvi, and cameos together in *Around the World in 80 Days* (Todd/United Artists, 1956). Most of his movie appearances in later decades were throwaways, but he guest-starred in countless TV series episodes and had running parts as the Joker in *Batman* (1966-68) and as Jane Wyman's husband on *Falcon Crest* (1985-87). It was on the latter series that he celebrated his eightieth birthday.

I had wanted to get in touch with Romero and invite him to reminisce about his time as Cisco but kept putting it off. He looked so vigorous and healthy in his promos for the American Movie Classics cable channel that I figured there was no rush. As 1993 drew to an end, I made a resolution to write him care of AMC as soon as the holidays were over, but I was too late. He had gone into St. John's Hospital and Health Center in Santa Monica with severe bronchitis and pneumonia and, in the last hours of December 31, died there of complications from a blood clot. He was 86 years old. This book is the poorer for my procrastination.

DUNCAN RENALDO ENTERS 7

C isco left the nation's movie screens about eight months before Pearl Harbor and wouldn't return until a few months before World War II ended. But for one season during the war years he became the hero of a radio series on WOR-Mutual, debuting October 2, 1942. Jackson Beck played "O. Henry's beloved badman who rides the romantic trail that leads sometimes to adventure, often to danger, but always to beautiful señoritas." Louis Sorin portrayed his faithful sidekick Pancho, the first time Cisco's compadre was known by that name but hardly the last. Jock MacGregor directed the series, which left the air after a year or so.

Late in 1944 20th Century-Fox officially said *adiós* to Cisco by selling off its rights in the property. The buyers were independent producers Philip N. Krasne and James S. Burkett, who a year earlier had bought from the same studio the rights to carry on the long-running Charlie Chan detective series and then made a deal with Monogram Pictures to release new low-budget Chan features. Burkett was a newcomer to the B-movie game while Krasne had entered the field in 1939 and had formed Criterion Pictures to make half a dozen quickie exploits of Renfrew of the Royal Mounted, starring James Newill, for Monogram release. Now, five years later, Krasne arranged for Monogram to release a new series of Cisco Kid adventures. The original plan called for eight Cisco pictures but the studio then

opted to save money by committing only to four, filling the other four slots in its schedule with the first entries in a rock-bottom-budget singing-cowboy series starring Jimmy Wakely. As things turned out, the Cisco series in its first incarnation at Monogram lasted for just three films.

Reading what the most knowledgeable commentators on Westerns have to say about the trio, you have to wonder if they were all watching the same pictures. Jon Tuska claims in *The Filming of the West* that Krasne's financial backing gave the threesome "the best production values of any Western series Monogram made" (441). Don Miller, on the other hand, writes in *Hollywood Corral* that "Krasne's productions were a long distance from the solid look of 20th Century-Fox. Actually [this] was a blessing in disguise, for the low budgets moved the films closer to the traditional Western. But . . . [they] were no world beaters. . . . Main trouble with the productions was that they looked about ten years older than they were, even the photography having a sort of mildewed look" (184). William K. Everson in *The Hollywood Western* says just that Monogram's Cisco series "started off rather weakly with . . . three lackluster entries" (225). I tend to agree with Miller and Everson about the first and third of the trio but the second effort is somewhat better. In any event, it's Phil Krasne who deserves the credit for casting the actor still considered the definitive Cisco by most of those who remember the character at all.

Duncan Renaldo was often cast in Mexican roles, such as John Carroll's servant in Republic's *Zorro Rides Again* (1937).

Duncan Renaldo claimed not to know where or when he was born, thanks to having copies of six birth certificates with conflicting information, but late in life he told interviewers that he'd been born Renault Renaldo Duncan in Valladolid, Spain, on April 23, 1904. He never knew his parents and might have been of Romanian, Russian, or Portuguese heritage, or almost anything else. As an orphan he was shunted among foster homes in Spain, France, and Argentina until in his teens he signed up for a three-year hitch in the Brazilian merchant marine. One story has it that in 1921 or '22

John Carroll as Zorro in *Zorro Rides Again* (1937)

his ship burned while docked in Baltimore and he received a ninety-day seaman's permit to live in the United States. When the time was up he stayed in the country illegally, relocated to New York City, got small parts in a few silent features, and moved to the West Coast a few years later. His Hollywood acting career began at the Tiffany studio in 1928, but his strongest early roles were for MGM in *The Bridge of San Luis Rey* (1929), opposite Lily Damita and Ernest Torrence, and in *Trader Horn* (1931), which was shot largely in Africa and starred Harry Carey and Edwina Booth. Some time after his return to the States he was arrested as an illegal immigrant and spent two years in prison on McNeil Island, off the coast of Washington. After being pardoned by President Roosevelt he picked up the pieces of his movie career and in 1937 was signed by Republic Pictures to a nonexclusive seven-year contract.

Renaldo didn't know his nationality but proved most convincing playing Mexican roles in several Republic cliffhanger serials and B Westerns. His first two parts for the studio were as the bandit Zamorro in *The Painted Stallion* (1937), which marked the debut of master action director William Witney, and as star John Carroll's confidant and servant in *Zorro Rides Again* (1937), the first of the twenty-three consecutive serials Witney codirected with his best friend John English. In a later Witney-English cliffhanger, *The Lone Ranger Rides Again* (1939), the directors cast Renaldo as fiery Juan Vásquez in a move to convert the Ranger-Tonto partnership (Robert Livingston and Chief Thundercloud) into a threesome. Next Renaldo found himself alongside Livingston and Raymond Hatton and cast as Rico, the second lead in Republic's Three Mesquiteers trio Western series during its 1939-40 season, while continuing to do Latin parts in Gene Autry features like *South of the Border* (1939) and *Gaucho Serenade* (1940). His final roles at Republic were in the serials *Secret Service in Darkest Africa* (1943) and *The Tiger Woman* (1944) and the Westerns *Hands Across the Border* (1943, starring Roy Rogers), *The San Antonio Kid* (1944, starring Bill Elliott as Red Ryder), and *Sheriff of Sundown* (1944, starring Allan Lane). When not acting at Republic or elsewhere, Renaldo moonlighted as a State Department emissary to various countries below the Rio Grande, assigned to help boost support for the Allied cause in World War II among the people, many of whom were of German stock.

If we believe Renaldo's reminiscences of almost thirty years later, Phil Krasne had no clear idea what to do with the Cisco character he'd acquired from 20th Century-Fox. He did know that the hero would need a comic sidekick something like Chris-Pin Martin's Gordito and signed Martín Garralaga (1895-1981), a former opera singer who had played minuscule Latino parts in Hollywood movies through the thirties including at least one picture, *Rose of the Rio Grande* (Monogram, 1938), that also featured Renaldo. Garralaga was a wiry little fellow who couldn't possibly be called Gordito. The new name for Cisco's sidekick was lifted from the 1942-43 radio series and would last, with one interruption, for as long as Cisco films continued to be made. That name, of course, was Pancho.

With his Republic contract behind him by the end of 1944 and the war in Europe nearly over, Duncan Renaldo was free to accept Krasne's offer of the role of Cisco if he wished. He was willing but only—or so he claimed in conversation with Jon Tuska decades later—on one condition. "I told Phil how much trouble Romero had caused in Latin America playing the Kid as a vicious bandit" (441). Anyone who's seen Romero's Cisco pictures knows this accusation is nonsense: the character he portrayed is certainly an outlaw and something of a boastful poseur in the style of Mr. Toad from *The Wind in the Willows*, but he's never vicious and always ready to abort his own or someone else's criminal schemes for the love of a señorita. In any event, Renaldo suggested to Krasne an approach markedly different from Romero's. "Why not base the character on the greatest book in all Spanish literature, *Don Quixote de la Mancha*? Cisco is a modern knight; Pancho is his Sancho Panza, a delicate comedy character—not a buffoon—who always gets his partner in trouble when they try to help people" (441).

Near the end of his life Renaldo still remembered his first sidekick fondly. "Martín was perfect as Pancho. . . . His comedy was very, very human. But he just couldn't stand horses. He was allergic to them" (441). This, however, is a minority viewpoint, and when most viewers see Garralaga as Pancho what comes to their minds is not Sancho Panza but a weasel. "Every time you open your mouth," Renaldo tells him early in their first picture together, "you fall in it." In the first four Cisco films that followed the Renaldo trio, Garralaga was more appropriately cast in various Latino character parts.

And Renaldo in his first outings as Cisco hardly comes across as a Don Quixote. We never see him being a bandit as we usually did in at least the opening scenes of most of the 20th Century-Fox Ciscos, so it's a bit of a mystery why he's always the prime suspect whenever a crime is committed. He is of Mexican descent, not Portuguese like Romero's

Cisco. In the first of the Renaldo trio, which was written by Betty Burbridge, his name is Juan Francisco Hernández and Cisco is simply a shortened version of his middle name; in the second, also written by Burbridge, his name changes to Juan Carlos Francisco Antonio; and in the third and last he's just Cisco or sometimes, as in his first two exploits, "the Cisco." With his tiny mustache and neat bolero jacket he projects the image of a rogue and roué but not at all that of a knight.

The millions of us who grew up watching Renaldo as Cisco on the small screen know that he rode a pinto stallion called Diablo, but his horse in the first three Cisco features was a palomino. "He was a fearful horse," Renaldo told Jon Tuska. "He tried to break a double's legs by smashing against trees. I learned to ride very carefully because when I was at Republic working on those Mesquiteers pictures with Bob Livingston, a camera truck skidded into me and pushed both myself and the horse I was on through a barbed-wire fence. Well, they told me about this palomino, but we became good friends and I never had any trouble with him. Later, when we did the television episodes, I bought a paint. I called him Diablo, too, after the palomino" (443).

Besides signing Renaldo as Cisco and creating the original screen version of Pancho, Krasne assembled many of the behind-the-scenes people who kept working regularly in the series well into its long run on TV, notably assistant director Eddie Davis, film editor Martin G. Cohn, composer Albert Glasser, and scriptwriter Betty Burbridge. All four were on the team that made the first of Monogram's Cisco features, *The Cisco Kid Returns* (1945). The film's director, John P. McCarthy (1885-1962), a veteran of low-budget productions since 1919, had spent the first half of the thirties helming super-cheap Westerns with stars like Bob Steele, Tom Tyler, or Rex Bell, often for Monogram release. He was unaccountably out of the business between 1937 and 1943 but came back to direct three more Monogram shoot-'em-ups: *Raiders of the Border* (1944) with Johnny Mack Brown, *Marked Trails* (1945) with Bob Steele and Hoot Gibson, and *The Cisco Kid Returns*, which was the best of an indifferent trio and the last film of his career.

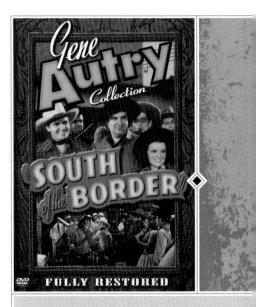

Renaldo also portrayed Latinos in Gene Autry films, such as *South of the Border* (1939).

The picture opens with what was supposed to be the marriage of Cisco's former sweetheart, Rosita Gonzales (Cecilia Callejo), to businessman John Harris (Roger Pryor), but the ceremony is broken up when Cisco charges in and claims that he's been Rosita's husband for years. Along with Cisco are Pancho and a four-year-old girl who calls the bride Mamacita. At this point Rosita faints—partly no doubt because the child's hair is golden blonde—and Cisco carries her away. The little girl, Nancy Page (Sharon Smith), was borrowed by Pancho from his friend Antonio, who was helping her father raise her. Safely away from the Harris ranch, Cisco explains to Rosita that he broke up the wedding

Hoot Gibson and Bob Steele become U.S. marshals to save a town from a cutthroat gang in *Marked Trails* (1944). Director John P. McCarthy went on to direct *The Cisco Kid Returns* (1945).

because the man was no good for her and vows he'll be faithful to her forevermore. "On my heart I swear it!" he proclaims, the first of many times we'll hear Renaldo making this pledge to a señorita.

Cisco rides with Pancho and Rosita to return Nancy to her father but finds both Stephen Page and his servant Antonio lying shot and near death in the living room of Page's ranch house. He sends the others away, explaining the situation to them in Spanish so Nancy won't understand, then goes back inside to investigate. He promises Antonio that he'll take care of Page's child and, in one of the few Catholic touches in the entire Cisco series, helps the dying servant make the sign of the cross. The sheriff (Bud Osborne) and a posse ride up, and from a hiding place in the house Cisco overhears enough to know that Harris is trying to pin the murders on him. He dashes out of the house, pausing for no earthly reason to put on a Zorroesque black cloak, and races away with the posse in hot pursuit. Meanwhile, we learn from a conversation between Harris and his gunman Jennings (Cy Kendall) that Rosita's jilted fiancé is behind the murders.

Cisco sneaks into his rival's house, gets the drop on Harris, and makes him admit to having told the sheriff that Cisco was in the area, but Harris swears he didn't give the lawman any physical description of his enemy. (If you're wondering why not, nothing in the film relieves your curiosity.) Cisco takes Harris out to meet the posse on the trail and forces him to describe the bandit to the sheriff as a short, fat, bearded hombre missing a finger. After joining the posse and spending some time hunting for himself, Cisco rejoins Pancho, Rosita, and Nancy at the home of Tía Jiménez (Eva Puig), bringing a necklace for the grown woman and a blue dress for the child. Then he and Pancho head for the local mission, where the padre (Fritz Leiber) calls him Francisco and, in another of the film's Catholic touches (director McCarthy's contribution?), asks Pancho how long it's been since his last confession. While they're talking, two women stop at the mission, claim to be Stephen Page's widow (Vicky Lane) and her French maid Jeanette (Jan Wiley), and ask directions to the Page ranch. Cisco agrees to take the women to their destination but for reasons that are never explained he doesn't bother to tell them either that Nancy isn't at the ranch or that he is watching out for her. Instead he focuses on romancing the maid Jeanette. When Julia Page discovers that her daughter is missing she offers a large reward for the child's return, but Cisco still says nothing. At this point we learn that the two women are impostors sent by Page's

Pancho (played by Martín Garralaga) seeks cover behind Cisco (Duncan Renaldo) in this scene from *The Cisco Kid Returns* (1945).

corrupt business manager Paul Conway (Anthony Warde), who is behind the murders, to get custody of Nancy so he can control the Page fortune.

That night Cisco and Pancho slip away from the home of Tía Jiménez and Rosita, suspecting that Cisco's going to make love to another woman, shadows him. Cisco sneaks into Stephen Page's study, finds and pockets a four-year-old letter in the handwriting of the dead man's estranged wife, then makes his presence known and again makes a play for Jeanette. Rosita catches him and throws dishes at the lovebirds until Cisco and Pancho manage to drag her away.

A furious Rosita goes back to Harris and reveals to him that Nancy is with Cisco. Conway arrives on the scene and he and Harris decide they can best trap Cisco and recover Nancy by having the sheriff keep an eye on the Page ranch. Sure enough Cisco and Pancho pay a return visit. Pancho strums a guitar while Cisco once more flings sweet nothings at Jeanette. The sheriff and his posse charge into the house and chase Cisco and Pancho through the rooms and out onto

the trail. Cisco stops in mid-flight to pick Nancy up from Tía Jiménez and carry her off in his black cloak.

To force a showdown, Cisco sends Pancho to the sheriff with an offer to lead the lawman to Cisco and Nancy, provided that Conway and the two women at the Page ranch are made to come along. Then Cisco goes to the mission and enlists the padre's help. The sheriff and his party arrive and the padre admits that Nancy is staying there but insists that "Mrs. Page" must sign a receipt of sorts before he turns the child over. Cisco and Nancy reveal themselves and Cisco exposes the scheme by showing the difference between the genuine Mrs. Page's signature on the stolen letter and the impostor's signature on the padre's receipt. With all the conspirators except Harris and Jennings actionlessly rounded up, Cisco and the sheriff go on to the Harris ranch where, again without any action to speak of, they round up the

MONOGRAM PICTURES
presents
DUNCAN RENALDO   "THE CISCO KID "in Old New Mexico"

45/137

In Old New Mexico (1945) is touted as one of Duncan Renaldo's best Cisco Kid features. Martín Garralaga holds the gun,
Bud Osborne is in the driver's seat, and the two nearest Renaldo are Gwen Kenyon and Frank Jaquet.

last two criminals. With Nancy back in the meaty arms of Tía Jiménez, Cisco carries Rosita away for another interlude of romance as the picture ends.

Soon after completing that picture, the same team started work on the second and by all odds best of the Renaldo trio, *In Old New Mexico* (1945), which far outdid its companion films in both action content and story complexity, so much so that at one point in the Betty Burbridge script Cisco is (not very plausibly) compared by another character to the king of mid-1940s screen sleuths, Sherlock Holmes. Phil Rosen was perhaps a strange choice to direct this adventure but, as events proved, not a bad one. Born in Marienburg, Russia, on May 8, 1888, Rosen had emigrated to the United States as a child and had begun his film career in 1912, working as a cameraman at Edison, Fox, Universal, and other studios and serving as first president of the American Society of Cinematographers, the "A.S.C." frequently found after the cameraman's name in movie credits. He'd

been making silent features since 1920, occasionally working with major stars (for example in Paramount's 1922 *The Young Rajah* with Rudolph Valentino) but usually on less prestigious projects. At the end of the twenties he moved from silents into talkies without missing a beat and picked up his first and only extensive experience making B Westerns in 1931-32 when he directed eight in a row with Ken Maynard at Tiffany and two with Hoot Gibson at Allied, followed by the somewhat higher budgeted *The Vanishing Frontier* (Paramount, 1932) with Johnny Mack Brown. A dozen years later, as luck would have it, Rosen and all three of these cowboy stars were working at Monogram, which was the director's principal employer from 1940 on. Most of Rosen's pictures after 1932 were adventure or detective programmers, and he directed Monogram's first four Charlie Chan quickies after Krasne and Burkett bought the property from 20th Century-Fox. He all but retired at the beginning of 1946 and died five years later.

In Old New Mexico opens most strikingly with an excellent action sequence that runs under the principal credits. Cisco and Pancho chase and stop a stagecoach, rob the male passengers, and take away with them the only woman on the coach, Ellen Roth (Gwen Kenyon). Cisco tells her what at one time or another he tells every female in the film—"You are the most beautiful señorita in all this world. On my heart I swear it!"—but anyone who thinks he's kidnapped her for romantic reasons has another think coming. In the nearby town of Gila, Sheriff Clem Petty (Lee "Lasses" White) is waiting to arrest her for murder. It seems that Ellen was nurse to Mrs. Prescott, a wealthy old lady in Denver whose will left her a great deal of money, and that she fled after the old lady was killed by an overdose of sleeping pills. When the stagecoach reaches town and the driver reports Cisco's kidnapping of the female fugitive, the sheriff forms a posse and rides out in pursuit. Cisco and Pancho encounter the posse but escape by hiding in the usual rocks. They leave Ellen at a mission—where Padre Ángelo (Pedro de Córdoba) calls Cisco by his full name, Francisco, and describes his father as the most prominent man in the province of Jalisco—and ride into Gila to return the stagecoach loot at the empty sheriff's office, although Cisco catches Pancho trying to hold back a watch he likes. It's clear by now that Cisco knows a lot about the murder of Mrs. Prescott but how he learned it and why he cares is never revealed to us.

One of the things he mysteriously knows is that the dead woman had often sent letters to Post Office Box 17 in Gila. While watching to see who is renting that box, he bumps into Belle (Donna Dax), a dance hall girl, and instantly starts to flirt with her. Then he observes saloonkeeper Will Hastings (Norman Willis) opening the box and removing a letter, so while Pancho trips Hastings, Cisco picks his pocket. The seemingly innocuous document is signed by someone calling himself Doc and refers to a woman named Dolores. Back at the mission, Ruth tells Cisco her side of the story, claiming that Mrs. Prescott was given the overdose of sleeping pills by a man who called at her house and claimed to be her new doctor. Ruth insists that she fled from Denver to find this man, investigate Mrs. Prescott's letters to Box 17, and clear herself.

Cisco and Pancho visit Hastings's saloon in Gila, where a Broadway-style Latin musical revue is in progress, complete with a line of chorus girls in scanty costumes kicking their legs. Cisco learns from Belle that one of the saloon entertainers is named Dolores and that Hastings considers her his property. Dolores (Aurora Roche) comes out and performs a number in the style of Carmen Miranda. No sooner is she done than Cisco takes her aside and starts romancing her and learns that Hastings is the late Mrs. Prescott's nephew, that he claims to have inherited money from her, and that one of his cronies is a man who calls himself Doc Wilson but isn't really a doctor. Hastings, furious at Cisco's playing up to Dolores, accuses him of having taken Ellen Roth from the stagecoach. The fight between them, perhaps the best-directed brawl in any Cisco feature, ends with the sheriff and posse returning to town and Cisco having to make a daredevil escape from the saloon. The chase sequence as the posse goes after Cisco and Pancho is another gem, full of running inserts and tracking shots. After eluding the pursuers, Cisco returns to Gila, bullwhips a gun from Hastings's hand, and, knowing that Ellen must be convicted of murder in order for the saloonkeeper's plot to work, offers to turn her over to the sheriff for ten thousand dollars. When Hastings agrees, Cisco drops in on Sheriff Petty and makes a deal to hand Ellen over in return for the dropping of all charges against himself. Ellen is arrested at the mission and carted off to jail.

Back in Gila, Cisco buys Dolores a fancy gown and the dressmaker's dummy that goes with it. Then he reminds Hastings that if Doc Wilson is ever found and made to talk, Ellen will be cleared. Next he calls on the editor of Gila's newspaper (Edward Earle) and forces him at gunpoint to print a story in the next edition to the effect that Doc Wilson has been arrested in Denver for Mrs. Prescott's murder. Once the paper hits the street, Hastings panics and starts packing his bags. Cisco makes a new proposition: while Ellen is being taken to Denver to identify Doc, why not kill her? Hastings agrees, and when a deputy and Ellen leave town in a buckboard, Cisco and Hastings's gunman Al Brady (John Laurenz) get ahead of them. Cisco apparently downs Ellen with a well-aimed rifle shot, the buckboard goes over a cliff, and Brady reports to Hastings that the job is done.

The next stage brings into Gila none other than Doc Wilson (Richard Gordon), who has read the phony story of his arrest. Spying on Hastings's saloon, Pancho sees a man fitting Ellen's description of the fake doctor go in and tells Cisco. The two of them watch Doc go to the newspaper office. Cisco strolls past the window, the editor points him out to Doc as the man who made him run the arrest story, and Doc follows Cisco to a stable where Pancho conks him from behind. While they're taking their prisoner to the mission, Dolores tells Hastings that someone stole her new gown and the dressmaker's

William S. Hart's silent Westerns, such as *Square Deal Sanderson* (1919, directed by Lambert Hillyer), brought complex good-bad characters to the screen.

dummy it came with, and Hastings suspects that he's been scammed, that it was not Ellen but the dummy that Cisco shot and sent over the cliff. He and Brady ride out to investigate and are captured by Cisco without a struggle and taken to the mission where, with the sheriff listening from a peephole, Doc is confronted with Ellen and makes a full confession.

The last of Renaldo's first three Cisco films and the only one that looks and sounds like a typical Monogram B Western of its period was *South of the Rio Grande* (1945). Krasne was still the producer but this time hired a new slate of production people. William Sickner, veteran of countless B pictures at Universal, served as cinematographer; the script by relative newcomers Victor Hammond and Ralph Bettinson was based on a story by Zorro creator Johnston McCulley; and the uncredited music score consisted of

Monogram's standard Frank Sanucci agitato themes, with the studio's other regular composer, Edward J. Kay, billed as music director. The cast included the usual assortment of Latin players plus some B Western stalwarts like George J. Lewis, Francis McDonald, and Charles Stevens, who was a grandson of Geronimo and portrayed Indians, Mexicans, and other ethnic characters in an endless array of Westerns including, as we've seen, Fox's 1931 *The Cisco Kid*.

To direct the picture Krasne brought in a prolific professional who actually had devoted much of his life to making Westerns. Lambert Hillyer was born sometime between 1888 and 1895 (depending on which reference book you consult) in northern Indiana, the son of actress Lydia Knott. After short stints as a newspaperman and actor in summer stock and vaudeville, he moved into the Hollywood community and began writing and directing silent Westerns starring William S. Hart such as *Square Deal Sanderson* (1919), *Wagon Tracks* (1919), *The Toll Gate* (1920), *O'Malley of the Mounted* (1920), and *Three Word Brand* (1921). He spent most of the twenties alternating between Tom Mix or Buck Jones Westerns for the Fox studio and non-Westerns for other companies. As we've seen, his first talkie, *Beau Bandit* (RKO, 1930), was the earliest "imitation Cisco" picture released by a Fox rival after the success of *In Old Arizona*. From 1931 through 1934 Hillyer wrote and directed most of Columbia's superb series of Buck Jones Westerns including *One Man Law*, *South of the Rio Grande* (in which Buck played a Mexican), and *The Sundown Rider*, all made in 1932. Most of his Columbia features after Jones left the studio were contemporary action pictures but his best known work of the decade was the pair of horror films he directed at Universal: *The Invisible Ray* (1935) with Boris Karloff and Bela Lugosi and *Dracula's Daughter* (1936) with Gloria Holden and Otto Kruger. He began turning out the occasional B feature for Monogram in 1938. From 1940 through late 1942 he was back at Columbia doing Charles Starrett and Bill Elliott shoot-'em-ups, perhaps the finest of them being *Prairie Gunsmoke* (1942) in which Elliott costarred with Tex Ritter.

In 1943 Hillyer moved virtually full-time to Monogram, where he worked almost exclusively on Johnny Mack Brown B Westerns until Krasne tapped him to direct *South of the Rio Grande*. Afterwards he returned to the Johnny Mack series and later in the forties to even more routine horse operas starring Jimmy Wakely or Whip Wilson. Anyone who sits through enough of Hillyer's Monogram output will find a huge number of routine yawners and every so often an unsung little gem like the Johnny Mack Brown entries *The Gentleman from Texas* (1946) and *Land of the Lawless* (1947), both of which are connected with the Cisco saga in a way we'll explore in chapter 9. At the end of the decade, like many another B movie director, Hillyer migrated into series TV. As we'll see in chapter 10, he wound up rejoining Renaldo and the Cisco series, contributing more of the character's adventures than anyone else who ever helmed a Cisco feature.

Unfortunately, his only full-length Cisco outing was as dreary as the vast majority of his other Monogram oaters. *South of the Rio Grande* opens with Cisco, dubbed of course by someone with a better voice than Duncan Renaldo, serenading a lovely señorita. The song is interrupted by Pancho with a letter from old Gonzales, who had been kind to Cisco as a child, asking for help in saving him and other rancheros from Miguel Sánchez (George J. Lewis), the corrupt *apoderado* (district governor). Cisco and Pancho arrive in the troubled area just in time to wipe out the squad of *caporales* who are about to execute old Gonzales's son Manuel (Tito Renaldo). The young man tells them that his parents have been murdered and that he's sent his sister Dolores (Armida) to the nearby town for safety, and asks Cisco to lead the rebel group fighting against Sánchez. The next day the rebels come upon and wipe out another squad of *caporales* on a murder mission, but they are too late to help the victim. Searching the dead man's papers, Cisco learns that he was Domínguez, a new official sent by the government to replace Sánchez as *apoderado*, and decides to take Domínguez's place, with Pancho posing as his servant. Within a few minutes of their triumphal entry into town, Cisco discovers that Dolores Gonzales is singing and dancing at the local *posada*, that Sánchez is making a play for her, and that the *apoderado*'s previous girlfriend, the dancer Pepita (Lillian Molieri), is jealous as only a Mexican spitfire can be. Still passing himself off as the new *apoderado*, Cisco works on Pepita and gets her to talk freely about Sánchez's crimes. Meanwhile, Sánchez offers his apparent successor a partnership in his graft, tries to kill him in the middle of the night, gets caught, is made to sign a confession, and gets blown away by Cisco when he makes the mistake of reaching for another gun. Pancho and the rebel force rout Sánchez's men in about thirty seconds of routine action. If one leaves out all the romance and Mexican songs and wine, that's all there is to this lame excuse for a south-of-the-border Western.

Director Lambert Hillyer was well known for his Buck Jones Westerns, such as *One Man Law* (1932). He later directed the Cisco Kid feature *South of the Rio Grande* (1945).

Thornton Wilder's novel *The Bridge of San Luis Rey* inspired three movies of the same name. The poster here is for the second, released in 1944 and starring Lynn Bari, who also played opposite Warner Baxter in *The Return of the Cisco Kid.*

HI-YO
SILVER

CHAPTER **1**
THE **LONE
RANGER
RETURNS**

The **LONE RANGER**
Rides Again

with
ROBERT LIVINGSTON
CHIEF THUNDER-CLOUD
SILVER CHIEF • DUNCAN RENALDO
Directed by WILLIAM WITNEY • JOHN ENGLISH
Associate Producer - ROBERT BECHE

BASED ON THE RADIO SERIAL
"THE LONE RANGER" *by* FRAN STRIKER

Republic SERIAL
IN **15** *Whirlwind* CHAPTERS

REPUBLIC
SERIAL

Duncan Renaldo was cast as Juan Vásquez in *The Lone Ranger Rides Again* (1939), giving the serial a trio of roving crime fighters.

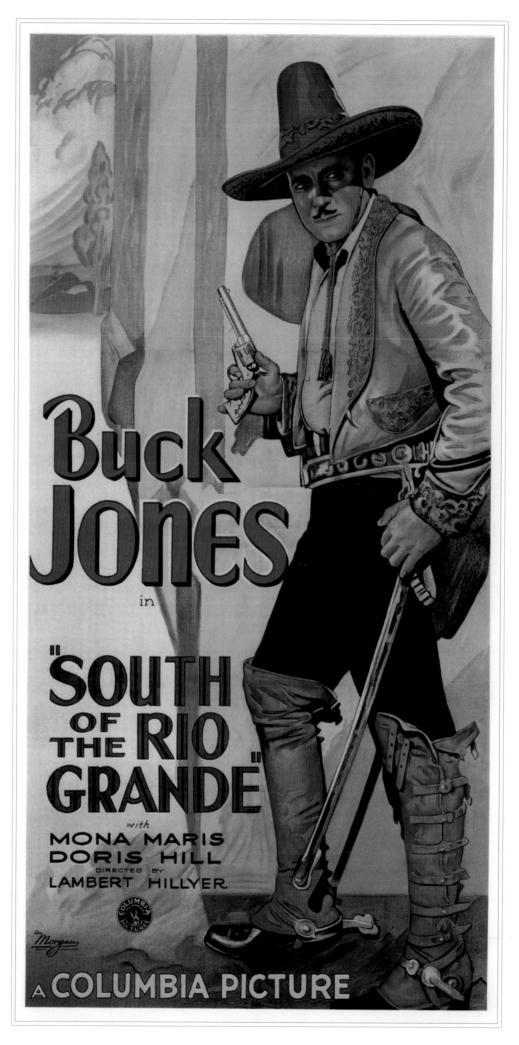

In *South of the Rio Grande* (1932), Buck Jones reprised his role as a Latino,
this time playing a Mexican *rural* who pursues Consuela, played by Mona Maris.

Lobby card from *Romance of the Rio Grande* (1941), featuring César Romero (left), Ricardo Cortez (center), and Raphael Bennett (right)

Title card for *In Old New Mexico* (1945). The film was noted for its action and story complexity.

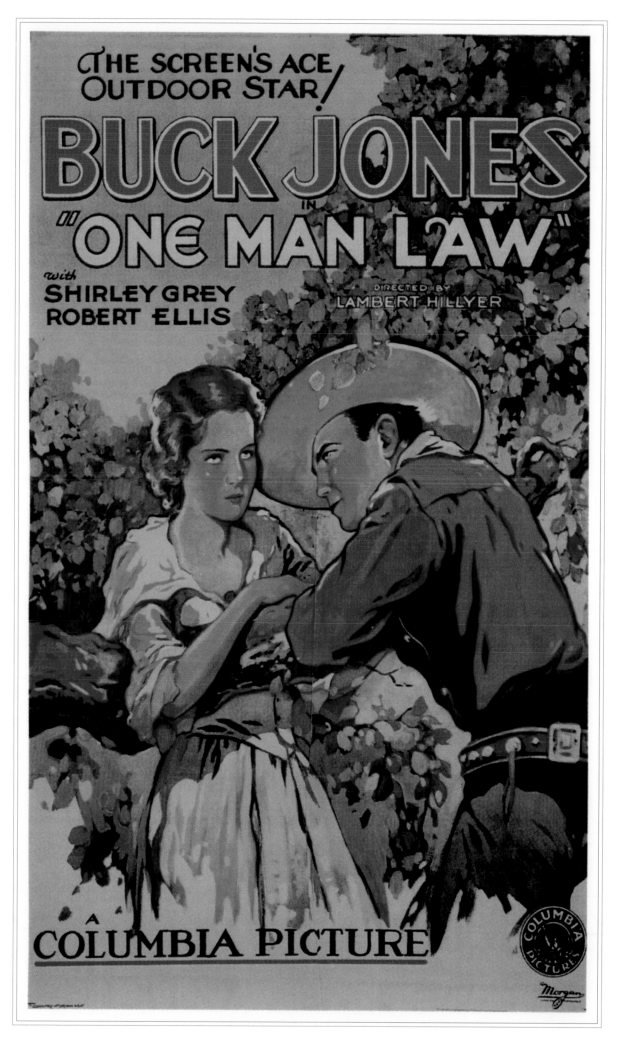

Buck Jones played a sheriff trying to stop a land swindler in *One Man Law* (1932).

The Toll Gate (1920) starred William S. Hart and was directed by Lambert Hillyer, who would later direct the Cisco Kid feature *South of the Rio Grande* (1945) and many episodes of the Cisco TV series.

In *The Gay Desperado* (1936), Nino Martini and Ida Lupino kiss under the admiring gaze of Leo Carrillo's bandido character Pablo Braganza.

Duncan Renaldo's Cisco sweet-talks barmaid Rosita (played by Armida) in a scene from *The Gay Amigo* (1949).

Romance often took a dangerous turn in Cisco Kid features, such as in this scene
from *South of the Rio Grande* (1945) with Lillian Molieri and George J. Lewis.

In this photo still from *The Cisco Kid Returns* (1945), Duncan Renaldo pledges fidelity to Jan Wiley: "On my heart I swear it!"

Gilbert Roland played a smoldering Cisco Kid in the mid-1940s, examples of which can be seen in these stills from *Riding the California Trail* (1947, top) and *South of Monterey* (1946, bottom, with Marjorie Riordan [left] and Inez Cooper).

A revamped version of the Cisco radio series returned to the airwaves in 1946 on the Mutual-Don Lee network, with Jack Mather playing Cisco and Harry Lang as a bullwhip-wielding Pancho. (Had the creators of this series seen some of the PRC Western features with Eddie Dean and Lash LaRue?) According to John Dunning's *On the Air: The Encyclopedia of Old-Time Radio* (Oxford University Press, 1998), each episode would open with Pancho exclaiming, "Ceesco! The shereef, he ees getting closer!" To which Cisco would reply: "This way, Pancho, vámonos!" Whenever Cisco got up close and personal with a young woman, organ music would accompany the following deathless lines. Woman: "Ohhh, Cisco!" Cisco: "Oooooooh, señorita!" And every adventure would close with the same four bits of dialogue, the first two destined to live forever in the minds of millions of kids who hunched in front of their 12½-inch TV sets a few years later.

"Oh, Pancho!"

"Oh, Ceesco!"

"Up, Diablo!"

"Up, Loco!"

But first came two more cycles of Cisco theatrical features, the earlier produced by a canny veteran of low-budget Westerns whose name will be familiar to many fans of the genre.

Scott R. Dunlap was born in 1891 and, like many young men in Hollywood's pioneer days,

started his movie career early. In 1915 he was a location scout for Universal. Four years later, possibly after service in World War I, he moved to Fox and became a director. In 1920 he made his first Western starring the man with whom he forged a permanent bond, Buck Jones. Dunlap directed eight silent features with Buck between 1920 and 1923, then left Fox to freelance—a period during which he directed six shoot-'em-ups starring Harry Carey—then came back to Fox for three final Westerns with Buck in 1926-27. When silent films were made obsolete by talkies, Dunlap gave up directing to work as Buck's manager and agent. In 1937, when Monogram Pictures split from the Republic organization and resumed independent existence, Dunlap was hired as executive in charge of production on the studio's short-lived Tom Keene series (1937-38), the Jack Randall Westerns (1938-39), and the Mr. Wong whodunits with Boris Karloff (1938-39), as well as a few non-series B movies.

In 1941 Dunlap returned to work as an active producer, bringing together Buck Jones, Tim McCoy, and Raymond Hatton for the legendary Rough Riders series, which ended after only eight films when McCoy, a longtime army reserve officer, volunteered for active duty in the Second World War. Late in 1942 Dunlap and Buck went east on a war bond sales tour that culminated in the disastrous fire at Boston's Cocoanut Grove nightclub. Dunlap managed to get out of the club without serious injury, but Buck was critically burned and died in Massachusetts General Hospital on November 30, two days after the fire that took the lives of almost five hundred people. Returning to Monogram, Dunlap produced about half a dozen of the early entries in the new Western series with Johnny Mack Brown and Raymond Hatton that was devised as a substitute for the Rough Riders pictures. Then, in late 1945 or early 1946, he took over the production reins on Monogram's Ciscos and started hunting for someone to replace Duncan Renaldo in the part.

The actor he settled on was known for more than seventy years as Gilbert Roland, but the name his parents gave him was Luis Antonio Dámaso Alonso. Exactly when and where he came into the world is a bit of a puzzle. His birth date is usually given as December 11, 1905, but a number of sources leave off the year, which suggests that he may have been born a few years earlier. Every reference I've consulted gives his birthplace as Ciudad Juárez in the Mexican state of Chihuahua, but in a 1931 interview his father, former bullfighter Francisco Alonso, claimed that his already famous second son had been born in Bilbao, Spain. All the son had to say was, "I am a Spaniard but Mexico is my second fatherland." The family fled from Ciudad Juárez across the border to El Paso to escape the violence of Pancho Villa's revolution, and when he was fourteen Luis drifted out to Hollywood and quickly got hired for unbilled bit parts in all sorts of movies. By 1923 his parents and five brothers and sisters were also living in the Los Angeles area. More than sixty years later, in an article for *Sports Illustrated*, Roland described his father as "a brave matador, his mouth always dry on the day of the bulls. Sixteen horn wounds in his body. . . ." Francisco Alonso eventually returned to his native soil, and in 1936, during the Spanish Civil War, he was shot to death by a machine-gunner on a church roof.

Choosing a new name in honor of silent stars John Gilbert and Ruth Roland, Luis earned his first screen credit in *The Plastic Age* (Schulberg, 1925), which was directed by Wesley Ruggles and starred Donald Keith and Clara Bow, the first of many famous actresses with whom young Roland enjoyed short and passionate affairs. His big break came

Gilbert Roland, Marsha Hunt, and Charles Bickford in *Thunder Trail* (1937)

two years later when director Fred Niblo cast him as Armand opposite Norma Talmadge in *Camille* (Schenck/First National, 1927). Roland costarred with Talmadge in several other late silents and one early talkie, *New York Nights* (Schenck/United Artists, 1929), where under the direction of Lewis Milestone he played a gangster. A year later he appeared for the first time as a macho star in the English and Spanish language versions of *Men of the North* (MGM, 1930), both of which were directed by, of all unlikely people, Hal Roach.

Between 1932 and 1935 Roland was under contract at Fox. If the studio had been making Cisco features during that period, he almost surely would have been in them; as it was, he alternated between starring roles in romances shot in Spanish and thrillers filmed in English. After his time at Fox he freelanced. His most prestigious parts were opposite Paul Muni and Bette Davis in *Juárez* (Warner Bros., 1939, directed by William Dieterle) and with Errol Flynn in *The Sea Hawk* (Warner Bros., 1940, directed by Michael Curtiz). But his performances were just as intense and his roles far meatier in two Westerns, *Thunder Trail* (Paramount, 1937) and *Rangers of Fortune* (Paramount, 1940), which were covered in chapter 5.

In 1941 Roland married actress Constance Bennett, with whom he had costarred in *Our Betters* (RKO, 1933, directed by George Cukor) and *After Tonight* (RKO, 1934, directed by George Archainbaud). The following year he became a U.S. citizen and, like many other Hollywood personalities, joined the military. The day after his discharge from the Army Air Corps he started work in *The Desert Hawk* (Columbia, 1944, directed by B. Reeves Eason), a fifteen-chapter serial about a sort of Arab Zorro figure. Jimmy Ellison was to have played the title role but had to be hospitalized after a fall from a horse on the first day of shooting. Roland went on from that cliff-hanger to a substantial part opposite Charles Laughton and Randolph Scott in *Captain Kidd* (1945) and from there, after he and Constance Bennett were divorced, to Monogram and the Cisco series.

Duncan Renaldo is reported to have coached Roland in how the part should be played, and one can be pretty certain that Scott Dunlap made suggestions too, but it was Roland himself who called most of the shots. The Cisco he portrays makes Renaldo's version seem light as a feather by comparison. He is a firebrand of antiestablishment ardor, riding at the head of a singing guerrilla band on a magnificent palomino with a flowing white tail that almost touches the ground. (The horse was Don

J. Carrol Naish and Gilbert Roland in *Thunder Trail*

Juan, a national parade champion in 1944 and 1945.) He and his followers roam the countryside, robbing wealthy oppressors and giving to the persecuted poor. But he's also a smoldering sexual volcano who will swagger into a cantina with a cigarette behind his ear, perhaps even a rose in his teeth, and order tequila, drinking it in the Mexican ritual manner with salt and a slice of lime or lemon, while his eyes burn with desire for every beautiful woman in the room. From an Anglo male perspective it may look absurdly overdone, but remember, guys: that seething sexuality isn't being aimed at us. If you doubt it's real, watch a Roland Cisco with a woman you trust and ask her.

Other aspects of characterization and costume were also Roland contributions. The two-inch leather wristband he wore as Cisco was and continued for years to be part of his own wardrobe. Although he never wrote a script for the series, he was credited at times with "additional dialogue" in which, to quote Don Miller in *Hollywood Corral*, he "would declaim lyrically about the beauty of women, or nature, or both, or some such flowery verbiage" (184). It was Roland who suggested that between bouts of thievery and amor Cisco should be shown reading Shakespeare by a river bank. "I wanted to be sure the Mexican was not portrayed as an unwashed, uneducated savage clown," he told interviewer Al Martínez. "I refuse roles that picture Mexicans as ridiculous, quaint, or foolish." (The interview is included in Martínez's book *Rising Voices*, New American Library, 1974.)

It seems that those who enjoy and write about Western series either love the Roland Ciscos or hate them. In the latter camp is Jon Tuska, who writes in *The Filming of the West*: "Roland made the Kid a dashing lover, a friend of the poor, an enemy to the rich, a savage killer and robber when necessary, an infidel, a vagabond. His interpretation owed nothing to Duncan [Renaldo], nothing really to O. Henry, and very little to either [Warner] Baxter or [César] Romero. The Latin American market that had been developed by the Renaldo series began to dry up" (443). Among Roland's staunchest champions is William K. Everson, who tells us in *The Hollywood Western* that the involvement of Dunlap and Roland and an increase in the films' budgets "not only salvaged the series but also turned it into an entirely superior one. The Ciscos of Roland had genuine charm, a quality not often found in smaller Westerns, pictorial qualities were often exceptional and even near-poetic . . . and action, while never excessive, was often extremely well staged" (225).

Having seen all six of the Ciscos with Roland in the lead, I fall somewhere in the middle. Certainly Roland is the finest actor ever to take the role, surpassing even Warner Baxter, thanks to not having to fake a Mexican accent. His characterization is the fullest and most unusual of any of the Ciscos, although the Baxter of *In Old Arizona* perhaps runs him a close second. With fourteen- to sixteen-day shooting schedules and considerably higher budgets than any other Monogram Western series of the forties, these films could have been just as exciting as Roland's personal contribution to them was. By and large, however, they're not. Action is rare and not terribly well directed when it comes, the storylines are routine, most of the dialogue is forgettable except perhaps for Roland's poetic effusions, and the singing guerrillas quickly become laughable because they never do anything but sing.

Ride
　Amigos ride
　　And as we ride we sing a song of victory.
　　　We'll do or die
　　　　For those we love
　　　　And that is why
　　　　The skies above
　　　　　(Ride, amigos, ride)
　　　　　And fate decide the price we pay
　　　　　for liberty.
　　　　　The call to arms
　　　　　Rings far and wide
　　　　　We ride along.
　　　　　Amigos ride!
　　　　　Ride! Ride! Ride on!

These lyrics were composed by Eddie Cherkose, who had also written the theme song for the magnificent serial *Zorro's Fighting Legion* (Republic, 1939), and the male chorus belting out the words over the credits of the Roland Ciscos sounds like the group that sang in the serial. With Edward J. Kay's music the lyrics are much more impressive, almost leading one to expect the same level of action and excitement William Witney and John English brought to that *Citizen Kane* of cliff-hangers. Unfortunately, the Roland Ciscos were directed by a different William.

William Nigh was born in Berlin, Wisconsin, on October 12, 1881, and began directing movies in 1915. In Hollywood's pioneer days he made at least a few relatively prestigious pictures like *A Yellow Streak* (Metro, 1915), starring Lionel Barrymore, and *The Kiss of Hate* (Columbia, 1916), with Lionel's sister Ethel in the lead. When other leading men were unavailable he liked to cast himself, starring in four silents that he also directed. Between 1927 and 1930 he worked at MGM, directing stars like Lon Chaney (in *Mr. Wu*, 1927, and *Thunder*, 1929), John Gilbert and Joan Crawford (in *Four Walls*, 1928), and Tim McCoy (in *The Law of the Range*, 1928). Once silent pictures had fallen to the onslaught of talkies, Nigh found himself helming bottom-rung pictures for marginal outfits. He squeezed in a shoot-'em-up with Ken Maynard at Tiffany (*Fighting Thru*, 1931) and three with Harry Carey at Artclass before carving a niche for himself at Monogram, where he stayed for the rest of the thirties, turning out junk. Perhaps the quintessential William Nigh film is *The Mysterious Mr. Wong* (Monogram, 1935), starring Bela Lugosi as a pig-tailed, silk-robed Fu Manchu clone desperate to possess the legendary twelve coins of Confucius. "My name is Vong," he intones. "Vhere is the tvelfth coin?" Or words to that effect. A few years later Nigh directed Lugosi's horror-film partner Boris Karloff as a completely different character with the same last name, James Lee Wong, a grade-Z Monogram version of Charlie Chan. Karloff's Asian makeup and accent were just as ludicrous as Lugosi's. How Nigh got to direct the first four of the Gilbert Roland Cisco features is a mystery more baffling than any that ever faced Mr. Wong.

Except for their casts, the credits of the first four Roland Ciscos are fairly standard. All were photographed by Monogram veteran Harry Neumann and featured background music by regular Monogram composer Edward J. Kay. Many of the actors had little or no experience in Westerns but there were a few familiar faces like Tristram Coffin,

Gilbert Roland and Nacho Galindo in *The Gay Cavalier* (1946)

John Merton, George J. Lewis, Harry Woods, and Terry Frost. Cisco's sidekick is called "Baby" throughout the quartet but is played by two different actors: Nacho Galindo in the first film, Frank Yaconelli in the next three. Three of the four films run between 59 and 65 minutes; *Beauty and the Bandit* clocks in at 77 minutes.

The cycle begins with *The Gay Cavalier* (Monogram, 1946), which was directed by Nigh from a screenplay by newcomer Charles S. Belden. Everson in *The Hollywood Western* describes its "pictorial qualities" as "exceptional and even near-poetic" (225), while Don Miller in *Hollywood Corral* writes that its "climax was more exciting than usual, but aside from Roland's welcome charm there was little else to merit comment" (184). As usual I find myself somewhere in the middle.

The scene is California in 1850 and we open with some dramatic shots of Cisco carving a notch in the cross on the grave of his father, the greatest bandit of old California, to atone for whose crimes Cisco, in the words of his sidekick Baby (Nacho Galindo), "steals only from the rich who are bad and

gives to the poor." Between crimes Cisco has a tendency to philosophize. "Time is a wonderful thing. It ages wine and mellows women." He and Baby and his outlaw band head for the village of El Monte, where a fiesta is under way at the hacienda of Don Felipe Peralta (Martín Garralaga) to celebrate the expected arrival of Lawton (Tristram Coffin), a wealthy Anglo who is going to pay off Don Felipe's many debts and marry his younger daughter Angela (Helen Gerald). The señorita's true love is Juan (Drew Allen), a sort of Latino Clark Kent, but she's ready to marry Lawton if that's what it will take to save the Peralta property. Her older sister Pepita (Ramsay Ames), who has no man in her life, fantasizes about that romantic rogue the Cisco Kid.

Meanwhile, a wagonload of donations from the poor of Monterey to build a mission in El Monte is held up by Lawton and a gang of masked bandits, who kill all but two of the men escorting the wagon and make off with "enough silver to break the backs of the men who lift it." Lawton's henchman Lewis (John Merton) calls him Cisco so that the wounded driver will blame California's Robin Hood for

Iris Flores and Marjorie Riordan stand by as Gilbert Roland confronts Harry Woods (held back by Frank Yaconelli) in *South of Monterey* (1946).

the crime. They take the one surviving guard (Frank LaRue) with them to Don Felipe's hacienda.

Elsewhere on the trail, Cisco and his legion are galloping along and lustily belting out their theme song, including a few stanzas that aren't sung again in later Cisco films. In El Monte, Cisco distributes alms to the poor, enjoys a drink of tequila with lime and salt—the ritual that is repeated over and over during Roland's time in the lead—and stops off on the way out of town to leap onto a balcony and romance the lovely Rosita (Iris Flores) while Baby serenades them. Cisco himself doesn't sing, he explains, because "I have a voice like a frog with a sore throat." As a parting gift he leaves Rosita with a necklace, another little action we'll see Roland perform again and again.

Riding across the countryside, the singing legion of good badmen finds the dying wagon driver, who reports with his final breath that the robbers who stole the mission's silver were led by Cisco and that the wounded guard was taken to Don Felipe's ran-

cho. By this time Lawton has reached the hacienda with his party and also claimed that Cisco was behind the robbery and murders. Pepita, who wants to save her sister from a marriage without love, encourages the spineless Juan to pick a fight with Lawton but gets nowhere.

Cisco comes to the fiesta calling himself Luis Antonio Dámaso Alonso Smith, makes a play for Pepita, catches Lawton alone, warns him to be careful what he accuses Cisco of doing, and slips away. While Don Felipe's men search the grounds for the intruder, he hides in Pepita's room, sips her hot chocolate, and listens to her sing a romantic song that Ramsay Ames wrote for herself and that is about as Latin as kung pao beef. When he comes out of hiding, Pepita recognizes him as the romantic rogue of whom she's dreamed. Juan disturbs their interlude and is knocked out for his troubles. After Cisco rides into the night, Pepita sends Juan after him, but before he leaves the hacienda Juan happens to overhear Lawton and Lewis discussing the robbery they pulled and mentioning that the stolen silver is at their hideout on the Mountain of the Shadows.

Juan somehow manages to follow Cisco to where his men are camped for the night, singing a mournful version of "Ride, Amigos, Ride." He tells Cisco what he overheard and asks for a chance to help recover the silver. Cisco, Baby, and Juan sneak up on the mountain hideout. During the clumsily directed fight between the trio and the gang, Cisco does nothing and Juan proves his manhood. One outlaw (Raphael Bennett) escapes and reports back to Lawton and Lewis at the hacienda. Lawton tells Don Felipe that Cisco stole the money he was going to use to pay the Peralta debts and then unaccountably asks to marry Angela and take over the rancho immediately. Rosita, helping to prepare Angela for the wedding, pays Cisco a glowing compliment that tends to make viewers roll on the floor today: "He rides like the wind and makes love just as fast. He is the greatest of all caballeros!" Pepita tries to persuade Angela not to go through with the ceremony, but Angela insists it's the only way to save the family property.

Cisco brings the silver to the padre at El Monte, learns that the wedding is about to take place, rides to the hacienda, accuses Lawton of the robbery, and disposes of him in a sword duel that is competently enough staged but can't hold a candle to the sword fights William Witney directed in *Zorro's Fighting Legion*. What no one seems to realize, certainly not the film's director or screenwriter, is that without Lawton's money Don Felipe and his daughters are going to lose their happy hacienda. Cisco leaves Pepita with romantic words and a necklace from his seemingly endless supply and rides out of the picture with his useless guerrillas.

Next in release came *South of Monterey* (Monogram, 1946), which was also directed by Nigh from a pedestrian if socially conscious screenplay by Belden. Don Miller in *Hollywood Corral* says of this picture only that it "moved fairly well" (184). Everson and Tuska don't mention it at all. Its only historic significance is that Frank Yaconelli replaced Nacho Galindo in the sidekick role.

While the legionnaires are singing around the evening campfire and Baby strums a guitar, Cisco philosophizes about what has brought him and his compañeros to the area. The Indians and the Latino powerless are being robbed by tax collectors and loan sharks. "The rich get richer and the poor—the poor get children." He sends Baby into town to pose as a blind minstrel and collect information.

Now the situation in the area is presented to us directly. Carlos Madero (George J. Lewis), one of the few ranchers who's been able to pay his taxes, is also the local firebrand. He's in love with María Morales (Marjorie Riordan), the lovely sister of Arturo (Martín Garralaga), the comandante of police, who is in a corrupt alliance with the tax collector, Bennet (Harry Woods), and is trying to pressure María into becoming Bennet's wife. (The name of Woods's character seems to be an inside joke on action director Spencer Bennet, who had made several excellent B Westerns for Monogram while Scott Dunlap was in charge of production.) María's heart, however, is with Arturo's and Bennet's victims. "Be sorry for the poor," her brother advises her, "but do not suffer with them. They belong to the lower class, which must always suffer."

Carlos has sold the people's cattle for enough money to pay their taxes and the money is on the way to them by coach, but many coaches have been robbed by a character known as the Silver Bandit, who wears a black cape and rides a horse with a silver saddle and who Carlos suspects is a tax collector. When Carlos knocks Bennet down on the street for beating up an old farmer who had seen his taxes triple overnight, Arturo arrests Carlos for disturbing the peace. The comandante is infatuated with Carmelita (Iris Flores), the local cantina singer, but won't invite her to his house because, as he tells her, "my sister is a lady." Bennet and Arturo conspire to frame Carlos for some crime or other.

While Baby in his blind minstrel guise is picking up this information, Cisco comes swaggering into the cantina and orders a tequila, which he drinks with the usual lemon and salt. A local peasant offers to buy him a drink and Cisco accepts. Arturo, curious who this stranger is, offers to buy him a drink and Cisco refuses. "That is an insult to a gentleman," Arturo protests. "Where is he?" Cisco asks. The look on Carmelita's face during this scene suggests that she knows who the stranger is even if Arturo doesn't. Cisco meets with Baby in the plaza and learns most of what we've already seen.

The coach that was carrying the cattle money comes into town and the driver announces that he was robbed by the Silver Bandit. A posse is formed to go after the thief, stopping at Arturo's hacienda to pick up the comandante and Bennet. Cisco follows the posse, but unfortunately he's riding a horse with a silver saddle. The posse members spot him, think he's the outlaw they're after, chase him and wound him in the shoulder, but he manages to elude them. A wretched María is preparing to move out on her brother when the wounded Cisco sneaks into the Morales hacienda and passes out on her bed. He comes to and is delighted to find himself with his wound bandaged and in the company of a beautiful señorita. He kisses María, helps himself to Arturo's tequila, learns that María loves the jailed Carlos, hides when Arturo returns from the disbanded posse, and overhears him tell María that Carlos will stay locked up until she marries Bennet.

That night Cisco pays another visit to the cantina, where Carmelita confronts him and we learn that he had romanced and jilted her in Monterey but that she's still wild about him. Maria comes to the cantina and tells Arturo that she's going to marry Bennet. The tax collector, for no particular reason, starts slapping Carmelita, who for no better reason blurts out that the swaggering stranger is, as she persists in calling him, "the Cisco." Arturo arrests Cisco and locks him in the cell next to Carlos, to whom he describes himself as "a prisoner of the government and a friend of the people." María comes to the jail to visit Carlos and Carmelita comes to give Cisco the key to the cells, which she stole from Arturo

after getting him drunk. Cisco releases Carlos, and both men, along with Baby, gallop out of town and rejoin the legion. Planning to murder both their prisoners, Bennet and Arturo discover them gone.

The climax of this draggy film is at hand, and none too soon. Cisco, Baby, and Carlos leave the legion behind and head for the mountain cabin to which Carlos had once followed Arturo. The Silver Bandit, who of course is Arturo himself, robs another coach and makes for the cabin with his loot, followed by Bennet, who shoots down his former partner in crime as he's about to take off with all the money the pair had stolen. Cisco comes on the scene and kills Bennet after a short and stodgily directed fight. Returning to the Morales hacienda, he spares María's feelings by telling her that Bennet was the Silver Bandit and that her brother died heroically while struggling with him. With Carlos and María reunited, Cisco and Baby rejoin the useless legion and everyone gallops off to the tune of "Ride Amigos Ride."

Beauty and the Bandit (Monogram, 1946), third and, at 77 minutes, by far the longest of the Roland Ciscos, is distinguished by Ramsay Ames, who is definitely a beauty, and by another heaping helping

Still photo for *Beauty and the Bandit* (1946), starring Gilbert Roland (right), Ramsay Ames (center), and William Gould (left)

Gilbert Roland with Ramsay Ames in *Beauty and the Bandit* (1946)

of thirties-style social consciousness. Everson ranks it on the same level with *The Gay Cavalier*. This may be a bit excessive, but it's certainly one of the more interesting pictures of the six.

The film opens with Cisco at the head of his band of merry muchachos riding to a California mountaintop and observing a ship as it approaches the port of San Luis. What he's looking for is a rich newcomer to rob, as becomes clear that night when he visits a sailors' hangout where his old pal Bill (Glenn Strange) in a striped jersey is singing "Blow the Man Down." Bill tells him that the only passenger who left the ship at San Luis was a young Frenchman on his way to the town of San Marino with a strongbox full of silver. Cisco joins the Frenchman on the night coach to San Marino but, when he lights a cigarette for his fellow traveler, he realizes that his companion is a woman (Ramsay Ames). Cisco's men hold up the coach, take the strongbox, shoot it open, and remove the pouch of silver from among a bed of rocks. Cisco goes after them, tells them to lock the chest again, and returns to the coach with it, pretending to have driven the bandits off. His

disguised traveling companion doesn't bother to open it and see if the silver is still there.

In San Marino, Doc Walsh (William Gould), a former medicine show performer who runs the town hotel, is waiting for the coach with his partner in crime, a disgraced doctor named Juan Federico Valegra (Martín Garralaga). We learn from their conversation that Valegra at Walsh's behest has been poisoning the Mexican peasants' crops and that the peasants have sold their land for next to nothing to Walsh, who in turn has sold the property to a Frenchman named Dubois, whose emissary is supposed to be on the night coach with the purchase money. When it arrives, the disguised woman takes a room in Walsh's hotel and has the strongbox deposited in his vault. Cisco, calling himself Luis Antonio Tomás Alonso Gonzales, invites the disguised woman to have a drink with him in the hotel bar. After the usual tequila ceremony Cisco has an unmotivated quarrel with the drunken Dr. Valegra, then enjoys himself playing mind games with the disguised woman, telling her that tequila will put hair on her chest and suggesting that she make a pass at the barmaid

Rosita (Vida Aldana). When she finally retires to her room, Walsh is waiting to tell her that he opened the strongbox and found it held nothing but rocks. This is supposed to be a huge surprise to her, but she reacts calmly and tells him that the purchase money from Dubois will arrive the next day. Then she lets her hair down for Walsh, identifies herself as Dubois' daughter Jeanne, and tells him that her father died recently. Cisco is listening in on this conversation out on Jeanne's balcony. When Walsh has left he slips in, romances Jeanne, and invites himself to spend the night in her bed—with her on the couch!—until she pulls a derringer on him and makes him leave.

The next day Cisco encounters a peasant boy with a sick lamb and takes them to Dr. Valegra, who demands an exorbitant fee for a bottle of the antidote to the poison that he himself has been spreading among the farmers, but Cisco takes the medicine from him by force. By this time Baby (Frank Yaconelli) has gotten hired as a cook in Walsh's hotel. Jeanne, now undisguised and beautiful, comes down for breakfast, and Cisco flirts with both her and the barmaid Rosita in the kitchen. Meanwhile the police captain from San Luis (George J. Lewis), who is an idiot, has arrived in San Marino to investigate the coach holdup. He comes close to figuring out that the second passenger on the coach was the notorious Cisco Kid until Walsh covers for Cisco by claiming that he and "Gonzales" are old friends.

Cisco takes Jeanne out for a horseback ride and another spot of romance, but the love session is cut short when Baby races up with the news that the captain has arrested two of the merry muchachos. This development triggers the only real action sequence in the film as Cisco rides into town and enables his men to escape by getting the troops to chase him, a quite decently directed few minutes of pursuit footage accompanied by Edward J. Kay's agitato music from Monogram's Rough Riders series of 1941-42.

That night Cisco rejoins Jeanne and brings her to the location where his men are camped. Instantly she becomes the dominatrix of the entire gang, cowing them with her shooting and knife-throwing prowess, but then she washes Cisco's shirt for him and generally acts like his slave, telling him that she's known all along that he stole her silver but didn't turn him in because he'd also stolen her heart. Claiming to be a cold-blooded businesswoman, she says she doesn't care that the land her silver was to buy had been stolen

from the peasants. "I live only to destroy those who take advantage of the poor people," Cisco tells her, and proceeds to give her a vigorous spanking, after which she bows to him and calls him "Master"! This is not a film I would recommend to feminists.

The next day Cisco and his men come across a farmer (Felipe Turich) who's been poisoned by eating his own crops. They bring the sick man to town and force Dr. Valegra to treat him, but the man dies in Valegra's office. Cisco finds the incriminating poison in Valegra's closet, substitutes castor oil, makes Valegra drink what he believes will kill him, and leaves him to suffer the pangs of conscience. The captain and his troops chase Cisco and his men out of town and Jeanne manages to slip away from the legion, taking the silver with her. Discovering the loss and suspecting that she's planning to buy the peasants' land, Cisco heads for Walsh's hotel.

Meanwhile, Jeanne has in fact purchased the property, but then she burns the deeds and says she's going to return the land to the farmers, which proves, I suppose, that there's nothing like a spanking to bring out a woman's social consciousness. Walsh grabs her and locks her in one of the hotel rooms, planning to kill Cisco for the price on his head when he comes to rescue her. That spanking Cisco gave her also seems to have taken away all her fighting prowess, for she doesn't resist Walsh in the least. When Cisco arrives, Walsh uses his skill as a medicine show ventriloquist to lure him into the pitch-dark hotel lobby and into a murky gun battle that would have made a marvelous climax with a director like Joseph H. Lewis but that Nigh reduces to a throwaway. Both Walsh and Valegra wind up dead, Jeanne returns their land to the peasants, and Cisco and his legion once again elude the taco-witted police captain and ride off to new adventure.

Riding the California Trail (Monogram, 1947) was directed by Nigh from a screenplay by Clarence Upson Young, who had written a few of Monogram's Johnny Mack Brown B Westerns. Similar to earlier Roland Ciscos, it is marked by strong social consciousness and a few excellent lines of dialogue, but the main virtue is Roland himself. The film opens with Cisco, Baby, and the legion galloping pell-mell out of yet another town after Cisco, saying "I do not like angry women," has jilted yet another señorita. Reaching a different part of California he's never seen before, he finds a "wanted" poster offering a reward for him of 500 pesos, an amount he considers insultingly small. After stopping off at the mission near the pueblo of San Lorenzo and learning from the padre that the place is a little Eden, with no oppression of

Raoul (Ted Hecht) and Cisco (Gilbert Roland) duel over a woman in *Riding the California Trail* (1947).

the poor or political corruption—"Oh, then this is no place for us," says Baby—Cisco contemplates settling there for good. Riding into the town, he buys a rose from a flower girl in the plaza, and with the rose in his mouth and a cigarette behind his ear, he swaggers into the local cantina and orders tequila and then a meal. The dancer Raquel (Teala Loring) comes out and performs, wiggling up a storm all around him. He ignores her and goes on eating his frijoles, but when she goes back to her dressing room he's waiting for her with the rose and words of romance.

At a knock on her door he hides behind a curtain and listens as she gets rid of her regular suitor, Raoul Reyes (Ted Hecht), by claiming to have a headache. Returning to Cisco's embrace, she tells him that though Raoul really loves her, he's going to marry the wealthy and beautiful Dolores Ramírez (Inez Cooper), who loves the poor and is known locally as the Angel of San Lorenzo. Cisco gives the dancer one of the necklaces he hands out to every attractive woman he meets. A suspicious Raoul barges in on them and finds them kissing. "Oh, so you had a headache," he says to her, then turns to Cisco, demanding: "Who are you?" "I am the

headache," he replies. They brawl, Raoul summons help, and Cisco is about to be taken to jail when Baby and his men pull their guns and free him. On the way out of town, Cisco catches a glimpse of Dolores in her coach and is entranced. Raoul and his men chase Cisco and the legion to some excellent and unfamiliar Edward J. Kay agitato music.

Deciding that Dolores should get to know him better, Cisco pays a visit to the Ramírez hacienda in a stolen coach, impersonating the wealthy San Francisco playboy and master swordsman Don Luis de Salazar, with Baby posing as his servant. Dolores's uncle, Don José Ramírez (Martín Garralaga), welcomes the guest and introduces his niece. Cisco learns of her great generosity to the poor and of course starts making love to her the first moment they're alone. She resists him, admitting she doesn't love Raoul but is marrying him because Don José told her it was her father's dying wish. The poor come bearing small gifts and hopes for her happiness. "I have the same weakness you have," Cisco tells her. "I cannot see other people suffer." Meanwhile the coachman whose vehicle Cisco hijacked makes it to San Lorenzo and reports the theft to the *policía*.

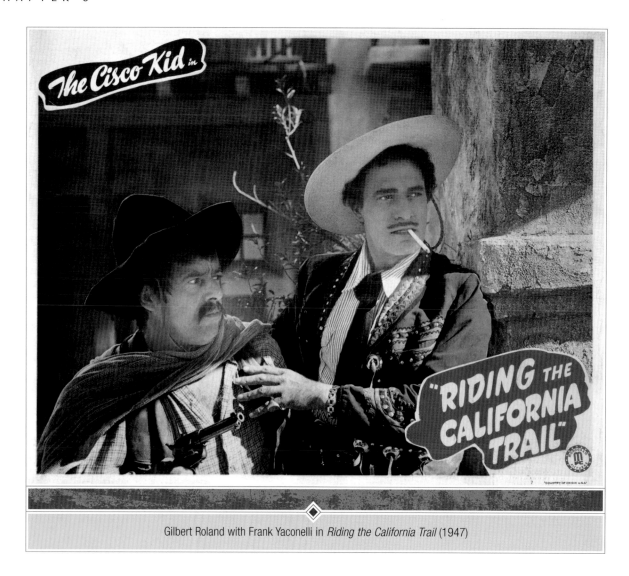

Gilbert Roland with Frank Yaconelli in *Riding the California Trail* (1947)

That night, after Dolores has sung a Latin melody for Cisco, Raoul shows up, is introduced to the newcomer, and claims not to have met him before. The two men duel verbally. After some pointed remarks about "the Cisco"—Dolores's comment is "I have heard that he only offends the law helping the poor"—Raoul calls "Luis" an impostor and challenges him to a duel with swords. Cisco's skill with the blade makes Raoul look ridiculous. He and Baby slip away, though no farther than the courtyard of the hacienda, when the policía arrive. In the middle of the night, Dolores's duenna, Mamá Rosita (Marcelle Grandville), tells Cisco that Don José and Raoul are in a conspiracy to get Dolores married to Raoul and split her fortune. Cisco vows to stop the wedding.

Very late, after the cantina has closed, Cisco goes back there and once again romances Raquel, who admits that she's in on the plot and that Raoul and Don José have a secret written agreement proving the conspiracy. He visits Raoul's house, ties him up, rummages through his papers, and in five seconds locates an IOU from Don José to Raoul for half a million pesos. Raquel, who's followed Cisco, releases Raoul,

who guesses that Cisco's next stop will be the Ramírez hacienda and heads out there to kill him. Cisco slips into the hacienda, breaks into the box containing Don José's secret papers, and discovers a forged will supposedly signed by Dolores's father and providing that her inheritance will pass to Don José if she marries Raoul. Caught red-handed by the Ramírez household, Cisco exposes Don José by showing Dolores the false will. When Raoul arrives he and Cisco settle accounts with another stodgily directed swordfight. Dolores helps Cisco escape as the policía arrive and he rejoins his warbling amigos.

Riding the California Trail was the last of Scott Dunlap's and William Nigh's contributions to the Cisco saga. Nigh directed two more Monogram quickies—neither of them Westerns, both released in 1948—and then retired. He died in 1955. Dunlap worked very little after the Cisco films, although he did keep his hand in by producing an occasional non-series Western or adventure flick for release by Allied Artists, which bought Monogram in the early fifties. His last films as a producer—*Johnny Rocco* and *Man from God's Country*, both released in 1958—were directed by Paul Landres, who had helmed more Cisco TV episodes than anyone else. Dunlap died on March 30, 1970, at age seventy-eight.

The production reins on what was left of Monogram's Cisco series were turned over to a newcomer with minimal credentials in the Western genre. Jeffrey Bernerd, born in London around 1892, had worked in the business end of the English movie industry since before the First World War. He became managing director of the Stell film company and later moved to Gaumont-British, where he served as general sales manager and newsreel producer. He came to the United States in 1941 and to Monogram three years later, producing low-budget social problem pictures, weepers, and one horror flick. The only film he worked on that is still of some interest today is *Black Gold* (Allied Artists, 1947), a contemporary Western of sorts, directed in Cinecolor by Phil Karlson (with second-unit work by B. Reeves Eason), and starring Anthony Quinn and his then wife Katherine DeMille. Bernerd died in his Beverly Hills home on August 10, 1950.

Under his brief regime a number of changes were made in the Cisco films. Thrown on the trash heap were Roland's tequila rituals, most of his swaggering machismo and social consciousness, and the legion of singing guerrillas. His comic sidekick was both rechristened and recast, with Chris-Pin Martin from the 20th Century-Fox Cisco cycle brought in to replace Frank Yaconelli. As in Monogram's earliest Cisco films, the character was again called Pancho. Bernerd unaccountably replaced William Nigh, who had directed more of the Monogram pictures Bernerd had produced than anyone else, but chose another wrong William to take Nigh's place.

Born in St. Louis on April 16, 1888, W. Christy Cabanne was established in movies as an actor and assistant director under the legendary D. W. Griffith before he was old enough to vote. Raoul Walsh, the first director of a Cisco feature, knew and worked with Cabanne for a few years around 1910 and makes a dozen references to him in his 1974 autobiography *Each Man in His Time*. By 1914 Cabanne was a director in his own right, although Griffith is billed as "supervisor" on a number of his early films. Like William Nigh, Cabanne had the highest-powered stars of his career in some of his first silents. In 1915 and 1916 alone he directed four pictures with Lillian Gish in the lead and another four with Douglas Fairbanks Sr. Also like Nigh, Cabanne put in a brief stint at MGM during the mid-to-late twenties and was kicked to the bottom of the directorial ladder with the coming of sound.

Most of his thirties films are B melodramas with an occasional Western sandwiched among them like *The Dawn Trail* (Columbia, 1930), starring Buck Jones. He made his best known contribution to the genre while a contract director at RKO. *The Last Outlaw* (RKO, 1936) starred Harry Carey and Hoot Gibson in a remake of the 1919 two-reeler of the same name that had been directed by John Ford. To quote Everson's *The Hollywood Western*, the story was "about an old-time outlaw returning from jail to his home in the modern West, encountering prejudice, contemporary racketeers, and . . . a grown daughter entranced by a singing cowboy in the movies!" (196). As luck would have it, the Autry parody in the movie-within-the-movie was played by Fred Scott, who began starring in his own musical shoot-'em-ups that same year. Cabanne, says Everson, "did a competent enough job with it, but totally failed to inject the kind of magic that Ford would have added intuitively" (196). The following year Cabanne directed Preston Foster, Jean Muir, and Van Heflin in *The Outcasts of Poker Flat* (RKO, 1937), another remake of a Ford silent. These are the high spots in Cabanne's meager output of Westerns.

From 1939 till 1942 he worked primarily at Universal cranking out quickies starring Richard Arlen and Andy Devine or, every so often, Andy Devine and future Cisco sidekick Leo Carrillo. By 1945 he was relegated to unprestigious outfits like Monogram, whose final pair of Ciscos, like just about everything else Cabanne directed, were lackluster.

Grizzled B movie scripter Bennett Cohen furnished the screenplay and story and Roland some "additional dialogue" for *Robin Hood of Monterey* (Monogram, 1947). With a running time of only 55 minutes and the principal villains being played by veterans Evelyn Brent and Jack LaRue, it's understandable that Don Miller in *Hollywood Corral* described the picture as "slight but short and swift . . . with dependable skullduggery . . ." (184). It's tolerable today only because of Roland's performance and a storyline heavily influenced by a type of movie that in 1947 was enjoying its golden age: film noir.

We open on Cisco reading Spanish love poetry to Pancho. (No, amigos. Don't say it. Don't even think it.) The interlude is broken up by gunfire and Cisco, riding to the rescue, finds Eduardo Belmonte (Travis Kent) wounded and about to be murdered by the Mexican posse that has been chasing him. Cisco fools the pursuers into thinking their young target is already dead, then he and Pancho patch Eduardo up and take him to the cabin of Pablo (Ernie Adams). As Eduardo tells them his story, which has strong

The Cisco Kid (Gilbert Roland) holding a gun on the alcalde (Nestor Paiva) in *Robin Hood of Monterey* (1947)

noir overtones, the movie shifts into flashback. Although he was running from the law after being charged with the murder of his father, Don Carlos (Pedro de Córdoba), Eduardo claims that the real killers are the Don's scheming second wife María (Evelyn Brent) and her lover Ricardo Gonzales (Jack LaRue). Cisco and Pancho leave the young man in Pablo's care and pay a surreptitious visit to the Gonzales hacienda where they run into Eduardo's fiancée Lolita (Donna DeMario). Then Cisco drops in on María Belmonte and discovers that she is María Sánchez, an avaricious cantina dancer he once knew. Instantly he knows that Eduardo's story was true, and he's even more certain when María pulls a derringer on him. As soon as Cisco is gone, María and Gonzales conspire to have him arrested by the local authorities, and Gonzales makes tracks for the pueblo of San Blas to tip off the idiot alcalde (Néstor Paiva) that the notorious Cisco is in the area.

Cisco comes to town and learns from the local doctor that Don Carlos was killed by a very small bullet, but he is cornered by the alcalde's troops and forced to make a run for his life with Pancho. The

film's only genuine action sequence, and not a bad one either, comes abruptly and not too credibly to an end when Cisco stops along the trail to chat with Lolita. Thanks to this blunder he and Pancho are caught by the soldados and tossed into the *calabozo*. The next day Cisco is marched out and executed by a firing squad, with María and Gonzales as witnesses. Mother of Mercy, is this the end of Cisco? Far from it! We soon learn that he happens to be an old friend of the firing squad leader and paid him to have the men's rifles loaded with blanks.

That night he breaks Pancho out of jail and the two of them flee to Pablo's cabin, where they find out that Eduardo, believing naturally enough the reports of Cisco's execution, has gone to the Belmonte hacienda to settle the score on his own. Unfortunately the young man gets himself captured by the troop of soldiers who are hunting for the escaped prisoners, so that Cisco and Pancho have to rescue him from the alcalde's troops all over again. Finally the burrito-witted official understands Cisco's point that if Don Carlos was killed by a derringer the killer must have been María, and they prepare a rather

King of the Bandits (1947) was Gilbert Roland's last Cisco Kid film. Here Roland and Chris-Pin Martin make a stand in front of a saloon.

simple-minded trap. Cisco returns to the hacienda and gets her to admit her guilt within earshot of the hidden alcalde and his men, who arrest her and Gonzales without a nanosecond of action. With the killers caught and the young lovers reunited, Cisco goes back to reading Spanish love poems to Pancho.

Roland's time as Cisco came to an end with *King of the Bandits* (Monogram, 1947). Cabanne not only directed but furnished the film's original story (turned into a screenplay by Bennett Cohen, with Roland again credited for additional dialogue) and cast his son Bill in a bit part as an orderly. Visually the picture is dull as dishwater and its plot has more holes than a slab of Swiss *queso*.

The scene is Arizona and the film opens abruptly with Cisco and Pancho being executed by a firing squad just as they had been in Cabanne's *Robin Hood of Monterey*. They're not really dead this time either: the sequence turns out to be a dream brought on by Pancho's consumption of sixteen enchiladas. On the trail that day, our heroes find a poster nailed to a tree, offering a $500 reward for Cisco even though he's

never been in Arizona before. (So much for any continuity between this film and the earliest Cisco features.) A few seconds of screen time later they save the life of Pedro Gómez (Pat Goldin), a little saddlemaker who was about to be lynched after being falsely accused of having helped the notorious Cisco Kid and his gang rob a freight wagon. Anyone who doesn't have frijoles for brains understands that, as in so many other Cisco films, an impostor has been committing crimes in the caballero's name.

Cisco, Pancho, and their newfound amigo are riding peacefully along when a runaway stagecoach speeds by. Cisco overtakes and stops the coach (with Roland himself making the transfer from saddle to driver's box in medium close-up) and learns from Alice Mason (Angela Greene) and her injured mother (Laura Treadwell) that the coach was robbed and the women's heirloom jewelry stolen by—you guessed it—the nefarious Cisco Kid and his gang. Cisco prudently declines to identify himself except by his real name, Luis Antonio Dámaso Ramón Alonso. Leaving the coach and women at a nearby

Gilbert Roland plays Major de Roja in *Pirates of Monterey* (1947).

mission with Pedro to guard them, Cisco and Pancho ride off to summon Alice's brother, Captain Frank Mason (William Bakewell), who is stationed at Fort Roberts.

Stopping off in the town of El Rio for a cigarettes-and-tequila break (though this time he doesn't perform the drinking ritual with lime and salt), Cisco notices a locket around the neck of a dance hall girl (Cathy Carter) and, magically intuiting that it was part of the jewels stolen from Alice, starts to flirt with the dancer. A few minutes of love murmurs and she tells him she was given the locket by Smoke Kirby (Anthony Warde), who's playing poker across the room. Cisco is buying the locket from her for $100 in gold when Kirby sees what's going on, comes over, and slaps her face. Cisco knocks him down, finds the rest of the jewels in Kirby's pocket, and he and Pancho race out of town in an unexciting chase sequence that ends as usual with their hiding behind some rocks until the pursuers go by.

At Fort Roberts, Colonel Wayne (Boyd Irwin) dispatches Alice's brother and some troopers to search for the overdue coach containing the captain's sister and mother, who at the same time are being escorted to the fort by Cisco, Pancho, and Pedro. Cisco by now has fallen deeply in love with Alice. "Life is beautiful," he rhapsodizes as he drives the coach with Alice beside him. "There is beauty everywhere. In the trees, in the mountains, in the sky. Do you know how a cloud is born?" That night at their campsite he romances her again but still doesn't reveal who he is except indirectly, talking about a fantasy hero of his who "hates injustice so he makes his own laws" and saying he'd like to settle down with a woman "with eyes soft like the sky and hair soft like golden wheatfields." Kirby breaks up this adolescent poetry by riding into their camp and challenging the Mexican who hit him in the saloon to a gun duel. When his adversary identifies himself as Cisco, Kirby tries to cheat in the duel but fails. At this point Captain Mason and his troops come on the scene. Kirby tells the soldiers that his adversary is Cisco and, with the jewels he took back from Kirby found on him, Cisco and Pancho are arrested. This development doesn't make a taco's worth of sense since Alice and her mother are on the spot and can swear that these aren't the men who robbed them, but logic is not this picture's strong point. (Neither is anything else.)

The troops and their prisoners reach Fort Roberts after dark, and Captain Mason is ordered to take Cisco and Pancho to the U.S. marshal in El Rio the next morning. In a cell, Cisco recites a poem about a man condemned to hang. Little Pedro, who had slipped away from the campsite before the troops showed up, sneaks into the fort and steals some guns, which he slips to the prisoners in their cell. Just before her brother is to leave for El Rio with the prisoners, Alice begs him to let them escape. When Cisco gets the drop on the captain and forces him at gunpoint to escort them away from the post, Mason concludes that he got the gun from Alice. He tries to protect her by refusing to explain what happened, and Colonel Wayne orders him locked up.

Later in El Rio, Cisco happens to overhear the marshal (Gene Roth) talking in the saloon about the captain's imminent court martial and knows he has to save Alice's brother. He sends Pedro to the saloon with a threatening note for Kirby, whose henchman Burl (Rory Mallinson) takes the paper out of town to the gang's hideout cabin, followed of course by Cisco. The minute Cisco and Pancho fire one or two shots at the cabin, two members of the gang run for their lives. That night three others desert. When Burl makes a move in the same direction, a by now drunken Kirby shoots his henchman in the back. Then he comes out of the cabin, shooting wildly into the dark. Cisco stalks him back to town and the deserted saloon, where he collars his quarry actionlessly after Kirby runs out of bullets. With Captain Mason released and the misunderstanding between him and his sister cleared up, Cisco sadly concludes that he will always be "the wanderer, the restless one" and says goodbye to Alice.

After finishing his pair of Ciscos, Cabanne once more followed in the career path of his predecessor William Nigh. He directed two mediocre oaters for Monogram that came out in 1948 (*Back Trail* with Johnny Mack Brown and *Silver Trails* with Jimmy Wakely) and then retired. He died soon after he stopped working, on October 15, 1950.

Not long after he'd finished his stint as Cisco, Gilbert Roland's career once again went into orbit, thanks mainly to director John Huston, who gave him a major role opposite Jennifer Jones and John Garfield in *We Were Strangers* (Horizon/Columbia, 1949). "If Huston hadn't had faith to cast me in his picture," Roland told an interviewer years later, ". . . I might be back where I started as a kid, selling cushions at the Juárez arena." From that part he went on to appear alongside Spencer Tracy and James Stewart in *Malaya* (MGM, 1950, directed by

Richard Thorpe); with Cary Grant and José Ferrer in *Crisis* (MGM, 1950, directed by Richard Brooks); opposite Barbara Stanwyck, Wendell Corey, and (in the final role of his life) Walter Huston in *The Furies* (Wallis-Hazen/Paramount, 1950, directed by Anthony Mann); with Robert Stack in *Bullfighter and the Lady* (Republic, 1951, directed by Budd Boetticher); side by side with a flotilla of stars including Lana Turner, Kirk Douglas, Walter Pidgeon, and Dick Powell in *The Bad and the Beautiful* (MGM, 1952, directed by Vincente Minnelli); and opposite James Stewart and Joanne Dru in *Thunder Bay* (Universal, 1953, directed by Anthony Mann).

Roland continued to appear in Westerns and other films through the rest of the fifties and well into the sixties while also making guest appearances in a number of TV series episodes, of which two in particular stand out. In the fall of 1960 he played El Cuchillo, a more roguish and larcenous offshoot of his version of Cisco, for two sixty-minute segments of *Walt Disney Presents* ("El Bandido," October 30, 1960, and "Adiós El Cuchillo," November 6, 1960) that brought back Guy Williams as the character he'd

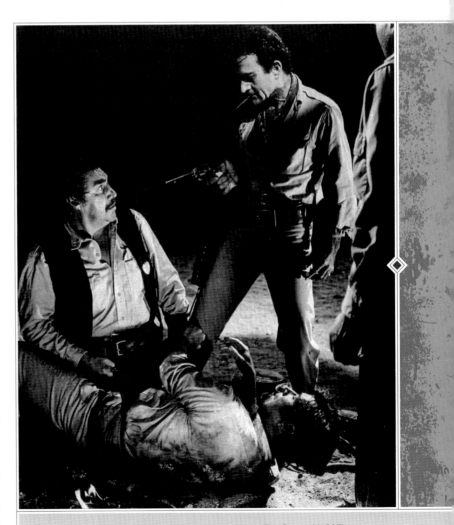

Gilbert Roland holds Emilio Fernández at gunpoint in *The Reward* (1965).

Ricardo Montalbán (left) and Gilbert Roland engage in swordplay in *Mark of the Renegade* (1951).

ing character if the series hadn't been canceled. Later in the decade Roland was featured opposite George C. Scott in *Islands in the Stream* (1977, directed by Franklin J. Schaffner), based on the posthumously published Hemingway novel.

His final movie role was in the offbeat Western *Barbarosa* (1982) starring Willie Nelson and Gary Busey. The film's director was Fred Schepisi, a then little-known Australian who went on to helm megahits like *A Cry in the Dark* (1988) and *The Russia House* (1991). When asked by a *New York Times* reporter what this living legend was like, Schepisi replied:

> A friend said to me: "When you're working with Gilbert Roland, you're like a little boy with a huge white wall, and somebody's given you a box of crayons." And it's true. As soon as he knows he can trust you, he opens up and offers you all the stuff he's ever learned. He comes prepared. He's gracious to everyone. And when he goes to the set, a man about his age follows him. The man is never in the way, but he gives Gilbert water, or honey and tea, and just before each take, he brings him a mirror. Obviously, Gilbert worked out a long time ago that, in the heat of things, with the best intentions in the world, people forget to give you water or a mirror, so he brings his own. (*New York Times*, August 6, 1982, sec. C, p. 8)

played in the Disney TV series of 1957-59: Zorro. This virtual movie for the small screen was directed by William Witney, the Hitchcock of the action film, and a succulent stuntfest it is. Five years later Witney directed and Roland guest-starred in the *Bonanza* episode "The Lonely Runner" (October 10, 1965), a dramatically powerful story of a man who becomes a fugitive rather than surrender his beloved mare to the person the courts have ruled her legal owner.

Roland kept a lower profile after turning sixty or so but still had no trouble finding movie work when and as he wanted. Between 1967 and 1969 he starred in four Westerns shot in Italy and one in Spain. On the sudden death of Frank Silvera, who had been playing Don Francisco de Montoya in *The High Chaparral* (NBC-TV, 1967-1971), Roland came aboard as the don's brother Domingo for the two-hour episode "The New Lion of Sonora" (Feb. 19, 1971) and would surely have stayed on as a continu-

Roland once summed up his philosophy of life by translating his mother's last words: "My son, don't rush yourself, don't worry yourself, goodbye, my soul." He had the words engraved on the gold ring he wore on his left pinky. His great good luck, he said, was to have "the blood of Spain, the heart of Mexico, and the freedom of America" (obituary of Gilbert Roland, *New York Times*, May 18, 1994, sec. B, p. 8). He also enjoyed excellent health, continuing to play championship-caliber tennis at the Beverly Hills Athletic Club when most men of his age, if alive at all, would be hobbling around on walkers. Early in 1994 I learned his address and sent him a letter, inviting him to look this chapter over, add whatever comments he might wish to make, and perhaps write an introduction for the book. As with César Romero, I made my move too late. He was suffering from cancer and died on May 15 at the age of at least eighty-eight.

Adiós, amigo. If we meet somewhere else and they serve liquor, I'll buy you a tequila.

During the more than three years when Cisco was being played by Gilbert Roland or no one at all, what was Duncan Renaldo up to? Apparently very little. He had a tiny part opposite Alan Ladd and Brian Donlevy in *Two Years Before the Mast* (Paramount, 1946, directed by John Farrow) and medium-size roles in two forgettable quickies, *Jungle Flight* (Paramount, 1947) and *Sword of the Avenger* (Eagle-Lion, 1948). Calling himself Renault Duncan, he collaborated with Jack DeWitt on the screenplays for a pair of Latin-themed Westerns, *Don Ricardo Returns* (PRC, 1946) and *Bells of San Fernando* (Hillcrest/Screen Guild, 1947), both produced by former Cisco owner James S. Burkett. As far as I can tell, these five pieces of work were all that came Renaldo's way between 1946 and 1948.

His career was pulled out of the doldrums by Phil Krasne, who in partnership with Burkett had bought the Cisco property from 20th Century-Fox in 1944 and sold it to Monogram. With that studio and Roland out of the Cisco business—permanently, as it turned out—Krasne organized a new company called Inter-American Productions, resumed control of the character, and closed a distribution deal with United Artists, which had been disappointed with the returns from the Hopalong Cassidy features it had released between 1946 and 1948 but was ready to try again with another Western series. Renaldo, who seems to have been a partner in Inter-American, agreed to play Cisco again as he had in 1945, as a carefree adventurer and righter of wrongs, without Roland's sexuality or tequila rituals or social consciousness, even without the trim mustache that every previous actor in the part including Renaldo himself had worn. His outfit is not the ornate regalia he wore later in the TV series but a functional sombrero and bolero jacket. As for his characterization, he told Jon Tuska late in his life, "When I played Cisco I wanted the world to see . . . a man of generosity. . . . Cisco was a friend to a better world. That's the way I saw him. . . . But he wasn't above breaking a señorita's heart" (444).

Cisco's compañero in the Inter-American films was again called Pancho, as he had been when the part was played by Martín Garralaga in the original Krasne-Renaldo trio and by Chris-Pin Martin in the last two films with Roland. But Krasne wanted someone different for the role, and finally settled on the actor who most of us would say was predestined for it.

Leo Carrillo was a native Californian, born in Los Angeles on August 6, 1881, to one of the state's most distinguished families. His great-grandfather, Carlos Antonio Carrillo, had been California's first provisional governor and his father was the first mayor of Santa Monica. Leo's parents wanted him to be a priest, but after studying for a while at Los Angeles' Loyola University, the young man joined the Southern Pacific Railway's engineering department and, when not on the job, amused himself drawing cartoons and imitating railroad laborers' accents:

Spanish, French, Italian, even Chinese. Then he took an art course, moved to northern California, and became a staff cartoonist for the *San Francisco Examiner*.

What developed into a new career that lasted half a century began one night at the Orpheum Theatre when a scheduled vaudeville act failed to show up and Carrillo suddenly found himself on stage as an instant replacement. He proved so popular that the Orpheum management sent him down to Los Angeles for a three-week engagement and that in turn led to years of touring the country in vaudeville. His specialty was humorous monologues delivered in foreign accents, and one day in Chicago he happened to take in the act of a young performer named Will Rogers and talked him into supplementing his riding and roping tricks with a monologue of his own.

Carrillo graduated from vaudeville to the legitimate stage with a part in the musical comedy *Fads and Fancies* (1915). His biggest stage hit was as a good-hearted Italian American dressmaker in *Lombardi, Ltd.* (1917), which was written expressly for him and in which he barnstormed the country for years. In the New York cast with him, as we've seen, was a young man named Warner Baxter, who went on to become the talking movies' first Cisco.

In 1927, at the dawn of talkies, Carrillo came to Hollywood to make a short series of comic monologues as "The Italian Humorist." He played an Italian in his first feature, *Mister Antonio* (Tiffany, 1929), and quickly became stereotyped as a gangster or nightclub owner in early talkies. His first appearance both as a Latin American and in a Western was opposite *In Old Arizona*'s Dorothy Burgess and John (not yet Johnny) Mack Brown in *Lasca of the Rio Grande* (Universal, 1931), which was discussed in chapter 5.

Anyone studying the credits of the more than seventy features Carrillo acted in before becoming Pancho must be struck by how many times he intersected with someone or something else that was to figure in the Cisco saga. In another Latin-themed Western, *Girl of the Rio* (RKO, 1932, directed by Herbert Brenon), he played opposite Dolores del Río and future Cisco director Norman Foster. The film, as it happens, was a remake of *The Dove* (Schenck, 1928), a late silent in which the same roles had been played by Norma Talmadge, Noah Beery, and the young Gilbert Roland. When the picture was remade yet again as *The Girl and the Gambler* (RKO, 1939), Carrillo repeated his part—with the other members of the triangle portrayed by Steffi Duna and Tim Holt—for a director who fif-

teen years later would be helming several episodes of the Cisco TV series, Lew Landers. In *Four Frightened People* (Paramount, 1934, directed by Cecil B. DeMille) Carrillo had a meaty featured part opposite stars Claudette Colbert and Herbert Marshall, while the actor he would eventually replace in the role of Cisco's sidekick, Chris-Pin Martin, had a bit as a native boatman. In the fifteen-chapter serial *Riders of Death Valley* (Universal, 1941) Carrillo can clearly be heard using the single word for which his Pancho is most fondly remembered: "Lezwent!" He actually played a character named Pancho later the same year, in *The Kid from Kansas* (Universal, 1941). And in his twenty years in movies before joining the Cisco team, he was directed at one time or another by half a dozen of the men who had done or were to do Ciscos: William Nigh (*Men Are Such Fools*, RKO/Jefferson, 1933, and *The Kid from Kansas* and *Escape from Hong Kong*, both Universal, 1941), Herbert I. Leeds (*Arizona Wildcat* and *Chicken Wagon Family*, both 20th Century-Fox, 1939), Lew Landers (*The Girl and the Gambler*, RKO, 1939, and *Crime, Inc.*, PRC, 1945), Irving Cummings (*Lillian Russell*, 20th Century-Fox, 1940), Ford Beebe (*Riders of Death Valley*, Universal, 1941, and *Frontier Badmen*, Universal, 1943), and Christy Cabanne (*Top Sergeant* and *Timber*, both Universal, 1942). Carrillo's last role before he became Pancho was one of his most prestigious, opposite Henry Fonda and Dolores del Río in John Ford's lavish *The Fugitive* (Argosy, 1947).

Apparently, acting in seventy-odd pictures wasn't enough to keep him overbusy. He involved himself in California politics, and in 1942 he crisscrossed the state with gubernatorial candidate Earl Warren, later to become chief justice of the U.S. Supreme Court. When Warren was elected governor, he rewarded Carrillo with an appointment to the State Park Commission, where Leo worked to restore California's old missions and to turn Will Rogers's ranch in Santa Monica into a recreation area. Somehow he also found time to run his own ranch and make it prosper.

Near the end of his life, in a conversation with Jon Tuska, Duncan Renaldo took credit for recruiting Carrillo into the Pancho role. "Leo refused. 'The part, amigo, is that of a buffoon,' he said. 'I am a serious actor, not a buffoon.' I explained to Leo that he wasn't to play it as a buffoon, but rather as a tragic and humane Sancho Panza. Leo said, 'All right. I do it. But only once!'" Carrillo wound up playing the part not once but 161 times: in the five last features and the 156 episodes of the TV series. And, as everyone knows who's seen him, he did play Pancho as a buffoon. "He overdid it," Renaldo admitted to Tuska, "but everyone liked him. His accent was so exaggerated that when we finished a picture no one in the cast or crew could talk normal English anymore" (444). In the features he's often seen smoking, but he dropped the habit when the series migrated to TV.

Of all the character actors and behind-the-scenes people from this last sequence of Cisco features who moved into television with Renaldo and Carrillo and the series itself, one who made a special contribution never received adequate credit and therefore deserves some attention here. Albert Glasser was born in Chicago on January 25, 1916, grew up in southern California, earned a music scholarship to USC and, when he graduated, talked his way into a copyist's job in the music department of Warner Brothers, working under titans like Max Steiner and Erich Wolfgang Korngold, later moving to MGM as an assistant to Dmitri Tiomkin. His first screen credit was for *The Monster Maker* (PRC, 1944), a Grade Z horror pic starring J. Carrol Naish, Ralph Morgan,

and Tala Birell. "For $250," he told an interviewer for *Filmfax* (February–March 1991), "I was to compose, orchestrate, copy, conduct, and work with the music cutter! If I didn't want it, they had ten guys waiting." The next year, as mentioned briefly in chapter 7, he was hired by Phil Krasne to write the scores for Monogram's first two Cisco features with Renaldo, *The Cisco Kid Returns* and *In Old New Mexico*. Four years later, with Krasne and Renaldo back as producer and star after the Gilbert Roland hiatus, Glasser was brought in again, this time as both composer and director of the Cisco score. The rousing Latinesque theme under the credits of all five Inter-American features became familiar to a huge audience during the fifties when it was used—without ever being credited to Glasser—for the opening of each episode of the TV series. Glasser died on May 4, 1998.

Brought in to direct the first three features was Wallace Fox, who was born March 8, 1896, in Purcell, a settlement in what was then Oklahoma Indian territory. His middle initial was W, and if his full name were something like White Fox or Walking

Duncan Renaldo reprised his role as the Cisco Kid in the 1949 film *The Valiant Hombre*, which featured Stanley Andrews (center) and John Litel (right).

Fox he would be the one and only Native American director of B Westerns, but I haven't been able to confirm this speculation. Fox studied at West Texas Military Academy in San Antonio, served in the navy during World War I, and in 1919 got a job as prop man at a movie studio in Fort Lee, New Jersey. After working as an assistant director at First National (1921-25) and FBO (1926-27), he became a full-fledged director, making several FBO Westerns that starred Bob Steele. With the coming of talkies and FBO's mutation into RKO, Fox started drifting from one small studio to another and directing whatever came along, which happened to include a hunk of junk called *Trapped in Tia Juana* (Fanchon Royer, 1932), starring Edwina Booth and the young Duncan Renaldo.

Fox spent the middle 1930s at RKO, where he directed two rather dull non-series Westerns that are probably his best known films: *Powdersmoke Range* (1935) with Harry Carey and Hoot Gibson and *Yellow Dust* (1936) with Richard Dix. Between 1938 and 1945, Fox's principal base was Monogram and his chief job was directing East Side Kids flicks. In between times he'd do a few B Westerns like *The Mexicali Kid* and *Gun Packer* (both 1938) with Jack Randall and, on loanout to Columbia, *The Lone Star Vigilantes* (1941) and *Bullets for Bandits* (1942) with Bill Elliott and Tex Ritter. Historically perhaps his most important B Western was *The Ghost Rider* (Monogram, 1943), first of the almost endless Johnny Mack Brown series with which the studio replaced the Buck Jones cycle after Buck's tragic death. In 1945 and 1946 Fox produced and directed all seven entries in Universal's short-lived B Western series starring Kirby Grant, then spent a brief stint at Columbia directing yawnful serials like *Jack Armstrong* (1947, starring John Hart) and *The Vigilante* (1947, starring Ralph Byrd). None of his features for Monogram seems to have been produced by Phil Krasne, but it was probably the Monogram connection that led to his being hired by Inter-American.

First and best of the three Cisco features Fox directed was *The Valiant Hombre* (1949), a neat little picture with exactly what any good B Western needed: a simple story (scripted this time by Adele Buffington) and plenty of action. The main villain and the female lead were played respectively by John Litel and Barbara Billingsley, neither of whom had appeared in many Westerns, but the cast was filled out by shoot-'em-up regulars like Stanley Andrews, Lee "Lasses" White, and Gene Roth, with Terry Frost and stunt wizard David Sharpe in unbilled bit parts.

The picture opens with a nice little burst of action as Cisco and Pancho are chased by a posse across the desert landscape to the New Mexico border. Actually, the sheriff (Hank Bell, uncredited) just wants to tell this latest and most law-abiding version of Cisco that he's entitled to a reward for capturing an outlaw gang two years before, but our heroes are so used to running from men with badges that they do it by instinct. When they pull up at an unlikely road crossing sign in the middle of the New Mexican wilderness, Cisco determines their next destination by tossing a knife at the various signposts with his eyes shut. This is how they wind up in the town of Brownsville.

On the sidewalk in front of the Red Slipper saloon they encounter Joe Haskins (Guy Beach), an old codger who's vainly trying to coax a despondent little dog called Daisy into taking some meat. When Cisco gets the pooch to eat, Haskins explains that Daisy belongs to Paul Mason, a young mining engineer from Boston who disappeared a week ago after announcing in the Red Slipper that he'd struck gold. On orders from saloonkeeper Lon Lansdell (John Litel), Pete the bartender (Gene Roth) shoots the old man on the street before he can say any more, then claims he saw Cisco commit the murder.

Cisco and Pancho are locked up by Sheriff George Dodge (Stanley Andrews) but stay behind bars only briefly thanks to Daisy, who brings them the keys to their cell in her mouth while Deputy Clay (Ralph Peters) is snoring up a storm. Instead of racing out of town as we might have expected, Cisco and Pancho visit the local undertaker, a genial soul who comes out with one-liners like "It's never too late to be dead." Cisco borrows the bullet that killed Haskins, goes back to the sheriff's office, and proves his innocence by showing that the old man was killed not by a .45 like his own guns, but by a .38.

While the sheriff arrests Pete the bartender, Cisco learns at Brownsville's land office that no new claims have been filed in the past week and concludes that Paul Mason is still alive and being held prisoner somewhere. When gunman Red (Terry Frost, uncredited) kills the bartender in his cell, Cisco becomes certain that the man behind the two murders and Mason's disappearance is Lansdell. In a sequence that adds nothing to the plot, Pancho manipulates two gamblers in the Red Slipper (one of them ace stuntman David Sharpe, uncredited) into a fierce brawl. Where earlier features in the series tended to avoid action, this one throws it in on every possible occasion.

The next day, while searching Mason's cabin, Cisco discovers that the missing man has a sister

In *The Gay Amigo* (1949), Duncan Renaldo and Leo Carrillo appear with the diminutive Armida Vendrell, a four-foot-eleven actress who was born in the Mexican state of Sonora and became a leading lady in low-budget adventure films of the thirties and forties.

named Linda. On the trail again, he stops for a chat with Whiskers (Lee "Lasses" White), the driver of a passing stagecoach on the way to Brownsville with a beautiful but imperious female inside. Only when the coach reaches town does Cisco learn that the woman is Linda Mason (Barbara Billingsley), and that she's been sent for by Lansdell. Unfortunately, she's too stubborn to believe anything Cisco tells her. Meanwhile, Lansdell rides out, crosses a swaying suspension bridge familiar to all lovers of Westerns and serials, and enters the shack where his men have been trying to make Paul Mason (John James) reveal the location of his gold strike. Mason refuses to take Lansdell's word that Linda is under his control. Later back at the Red Slipper, Daisy keeps sniffing at Lansdell's trouser legs and Cisco figures the saloonkeeper has seen Mason recently.

Before Lansdell can kidnap Linda, Cisco and Pancho spirit her from the town hotel on a pretext and bring her to Mason's cabin, where all three are then captured by the gang. Lansdell leaves three men to guard Cisco and Pancho while he and the others escort Linda to where they're holding her brother. From this point on the action never stops. Cisco and Pancho overpower the three guards, tie them loosely, wait for them to get free, and trail them to the shack on the far side of the suspension bridge. They besiege the place and kill or capture the outlaws, with Cisco tossing Lansdell into the river far below after a decently directed fistfight along the bridge. Later, when Paul offers his rescuers a share in the gold mine, Cisco refuses and explains to Pancho, in words that might have been written by Gilbert Roland, "Pancho, we have the richest mine in the whole world. Every morning and every evening it fills the sky with gold. And no man can take it away from us." On this note they ride out of the frame.

Their next adventure was *The Gay Amigo* (1949), a weaker effort directed by Fox from a screenplay by Doris Schroeder that borrowed two characters (the mercenary dance hall girl and the bumptious cavalry sergeant) and at least one scene from 20th Century-Fox's 1940 *Lucky Cisco Kid*. The cast included B Western fixtures like Joe Sawyer, Fred Kohler, Jr., and Kenneth MacDonald, with the tiny part of the lieutenant going to Clayton Moore, who later in 1949 began his long and legendary TV career as the Lone Ranger.

This film also opens with a chase, but for once Cisco and Pancho aren't the ones pursued. At the Arizona-Mexico border they see a cavalry troop chasing what seems to be a gang of Mexican bandits, who get away across the line but lose one man in the running gun battle. If Captain Lewis (Kenneth MacDonald) had bothered to recover the bandit's body, this picture would have been over in a few minutes. Instead he watches through field glasses, recognizes Cisco as he and Pancho ride up to the fallen outlaw, and jumps to the conclusion that Cisco is the leader of the gang. As they examine the body, Cisco recognizes the dead man as outlaw Vic Harmon in Mexican disguise and feels an obligation to help the cavalry capture the bandits who are framing his people for their crimes. At the cavalry post Cisco encounters loudmouthed Sergeant McNulty (Joe Sawyer) and makes a fool of him by breaking a horse that bucked the sergeant off. Before they can report what they've discovered, a lieutenant (Clayton Moore) recognizes Cisco and sounds the alarm. In the film's second chase, Cisco and Pancho escape as usual by hiding in the rocks.

As they enter the nearby town, the cavalrymen once again are on their heels. Cisco takes cover in a deserted cantina, starts flirting at once with the barmaid Rosita (Armida), and, in a sequence more or less borrowed from *Lucky Cisco Kid*, hides in her room while McNulty, who thinks Rosita belongs to him, tries vainly to search the place. Just when Cisco and Pancho think they've tricked the troops into riding out of town, McNulty returns and gets the drop on them. At the post they insist on their innocence to Captain Lewis, who pretends to accept their story and lets them go, but Cisco recognizes that Lewis doesn't believe him and so doesn't bother to report that the Mexican bandits are gringos. On Lewis's orders, McNulty follows Cisco and Pancho into town.

At the offices of the Arizona *Globe*, while editor Stoneham (Walter Baldwin) is letting him read back issues of the paper covering the Mexican bandit raids, Cisco overhears Ed Paulsen (Sam Flint) drop in and tell Stoneham he's going to leave on the afternoon coach with a petition for Arizona's statehood that he's taking to Washington. When they see McNulty ineptly shadowing them, Cisco and Pancho decide to make him look ridiculous again and march him to the cantina where Rosita is singing. Cisco notices that she's wearing a belt identical to the distinctive belt worn by the dead Pete Harmon—whether it's the same one or a twin is never explained—and learns that she was given hers by Bill Brack (Fred Kohler, Jr.), the local blacksmith. Leaving McNulty tied up and fuming in the empty cantina, they drop in at the blacksmith shop, where Brack lets slip that he knows Harmon is dead. McNulty stops them as they're leaving and challenges Cisco to a fistfight, the only such scene in the film, with Fox relying heavily on long shots to mask Renaldo's double. Cisco and Pancho leave town but come back that night and, while in the barber shop, see a special edition of the *Globe* reporting that Paulsen was killed in the stagecoach but saying nothing about the statehood petition he was carrying. On this flimsy evidence Cisco concludes that editor Stoneham is behind the fake Mexican bandits.

The next day our caballeros launch a complex plan to trap the gang. First they intercept a stagecoach, and while Pancho amuses the passengers with his antics, Cisco sneaks into town and forces Stoneham to print another special edition with the news that the Mexican gang has attacked the coach. He locks the editor in a closet, steals a strongbox from his safe, and rides through town distributing the paper, then rejoins Pancho and lets the coach continue on its way. Stoneham refuses to believe that Brack and his fake Mexicans didn't attack the coach, and Brack refuses to believe that the strongbox with all the gang's loot was hijacked from Stoneham. The coach reaches town and everyone learns that there were only two holdup men. Suddenly the cavalry troop rides in, and Cisco and Pancho let themselves be seen and chased away, a well-directed—if all too brief—sequence. That night Cisco surprises Brack at home and convinces him that Stoneham faked the newspaper office robbery but claims that he himself has a new crime set up that will require all of Brack's men. The gullible blacksmith shows him the way to the gang's hideout. Meanwhile in the cantina, Pancho pretends to have broken with Cisco and tells Rosita that his former compadre is going to rob the mine wagon at Lopez Rocks the next day at noon. As expected, Rosita tips off McNulty and the cavalry.

In the morning Brack and his men in their Mexican outfits come across the border to pull the job. The driver of the "mine wagon" is Pancho, who pretends to be shot when Cisco fires at him and sends the wagon into a furious runaway with everyone in the gang giving chase. When the wagon is halted, Cisco and the "dead" Pancho get the drop on the outlaws without a scintilla of action. The cavalry troop rides up according to plan and Cisco turns over his prisoners—including Stoneham, whom Pancho had kidnapped and stuffed in the ore wagon—with the mischievous claim that the entire scheme to capture the gang was the brainchild of McNulty.

Third and last of Wallace Fox's contributions to the saga was *The Daring Caballero* (1949), from a screenplay by Betty Burbridge based on an original story by Frances Kavanaugh. Most of the featured cast members were strangers to the shoot-'em-up genre, and action took a back seat to plot, but, as Don Miller said in *Hollywood Corral* about the Inter-American Ciscos in general, "there were worse Westerns on the market . . ." (184).

Stopping at a mission as is their custom, Cisco and Pancho find Padre Leonardo (Pedro de Córdoba) worried about Bobby Del Río (Mickey Little), a young boy who's been staying at the mission but has run away. When they locate the boy, he says he left to find his father and they agree to do the job for him. Back at the mission the padre tells Bobby that his father is going on a long journey he must make alone. Once the boy is safely out of earshot, the priest explains to Cisco and Pancho that Bobby's father, Patrick Del Río (David Leonard), formerly the town banker, is to hang in the morning for a murder he swears he didn't commit.

A title card for *The Daring Caballero* (1949), director Wallace Fox's last Cisco Kid film

Norma Talmadge, Noah Beery, and Gilbert Roland starred in *The Dove* (1928).

In *Lasca of the Rio Grande* (1932), Leo Carrillo appeared with Dorothy Burgess, who played
the love interest fought over by the Cisco Kid and Sergeant Dunn in *In Old Arizona* (1929).

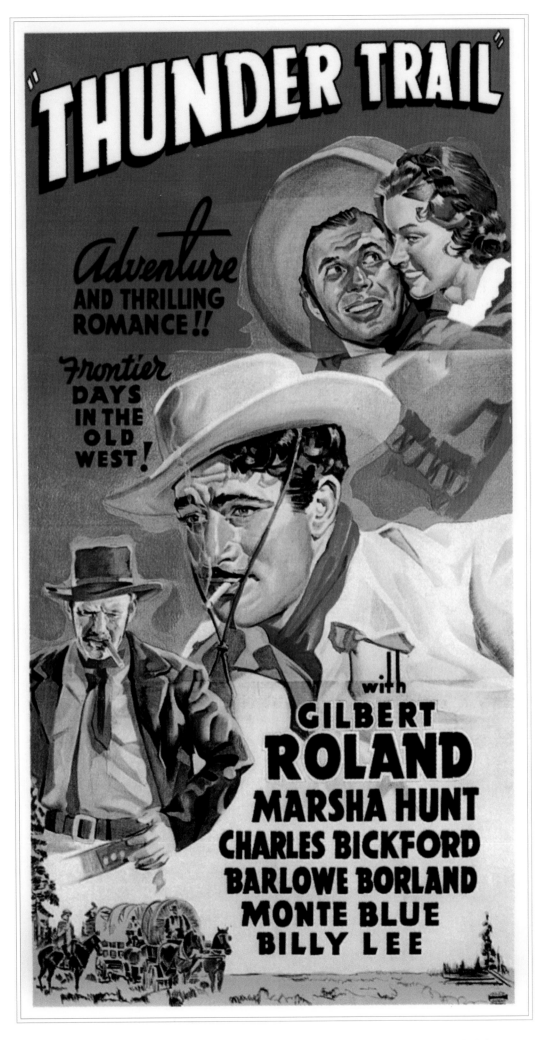

In *Thunder Trail* (1937), Gilbert Roland, with the ubiquitous cigarette in his mouth, played Arizona Dick Ames, the same sort of romantic and virile character that was typical of his Cisco Kid roles.

Cisco (Duncan Renaldo) offers to help a damsel in distress (Barbara Billingsley) in *The Valiant Hombre* (1948). The stagecoach driver is Lee "Lasses" White.

Cisco (Duncan Renaldo, right) and Pancho (Leo Carrillo, left) get the upper hand in *The Valiant Hombre* (1948).

Lobby card from *The Daring Caballero* (1949), featuring Duncan Renaldo, Leo Carrillo, and Charles Halton

The Cisco Kid (Duncan Renaldo) connects with a rival in *Satan's Cradle* (1949).

T he noble bandit films in general and Cisco Kid features in particular made ample use of romance (or a more intense version of the same) as well as peril. In fact, in much of their content and publicity, the amorous and the perilous were intertwined.

Title card from *The Return of the Cisco Kid* (1939)

Title card from *The Gay Caballero* (1940)

Title card from *The Girl from San Lorenzo* (1950), starring Duncan Renaldo and Leo Carrillo

Title card from *South of the Rio Grande* (1945), starring Duncan Renaldo, Martín Garralaga, and Armida

Title card from *King of the Bandits* (1947), starring Gilbert Roland and Chris-Pin Martin

Title card from *South of Monterey* (1946), picturing Marjorie Riordan, Gilbert Roland, and Frank Yaconelli

Title card from *Robin Hood of Monterey* (1947)

Title card from *Riding the California Trail* (1947)

A t first blush, the sword does not appear to be a likely weapon for the Western. Of course, Westerns make use of six-shooters, derringers, rifles, and other firearms, as well as whips, which became the trademark of some characters. The sword, however, has a special place in Latina/o good bandit narratives, and it can be traced to earlier, classic works such as *The Three Musketeers*.

Douglas Fairbanks played Zorro and Don Diego in this 1920 film. Fairbanks initiated the elements of sword fighting, daring escapes, and exceptional athleticism that would characterize all filmic Zorros.

Gilbert Roland demonstrated his swordsmanship in *The Gay Cavalier* (1946) and *Riding the California Trail* (1947).

Our amigos need to know no more. That evening at suppertime Cisco ties up and then impersonates the guard bringing the prisoner his last meal. He and Pancho break Del Río out of jail, elude the posse that chases them, return to the mission, hide Del Río in the wine cellar, and listen to his story. He was convicted of the murder of one of his tellers and the embezzlement of $90,000 on the perjured testimony of E. J. Hodges (Charles Halton), who is now president of the bank, and of Deputy Scott (Edmund Cobb), who is now the town marshal, with the connivance of prosecutor Brady (Stephen Chase), currently the mayor.

The next morning as Marshal Scott is sending out several posses to hunt for Del Río, Cisco and Pancho ride into town. Pancho goes to buy food for Del Río and Cisco and, dropping in at the mayor's office, recognizes Brady as Barton, an outlaw he used to know. Brady suspects that Cisco was behind Del Río's escape and orders Marshal Scott to arrest him. While Cisco is at the bank exchanging $1,000 in gold for paper money he hopes will prove to be part of the missing $90,000, Pancho meets an attractive young woman (Kippee Valez, playing a character of the same name) and tries to impress her by claiming to be the famous Cisco Kid—just at the right moment for Marshal Scott to overhear and throw him in jail. Cisco gets his partner out by forcing Mayor Brady at gunpoint to phone the marshal's office—lucky for him this frontier town has telephone service—and order Scott to release the prisoner. Two of the conspirators' gunmen trail Cisco and Pancho out of town but are caught and left unhorsed and hogtied to each other.

Mayor Brady suspects that Del Río is hiding at the mission to be near his son and sends out Marshal Scott with a search warrant. In the padre's wine cellar, Del Río tells Cisco and Pancho that before the $90,000 turned up missing he had made a list of the serial numbers on some of the bills and entrusted it to Kippee, who is a bank employee and the daughter of his dearest friend. He writes a note asking her to give Cisco and Pancho the list, but as they're leaving the cellar they hear the sounds of the marshal's search party approaching and hide behind wine barrels with Del Río until the danger is past.

Pancho takes the note to Kippee, who of course is the woman to whom he'd passed himself off as Cisco, and learns that she keeps the list at the bank. Meanwhile Cisco burglarizes the mayor's office, finds the key to a bank safe deposit box, and is caught red-handed by Brady himself. After a well-staged brawl between the two, Cisco escapes and rejoins Pancho, with the marshal and a posse hot on their horses' hooves. This neatly directed chase sequence ends as usual with Cisco and Pancho taking cover behind tall rocks as the posse gallops by.

They return to Kippee's house and persuade her to let them into the bank in the middle of the night so they can look at the list of serial numbers, which turns out not to match the numbers on the bills Cisco got at the bank earlier. Cisco then gets Kippee to open the bank vault so he can use the key he stole and take a peek inside the mayor's safe deposit box, which of course turns out to be the hiding place of the missing $90,000. Mayor Brady, who realizes that Cisco took his key, makes a late-night visit to the bank with Hodges. Cisco, Pancho, and Kippee hide behind some furniture and, when the mayor and banker enter the vault to see if their loot is still in the deposit box, lock them in. Then Cisco sends Pancho for Judge Perkins (Frank Jaquet), the jurist who presided at Del Río's trial. The best line in the movie is Pancho's description of this portly man as "the circular judge." Marshal Scott returns to town from the earlier chase sequence and is killed shooting it out with Cisco in the street.

In the morning, with the judge and a jury sitting in the bank, Cisco opens the vault, releases the mayor and Hodges, opens Brady's deposit box, and finds it empty. It takes him only a moment to figure out that during the night, after Hodges had passed out for lack of air, Brady had taken the key to the banker's own deposit box and hidden the money there. A split-second action flurry leaves the mayor dead and Hodges in custody. With Bobby and his father reunited, Cisco and Pancho gallop away to new adventure elsewhere.

For Wallace Fox, that fadeout was the end of the Cisco trail. He returned to Monogram and spent the next two years producing and directing low-budget oaters starring Johnny Mack Brown or Whip Wilson, most of them drearily routine but at least one (*Silver Raiders*, 1951, with Whip Wilson) surprisingly watchable. Then Fox moved to TV and joined the directorial stable at Gene Autry's Flying A Productions, churning out episodes of *The Gene Autry Show* and the Jock Mahoney series *The Range Rider*, then contracting with Poverty Row producer

Rudolph C. Flothow to direct the first (and most hackneyed) thirteen episodes of the Jon Hall series *Ramar of the Jungle*. Fox died on June 30, 1958.

The director of the fourth Inter-American Cisco feature was another old-timer with a long track record. Ford Beebe was born in Grand Rapids, Michigan, on November 20, 1888, and, like his contemporary Raoul Walsh, enjoyed a freewheeling and adventurous young manhood on both sides of the Rio Grande. In 1914 he was hired by Universal as a $25-a-week press agent but soon graduated to writing scenarios for the studio's two-reelers. He spent most of the twenties writing scripts and, to use his phrase, serving as "director general" for a long string of silent shoot-'em-ups starring and nominally directed by Leo Maloney, who died in November 1929 after a booze binge to celebrate the sale of his first talkie. Beebe spent the early years of the Depression and the transition to talking films working as and where he could and wound up at Nat

Levine's Mascot Pictures, writing and later directing cliffhanger serials like *Shadow of the Eagle* (1932), starring John Wayne, and *The Last of the Mohicans* (1932, codirected by B. Reeves Eason), starring Harry Carey. Between 1936 and 1945 he was back at Universal, directing ten features (including three B Westerns with Johnny Mack Brown) and codirecting a staggering twenty-three serials, five of them Westerns. When his Universal contract ran out, he started freelancing at Monogram and other small studios and was hired by Krasne to direct the next Cisco adventure, *Satan's Cradle* (1949).

The screenplay for this one was credited to Jack Benton, but the name is a transparent disguise for veteran B Western writer J. Benton Cheney, and the script is yet another version of an old Cheney standard in which the tough dance hall girl who heads the town's corrupt element falls in love with the hero trying to bring her down and ends up taking the bullet her jealous male partner-in-crime has

Title card from *Satan's Cradle* (1949), featuring Duncan Renaldo, Leo Carrillo, and Ann Savage

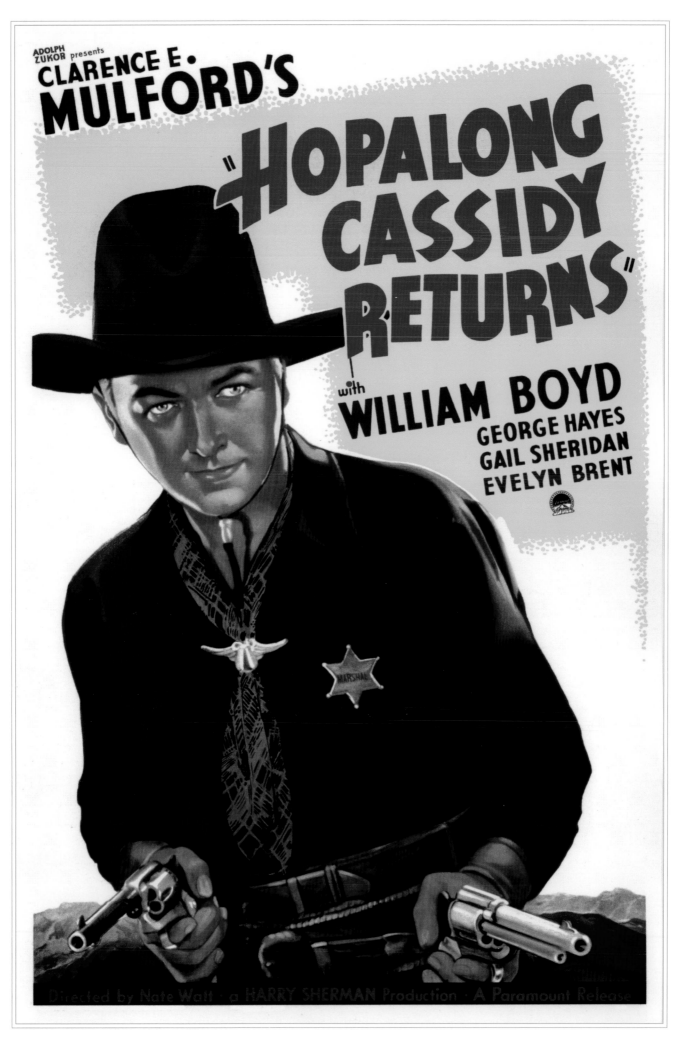

William Boyd, George Hayes, and William Janney (as Hopalong's kid brother) starred
in the seventh film in the Hopalong Cassidy series, *Hopalong Cassidy Returns* (1936).

fired at his honest rival. This storyline was first brought to cinematic life in *Hopalong Cassidy Returns* (Paramount, 1936), starring William Boyd (who else?) and directed by Nate Watt from a screenplay by Harrison Jacobs. The dance hall woman attracted to Cassidy was portrayed by Evelyn Brent and the spurned partner who kills her by Stephen Morris, later and better known as Morris Ankrum. Cheney got into the act five years later when he was hired to rework the 1936 script for another Cassidy picture, *Wide Open Town* (Paramount, 1941), directed by Lesley Selander. Evelyn Brent reprised her role as the dance hall woman and Morris Ankrum had a character part, but the role of her furious ex-lover went to Victor Jory and this time she survived the climactic gunbattle. Cheney grew so attached to the plot that from here on he treated it as his own and recycled it for at least two of Monogram's Johnny Mack Brown films, both helmed by once and future Cisco director Lambert Hillyer. In *The Gentleman from Texas* (Monogram, 1946), Claudia Drake played the saloon lady and

Tristram Coffin her partner. Hillyer gave the role to Coffin again in *Land of the Lawless* (Monogram, 1947), but the female lead went to June Harrison.

Two years later, in *Satan's Cradle*, the dance hall gal was portrayed by Ann Savage, who is best known as the psychotic woman in Edgar G. Ulmer's zero-budget film noir classic *Detour* (PRC, 1945), and her spurned lover by B-movie gangster Douglas Fowley. What distinguishes this version is the overtly religious element Cheney added to the basic script and the abundance of action scenes, far more than usual in B Westerns of the late forties or in any other Cisco feature except perhaps *The Gay Caballero*.

The film opens with Reverend Henry Lane (Byron Foulger) preaching on the main street of Silver City, proclaiming that the town has become a den of iniquity since being taken over by Lil (Ann Savage), the owner of the Silver Lode Saloon. Gunmen summoned by Lil's lawyer and lover Steve Gentry (Douglas Fowley) beat up the parson and kick him out of town while Gentry in celebration buys drinks for the house.

The Cisco Kid and Pancho save Silver City from the schemes of a crooked lawyer (Douglas Fowley, in business suit) in *Satan's Cradle* (1949).

Cisco and Pancho are heading for Silver City because Cisco has heard that a wealthy widow has moved in. Despite having *enamoradas* all over the West, our caballero wants to try his luck with this one too. "Just because a man has enjoyed a plum and a few grapes, must he turn his back on a peach when he finds one?" They come upon Lane, beaten and left for dead on the trail, and care for him in a manner recalling the story of the Good Samaritan. (This may be the only Western in which two men of Catholic background refer to a Protestant minister as "padre"). Lane tells his rescuers how Lil and Gentry took over the town on the basis of Lil's claim to be the widow of Silver City's founder, Jim Mason, who was killed in a supposedly accidental cave-in at his San Miguel mine. A scene back in town, with Lil reminding Gentry that she won't stand for any killings in the course of their scheme, reveals to us that she's a fake with a forged marriage certificate.

Cisco and Pancho accompany the preacher back to Silver City, where Lane announces in the saloon that Sunday services will be held as usual. Cisco engages in a long, drawn-out brawl with Idaho (George De Normand), one of the gunmen who beat the parson, and then starts flirting with Lil, telling her, "I shall see you in church—I hope." Lil forbids Gentry to kill Cisco and promises to use her own wiles on him instead. While Cisco and Pancho are helping to rebuild Lane's church, Lil saunters by and swaps romantic banter, with Cisco refusing the invitation to join her and she likewise turning down his offer to reform. A little later Idaho tries to shoot Cisco on the street and winds up dead himself. Lil threatens to expose Gentry's whole scheme unless he leaves Cisco alone.

To keep Lane safe until Sunday, Cisco and Pancho camp out with him in a place known as Satan's Saddle. Cisco is convinced that Lil was never married to Jim Mason but can't prove it and decides to reach her by appealing to the spark of good that both he and Lane believe to be in all of us. (Why this doesn't apply to Gentry and his gunmen is never explained or even explored.) Returning to the saloon, Cisco finds Lil in a revealing black evening

Lobby card from the final Duncan Renaldo Cisco feature, *The Girl from San Lorenzo* (1950). The Cisco impersonator (center) is master stuntman David Sharpe.

gown, plays blackjack with her, and catches her in a slip when she claims to have married Mason on a different day of the month than stated in her forged certificate. Gentry gets the drop on Cisco with a concealed pistol, but a warning to Pancho in Spanish allows the amigos to get away unscathed.

Some time later, one of the gang locates the camp at Satan's Saddle. In an action sequence that runs close to ten minutes, the outlaws raid the camp but are outgunned, and everyone except Gentry and his henchman Rocky (Buck Bailey) is killed. The two survivors trail Cisco and Pancho to the San Miguel mine. Cisco finds a piece of burnt fuse in the tunnel where Jim Mason died, but just then Gentry sets off another dynamite charge like the one he used to kill Mason. Of course, Cisco and Pancho are unhurt and find another way out of the mine shaft.

Back in town, Gentry boasts that he's killed Cisco and the outraged Lil decides to dump both him and their scheme. That night Cisco and Pancho return for a showdown but are spotted on their way to Lil's house, where she's packing her clothes. Lil is so glad to see him alive and so disgusted with Gentry that she agrees to tell the sheriff all she knows. Gentry shoots at her through the window. In the original version of this story, *Hopalong Cassidy Returns*, the woman was killed at this point, and in most of Cheney's subsequent rewrites she was at least wounded. This time she isn't even scratched. Cisco pursues Gentry and shoots him dead after another ten-minute action sequence with a chase on foot through a nightbound wood. Returning to town, he discovers that Lil is waiting for him in the church and expecting him to turn her over to the law but decides that her repentance is punishment enough and sets off with Pancho for a new adventure.

Ford Beebe was in his early sixties when he made this fine little Western but was nowhere near ready to call it quits. He went on to direct the first two entries in a new Don Barry series at Lippert—*The Dalton Gang* and the magnificent *Red Desert* (both 1949)—then returned to Monogram where he made eleven features in the Bomba the Jungle Boy series starring Johnny Sheffield. In the middle fifties he directed some episodes of the *Adventures of Champion* TV series (1955-56) for Gene Autry's Flying A Productions. When he was over eighty he came out of retirement to direct a pair of Alaskan wildlife movies, one on his own and the other in tandem with Tay Garnett (1894-1977), another old-time action director who didn't know how to stop working. Beebe died in 1978 at the age of eighty-nine.

At the end of *Satan's Cradle* Cisco had told Pancho that their next stop would be a town called San Lorenzo. Beebe knew this because he'd already written and sold the script for what would become the final Cisco feature, *The Girl from San Lorenzo* (1950). But his commitments at Lippert and Monogram made it impossible for him to direct this one himself and the man Krasne hired in his place proved a huge disappointment.

Derwin Abrahams was born in 1903 and learned what he knew of the B Western business during the years between 1936 and 1941 when he worked as an assistant director on Paramount's Hopalong Cassidy series. The first films he directed were a pair of lackluster Cassidys, *Border Vigilantes* and *Secret of the Wastelands* (both 1941), which were as good as his work ever got. He spent most of the forties at Columbia churning out four dull serials and nine routine entries in the Durango Kid series starring Charles Starrett, with an occasional detour to Monogram for a yawnful oater with Johnny Mack Brown or Jimmy Wakely. Like everything else he directed, *The Girl from San Lorenzo* is a bore. Its main interest for us is that it became the bridge on which the Cisco series crossed over from the large to the small screen.

The picture opens with a montage of stock footage and newspaper headlines blaming Cisco and Pancho for an epidemic of stagecoach robberies in the Cactus Wells area and the murder of a local resident named Steve McCarger. The next thing we see is Cisco and Pancho being chased across desert scenery, for no reason they can figure out, by a low-budget posse of three men. This sequence, in which they elude their pursuers by hiding behind a huge rock, provided the footage for the opening credits of the Cisco TV series.

Later in the town of San Lorenzo, they receive a letter in Spanish claiming that Pancho's grandmother is sick in Cactus Wells and needs to see them at once. Cisco recognizes the letter is a fake because the number 7 in the dateline doesn't have a cross-stroke in the Spanish manner, and Pancho also spots the message as a phony for the simple reason that his grandmother died years ago. Before they can leave San Lorenzo to investigate the decoy letter, Tom McCarger (Leonard Penn) starts shooting at

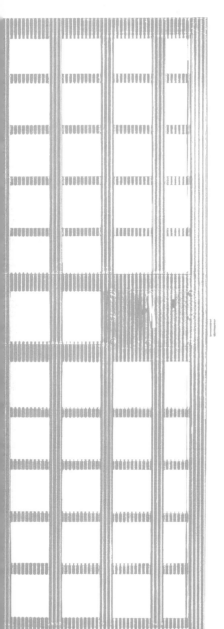

Cisco on the street. Nora Malloy (Jane Adams) saves Cisco's life by grabbing McCarger's arm, and Cisco wounds the man who tried to kill him. While the assailant is being treated by a doctor, Nora tells Cisco that she's on her way to Cactus Wells to marry stagecoach driver Jerry Todd (Bill Lester). When McCarger is well enough to talk, he accuses Cisco of having killed his brother Steve in Cactus Wells and shows a letter from the town's sheriff (Lee Phelps) blaming Cisco for the murder. The compañeros head for Cactus Wells to see what's going on.

Not far from their destination, the outlaws Blackie (David Sharpe) and Wooly (Edmund Cobb), dressed in the Cisco and Pancho outfits they've been using for their crime wave, pull yet another stage holdup, killing the guard and seriously wounding the driver, who happens to be Jerry Todd. The real Cisco and Pancho are riding by at just the right time and place to observe the crime. "Cisco, look at us down there holding up the stagecoach!" Pancho exclaims. Instead of going after their impersonators, they chase the runaway coach and bring it to a halt. Blackie and Wooly see them and know that the men they've framed for their crimes are in the area. The badly wounded Jerry tells Cisco that he's engaged to Nora Malloy, and Cisco and Pancho, despite knowing there's a price on their heads, drive the stagecoach into town.

The sheriff rides out to meet the coach, finds Cisco at the reins, and tries to arrest him, but Cisco throws a tarpaulin in his face and he and Pancho make their getaway. Word goes out over the telegraph wires that Cisco and Pancho have robbed another stage. They stop at Jerry's ranch where Nora is staying and tell her that they had nothing to do with shooting her fiancé. Nora believes him and, when the sheriff and deputies show up with the wounded Jerry, she hides the fugitives in the kitchen, where they later hear a despairing Jerry tell Nora that without an expensive operation he'll never be able to walk again. Cisco and Nora arrange a charade so that Nora will seem to have captured the fugitive pair and earned the reward for them, but the game is interrupted by the sheriff and his deputies, who come back to the ranch and capture them for real.

Cisco and Pancho sit tight in jail until Nora has been paid the reward money, but before they can break out, the job is done for them. Three masked men—Blackie, Wooly, and their sidekick Rusty (Wes Hudman)—slip into the jailhouse, slug the sheriff, lock him in a cell, release Cisco and Pancho, take them to their hideout, and leave them tied up and guarded by another outlaw called Kansas (Don C. Harvey) while they change into their Cisco and Pancho costumes and go off to commit another stage robbery for which our heroes will be blamed. Kansas, keeping watch over the prisoners, lets it slip that the outlaws have secret information about a shipment of gold bullion on the night stage. Pancho wheedles Kansas into giving him a cigarillo to smoke while he's tied up, then drops the smoke and pretends he's on fire, luring Kansas into a position where Cisco can overpower him. They find their horses, intercept the night stage before their impersonators do, and take the express box. When they shoot it open, they discover it's empty, while down the trail the fake Cisco and Pancho stop the coach and find they're too late.

Cisco and Pancho slip back into Cactus Wells, release the sheriff from jail, and explain the whole situation, convincing him that the empty strongbox proves that the man behind the robberies must be the express agent, Cal Ross (Byron Foulger). The three men set a trap. A rock is tossed through Ross's window with a note from Cisco wrapped around it that reads, "I will come for the loot in your office safe before daylight." Ross and Kansas post themselves in the express office and wait to kill Cisco when he shows up. The person who slips into the office, however, is Pancho, who pretends to have broken with his partner, tips them off to what he says is Cisco's plan, and tricks Ross into opening his safe, at which point Cisco and the sheriff effortlessly get the drop on the thieves. The fake Cisco and Pancho and the rest of the gang ride into town just in time to crash the party and add a few minutes of routine climactic action to the picture, culminating in a one-on-one between Cisco and the man who impersonated him.

The final scene of the last Cisco feature is in the quixotic Robin Hood vein. Nora, who has just married Jerry, comes to town and tries to give back the reward money. Cisco and Pancho conspire with the sheriff to put on another charade so that Nora won't feel guilty about using the money for Jerry's operation. The sheriff pretends to have the pair in custody again, Cisco and Pancho pretend to get the drop on him, and, in a rather nice closing shot, they ride off into the rising sun to continue their adventures on the small screen.

The Cisco series migrated to TV under the Krasne regime, but the person most identified with the move was a shrewd businessman named Frederick Ziv (1905-2001), who founded his own advertising agency in Cincinnati around 1931 and got into the entertainment media by developing a country-Western musical show that he sold to both a local radio station and a local sponsor. He soon became a specialist in the packaging and later in the nationwide syndication of radio entertainment, using the money he made from that venture to buy up other businesses that would make syndication even more profitable. One of his acquisitions, for example, was the World Library, a huge collection of recorded music that enabled him to add background scores to his syndicated programs without the hassle of squabbling with ASCAP over royalty payments.

By the late forties Ziv had moved to Chicago and recognized that the syndication of TV shows was the wave of the future. He bought out the General Film Library, a vast assortment of old newsreel and sports footage, and turned the millions of feet of film into *Yesterday's Newsreel* and *Sports Album*, two 15-minute series which he then syndicated around the country as he'd done in the past with his radio programs. The profits from these operations he used to launch his own TV film production company, which took over the Cisco series from Krasne while the earliest episodes were being shot. Ziv sent his salesmen across the country in search of local stations to broadcast the series, reportedly making them wear Cisco sombreros at any out-of-town meetings they attended. Meanwhile, he sold the commercial slots built into each Cisco episode's running time to Interstate Bakeries, whose bread products were distributed to firms around the country for resale to the consumer under those firms' brand names. (In the New York City area where I grew up, the original sponsor was Tip Top bread.) The studio and outdoor facilities needed for production were leased on a short-term basis from various studios until 1955, when Ziv took over the financially troubled Eagle-Lion company with the profits from *Cisco* and other syndicated series like *Boston Blackie* and *I Led Three Lives*. By 1960, having grossed about $11,000,000 from his operations, Ziv sold out to United Artists and retired from TV series production.

Clearly the intent of the Cisco TV series was to continue the movie series seamlessly but on the small screen and at a running time of slightly under thirty minutes per segment rather than slightly over sixty. Not only did Duncan Renaldo and Leo Carrillo carry on their roles as Cisco and Pancho, but all sorts of people out of camera range—director Derwin

Duncan Renaldo and Leo Carrillo starred in 156 television episodes of *The Cisco Kid* from 1950 to 1956.

Abrahams, assistant director Eddie Davis, scriptwriter J. Benton Cheney, cinematographer Kenneth Peach, and composer Albert Glasser, just to name a few—moved straight from the last Cisco feature, *The Girl from San Lorenzo*, into the first Cisco TV episode, "Boomerang," taking part of the feature's storyline with them to boot.

Dave Sharpe doubled Renaldo in the earliest episodes of the series but left for a stunting gig in Europe and was replaced by one of the men who contributed hugely to this book. Troy Melton was born in Jackson, Tennessee, in 1921, moved with his family to southern California during the Depression, served in the Army Air Corps during World War II, then began a career as an actor and stuntman that lasted several decades. He was one of the founding members of the Stuntmen's Association of Motion Pictures, and between 1962 and 1988 he owned the Playboy Restaurant next door to the Paramount studio on Hollywood's Melrose Avenue. He died of cancer on November 15, 1995, but during the last months of his life we spent several hours on the phone talking about his experiences as Duncan Renaldo's double.

"I was working on a Cisco," Melton told me, "doing a small part and working as a utility double," when Dave Sharpe left for Europe and the job opened up. Krasne and his associates

tried out two or three guys, trying to get someone who looked like Duncan who could work with him. I did not look like him. They tried out one or two people who could do the horseback riding, who were good cowboy types, but when it came to fight scenes and the stunts they weren't so good. A couple of others did those things fine but weren't so good with their horseback riding and certain tricks that you needed to do working with horses. I being on the show, they let me try out doing some of the little things like crupper mounts, jumping over the back of the horse, and side mounts and whatnot. I was quite acrobatic. I don't know how it happened, but they informed me that they were going to take me up on location to Pioneertown to do maybe a small part and utility double, but at the same time they were going to test me out in Cisco's outfit. Which they did.

It happened that my first stunt doubling him was a runaway stagecoach that actually did run away. I was supposed to catch it, so I was horseback-chasing it. At a certain point they wanted to see me transfer to the stagecoach, get up on it, and help stop it. They had a tree or a bush as a marker [where filming the scene later was supposed to begin]. Frank Matts was driving and I was trying to catch the coach. When I was finally getting to the point where I could overtake it, I saw that bush and decided that as long as I was doing it I might as well get it on film. So I made my jump and came up over the top. I took two of the horses and Frank took the other two and we stopped the coach. When they got the film back they were happy with it and informed me that I was now Cisco's double.

Meanwhile, Texas-born Bill Catching (1926-2007), who had started out as the horse wrangler for the series, became the double for Carrillo. "They made a body pad for me to double Leo," he remembered when I interviewed him. "I loved it because you'd bounce around in it when you hit the ground."

Bill Catching doubled for Leo Carrillo in the Cisco TV series and played small parts in countless episodes.

One day early in 1950, Catching and Melton were doing a fight on top of a building when they saw two men watching who turned out to be Fred Ziv and Maurice Unger, the new owners of the production company.

"When Ziv came out here," Melton told me,

> he had the rights to a lot of radio. Among his rights was *Boston Blackie,* and Phil Krasne had the rights to *Cisco.* Prior to Ziv coming in here, Phil had made a deal with Jack Gross to do his interiors at California Studios, which used to be Pop [Harry] Sherman's studio. So Krasne and Gross formed a partnership, which later included Ziv when he came out here with *Boston Blackie.* They joined forces and became a unit. As time went by, Ziv took over.
>
> We were operating out of an office on Carroll Drive in Beverly Hills, right off Sunset and Doheny. That's where Phil Krasne's office was, that was where the writing was done. The preparations, shooting boards, and everything were taken care of there. Then we would go out on location to Chatsworth or wherever and shoot our location shots. When there were some interiors that we had to have, we would rent from some independent studio.
>
> We would shoot a lot of location stuff up at Pioneertown. They had prop buildings there, like the exterior of the Red Dog cafe or a Chinese restaurant or whatever. Inside was actually a practical setting. In the Chinese restaurant they had a very good place to eat, and the Red Dog was a beer bar. On weekends or even during the week they sold beer to people who were visiting but we also used it as a set.
>
> Pioneertown was named for the Sons of the Pioneers, Roy Rogers' group. They got the idea of building a location where they could shoot Westerns. Unfortunately they built the street wrong so that you had the sun coming from the wrong direction. Instead of down the street it was coming across, so that you could only shoot certain things in the morning, and then you had to wait and shoot the other things in the afternoon instead of shooting straight down the street with sun. That was a problem we had, but we shot a lot of things on a little insert road below the town.

During production on the first season's episodes, Krasne began looking for a new assistant director to replace the veteran Louis Germonprez, who had started with the series. The producer asked Troy Melton if he could recommend anyone for the job. Melton told me,

> There was a guy named Bob Farfan, a friend of mine who was an assistant director. I recom-

A publicity still of Troy Melton, stunt double for Duncan Renaldo

> mended him and he got an interview. We weren't shooting on that day so I went over to the office. While I was there someone spoke to me and I looked around and it was Eddie Davis. I had worked with him at Monogram. How he came on the interview I don't know.
>
> A little later Phil called me into the office and said, "I saw you talking to Eddie Davis out there. How well do you know him?" I said, "I know him pretty well. I've worked with him." He said, "You know the kind of work we're doing here. What kind of an assistant director is he? With the speed and the kind of stuff we have to do, how do you think he fits in with our program?" Well, I asked Bob Farfan to come down on the interview but I told Phil the truth. "Eddie's a very good assistant director. I've worked with him on those quickies at Monogram. I've even worked with him on

some second units when he's directed on them. He's very good and he would fit in with our program very well."

This was how Davis got the job as assistant director, but he soon found himself promoted. "When Ziv took over," Bill Catching explained to me, "Babe Unger was left as the head of the studio, and he didn't know anything about movies and studios. So after they'd been wandering about the sets with stopwatches and talking to people, they realized that the most knowledgeable man in the company was Eddie Davis, so they made him production manager. . . . Eddie's desk was in the front of the room and Babe's desk was behind him. Every transaction that took place went through

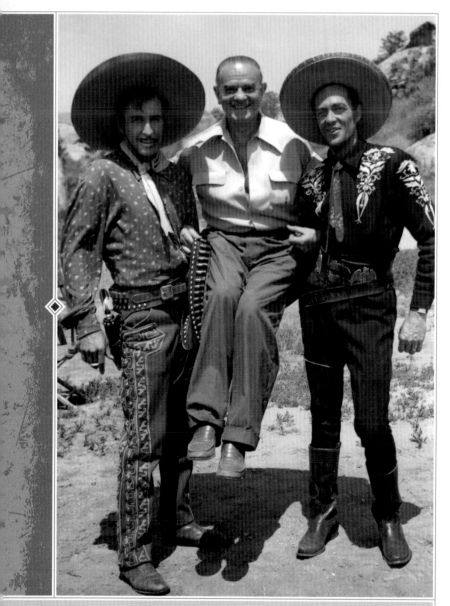

Bill Catching (left) and Troy Melton (right) on the set with a visiting Chrysler Motors executive in 1950

Eddie Davis. Babe sat behind with a secretary, and all he did was listen and make notes for possibly six months." During that time Davis "ran the studio. That guy could—oh, he did a ten-man job and did it well. Today in films there's ten guys doing what Eddie used to do." The first twenty-six episodes of the series were ready for broadcast by the fall of 1950.

Looking back from almost sixty years' distance, most Western enthusiasts would probably agree that the smartest money spent on the series was what it took to shoot every episode in color, even though color TV didn't exist at the time. "It was Kenny Peach's idea," Bill Catching told me. "Sixteen mm Cinecolor was cheaper than 35 mm black and white. You could open the lens up and you got much more light out of 16 mm than you could get out of the flat lenses. . . . With the 16 mm you could speed the camera up a little and have the people walk slow. We used to do a fight in slow motion."

Not so smart was the decision to cut costs by organizing each season's work so that the same director would shoot two, three, and occasionally four thirty-minute episodes at a time with the same core group of actors who would often have the same character names in each episode even though they were supposed to be different people. This ploy boggled the minds of the youngsters in the audience and was recognized as a cheapskate gimmick by the older kids and adults. But at least the actors who played these multiple parts were welcome friends to viewers who had grown up on theatrical B Westerns. Much less welcome was the decision to use the boring music of Albert Glasser for the sound tracks of the first season's twenty-six episodes, and the worst move of all was to entrust the initial thirteen segments to Derwin Abrahams, a director whose work never rose above routine competence.

There isn't a single visually exciting moment in the entire six and a half hours of footage Abrahams contributed to the series, and the amount of sloppiness he perpetrated has to be seen to be believed. Take the third episode, "Rustling," whose vanishing cattle herd plot was lifted from a Hopalong Cassidy feature, *Twilight on the Trail* (Paramount, 1941), on which Abrahams had served as assistant director. In one scene in a rancher's office he shows us a 1950s lead pencil complete with eraser. Later in an outdoor sequence, a single shot is fired and a character in the distance exclaims, "Those shots came from Hidden Valley!" The showdown between Cisco and the rustlers features several shots being fired without bangs being heard. That the series survived goofs like these is little short of a miracle.

Abrahams, so Bill Catching told me, was

> very strict, and knew exactly what he wanted, and had very little patience. If he rehearsed a scene and you did it and you goofed it up, he had very little patience with a person who did that a couple of times, because he was a professional and expected everybody else to be a professional. But he did have a sense of humor. When we were doing one of the first [episodes], I was wrangling on it and we worked at the old Harold Lloyd studio, a little tiny studio, and the stage was not much bigger than somebody's dining room. They had a little old cabin set, with greens and stuff, and Derwin would say, "Okay now, Duncan and Leo, you guys come charging in and dismount and go in the cabin." And the horses only had—there was two lengths of horses behind them and there was the wall from the front of the stage. They couldn't even get 'em to lope two jumps, that was all the space they had, and they'd be trotting when they came in. But he'd say, "Now I want you to come charging in."

Troy Melton and Leo Carrillo (on horseback) in 1952

On the positive side, Abrahams did fill out his casts with fine B Western female leads like Peggy Stewart, Gail Davis, and Noel Neill; former stars and stuntmen like Robert Livingston (Renaldo's former partner in Republic's *Three Mesquiteers* series during the 1939-40 season) and Dave Sharpe; and veteran shoot-'em-up character actors like Raymond Hatton, Earle Hodgins, Forrest Taylor, and Jack Ingram. Most of the scripts for Abrahams's thirteen segments were by J. Benton Cheney, and all of them were drearily routine, if not before then after the director got through with them, but some at least have aspects of historical interest to dedicated Ciscophiles. "Boomerang," the debut episode of the series, overlaps in both cast and storyline with *The Girl from San Lorenzo*, the last Cisco feature and the only one Abrahams directed. In this and other very early episodes Pancho is not just a lovable language-mangling buffoon but also a petty thief, and every so often Cisco gets genuinely angry at him. It was under Abrahams that the "Oh, Pancho!" "Oh, Cisco!" routine, with Renaldo and Carrillo laughing uproariously, evolved from an occasional novelty into the standard closing of every segment. Two of the Abrahams baker's dozen, "False Marriage" and "Renegade Son," both scripted by Betty Burbridge, are clearly rewrites of Burbridge's screenplays for *The Cisco Kid Returns* and *In Old New Mexico*, the

Monogram features in which Renaldo had first played the Robin Hood of the old West. And one of his episodes, "Cattle Quarantine," is graced by a classic Panchoism: "The she-male of the specimen is more deader than the male." [This one we can trace back to long before Carrillo began playing Pancho. In *History Is Made at Night* (Wanger/United Artists, 1937), directed by Frank Borzage and starring Charles Boyer and Jean Arthur, Carrillo as an Italian chef exclaimed, "The female of the spices is more dead than the male."] Picking up on items like these helps us sit through Abrahams's contributions without nodding off.

Once Abrahams got the Cisco series off the ground (a few inches anyway) he went elsewhere. A few years later he changed his name to Derwin Abbe and, with an equal lack of distinction, directed episodes of other early TV Western series like *Hopalong Cassidy* and *Judge Roy Bean*. He died in 1974, totally forgotten. The Cisco series improved hugely when two other directors, one with a long track record and the other new to the game, came aboard to helm the final thirteen segments of the first season.

The experienced hand was Albert Herman, who was born Adam Foelker in Troy, New York, on February 22, 1894, and got his start in the movie business in 1913. During the twenties he directed dozens

Clayton Moore (left) and Jay Silverheels (right) as the Lone Ranger and Tonto in an episode of the popular television series

Texas Rangers series that costarred Dave O'Brien and Guy Wilkerson. Herman's last films were released in 1945, which as chance would have it was the year Tex Ritter signed with PRC and took over Newill's role in the Texas Rangers series. He made no more films until the 1950-51 season, when he directed half a dozen Cisco segments. Bill Catching remembered,

> He used to be a fighter. And strong! When he'd shake hands with you, whenever he'd grip something tight, it would make his arms pull back, so if you shook hands with him, when he grabbed your hand and squeezed it, that would automatically drag you towards him. We were down in Pioneertown and he was standing across a little ditch and somebody came and said, "Is that Al Herman?" I said, "Yes. Come on, I'll introduce you to him." And he was standing across this little ditch and he stuck out his hand. And before I could cry "Don't shake hands with him!" they shook hands and he drug the guy right across the ditch.

Herman's segments were filmed in two packages of three episodes apiece, with B Western stalwarts Dennis Moore, Bill Henry, Steve Clark, and Ted Adams in one triad and Tristram Coffin, Zon Murray, Hank Patterson, and Kenne Duncan in the other. None of the six ranks with the finest Cisco TV episodes, but they're a huge improvement on the first thirteen, mainly because Herman took care to invest his action sequences with some visual excitement. It was on his watch that Leo Carrillo perpetrated two of his nuttiest Panchoisms. From "The Old Bum": "Some day, Cisco, you are going to find out that the moon is a mousetrap and you are the green cheese." From "Water Rights": "Cisco, my bones tell me something don't smell so good." Apparently Herman never worked in TV again. He died on September 28, 1958, after a long illness.

of silent two-reel comedies, including more than thirty in the Mickey McGuire series whose star, born Joseph Yule, Jr., but best known as Mickey Rooney, was a Herman discovery. After talkies put an end to the pie-in-the-face genre, Herman switched to directing ultra-low-budget Westerns with stars like Rex Lease, Big Boy Williams, and Bill Cody. In 1937 he joined the short-lived Grand National studio and directed James Newill as a singing, fighting Mountie in *Renfrew of the Royal Mounted* (1937) and *Renfrew on the Great White Trail* (1938). Then he helmed the studio's last two B Westerns starring Tex Ritter and, when the Ritter series moved to Monogram, he went along. Action master Spencer Bennet, who was directing the rest of Monogram's Ritter pictures, once described Herman to me as a big bull of a man, built like a wrestler. The features with Tex that Herman directed included some routine entries but also some gems like *Sundown on the Prairie* (1939), *The Man from Texas* (1939), *Pals of the Silver Sage* (1940), *The Golden Trail* (1940), *Take Me Back to Oklahoma* (1940), and *Rollin' Home to Texas* (1941).

During the war years Herman hung out at PRC, specializing in zero-budget contemporary thrillers and rejoining his former Renfrew, James Newill, for *The Rangers Take Over* (1943) and *Bad Men of Thunder Gap* (1943), the first features in PRC's

The remaining seven Cisco segments for the first season were the work of a relative newcomer to the director business. Paul Landres was born in New York City on August 21, 1912. After attending California Christian College and UCLA, he found a job as assistant film editor at Universal in 1931. Six years later he was promoted to full-fledged film editor, and B Western fans lucky enough to have DVDs or cassettes of entries in Universal's Johnny Mack Brown series like *The Bad Man from Red Butte* (1940), *Pony Post* (1940), and the magnificent *Arizona Cyclone* (1941) will find Landres listed in the credits in that capacity.

His career as a director began with *Grand Canyon* (Lippert, 1949, starring Richard Arlen and

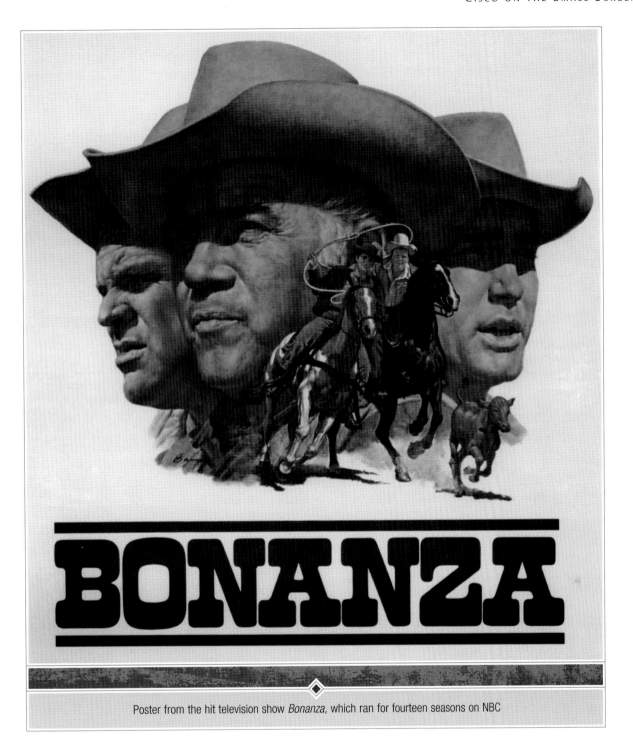

Poster from the hit television show *Bonanza*, which ran for fourteen seasons on NBC

Mary Beth Hughes), but he quickly recognized that the theatrical B feature was a dying breed and joined the first wave of directors who began making thirty-minute episodes of series for TV. "I was looking around for work," he told me when I interviewed him, "and a friend of mine [Mel Mark] was working as production man for Phil Krasne. He was also related to Krasne—his nephew I think—and prevailed upon him to see *Grand Canyon*. Phil saw it and turned around to Mel and said, 'What the hell am I looking at this for? This guy is a comedy director!' But Mel talked to him and convinced him, and that's the way it happened." Landres turned out a total of twenty-seven Cisco segments and seventeen episodes of the Kent Taylor action detective series *Boston Blackie*. Then he hip-hopped from one Western, adventure, comedy, or anthology series to another: *Cowboy G-Men*, *The Lone Ranger*, *Sky King*, *Mr. and Mrs. North*, *Adventures of Kit Carson*, *Ramar of the Jungle*, *Topper*, *Waterfront*, *Brave Eagle*, *Soldiers of Fortune*, and the list goes on and on.

By the late fifties and early sixties he had made the transition to prime-time adult Western series like *Bonanza*, *Law of the Plainsman*, *The Life and Legend of Wyatt Earp*, *Maverick*, *The Rifleman*, *Bronco*, and *Cheyenne*, not to mention Warner Bros.

Publicity photo of Chuck Connors, who played Lucas McCain in ABC's dark Western *The Rifleman* (1958 to 1963)

close shots, close shots. I said: 'Babe, how close do you want me to get?' He said: 'When I see their tonsils, that'll be close enough.'" Marshall Reed, Lane Chandler, and I. Stanford Jolley were featured in Landres's triad, and Phyllis Coates, Bill Kennedy, Mike Ragan, and Tom Tyler in his quartet. These seven were the best episodes in the first season, and one of them, "Pancho Hostage," boasts one of the wackiest aphorisms ever to issue from the mouth of Leo Carrillo: "If a monkey had wings instead of a tail, he could swim in the water like a rabbit."

Whatever Duncan Renaldo owed to others, he clearly owed the most to Leo Carrillo. "In the first year," Bill Catching told me, "Duncan got $320 per week, $160 per episode, and Leo got $1,000 plus a percentage. The second year Leo got Duncan to sign with Leo's agent, William Morris, and Duncan's salary was increased." Without Carrillo's intervention there never would have been a second year for Renaldo in the series, because he was still in the United States illegally. "I was on the set when they came and picked him up," Catching remembered. "I think it was the end of the first year or the beginning of the second year that the immigration department came to the studio and picked him up. . . . Leo Carrillo, who had more important connections in politics than anyone else in Hollywood, pulled strings and helped him to become a legal citizen."

Carrillo, Paul Landres told me,

was one hell of a rider, and he spoke English as well as I did, but he was always talking in the Pancho dialect. After the first episodes he started to have fun. I'd have a shot of him coming up over a low hill. . . . He knew I'd be in front of the camera, so when he's coming up the hill, he flicks the horse's head towards the camera, and the horse is coming right for me, and just at the last moment he flicks him away and rides by the camera. It was quite a shot but it was always a scary thing, because if that horse was a fraction of a second later he'd be into me. That was going on constantly.

PI series like *Hawaiian Eye* and *77 Sunset Strip*. All this in addition to a dozen or so theatrical features! No one so prolific can always be in top form, but some of his best early TV work—including some *Cisco* and *Boston Blackie* segments and his three episodes of *Cowboy G-Men*—hold up extremely well more than fifty years later, and his *Bonanza* episode "The Paiute War" is simply one of the most powerful Westerns I've ever seen. He lived to be 89, but in view of all the pictures he made in his prime it's a wonder he didn't drop dead of exhaustion long before 2001.

Landres began his association with the Cisco series by one-upping his directorial colleagues. Abrahams and Herman had made two or three segments at the same time with identical or overlapping casts, but Landres made first a group of three and then a brace of four. Babe Unger, he recalled during our interview, "would tell me what his plans were and how I should do it. He wanted close shots,

During the 1951-52 season Landres was probably the most overworked director in America, making twenty of the twenty-six episodes that comprised *The Cisco Kid*'s second season plus seventeen segments of the *Boston Blackie* series that Ziv launched that year. That one man could turn out approximately $18\frac{1}{2}$ hours of footage in less than twelve months is amazing enough. Even more astonishing is that the best *Cisco* episodes Landres directed that season were easily the finest in the series and arguably the most exciting exploits of the character ever committed to film. Scads of action, bizarre storylines, excellent supporting casts, Panchoisms galore—these episodes had it all.

One of the luckiest innovations in second-season Cisco was the replacement of Albert Glasser's threadbare background music with a fine new score. Early in the season's first episode, "Phoney Heiress," Cisco and Pancho race after a runaway buckboard with a young woman in it. Every B Western fan has watched hundreds of scenes very much like it, but what makes this rendition special is the superb agitato score, which continued in use not only for the rest of *Cisco*'s second season but, with additions by other composers, throughout the rest of the program's run. Anyone with ears can tell that the music isn't by Glasser, but since music scores are never mentioned in Ziv credit crawls, I can't identify the person who so enriched the rest of the Cisco saga.

The single weakness in the season's output was that too many outdoor scenes were shot indoors on a cramped soundstage garnished with ugly fake trees and rocks in the manner of *The Lone Ranger*. A case can be made for filming TV Western episodes this way, and veteran director Thomas Carr made it when I taped a conversation with him several years ago.

> You'd do your establishing shots [outdoors] and then you'd go into what we called a green set . . . built inside on the stage, where you have rocks, you have trees, you have big cycloramas of scenery. You can do wagon train scenes or anything in that space. . . . You're restricted, you can't expand, you can't see into the distance, you have a painted cyclorama in the background, not the horizon. . . . [But] it was easier for me because I had more control. You didn't have to worry about the elements or moving heavy equipment or terrain or anything. You just moved the dirt or moved a rock. In the outdoor pictures, when you wanted to climb up rocks you had to pull the cameras up by ropes. [Shooting indoors,] you just put the camera on a crane and got it up high and shot down.

As the fifties went on and the TV Western grew into a gigantic industry, most series followed the lead of *The Lone Ranger* and second-season *Cisco* when it came to shooting street and trail scenes on a closed set. Directors had more control and saved time and money but deprived us in the audience of what had been one of the central pleasures of watching Westerns: seeing the real outdoors.

Usually the loss of the land's beauty wasn't worth the gains in efficiency, but Paul Landres invested his finest Cisco segments with such visual flair that you hardly notice how much footage was shot on a soundstage. Perhaps Landres's second-season casts boasted fewer old favorites from theatrical B Westerns, but they did include, among a host of less familiar names, stalwarts like Reed Howes, Pierce Lyden, Stanley Andrews, Bud Osborne, Myron Healey, Steve Clark, Terry Frost, John Merton, Earle Hodgins, Edmund Cobb, Milburn Morante, John Cason, Raphael Bennett, and Kermit Maynard. First-season workhorse J. Benton Cheney also wrote most of the brace of scripts for 1951-52 but transcended his usual lack of imagination and came up with some memorably weird storylines. In "Jewelry Store Fence" a crazy old man tries to kill Cisco and Pancho with a crossbow built into an ornate clock. "Foreign Agent" dealt with spies from a nameless evil empire (a surprisingly common element in TV Western episodes from the HUAC-Red Menace era) seeking control of a tungsten lode in the old West. "Sleeping Gas" pitted Cisco and Pancho against a family of bank robbers whose modus operandi involved a high-pitched fiddle and an ornamental globe full of the titular gas. "Buried Treasure," with its witchcraft and reincarnation motifs, is perhaps the most bizarre episode in the entire series, with Cisco, revealed to be the living image of pirate Jean Lafitte, trying to save Lafitte's cabin boy, now a very old man, from being tortured by an ancient hag and her sons, who are after Lafitte's lost booty. If I had to pick a handful of *Cisco* episodes to be preserved for future generations while the rest were destroyed, this is definitely one I'd save, along with "Protective Association," which is stagebound but crammed with action, and "Water Toll," which was filmed in the open and includes the single finest sequence in the entire Cisco series as Landres's tracking shots follow Renaldo chasing outlaw leader Michael Whalen into a swamp.

Landres's workload came vividly to life in the course of my conversation with him. "One month we were doing seven shows with *Cisco* and six with *Boston Blackie*, the next month we were doing seven with *Blackie* and six with *Cisco*." The episodes were organized in groups of two or three, featuring the same character actors and often the same character name for the same actor in different segments. What made this assembly-line method possible was the master scheduling board prepared by production manager Eddie Davis. Babe Unger, says Landres, "was as sharp as they come but he didn't know anything at all about production. As far as he was concerned, that board was sacrosanct. . . . Eddie never came out on location. He stayed in and he was

always there with Babe, holding Babe's right hand. Which I didn't like, because I knew damn well he was cutting my throat behind my back." Everything on the scheduling board "was broken down according to locations. They had scenes that were being done outside, up at Pioneertown, and they had stuff that was being done on the sets inside. When we went out on location it was crazy. When we were shooting six or seven episodes we might spend a week up in Pioneertown. The rest we'd do on stage, on the sets." Landres at first had a problem keeping his actors' names straight, but he solved it by calling them by their cast names, which were usually the same in each episode within a group. "I started keeping a list of all the actors I ever worked with, and from that I could cast anything, anytime, anywhere. The bad ones I never called back."

Most of the scripts Landres directed were written by J. Benton Cheney.

> They were designed for three action scenes per script, and they were usually impossible to do. They just couldn't be done on our schedule. . . . I would read these things and I'd go in screaming to Joe Cheney and his answer always was, "Well, that's what Babe wants." So I'd go in to see Babe, and every time I told him that it was impossible to do what was in the script because of the schedule, he'd look me dead in the eye and say, "Well, what *can* you do?" Now the ball was back in my court, so I would really have to extend myself and dream up something that would take the place of this. In effect it was pretty much the same thing, but it was in a doable way, and I'd go back and tell Joe what I was going to do and have him write it. It was a very tough situation for me because he had three of these things, one action scene every eight minutes I think it was.

Not all of these action scenes worked out exactly as planned. "One time," Troy Melton recalled, "I had to chase Bill [Catching], jump from my horse, land on the back of his horse, scissor him with my legs, and then catch a limb as we went under it and pull him off the horse. The force of gravity pulled my legs out and we both busted our butts on the ground."

The breakneck pace soon began to affect Landres's health. "I'd come home from a day's shooting and I'd have to prepare. Not the next day's work, because I'd have all seven of them done before I set foot on the stage, but I had to prepare the next group as soon as I was given the scripts. That meant that I'd come home,

say at seven o'clock at night, have dinner, work at home until twelve, get up around five or six o'clock in the morning, work for a couple of hours preparing, and get on the set." The demands on him were so great that "I didn't even have time to look at any of the shows as they were edited. . . . But I knew that everything went together because I shot it for the cutting room. That makes a vast difference. My background as an editor was of tremendous help to me."

How much was Landres being paid for this nonstop work? "I think I was getting $500 a week for directing three episodes a week. Then the Guild was able to get a deal where the director would get $520 per episode, and I went from $500 to more than $1500 a week. That was a hell of a bump." But he was pushing himself so hard that eventually "I had to accept Eddie Davis's help."

Davis, as we've seen, had joined the Cisco series as assistant director on its earliest segments after working in that capacity on some of the Monogram Cisco features and countless other B Westerns of the forties. That he was given a chance to direct in his own right came about largely through the recommendation of Troy Melton. "I said to Babe, 'You've got one guy on the lot right now who would make a fine director and that's Eddie Davis. The guy is very knowledgeable, he knows horses, he knows what you can get done with horses, he knows actors, he knows how to work with actors.' Babe said, 'Well, I'm going to keep that in mind, Troy.'"

In the middle of shooting the superb "Protective Association" episode Landres almost fainted from influenza and had to be sent home. With his permission, Eddie Davis took over as director. Troy Melton told me,

> It happened that everything we had the rest of that day was action stuff. Bill [Catching] and I had a fight to do on a balcony where I had to come through a rail and swing out on a chandelier. When I saw Eddie come in on the set I said, "What's doing here?" He said, "They're going to let me direct the rest of the show, Troy. You'll stick with me, will you?" I said, "You know that," because I liked Eddie. I got with Bill and said, "Bill, this is all action this afternoon. Let's try to do everything in one take, as fast as we can get things done." Then I talked to some of the crew and said, "Here's a chance to give one of our guys a break, so let's get in there and pitch." Which we did.
>
> A little later, maybe five-thirty or six o'clock, I was outside, the sun was shining down nice, and I ran into Babe. He said, "What's going on? What's happening?" I said, "We wrapped. We

finished for the day." He was flabbergasted and asked how we could be finished so early. I said, "You've got a director." That's when Eddie Davis was born.

The experience convinced Davis to direct full-time, with Unger taking over as production manager. "I think [Eddie] was a natural-born director or something," Bill Catching told me, "because he'd been an assistant so long and worked with so many of the good, fast directors. He put quality into the shows. He and Landres, I think, did some of the best." But Davis had his share of problems with the front office too. As production manager he had been "pretty tight with a dollar." But now that he was directing, "Babe starts using the tactics on Eddie that Eddie had used on the other guys. And Eddie says, 'Wait a minute! You can't do this! I'm the director!' "

Four of Davis's initial half dozen are rather ordinary, but the other two rank with the best in the series. "Hidden Valley," with Cisco and Pancho blundering into and becoming rebel leaders in the Western equivalent of a lost civilization, ruled with an iron hand by a tyrannical ex-sea captain and his terror squads, is so densely packed with action and incident (even a sword duel at the climax) that it might almost have been a condensed version of a twelve-chapter cliffhanger serial. And "Ghost Town" with its spooky elements menacing a young woman as she searches through the deserted town for her identity is a fine merger of Western action with the old-dark-house thriller. Studded through Davis's cast lists were fugitives from Monogram B Westerns like Stephen Chase, Dennis Moore, Tristram Coffin, I. Stanford Jolley, Keith Richards, Riley Hill, Denver Pyle, and Zon Murray. When not directing Cisco adventures, Davis spent his 1951-52 workdays turning out half a dozen episodes of *Boston Blackie*.

My own enthusiasm for second-season *Cisco* as a youngster and today was not universally shared. In fact, some of the season's most imaginative episodes generated a surprising amount of controversy. *TV Guide* for February 20, 1953, printed a letter from Sid Kipness of Dumont, New Jersey, condemning the "Buried Treasure" segment. "My five-year-old daughter was frightened by the old witch. If this is for children, I'll send the makers of Tip Top Bread a broom for an award." Viewers must have written in the same vein about this and other *Cisco* episodes either to the local bread company sponsors or to Ziv's offices. Before work began on the third season, Unger handed down some rigid new edicts to his staff. There will be no more knife fights as in "Romany Caravan." No more witchcraft or any

supernatural elements like the reincarnation motif in "Buried Treasure." Neither Cisco nor Pancho will ever again kill an adversary as they had in several episodes from the first and second seasons including "Vigilante Story" and "Romany Caravan." And so on until very little was left except the most simple-minded and juvenile material.

Small wonder that the third season was such a letdown. Most of the outdoor scenes were once again shot outdoors, but the front office edicts forced the storylines and direction into conventional patterns. Paul Landres had left Ziv to direct twenty-four of the fifty-two new episodes of *The Lone Ranger*, with John Hart replacing Clayton Moore as the masked rider of the plains and almost all the action staged on the same sort of excruciating indoor sets Landres had contended with during his Cisco period. Eddie Davis took over as the 1952-53 season's principal director and helmed eleven of the third set of twenty-six episodes—two simultaneously shot triads, a matched pair, two singletons without companion episodes, and one segment whose companion piece was unaccountably directed by someone else—but only the old-dark-house thriller "Fear" was in the same league with the best work of the second season. The casts of the Davis episodes were again heavy with veterans of Monogram's B Westerns like Marshall Reed, Zon Murray, Jack Ingram, Gail Davis (soon to star in her own series as Annie Oakley), Keith Richards, Bob Wilke, Kermit Maynard, John Cason, Hank Patterson, Myron Healey, Earle Hodgins, Forrest Taylor, and Bill Henry. The taboos laid down by Ziv's front office explain why so many third-season episodes emphasized circus elements: an equestrian clown show in "Monkey Business," a puppet theater in "The Puppeteer," a medicine wagon complete with elephant in "Pancho and the Pachyderm" and, as if to prove that the taste for the weird could not be totally stamped out, a ventriloquist with a living dummy in "Laughing Badman."

In "Pancho and the Pachyderm," Bill Catching told me, "I was doubling Leo on top of the elephant. The old gal's name was Emma. She was from the alligator farm up there in Thousand Oaks. I had never ridden an elephant before, and she was shuffling along pretty good and the camera car's in front, and the director told the trainer, 'Make her go faster.' And they speeded up the camera car and the trainer yelled, 'EMMA!!' Man, she shifted gears like a car, and started forward so fast, the leather thing around her neck that I was holding to broke, and I rolled backwards off her. That was the tallest saddle fall I ever did."

Directing three of these circus segments plus four others was George M. Cahan (19??-1991), a novice whose only previous Western experience seems to have been as director of three episodes of the low-budget *Cowboy G-Men* series starring Russell Hayden and Jackie Coogan. "He didn't last very long," Bill Catching says. "He didn't understand action Western shows." But at least he knew enough to cast lots of Monogram B Western veterans like Leonard Penn, Raymond Hatton, Mike Ragan, Ted Mapes, Tom London, House Peters, Jr., Zon Murray, Jack Ingram, and Guy Wilkerson, and he saw the potential in newcomer Sheb Wooley, who near the end of the fifties would stake out his claim to Western fame opposite Eric Fleming and Clint Eastwood in *Rawhide*. Two of Cahan's septet—scripted, as if you hadn't guessed, by J. Benton Cheney—were as off-trail as anything from the second season. "Face of Death" has Cisco and Pancho joining a murder-

plagued archaeological expedition hunting an Aztec high priest's tomb, and in "Lost City" they come upon an Inca community complete with beautiful princess and try to save its treasure from thieves. The budget and time constraints combined with Cahan's inexperience to keep these episodes from living up to the expectations of their premises. After cranking out his seven Cisco shows plus four adventures of Boston Blackie, Cahan decided that high-speed action stuff was not his forte and switched to directing episodes of sitcoms like *Gilligan's Island* and *The Brady Bunch*. Since he's best known as a comedy director, we shall take leave of him by quoting a Panchoism tossed off by Carrillo during Cahan's "Laughing Badman," which will delight anyone who was forced in high school to memorize gobs of speechifying from *Julius Caesar:* "The evil that men live do after them. The good is oft interrupted in the bones."

Of the third season's other director perhaps more could have been expected. Sobey Martin was born in Leipzig, Germany, in 1909 and, after attending the Sorbonne in Paris, emigrated to the United States where he worked in MGM's editorial department between 1936 and 1942. He served in the army during World War II and began directing documentary films when the war was over. As far as I can tell, he was the first person ever to direct a filmed episode of a TV series. The twenty-six-segment series known alternatively as *Your Show Time* and *Story Theater* was broadcast on NBC during the first half of 1949 and offered thirty-minute versions of short stories by writers like Stevenson, Conan Doyle, Mark Twain, de Maupassant, and Oscar Wilde. The first episode aired was an adaptation of de Maupassant's "The Diamond Necklace," directed by Martin and starring John Beal, which won the first Emmy ever awarded for best film made for television. (Not that there was much competition in this category at the time.) Martin also directed for this series the first telefilm adaptation of a Sherlock Holmes story ("The Adventure of the Speckled Band" with Alan Napier as Holmes), a half-hour version of Mark Twain's "The Celebrated Jumping Frog of Calaveras County," and short films based on tales by Dickens, Stevenson, and other greats. Less than three years later he was under contract at Ziv and churning out exploits of Boston Blackie and Cisco. There's nothing special in his eight *Cisco* segments except for a few featured players—Peggy Stewart, Roscoe Ates, a teenage Bobby Blake, John Pickard, Bud Osborne, Rand Brooks—and, from "Bell of Santa Margarita," one gorgeous Panchoism: "It will be like hunting for noodles in a smokestack!" Martin kept busy throughout the fifties

Photo still of James Arness, who played Marshal Matt Dillon in CBS's long-running *Gunsmoke* (1955-1975)

and early sixties directing episodes of *The Million-aire*, *United States Marshal*, *Gunsmoke*, *Rawhide*, and other series. In 1964 he became a contract director for Irwin Allen's small-screen fantasy factory and spent the rest of the decade on series like *Voyage to the Bottom of the Sea*, *Lost in Space*, *The Time Tunnel*, and *Land of the Giants*. He seems to have retired around 1970. He died on July 27, 1978.

Neither Cahan nor Martin lasted long on the *Cisco* series. Troy Melton told me,

> We put in long days, usually starting at four-thirty, five, six in the morning, and we never got home before dark, usually seven, eight, or nine at night. It was telling on the crew, on the cast, on Leo and Duncan, on everybody. This one particular night I came in on the lot, and as I walked in the front gate Babe Unger was standing there. He came over to me and said, "Hey, Troy, how's it going?" I said, "Well, you can see. The same old thing. Nothing's changed." He said, "What's wrong?" I said, "Well, I don't know where you're getting these directors. Like Sobey Martin, George Cahan. They don't know from nothing. They don't know which end to put the hay in. I don't know where you're finding 'em, Babe, but these are not directors for our kind of show. These guys ask us to do things that you can't do, the wranglers can't handle the stuff. You've got to find some action directors, some guys who have worked around horses, who know what you can do with a horse, who know Westerns."

Thanks at least in part to this conversation, the people brought in to direct the fourth season's adventures were of a higher caliber.

The 1953-54 quota of twenty-six episodes was split among five directors. Ten segments went to Eddie Davis and four to the briefly returning Paul Landres. Another four were assigned to old Cisco hand Lambert Hillyer, who had helmed *South of the Rio Grande* with Renaldo as Cisco back in 1945 and was now under contract to direct episodes of Ziv's new Red Menace series *I Led Three Lives* as well as a few segments of *Cisco*. "'Full Load Hillyer' they called him," Bill Catching told me. "You could use quarter, half, or full loads on the guns. Lambert was a little hard of hearing, and he thought you got bet-ter reactions if you used full loads. They finally had to get the SPCA after him to say that you couldn't fire a full load, you had to use a quarter load if you were riding a horse or close to a horse. Because, man, that noise just made them horses freak out! It just devastated their ears."

A pair of fourth-season episodes was directed by Herbert Leeds, who had done 20th Century-Fox's last Cisco feature with Warner Baxter and four of the sequels with César Romero. "He was determined," says Bill Catching.

> He told everybody what to do, and he had in his mind that the sky had to drop on Cisco. The bad guy had the gun pointed at Cisco's stomach, and Leeds had in mind that before the guy could cock the gun and fire it, Cisco would knock the gun away. And I said, "No, God damn it! These blanks will hurt you! I don't want to do it." And he said, "Here, I'll show you. Point the gun at me, and before you can cock it and pull the trigger, I can knock it away." And I said, "No, Mr. Leeds, I don't want to do that." He says, "Do it! Come on!" I cocked the gun and pulled the trigger and shot him right in the stomach. That wad burned the hell out of him. If I'd have been closer . . .

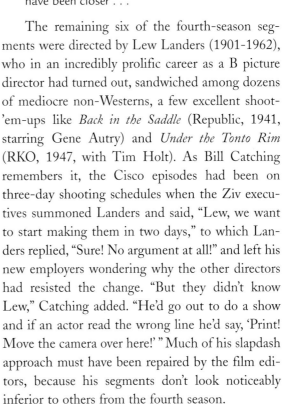

The remaining six of the fourth-season seg-ments were directed by Lew Landers (1901-1962), who in an incredibly prolific career as a B picture director had turned out, sandwiched among dozens of mediocre non-Westerns, a few excellent shoot-'em-ups like *Back in the Saddle* (Republic, 1941, starring Gene Autry) and *Under the Tonto Rim* (RKO, 1947, with Tim Holt). As Bill Catching remembers it, the Cisco episodes had been on three-day shooting schedules when the Ziv execu-tives summoned Landers and said, "Lew, we want to start making them in two days," to which Lan-ders replied, "Sure! No argument at all!" and left his new employers wondering why the other directors had resisted the change. "But they didn't know Lew," Catching added. "He'd go out to do a show and if an actor read the wrong line he'd say, 'Print! Move the camera over here!'" Much of his slapdash approach must have been repaired by the film edi-tors, because his segments don't look noticeably inferior to others from the fourth season.

Each of the directors organized his episodes in matched pairs with identical or overlapping casts and the work began. At first everything went well. Most rewarding of the early segments was a pair directed by Hillyer and featuring John Doucette, Francis McDonald, and former *Mesquiteers* star Bob Livingston. "Pancho and the Wolf Dog" dealt with a wild dog and skullduggery at the West's first ice house, and "The Faded General" was about a senile ex-officer who locks up Cisco and Pancho in his private stockade. The climax of the latter episode re-created a breathtaking stunt from the Buck Jones feature *One Man Law* (Columbia, 1932), which Hillyer had both written and directed. Herbert Leeds added to the interest of one of his segments, "Bullets and the Booby Trap," by casting Bobby (not yet Robert) Blake as a teenage inventor living in a ghost town with his shotgun-toting granny.

Then disaster struck. A scene in the Lew Landers episode "Battle of Red Rock Pass" went haywire and a flying boulder almost broke Duncan Renaldo's neck. According to Bill Catching,

That was Duncan's fault. There was a cute girl on the set, Nan Leslie, a really sweet, cute gal, and Duncan really liked her. He was single then and he was kind of pursuing her, and she kept teasing him and Leo that they were two old farts. . . . So when this scene came up, Troy [Melton] was supposed to do it. He was trailing this guy on foot and looking down at the tracks, and Red Morgan, the stuntman actor up in the rocks, rolled this rock at him. It was a big phony rock, but it weighed forty pounds or better. They made 'em out of plaster of paris with wire. And Duncan came walking along, and he insisted on doing this scene because Nan had teased him. Troy and I almost yelled, but he never looked up, and there's nothing Red could do. He rolled the rock off and Duncan—there was a sound made so Duncan would look up and see it and step back. Well, he never even looked up. He had his head down and it hit him in the back of the head and knocked him down. He got up and staggered around and leaned against a rock and started to walk on and then he fell. We rushed over to him and kept him from moving and got him in the—we didn't even have ambulances or anything, we had a station wagon that had a mattress in the back of it in case somebody got hurt. And we got him in it and took him to the hospital and found out that if he had moved a lot more . . . the vertebrae in his neck were just a fraction from being severed. He came within a fraction of being killed. He was in the hospital for about six weeks, I think, and in the interim Leo's wife died, and we did either two or three Ciscos without either Cisco or Pancho!

What would have paralyzed most series seemed to energize the people responsible for this one. While Renaldo was convalescing in the hospital, directors and writers scrambled to concoct new storylines that would keep the star's face out of sight. Where this wasn't possible, the director would cover by photographing Troy Melton from odd angles. "They shot me during the day," Melton recalled during our conversation. "I actually did the dialogue with the other actors, and I did the entire show. At night they would go to the hospital bedside. Duncan would read the dialogue that I had and do it over and they recorded him and put his voice on the soundtrack." When all else failed, the director would recycle footage of Renaldo from pre-accident episodes and later shoot a few extreme close-ups of him against a blue backdrop once he was on the mend. Not only did everyone survive the crisis but, according to Melton, "we hardly lost any time at all."

The segments made while Renaldo was recovering are marked in this book's filmography with an asterisk. Most of them were directed by Eddie Davis, and the most ingenious of the lot was "Bandaged Badman." A gunman hired to kill Cisco is blown up in an explosion, and Cisco has a friendly doctor identify the remains as his and cover his face with bandages so he can pose as the assassin, claim he was burned in the explosion but not killed, and try to connect with whoever paid for the murder. Not having to worry about keeping the double's face concealed, Davis crammed this episode with more action and stunts than one ever saw in a TV Western series of the time except for *The Range Rider*.

Different coping strategies were devised for other segments. In "The Black Terror," where Cisco invents a masked-bandit persona for himself so he can join a gang of outlaw brothers and break them up from within, Davis cast Reed Howes as the oldest brother so he could recycle Howes's fight scenes with Renaldo from two second-season episodes directed by Paul Landres, "Stolen Bonds" and "Protective Association." But as if to tell the world that he and no one else was in charge, he made sure that in one of the town scenes the camera focused on a sign reading ED DAVIS/FANCY SADDLES. Lew Landers, who clearly wasn't blamed for Renaldo's accident since he continued to work on the series as if nothing had happened, fused these ploys for "The Iron Mask." The outlandish storyline had Cisco replacing a sheriff who'd been locked inside the titular mask by outlaws, and Michael Whalen was cast as the gang leader so the episode could end with

Paul Landres's magnificent chase-into-the-swamp sequence from "Water Toll."

The series briefly experimented with a new approach after Renaldo recovered. In a matched pair of episodes directed by Landres, "Not Guilty" and "Horseless Carriage," José Gonzales Gonzales was introduced as Pancho's young nephew José with the evident intent of adding a younger continuing character loosely modeled on Dan Reid, the masked man's nephew in *The Lone Ranger*. The plan fizzled out and Gonzales never again appeared in a Cisco episode. "I couldn't understand him," Landres told me. "It didn't work out too well." Bill Catching, however, said that Gonzales "got more laughs than Pancho" and Carrillo couldn't tolerate being upstaged.

Of the twenty-six episodes shot for the 1954-55 season, two were directed by Eddie Davis, one by a newcomer to Westerns who will be formally introduced later in this chapter, and a staggering twenty-three by Lambert Hillyer, who brought to these fifth-season segments the abundant professional skills he'd acquired in almost forty years at his job but nothing special that made them stand out in a crowd. "Trouble in Tonopah," in which Cisco tries to figure out how someone learned the combination to the Tonopah express office's burglarproof safe and pulled off a series of baffling thefts, is historically interesting because it was the single Cisco script written by that prolific B Western hand Oliver Drake. If you think the storyline sounds familiar even though you've never heard of this episode before, there's a reason: Drake recycled it from his script for the George O'Brien feature *Trouble in Sundown* (RKO, 1939).

Long-memoried viewers who have seen a lot of B Western features may get the same sense of déjà vu from other fifth-season episodes. In "Pancho's Niece" Cisco has his *compañero* pose as the uncle of a young half-Mexican woman whose banker father apparently killed himself after losing most of the bank's money. The script for this one is credited to Barry Cohon but actually it's a condensed remake of the Buck Jones feature *The Fighting Code* (Columbia, 1933), which Hillyer had both written and directed. He borrowed from himself again in "Juggler's Silver," restaging for the second time in a Cisco episode the spectacular stunt Buck Jones or his double performed in the 1932 *One Man Law*. And in "New Evidence," in which Cisco sets out to clear a young man on trial for the murder of his girlfriend's father, Hillyer or scriptwriter Ande Lamb borrowed heavily from the courtroom sequence of John Ford's classic *Young Mr. Lincoln* (20th Century-Fox, 1939).

Aside from historical curiosities like these, fifth-season Cisco segments tended to be solid and reliable without any particular distinction. Most of the scripts were standard issue, Hillyer's casts were about the same as usual—Dennis Moore, Earle Hodgins, Zon Murray, Nan Leslie, John Cason, Bill Kennedy, Myron Healey, Kenneth MacDonald, Kermit Maynard, I. Stanford Jolley, Leonard Penn, Keith Richards, Lane Bradford, Eddy Waller, Jack Ingram, Raymond Hatton, Marshall Reed, Hank Patterson, Edmund Cobb, Rory Mallinson, Sam Flint, Terry Frost, Glenn Strange—and all in all the Cisco series seemed to be getting a bit stale. In the entire season's output there was only one memorable Panchoism, from "Extradition Papers": "Goodbye, little toes. The next time I see you, I won't be looking at you."

In the fall of 1955 the so-called adult Western began to dominate television with the debuts of *Gunsmoke* and *The Life and Legend of Wyatt Earp*, and it soon became obvious that the days of the more juvenile-oriented series were numbered. The 1955-56 season was the sixth for *The Cisco Kid*, and also the weakest and the last. Hillyer directed thirteen of the final twenty-six episodes, but the only one that comes close to his best work for the series was the action-packed "Gold, Death and Dynamite." By the time he had completed his sixth-season quota he was well into his sixties, perhaps almost seventy, and had put in close to forty years as a director. It was time to retire. He died on July 5, 1969. His best Westerns from all periods—with William S. Hart in the teens and early twenties, Buck Jones in the thirties, Bill Elliott in the early forties, Johnny Mack Brown in the middle and later forties, and at least a few of his *Cisco* TV episodes with Duncan Renaldo—will continue to be enjoyed as long as there is an audience for the genre.

The sixth season's remaining thirteen episodes as well as the final episode from the fifth season were directed by a newcomer to the shoot-'em-up. Leslie Goodwins, born in London on September 17, 1899, had begun his career as a director in the thirties, making comedy shorts at RKO. One of his assistants at that time was later superstar director Robert Aldrich. "You could learn more about comedy assisting Les Goodwins on a two-reel Leon Errol than you could spending two years at film school," Aldrich said near the end of his own life. Goodwins graduated to directing features in 1937. Most of his films from then until

Publicity photo of James Garner as Bret Maverick, a footloose and cowardly gambler in *Maverick* (1957-62). The show originated as a typical Western of the time but graduated to a dark comedy by the end of its first season.

But his episodes are graced by the last two Pancho-isms worth quoting. From "The Epidemic": "Cisco, we're kind of down the river without water, huh?" And from "Tangled Trails," the 156th and final installment of the series and the only one since early 1953 to be written by the pioneer *Cisco* TV scripter J. Benton Cheney: "If I had money I would have such a big garden I could be arrested for fragrancy."

Goodwins continued to direct for many years after the Cisco series came to an end. From 1959 through 1962, under contract to Warner Bros., he did episodes of *Maverick, Cheyenne, Bronco, Sugarfoot, The Alaskans,* and *Surfside 6.* Will Hutchins, the star of *Sugarfoot,* remembers Goodwins as "a round, bespectacled gent with a Cockney accent. . . . With a wry smile he referred to those days as the twilight of his career. He was a good bloke; no airs about him. He came to work and did his job. One morning [on a *Sugarfoot* episode] he shot fifteen pages before lunch." From Warners he moved on to direct for a number of well-known sixties sitcoms like *My Favorite Martian, F Troop,* and *Gilligan's Island.* He died on January 8, 1970.

When the shooting on *Cisco* stopped, Carrillo looked in his fifties but in fact was approaching his 75th birthday. His wife Edith had died in 1953 after a marriage lasting four decades. Having spent half a century in show business, Carrillo had no need or desire to work any longer. He retired to his Santa Monica ranch, managed his property, rode as grand marshal in civic parades, and spent his spare time writing an informal history of his state, *The California I Love,* which was published by Prentice-Hall in 1961, the year he celebrated his eightieth birthday. A month later, on September 10, with his daughter Marie Antoinette and his brother Ottie at the bedside, Leo Carrillo died of cancer.

Duncan Renaldo also retired after the Cisco TV series halted production. He bought a hacienda in Santa Barbara with a view of the Pacific, relaxed, put on some weight, and smoked more than was good for him. Jon Tuska, who interviewed Renaldo in the early and middle 1970s, described him in *The Filming of the West* as "one of the most charming men I have ever known. . . . White-haired, his lined countenance ruddy with a persistent youthfulness, . . . at peace with the world . . ." (438). On September 3, 1980, a week short of nineteen years after the death of his compañero, Duncan Renaldo died in Goleta Valley Community Hospital. The cause was lung cancer. His age, if you accept the one birth certificate he had whose date has been published, was seventy-six.

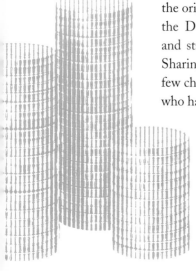

1946 were segments of unpretentious RKO comedy series, like the Mexican Spitfire pictures with Lupe Vélez and his two-reeler star Leon Errol, or forgettable low-budget musicals for the same studio. The closest he ever came to directing a Western was *The Singing Sheriff* (RKO, 1944), a croon-'em-up with Bob Crosby. The first TV series he worked on was the original version of *The Life of Riley,* broadcast on the Dumont network during the 1949-50 season and starring the then little-known Jackie Gleason. Sharing directorial chores on that series, as we saw a few chapters ago, was *Cisco* alumnus Herbert Leeds, who had killed himself a year or so before Goodwins unaccountably landed at Ziv.

Why he was asked or agreed to become the last director of *Cisco* episodes remains a mystery. Certainly he wasn't very good at this kind of film: his segments aren't weighted toward comedy as his background might have led one to expect, and in terms of drama and action they're hopelessly inept.

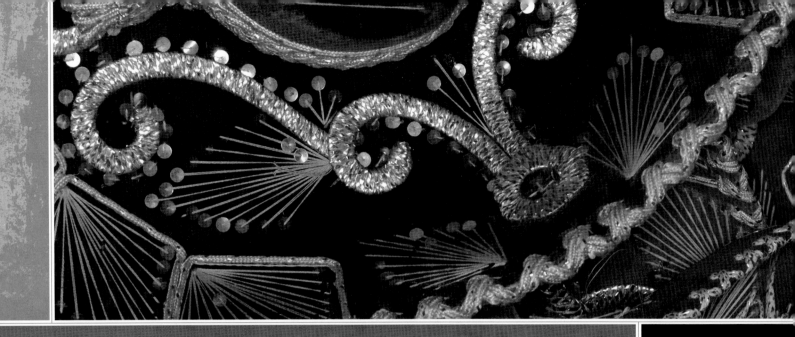

D uring the first run of the Ziv TV series, most of America's Ciscophiles were kids. Few if any who followed those 156 episodes were old enough to have seen César Romero, let alone Warner Baxter, in 20th Century-Fox's two cycles of Cisco features, and since the major studios including 20th Century-Fox were boycotting the new medium and not allowing their old pictures to be shown on the small screen, viewers had no way to compare the TV series with the Cisco movies of previous generations. The three Monogram features with Renaldo and Martín Garralaga and the six with Gilbert Roland were seen on countless local stations, as were the five Inter-American pictures with Renaldo and Carrillo. Usually the titles of these films were changed for TV: *The Cisco Kid Returns* became *The Daring Adventurer*, *The Gay Amigo* was switched to *The Daring Rogue*, *The Daring Caballero* got the new name of *Guns and Fury*, *Satan's Cradle* was altered to *The Devil's Den*, and *The Girl from San Lorenzo* found a second life as *Don Amigo*. As if that weren't confusing enough, all references to the Cisco character and even to O. Henry were blacked out of the credits of the TV prints, and whenever "the Cisco Kid," "Cisco," or "Pancho" occurred in the dialogue, either the words were erased so that the actor's lips would move with nothing coming out, or else the new speakers would recite "Chico Villa," "Chico," or "Pablo" onto the soundtrack in voices that even the deaf could tell were not those of the original cast. In *The Gay*

Amigo, the alteration resulted in Renaldo's explaining that his name, Chico, was short for Francisco. Why this nonsense was thought necessary I have no idea, but it did cost money: in one feature in which a reward poster for Cisco was nailed to a tree, someone actually took the trouble to insert a new shot, showing a poster for that notorious bandit Chico Villa! Videocassettes and DVDs copied from these old 16 mm prints still exist today and tend to cause giggling fits when a Western fan stumbles upon them. Thanks to the alterations in the Cisco features and to the use of Renaldo's and Carrillo's images from the TV series both in Dell's Cisco comic book (forty-one issues, 1950-58) and the daily Cisco comic strip by Rod Reed and José Luis Salinas (1951-68), the millions of us who first discovered the compadres on the small screen find it hard to accept anyone else in the roles— not even Renaldo himself when, as in the features, his looks and outfit are different. Ziv shut down production on the series in 1956 but, having been shot in color, it continued in syndication for decades.

The kids who had ridden the TV trails with Hoppy, Gene, Roy, Cisco, and the Lone Ranger all too soon grew up. Some looked back on those figures as heroes, others as jokes. It's anyone's guess how they were remembered by the rock group War, whose 1973 song about one of them (which Professor Keller discusses in further detail in chapter 12) rose to the number two spot on the pop charts.

> Cisco Kid
> Was a friend of mine
> Cisco Kid
> Was a friend of mine.
> He'd drink whiskey
> Pancho'd drink the wine.
> He'd drink whiskey
> Pancho'd drink the wine.

Sounds like the War-riors were thinking of Gilbert Roland and his tequila ritual, assuming Cisco really meant anything to them at all. But the makers of *Hill Street Blues* (NBC-TV, 1981-87), the premier TV cop series of the eighties, left no doubt about their affection for Cisco when they chose for the program's third-season debut "Here's Adventure!

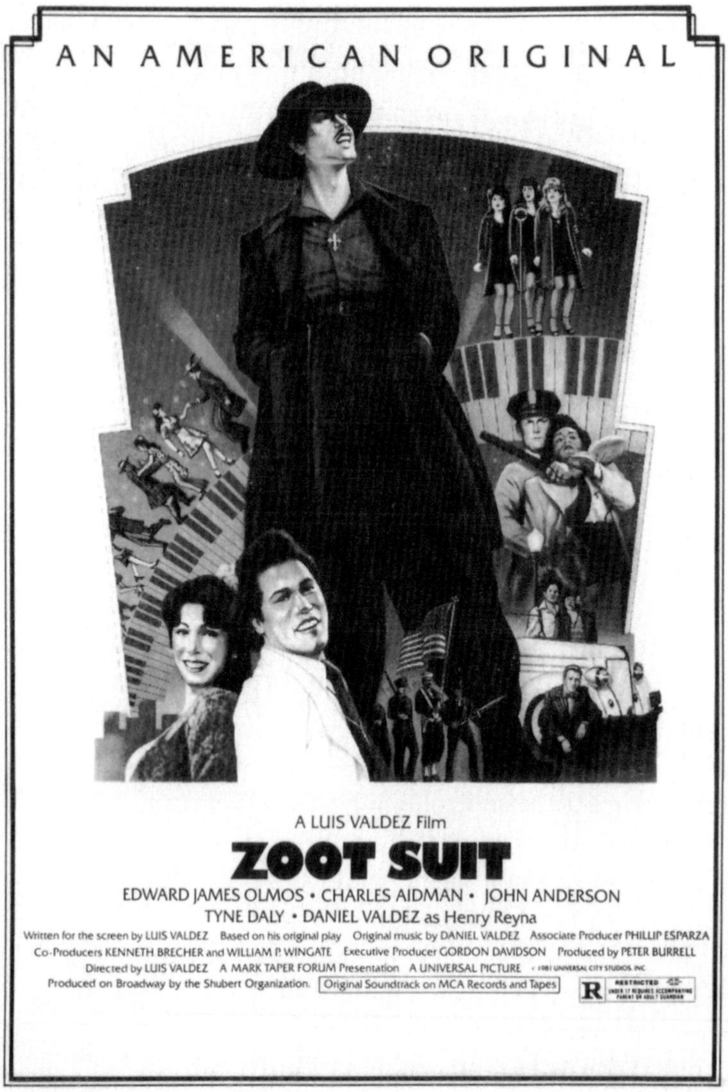

Poster for Luís Valdez's film *Zoot Suit* (1981), starring Edward James Olmos and Daniel Valdez

Here's Romance!" (October 13, 1983, directed by Christian I. Nyby II), a tale about a joyously demented Hispanic, played by Martín Ferrero, who's convinced that he *is* Cisco and, in an outfit like Duncan Renaldo's and astride a stallion that could be mistaken in dim light for Diablo, rides the mean streets of the city helping its cops keep the peace.

Early in the 1980s screenwriter Michael Kane made Cisco and Pancho the main characters in a script that borrowed from the period's most spectacular movie success by having the compadres hunt for an old West version of the lost ark. The project knocked around for more than a decade and wound up at Turner Pictures, the company formed to produce original features for Ted Turner's TNT cable network. Signed to direct the film and revise Kane's script so as to "kick it into the nineties" was the foremost Latino playwright-moviemaker north of the Rio Grande.

Luis Valdez (1940-) grew up in California's San Joaquin Valley, one of ten children born to a migrant worker couple. "When I was very young," he told a *Washington Post* reporter, "I was severely scalded and almost died. The local hospital refused to admit me because I was a 'farm labor' child. . . . So for six months I slept on my mother's stomach while the skin on my back came back into place." After Pearl Harbor the army offered the Valdez family and many other Mexican farm workers the properties that had belonged to California's Japanese Americans, now forcibly moved into detention camps. "So from 1942 until 1946 we had a ranch, we had land, we had money. I grew up with all that." The family lost the farm after the war and Luis was soon picking cotton for three dollars a day.

In the early 1960s, as a scholarship student at San Jose State College, Valdez discovered his twin careers as playwright and political activist, fusing them in 1965 when he organized El Teatro Campesino, a troupe that rode around the fields performing *actos* (propaganda skits) on the backs of flatbed trucks in support of the United Farm Workers strike to unionize migrant laborers. One of Valdez's sketches from this period was "El Bandido," which was loosely based on his childhood memories of the late-forties Cisco features and the TV series. In his version, as he described it, "Pancho finally asks the operative question: 'Cisco, why the hell are we always helping gringos?' " In 1971 he settled El Teatro Campesino in San Juan Bautista, a tiny farm town thirty-five miles south of San Jose.

The best known play Valdez wrote during his firebrand years was *Zoot Suit* (1978), a dramatization of the Sleepy Lagoon case of the 1940s in which twelve Chicano street kids were sentenced to life in prison for a murder probably committed by none of them. Costarring in the play were Valdez's brother Daniel and a young actor named Edward James Olmos, who went on to become a movie and TV star and won an Emmy for his role as Lt. Castillo on the *Miami Vice* series. The play won the Los Angeles Drama Critics Circle award and ran in southern California for almost a year. Valdez then became the first Latino dramatist to have one of his works produced on Broadway, but the play closed in New York after five weeks. The movie *Zoot Suit* (Universal, 1981), shot by Valdez on a two-week schedule and a $3,000,000 budget, was a disaster. As one sympathetic observer commented, "They might as well have given him a jar and said, 'Cross the ocean.'"

Both critically and commercially, Valdez did much better with *La Bamba* (New Visions/ Columbia, 1987), which propelled Lou Diamond Phillips to stardom playing Ritchie Valens, the Chicano rock-'n'-roll legend who died in a 1959 plane crash at the age of seventeen. "Our attempt now is to reach as large an audience as possible," Valdez said, meaning that he no longer identified himself as a Latino writing and directing for other Latinos but instead would work to balance his ethnic interests with his desire for mainstream commercial success. Former ideological comrades accused him of selling out to the gringos and started calling him "Tío Taco," which is the same as calling a black man "Uncle Tom." He apparently saw the Cisco project as a golden opportunity to prove he could be as anti-gringo as ever and still make a hit.

"Cisco and Pancho were fun characters," he told *TV Guide* (February 12, 1994), "and I was really taken with them [as a child] because they were the only Mexican heroes on the screen." When Turner Pictures hired him to direct and rewrite *The Cisco Kid* (1994), he aimed for it to be two kinds of picture in one: a wild Spielbergesque action flick and a strong assertion of ethnic pride and defiance like "El Bandido" and his earlier features. For the music beneath the credits he chose War's 20-year-old Cisco song. As Cisco he cast Jimmy Smits, the handsome young actor of Puerto Rican and Dutch descent who had become a household name playing attorney Víctor Sifuentes on the *L.A. Law* series. For the part of Pancho he signed Cheech Marín, best known as the costar of *Up in Smoke* and other marijuana-related comedies. The crew and cast were almost all Latino except, of course, for the Anglo characters, each of whom is a walking cesspool of

Cheech Marín as Pancho and Jimmy Smits as the Cisco Kid in Luis Valdez's 1994 film, *The Cisco Kid*

evil. "If the film is labeled as politically correct," pronounced one of TNT's senior vice-presidents, "that's not a bad brush to be tarred with." If TNT had bothered to season the storyline with some nonpolitical common sense or had hired a competent second unit director to shoot what passes in the picture for action sequences, *The Cisco Kid* might have turned into a watchable telefilm. As broadcast, however, it left much to be desired.

The year is 1867 and, as we learn much later, a dashing young Californio named Francisco Hernán Sánchez Aguilar de Solares, Cisco for short (Jimmy Smits), has led a grungy assortment of Confederate veterans into Mexico for the purpose of selling a wagonload of Civil War weapons, including a Gatling gun, to the revolutionaries under Benito Juárez, who are fighting to overthrow the French-supported puppet emperor Maximilian. Cisco has gotten into some never-specified trouble trying to rescue a woman named Libertad from a French army brothel and has wound up in a prison cell under sentence of death. In another cell awaiting the

Benito Juárez served five terms (1858-1872) as president of Mexico and became one of the country's most beloved leaders.

is traveling to the provincial capital of Chiloquín to marry Delacroix (Ron Perlman), a lieutenant colonel in the army of occupation.

Taken by Pancho to the mountain pass that the rebels must hold against the French at all costs, Cisco is introduced to the local Juarista generals, Montano (Pedro Armendáriz Jr.) and Gutiérrez (Honorato Magaloni), and to Doña Josefa (Teresa Lagunes), a plain woman with glasses who obviously holds a high rank in the rebel chain of command. "You are not part of us?" she asks. "No," Cisco replies, "I am not political, señora." "Neither are we," she tells him. "We just want our country back." Cisco and the Juaristas agree on a price for the weapons he's brought into Mexico. Meanwhile in Chiloquín, his Texan ex-partners Washam (Tony Amendola) and Lundquist (Tim Thomerson) double-cross Cisco and Juárez and make their own deal for the guns with Dupré. The general promises them a fortune if they and the other Texans will attack the enemy village of San Miguel de Oro and steal El Niño, a red-gold statue of the infant Jesus cast in the time of Cortez, which is exposed only on Christmas Day and without which the superstitious Juarista peasants will lose their will to fight and cave in to the French. Spookily awesome pseudo-John Williams music on the soundtrack signals to us that the next segment of this film's plot will be borrowed from Spielberg's *Raiders of the Lost Ark.*

On Christmas morning Cisco is taken into San Miguel and discovers that Pancho is not a priest but a married man with a pregnant wife (Yareli Arizmendi) and six children. The entire Rivera family and Cisco go to church for the ceremony and the exposure of El Niño—which is interrupted when Washam and Lundquist and their gang ride their horses into the building, shoot the altar to pieces, and grab the golden statue. Cisco is knocked out in the fight and the church catches fire, with Pancho's daughter Linda (Marisol Valdez) trapped in the choir loft. In a scene that reminds younger viewers of the so-called Lash LaRue stunt from *Star Wars* (1977) but that actually comes from one of the classic chapter endings of the serial *Zorro's Fighting Legion* (Republic, 1939), Cisco hurls himself and the child on the church bell rope through a stained glass window to the street below.

The next morning over a tequila breakfast Cisco and Pancho make plans to recover the statue. On their way to the governor's palace in Chiloquín, where they're convinced El Niño must have been taken, they stop for a meal at a cantina where the old proprietress (Valentina Ponzanneli) and every

same fate is Francisco Rivera, known as Pancho (Cheech Marín), a Juarista with a price on his head, disguised as a priest. (The French think he's a genuine priest and why they're about to kill him is something else Valdez never bothers to explain.) The film opens with its best scene as these two strangers are yoked together with a ball and chain and dragged through the foul prison corridors to the courtyard, where a firing squad is at work. Just as they're to be shot, Juaristas raid the prison. How the battle turns out we never learn, but as French general Achille Dupré (Bruce Payne) rides in from out of nowhere with a counterattack force, Cisco and Pancho steal a burro and manage to escape in the confusion.

On their way to the Juaristas' mountain stronghold in Devil's Horns Pass, they go through a town under Dupré's control where tax collector Alain Vitton (Tony Pandolfo) is squeezing pesos from the campesinos. Cisco and Pancho kill off the troops guarding Vitton and recover not only a fortune in taxes bled from the people but also Cisco's stallion Diablo, who somehow or other wound up being given to the collector after Cisco's arrest. Stopping off at the town during this encounter is General Dupré's lovely niece Dominique (Sadie Frost), who

one of her customers unaccountably sport grotesque facial scars. Van Hoose (Clayton Landey) and several others from the gang that attacked the church happen to drop in at the same cantina and get decimated by our amigos in the film's next shootout.

Once in Chiloquín, Cisco and Pancho learn that a rodeo is being held in the municipal arena and that the winner will be a guest at the governor's ball that evening. Seeing a heaven-sent opportunity to search the palace for El Niño, Cisco signs up as a contestant and effortlessly takes top honors in every event. Sharing a box at the games are General Dupré and his niece Dominique, who recognizes Cisco from the tax collector incident but says nothing.

At the lavish ball that night, while Cisco dances sensuously with Dominique under the furious glare of her cigar-chomping fiancé, Delacroix, Pancho slips upstairs and hides in Dupré's office just in time to see Washam and Lundquist arrive and turn over El Niño and to hear the general order an attack on Devil's Horns Pass. Pancho filches the statue, but meanwhile, downstairs, the tax collector Vitton has also recognized Cisco, and the compadres have to fight their way out of the palace in a comic action sequence that culminates in their being captured by Washam and Lundquist in the street. The Texans march their prisoners through a stable where a wagon with the U.S. guns is being kept and into the brothel, where the rest of the gringos are enjoying themselves. Washam tells his crew that Dupré has refused to pay the fortune promised for El Niño. They search Pancho, find the statue under his shirt, and are crowing over their good luck when in yet another played-for-laughs action scene they're set upon by all the women in the brothel, who in fact are patriotic Juarista spies. El Niño gets tossed around in the air like a golden football until Cisco and Pancho manage to escape with both the statue and the wagonload of guns. Needing something else to make Dupré pay what he's promised, the Texans then kidnap Dominique and hide her in an abandoned mine.

After delivering the weapons and El Niño to Devil's Horns Pass, Cisco demands the money he'd bargained for plus a receipt personally signed by Juárez. "You've been living with the gringos too long," Pancho spits at him. "Screw you, bandido." A fistfight breaks out between them that ends only when Cisco offers an explanation that explains nothing, claiming that he'd gotten into some trouble in California and was forced by federal agents to bring the guns into Mexico.

A Juarista spy from the governor's palace races into camp with the news that Dupré and the entire

Photo still from *Zorro's Fighting Legion* (1939), considered to be one of the finest movie serials ever made

French army will attack the next day at dawn. This shouldn't be news at all because Pancho had overheard the general giving the attack order, but if you want a plot with a little common sense, go switch channels to *Inspector Morse*. Pancho rides through the countryside like a Latino Paul Revere, shouting "The Frenchies are coming!" and displaying El Niño so that every farmer drops what he's doing and rushes to join the defense force. The nonpolitical Cisco (as he describes himself) is about to leave with his money when the spy tells him that Dominique has been kidnapped. He runs into several of the Texans in the scarred woman's cantina and, joined at the last moment by Pancho, wipes out all but Van Hoose, who is forced to tell where Dominique is being held. Cisco reaches the mine just in time to save her from a fate worse than death at the hands of her guard Haney (Charles McCaughan) and, for good measure, from a cave-in. The couple rejoin Pancho and apparently have sex that night.

The French troops attack the Juarista stronghold at dawn. While the battle is raging, Dupré, with a small force, captures the village of San Miguel. Unable to make anyone tell what happened to El Niño, he orders his Texan accomplices to massacre the women and children with the Gatling gun. (How come they're alongside the general when, the last time we looked, they were holding his niece for ransom? ¿Quién

Basil Rathbone (left) and Errol Flynn duel in *The Adventures of Robin Hood* (1938).

sabe?) Cisco and Pancho charge into the town square, seize the gun, lead the villagers in an assault on the French, and kill off Washam and Lundquist. As Dupré makes a break for it, Cisco chases him back into the heart of the battle at Devil's Horns Pass and knocks him off his horse. The general is killed when his head hits a rock. Suddenly the battlefield goes silent, and Delacroix engages in a flatly directed duel with Cisco that owes a great deal to the one-on-one between Errol Flynn and Basil Rathbone in *The Adventures of Robin Hood* (Warner Bros., 1938), even to the exchange of insults between sword thrusts. "You fight very well for a Mexican!" "You fight very poorly for a Frenchman." Pancho arrives with San Miguel villagers and the Gatling gun in time to mop up the remnants of the French army. "¡Viva Benito Juárez!" a suddenly politicized Cisco exclaims.

Juárez himself (Luis Valdez) visits the stronghold to thank Cisco and Pancho and plan for the final battle against Maximilian. At first Cisco wants to go back to California: "I'm thinking I like to be president." "Of what?" Pancho scoffs. "The Gringo States of America? Keep dreaming!" "I will," Cisco tells him. But as the film ends, after saying au revoir to Dominique, he rides off to rejoin the Juaristas and take part in the good fight with Pancho at his side.

The picture's storyline is chaotic, but what does more harm is a blunder that Valdez shares with many other recent directors: he sets out to make an old-fashioned action film and at the same time to show its superiority to a junk genre by making fun of his own work, hedging his bets, playing part of the film straight and the rest as a joke. For example, right after *The Cisco Kid*'s credits comes a prologue that will remind knowledgeable viewers of the opening of countless B Westerns—until the last line, where Valdez tries to make us laugh.

> The legend of the Cisco Kid begins in 1867. The Mexican forces of President Benito Juárez were locked in a life and death struggle with the occupying French armies of Napoleon III and his puppet Emperor, Maximilian. The fate of Mexico hung in the balance.
> Then along came a solitary hero . . .
> Well, maybe two.

Despite these flaws, as Professor Keller points out in chapter 12, there is important Chicano/Mexicano content in the film that resonates with the U.S. Latino community.

The reaction of film critics was mixed. While U.S. Latino critics took a more favorable view of the film, Anglo critics had a field day making it look ridiculous. Michelle Greppi of the *New York Post* described it as "full of hokey dialogue, accents so bad they're actionable, . . . action sequences that make professional wrestling look real, and hairdos that make Burt Reynolds's toupee look good . . . [Jimmy Smits] all but counts out loud as he clomps through his big ballroom scene . . . [In the action scenes] viewers can spot the stand-ins a mile away and count the number of times a punch or butt of a rifle misses its mark by a mile" (February 3, 1994). Gary Danchak of the St. Louis *Riverfront Times* stated, "For once, a TV movie where commercials will make it better. . . . There's plenty of deliberate bad overacting going on, especially with the secondary players. The fight scenes are straight out of *Batman*, lacking only the BLAMMO! BIFF! KAWHAP! cartoon balloons on the screen. . . . Pepe LePew does a better French accent [than Bruce Payne as Dupré]. Acts better, too. . . . The climactic battle between Cisco and the governor is risibly short, poorly staged, cheesily shot. . . . Oh, Cisco. Oh, Pancho. Vaya con queso, boys" (February 2-8, 1994, p. 31).

Plans for Valdez to direct a second Cisco telefeature with Smits and Marín were put on hold in the summer of 1994 when David Caruso quit his starring role in ABC's hit series *NYPD Blue* and Smits was signed to replace him. The Cisco saga may not be quite what we in our middle-to-golden years would have wished for, but chances are it will continue in the twenty-first century.

Lezwent!

THE CISCO KID FROM BAD GRINGO TO U.S. HISPANIC HERO

12

The Cisco Kid is a moving target. One that has grown neither old nor stale since he emerged 100 years ago from his origins as a bad but Mexicanized gringo, then a bad Mexican, eventually becoming a Hispanic hero who confronts assorted malefactors who would do harm to innocent and defenseless people. Ultimately, the 1994 Luis Valdez Cisco is transformed into a Mexican American persona who incarnates the challenge of being a hyphenated American and meets that challenge with gallantry and heroism. What is next? *¿Quién sabe?* He takes on new dimensions according to the tenor of the times and our nation's mutating needs for heroic vindication.

In 1994 I published a book about how the image of Hispanics developed in U.S. cinema over the past century. The epigraph of the book was

Y para la Raza, siempre

ai les va de cuento largo para que caigan en la cuenta y podamos iniciar

el ajuste de cuentas.

I didn't perceive it at the time, but the epigraph originally intended for the general development of the image of Hispanics in U.S. cinema fits the evolution of the Cisco Kid to a tee, and that's what this chapter is about, a *cuento largo que ajusta las cuentas.*

CISCO'S *PRIMERA SALIDA:* GRINGO IN A CORNUCOPIA OF ETHNICITY

Like Don Quixote, the Cisco Kid has had more than one *salida* in his development of a pedigree over the many years of his pop culture existence. However, he didn't begin with a pedigree; he started out as a mongrel. When O. Henry published the story "The Caballero's Way" in 1907, the character that emerged from the author's genial and ingenious but also bilious imagination was not Hispanic but a gringo with a Mexican demeanor. O. Henry's Cisco Kid lived and found refuge part of the time in a Hispanic world, had a Mexican lover, and above all had a sense of honor shaped by Hispanic culture.

His creator, William Sydney Porter (1862-1910), better known as O. Henry, was an odd duck. In addition to his twist endings, ironies, and rhetorical flourishes he was not averse to cultivating the discourse of the ethnic and racial superiority of the white race common to the late nineteenth and early twentieth centuries, some of it attached to specific currents of social Darwinism.

The influence of social Darwinism would appear to have an echo in "The Caballero's Way" in the story's preoccupation with Nordic versus Latin peoples.

Darwin's theories of evolution were used by others with peculiar vested interests to distinguish differences between the races of man based on genetic branching and natural selection. Genetic branching is the process that occurs in all species in which groups of a species become separated from one another, each developing its own genetic characteristics. Popular at the time of O. Henry's writings was the idea in one branch of social Darwinism that as a result of genetic branching and of natural selection working at a faster pace in the frigid north, the weak and unintelligent were eliminated more thoroughly than they were in warm climates. Nordicists reasoned that if animals adapted to their own climates, both physically and mentally, then humans did as well.

Another strand of social Darwinism expressed alarm about the status of the white race. In this view, it was the white race that had created the great Western civilization and therefore deserved to survive from the viewpoint of "survival of the fittest." However, in the modern world the white race was becoming a victim of internal politics while the yellow and brown races were gaining strength and threatening to overthrow the white man's domination of the globe. Many believed that it was only a matter of time before white people and Western culture would be supplanted by "inferior" races and cultures. This *voz de alarma* was being sounded by many influential individuals in the early twentieth century, including the American journalist Lothrop Stoddard in his

book *The Rising Tide of Color Against White World-Supremacy* (1920) and later the heroic aviator Charles Lindbergh, who believed that the white nations should keep technological advances, especially aviation, to themselves for their own advantage. Both these strands may have been given some play in "The Caballero's Way," the first in the imposing figure of Sandridge, a strapping Nordic type, particularly with respect to sexual selection (a key concern of social Darwinists) and his superiority over the Cisco Kid as an object of physical ardor in the mind of Tonia. The second current may be evoked in Cisco's triumph over Sandridge in the story.

The influence of these and similar currents of social Darwinism on O. Henry, or for that matter on his short story "The Caballero's Way," is subject to speculation. What is not is that the author was capable of the most injurious and prejudiced anti-Mexican verse imaginable. One of his poems, "Tamales," evokes a "greaser" who opens a tamale stand in Austin and avenges himself on the Texans for having killed his grandfather in the battle of San Jacinto. Don José Calderón serves his unwitting white victims tamales with fillings made of cat, terrier, and other such delicacies. Some of the poem is as follows:

> What boots it if we killed
> only one greaser,
> Don José Calderón?
> This is your deep revenge,
> You have greased all of us,
> Greased a whole nation
> With your Tamales . . .
> (*Complete Writings* 12: 257-58)

Notwithstanding verse such as that cited above, O. Henry was well acquainted with both Mexican culture and the Spanish language, to the degree, as we will review below, that some of his literary devices preceded and anticipated what Ernest Hemingway has become internationally recognized for with respect to the elaboration of Spanish through English. We need to examine the use of Spanish by O. Henry in some depth. In its invocation of Spanish, O. Henry's short story sets the stage for a characteristic that was at the heart of the first Cisco Kid sound film, *In Old Arizona*. Spanish was a major factor in the film, which earned an Academy Award for Warner Baxter as best actor. In fact, Spanish in all of its good, bad, and good-bad varieties is one of the elements that defined the Cisco Kid persona from its very inception.

The first *salida* of Cisco through the creative imagination of O. Henry was inspired by and mod-

Kris Kristofferson's Billy the Kid in *Pat Garrett and Billy the Kid* (1973) was an Anglo good-bad bandit.

eled somewhat on Billy the Kid. The element of "Kid" is notable in the nicknames of both Cisco and Billy. In Mexican culture, during the time frame of the latter figure's exploits and misdeeds and subsequently his first glorification, Billy the Kid was known as "el Bilito," with the Spanish diminutive -*ito* functioning as the Hispanic analog of the affix -*y* that makes William into Billy, Michael into Mickey, Thomas into Tommy, and so on. "Bilito" in Spanish simply adds to a Hispanicized pronunciation of Billy, in the form of Bili, the diminutive -*ito*, which stands for such attributes as "small," "young," or "dear," depending on the context. In the Mexican view of Billy the diminutive -*ito* may stand for all three: it certainly stands for youth, probably for small size, and possibly for affectionate feelings, given the folk claims of Billy the Kid's alleged affection for the Mexican communities of the Southwest. In the film *Pat Garrett and Billy the Kid* (1973), the view of Billy as an Anglo hero who was inextricably part of Mexican culture and a defender of Mexicans from some truly evil bandits is a significant factor that endows him with the bona fides of a good-bad bandit.

While the American view of Billy the Kid as a folk hero with high regard for individual Mexicans and Mexican communities is pretty consistent, from the Mexican side it is somewhat less so. It is a positive sign that Billy was called "el Bilito" in the time period contemporaneous with and shortly after his exploits and the formation of his persona, although it may be simply a convenient translation of Billy without any genuine affection attached to it.

On the other hand, we have identified two early New Mexican *corridos* composed by anonymous authors who claim that they aided Pat Garrett in the stalking and slaying of el Bilito. "Campaña de los Bilitos" ends in this fashion:

Pat Garrett ha sido el hombre
A quien todos le debemos
Este gran beneficio
Que nunca olvidaremos.

En fin jóvenes reflegen
La máxima del pasquín
Que ustedes han escuchado
Y tienen escrito allí.
Todo hombre que recio anda
Su carrera es muy cortita
Y antes que lo piense se halla
Rodeado en su casita
Como se hallaron los "Bilitos"
Y toda su pacotita.
(Lucero-White Lea 142)

The second *corrido* ("Muerte del Afamado Bilito") is primarily about el Bilito's escape from the Santa Fe prison after killing two guards "in cold blood" and how finally "the Kid" is killed by Pat Garrett. Billy is seen in a negative light and is described variously throughout the poem as "el Bilito malvado," "con criminal sonrisa," and with other such epithets. The *corrido* concludes:

Con la muerte del Bilito
Se halla este pueblo aliviado
Pues les daba temorcito
Hallerse por el rodeado.
Esta acción tan afamada.
. . . .
Ya concluyó el Bilecito
Después de tan corta vida
Cometió un delito
Que su muerte fué aplaudida.
Y así siguió Bilito
A sus compañeros buenos
Tom Foillard y Charley Bowdre
Pues no se podía menos.
(Lucero-White Lea 143-44)

Now let us turn to O. Henry's Cisco Kid. Three elements of "The Caballero's Way" that merit attention here are

the artful use of Spanish to develop the theme, including the use of Spanish for conveying intimacy and honor;

the characterization of the main characters and others through recourse to their ethnicity or race; and

the use of the motif of "the pear" and the "forests of pear" (prickly pear cactus) for various symbolic reasons, but particularly to distinguish the ingenuous Anglo, who is unfamiliar with the terrain, from the Hispanified Kid, who is an expert.

Spanish in the Service of Characterization in O. Henry's "The Caballero's Way"

While the folk hero Billy the Kid was called "el Bilito" by Mexicans during the late nineteenth and early twentieth centuries, keying on his first name, in contrast, in O. Henry's story the Mexican characters call Cisco "el Chivato," which refers to the *apodo* "Kid." Actually, although the character is a gringo, he has two *apodos*. Cisco is a nickname form of Francisco (as is Pancho). Francisco is a curious name for a gringo, but it is yet another reason that Cisco quickly became a Hispanic character. Putting the -*ito* on Cisco (e.g., Cisquito) is theoretically a possibility, but as a native speaker of Spanish I've never once heard it, probably because it is overkill, since "Cisco" itself is an endearing version of Francisco. So, in Spanish, keying on the element of the Kid is the obvious recourse. O. Henry's use of "el Chivato" and other Spanish locutions in "The Caballero's Way" points to a high level of understanding of the Spanish language and Mexican culture on his part in that the word *chivato* is not particularly common in Spanish and that O. Henry was able to use it accurately and with semantic resonances that enhance his short story. The primary meaning in Spanish of *chivato* is "kid" (baby goat, adult goat being *chivo*) between six months and a year old. Through the use of *chivato*, the O. Henry story confers youth on Cisco in the Spanish language in a connotative fashion. This connotative usage is analogous to but different from the specific designation of youth that is expressed by the name "el Bilito" in Spanish. Of course, at the same time we remind ourselves that "Billy" is the English analog of "Bilito" and that it customarily implies youth as well. In the English name, the quality of youth is overdetermined, being expressed both through the affix -*y* and the term "the Kid."

The nickname "el Chivato" works well in the text of "The Caballero's Way," for it does double duty. *Chivato* textually refers both to the human, Cisco, and to an animal, a baby goat, but it also conveys its meaning on an emotional level in an ingenious passage in which Tonia identifies a young, crippled goat as her companion and the object of her affections from which she wishes to "graduate" when the Anglo Sandridge comes into her life. (The following and subsequent citations of "The Caballero's Way" are to page numbers of this book, followed by the facsimile page number, e.g., 25: 195.)

> I play no spy; nor do I assume to master the thoughts of any human heart; but I assert, by the chronicler's right, that before a quarter of an hour had sped, Sandridge was teaching her how to plait a six-strand raw-hide stake-rope, and Tonia had explained to him that were it not for her little English book that the peripatetic *padre* had given her and the little crippled *chivo,* that she fed from a bottle, she would be very, very lonely indeed. (25: 195)

With respect to his youth, the Chivato/Kid is introduced in the second paragraph of the story as follows: "The Kid was twenty-five, looked twenty;

and a careful insurance company would have estimated the probable time of his demise at, say, twenty-six" (24: 191). Additionally and poignantly, the Kid as *chivato*, baby goat, is highlighted by the "other" recipient of Tonia's affection until Sandridge enters her life. That entity is none other than the "little crippled *chivo*" referred to above, which the Cisco Kid would *also* appear to take very much to heart, as evidenced by the following passage:

> On his way the Kid suddenly experienced the yearning that all men feel when wrong-doing loses its keen edge of delight. He yearned for the woman he loved to reassure him that she was his in spite of it. He wanted her to call his blood-thirstiness bravery and his cruelty devotion. He wanted Tonia to bring him water from the red jar under the brush shelter, and tell him how the *chivo* was thriving on the bottle. (25-26: 196-97)

A second, colloquial meaning in Spanish of *chivato* is *soplón,* a rat, canary, or informer. Obviously, both the primary meaning of baby goat and the colloquial meaning have resonance for "The Caballero's Way," inasmuch as the Cisco Kid accomplishes his ends not through the direct way of using his gun, but in the roundabout way analogous to that of a *soplón*. Thus, O. Henry's use of "Kid" in "The Caballero's Way" documents his understanding in depth of what is implied by the word *chivato*, the term that the Mexican characters in his story choose to describe the Kid.

In addition to this use of *chivato* and other examples of Spanish that we review below, an intensely Hispanic component of Cisco's character in "The Caballero's Way" is the form in which he devises an ingenious means of revenge in order to redress the transgressions of his lover, Tonia, despite the superficial and sporadic nature of his relationship with her. Using a form of Spanish that requires a deep knowledge of the language, the adverb *muy* with the noun *caballero,* a turn of phrase that is colloquially accurate, O. Henry describes the Kid as having, in addition to his marksmanship,

> another attribute for which he admired himself greatly. He was *muy caballero,* as the Mexicans express it, where the ladies were concerned. For them he had always gentle words and consideration. He could not have spoken a harsh word to a woman. He might ruthlessly slay their husbands and brothers, but he could not have laid the weight of a finger in anger upon a woman. (27: 203)

This *caballerosidad* and the quality of revenge that it determines is utterly alien to Sandridge, who is grief-stricken and foiled by the bad, Hispanified gringo.

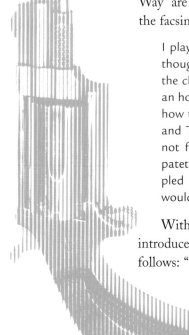

Just then all that Sandridge could think of to do was to go outside and throw himself face downward in the dust by the side of his hum-ming-bird, of whom not a feather fluttered. He was not a *caballero* by instinct, and he could not understand the niceties of revenge. (28: 208)

The successfully executed revenge plot is consistent with the Hispanic sense of aggrieved honor and is constructed within a Mexican and Latin frame of reference. Cisco's plot for exacting retribution for what he judges from his Hispanic sense of masculinity to be Tonia's perfidy with the Viking-like intruder, Sandridge, is not far removed from some of the honor plays of the Spanish Siglo de Oro, for example, Pedro Calderón de la Barca's *El médico de su honra* [The surgeon of his own honor]. In this, one of the most famous Calderón plays, the character successfully plots the murder of his wife, *even though she is innocent*, because his sense of honor has so warped his perceptions. Here we have a Spanish notion of marital honor that is pervaded with the ubiquitous and malicious "qué dirán," the "what will people say," that demands the saving of face. By the standards of Calderón's play, Tonia, guilty as hell from Cisco's point of view, clearly had it coming.

Race and Ethnicity in the Service of Characterization in "The Caballero's Way"

Generally, in both Hispanic art and in life, Spanish and Mexican notions of honor, transgressions of honor, and retribution for those transgressions rarely go outside the Hispanic world. However, interethnic rivalry is the norm for American popular cinema when Mexicans, Mexican Americans, or other Latinos are involved. Moreover, ethnicity is the coin of the realm in "The Caballero's Way." In this story, not only is interethnic rivalry cultivated, but the honor grievance, the matter of *pundonor* (point of honor) as it is expressed in the Hispanic world, is both felt and resolved by a Hispanified gringo. Extraordinary!

In addition to the Kid and Tonia, other characterizations on the basis of ethnicity abound in the O. Henry story. The Anglo rival, Sandridge, is described as "blond as a Viking, quiet as a deacon, dangerous as a machine gun. . . ." The family member with whom Tonia lived is "a father or grandfather, a lineal Aztec, somewhat less than a thousand years old, who herded a hundred goats and lived in a continuous drunken dream from drinking *mescal*."

Mexicans were an ambiguous lot in the eyes of the bad gringo, the Cisco Kid. As the opening of

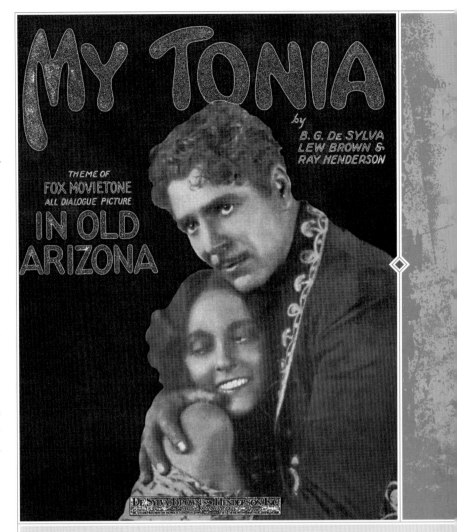

Warner Baxter and Dorothy Burgess, who starred in *In Old Arizona* (1929), were featured on the sheet music for a song from the film.

"The Caballero's Way" makes perfectly clear, the Kid's Hispanic sense of honor was no hindrance whatsoever to his murdering Mexicans: "The Cisco Kid had killed six men in more or less fair scrimmages, had murdered twice as many (mostly Mexicans), and had winged a larger number whom he modestly forbore to count. Therefore a woman loved him" (24: 191). The story also makes it apparent that the Kid killed for the fun of it, and Mexicans had taken cognizance of that fact. When Lieutenant Sandridge came around asking about the Kid, logically enough the first people he asked were the Mexicans, but their response was less than rewarding.

> Far more than the law, the Mexicans dreaded the cold and certain vengeance of the lone rider that the ranger sought. It had been one of the Kid's pastimes to shoot Mexicans "to see them kick": if he demanded from them moribund Terpsichorean feats, simply that he might be entertained, what terrible and extreme penalties would be certain to follow

should they anger him! One and all they lounged with upturned palms and shrugging shoulders, filling the air with *"quien sabes"* and denials of the Kid's acquaintance. (25: 193) [The phrase "Terpischorean feats" was not uncommon during the time O. Henry was writing. The etymology is from the Latin form of the Greek Terpsichorē, muse of dancing and dramatic chorus. Hence the theatrical slang "terp," "stage dancer, chorus girl."]

Just as the Kid had no qualms about killing Mexicans, he didn't have any about killing Anglos or anyone else, either. Mexicans were not his exclusive target. He was an equal opportunity murderer, and Mexicans simply happened to exist in force within his six-gun's range. O. Henry tells us that the Kid's "habitat was between the Frio and the Rio Grande" (191). This is south Texas and for centuries it has been and continues to be preponderantly Mexican, and, after the independence of Texas, the Mexican War and the Treaty of Guadalupe Hidalgo of 1848, Mexican American. Almost all of the rivers in Texas run on a diagonal from the northwest to the southeast and empty into the Gulf of Mexico. And almost all of these rivers retain their Spanish names. From north to south are the Guadalupe River, the San Antonio River, the Frio River, the West Nueces River (the Frio and the West Nueces join a short distance before the Gulf), and finally, the Rio Grande/Río Bravo (the latter is its name in Mexico.) The Cisco Kid lived in south Texas, south of where O. Henry lived for a number of years, which was San Antonio.

While the Kid was fine with killing Mexicans along with anyone else, he was attached to "the woman who loved him," who was a person of mixed race, Caucasian and Mexican. Tonia, the Kid's love interest, is a proto-Chicana, living on the hyphen. And she is a looker and a Carmen look-alike! It is worth noting that our broad Bold Caballero and Noble Bandida project is attentive to the enormous influence that the figure of Carmen—the archetypal and stereotypical Hispanic vamp created by Prosper Mérimée in his 1845 novel *Carmen*—had on the formation of the identity and character of Mexican, Mexican American, and other Latina female characters of popular culture, most especially in United States film. The shadow of Carmen looms large in the Cisco Kid's love interest: "Tonia Perez, the girl who loved the Cisco Kid, was half Carmen, half Madonna, and the rest—oh, yes, a woman who is half Carmen and half Madonna can

always be something more—the rest, let us say, was humming-bird" (24: 191).

Thus "The Caballero's Way" establishes the Cisco Kid as a Hispanified gringo in love with or at least attached to a half-Mexican of desirable physical qualities. She is attractive, particularly on the Spanish side, e.g., the Carmen half of the ledger; on the other hand, the Kid has a physical appearance and cultural features that could place him in the Mexican community and give him the conventional status in American pop culture of one who goes down to defeat in the "all's fair in love and war" game at the hands of an Anglo rival with Nordic features. The brown character defeated in love or battle by the white one is a classic American pop culture theme. This is precisely what happens to the Cisco Kid in his 1914 filmic appearance, this time as a Mexican.

The Motif of the Mexican Pear

I n O. Henry's story, the Kid is depicted as one who can hardly compete physically with his Anglo rival.

> Never before had Tonia seen such a man as this. He seemed to be made of sunshine and blood-red tissue and clear weather. He seemed to illuminate the shadow of the pear when he smiled, as though the sun were rising again. The men she had known had been small and dark. Even the Kid, in spite of his achievements, was a stripling no larger than herself, with black, straight hair and a cold, marble face that chilled the noon-day. (25: 194-95)

The Kid was short, dark, profoundly bilingual and bicultural, and unable to physically measure up to his "good-guy" albeit trickable gringo rival, the strawberry-complexioned Sandridge. What the Kid lacked in appearance, he made up for not only with his six-gun expertise, but in bicultural cunning of the eminently mongrelistic kind. The Nordic Sandridge may seem to Tonia to "illuminate the shadow of the pear," but he is in the wrong forest. This is not the pear forest of colder climes; it is the forest of the Mexican pear. The Kid is the master of this pear forest, and this particular milieu first appears when Tonia is introduced in the story:

> Back of the *jacal* a tremendous forest of bristling pear, twenty feet high at its worst, crowded almost to its door. It was along the bewildering maze of this spinous thicket that the speckled roan would bring the Kid to see his girl. And once, clinging like a lizard to the ridge-pole, high up under the peaked grass roof, he

had heard Tonia, with her Madonna face and Carmen beauty and humming-bird soul, parley with the sheriff's posse, denying knowledge of her man in her soft *mélange* of Spanish and English. (24: 192)

"Illuminating the pear forest" in "The Caballero's Way" is simply an *espejismo*. The pear forest by its very nature is not accessible to illumination, and for that matter, except for experts, it is not accessible to navigation. O. Henry uses a technique that is very common among Latin American writers (for example, the author José Eustasio Rivera in his 1924 novel *La vorágine*). In this work Rivera personalizes the adverse environment of the rainforest. As the novel communicates, *se los tragó la selva*, "they were swallowed by jungle." In similar fashion, O. Henry anticipates this sort of personalization and in fact associates the forest of cactus with the hardships of the Amazonian jungle:

> More weird and lonesome than the journey of an Amazonian explorer is the ride of one through a Texas pear flat. With dismal monotony and startling variety the uncanny and multiform shapes of the cacti lift their twisted trunks, and fat, bristly hands to encumber the way. The demon plant, appearing to live without soil or rain, seems to taunt the parched traveler with its lush gray greenness. It warps itself a thousand times about what look to be open and inviting paths, only to lure the rider into blind and impassable spine-defended "bottoms of the bag," leaving him to retreat, if he can, with the points of the compass whirling in his head. (26: 197)

O. Henry concludes, "To be lost in the pear is to die almost the death of the thief on the cross, pierced by nails and with grotesque shapes of all the fiends hovering about" (Ibid.).

It is from his secure hiding place in the pear that the Kid witnesses his betrayal by Tonia and in which he hatches the cunning scheme that is so alien to the culture and logic of Sandridge:

> Considering this extremely courteous idiosyncrasy of the Kid and the pride that he took in it, one can perceive that the solution of the problem that was presented to him by what he saw and heard from his hiding-place in the pear that afternoon (at least as to one of the actors) must have been obscured by difficulties. And yet one could not think of the Kid overlooking little matters of that kind. (27: 203)

Out of this prickly pear/nopalito environment the bad gringo Cisco first emerged, plotted maliciously and successfully, and got off scot-free. Nevertheless, this is the persona who over decades developed into

Zoot Suit writer and director Luis Valdez became the first Chicano director to have a play produced on Broadway (1979). In 1981 it was made into a movie starring Edward James Olmos.

a good U.S. Hispanic figure that thrilled children, gained the admiration of adults, and engendered the pride of ownership among Chicanos that was consummated in Luis Valdez's version. What a guy! What a country! *¡Ay bendito!*

GOOD SPANISH, GOOD-BAD SPANISH, BAD SPANISH

et us turn to some additional considerations of Spanish, both in "The Caballero's Way" and its abundant use in the early sound film *In Old Arizona*.

In this diglossic world of ours we have a multitude of forms of Spanish, such as the standard normal variety heard on Spanish-language television and the various vernaculars that populate the Hispanic world—including Mexamerica—used in relaxed and casual speech, in the baseball stadium and the *taquería*. An example of the latter is *fuímonos*, the Spanish construct that is the basis of "lezwent," which was used by Leo Carrillo in his interpretation of Cisco's sidekick, Pancho. It is a vernacular and idiomatic case of "good" Spanish, although it is hardly standard normal Spanish. But while *fuímonos* is certainly a colloquial form, it is intelligible and is used by native or otherwise fluent speakers.

Then we have various types of Spanish that cross la frontera of acceptance by the Spanish-speaking community. One of these is "no problemo," made famous by the current governor of California. If you google "no problemo" you get over a million hits. Another is "mucho macho." If you google this, you'll be surprised with 1,960,000 hits. My favorite of the dozen I sampled was "Williams College Mucho Macho MooCow Military Marching Band." Hooray for the Beatles, who live on in mock Spanish! "Mock Spanish" is the category in which examples of this kind are pigeonholed. If you google "mock Spanish" you get over four million hits! The dozen that I looked at were divided among the condemnatory and the exculpatory.

On the condemnatory side, the extremist view of linguistic anthropologist Jane Hill has received more attention than others. It has become common in American discourse for the far out to get the lion's share of attention. Hill condemns "mock Spanish" as a covert form of racism in her symposium presentation, "Mock Spanish: A Site for the Indexical Reproduction of Racism in American English" (1995). It is a rather weighty matter to decry as racist discourse the ilk of Arnold Schwarzenegger's "Hasta la vista, baby" and "no problemo" as well as numerous other "derogatory" phrases like "Adiós cucaracha." Hill claims, "It is important to emphasize that Mock Spanish is used almost entirely by Anglo speakers of English when addressing other Anglos. All parties to the usage can be (and usually are) monolingual speakers of English." That assertion is simply wrong.

On the exculpatory side is an interesting editorial (March 2, 2000) in the student newspaper, *The Daily Wildcat*, of the University of Arizona, where Hill teaches. Entitled "Editorial: Mock Spanish not racist, just natural," the newspaper takes issue specifically with Hill:

> A University of Arizona professor recently lectured on the use of "Mock Spanish"—Spanish words adapted into pop-culture expressions—as a form of racism, sparking a number of letters commenting on the idea. . . .
>
> Anthropology professor Jane Hill discussed varying levels of offensive speech, from racial

slurs, down to "Hasta la vista, baby." While the former is obviously more hurtful than the latter, Hill argued that all levels of Mock Spanish are potentially offensive and vulgar.

> It's true that with any mixture of races, misunderstanding of culture and ignorance of customs can hurt feelings. But in the real world, where a white teenager from a white town can come to school and live with someone directly from a reservation, for example, this is a risk that must be taken. In the daily struggle to understand each other and unearth internal stereotypes, words are thrown around and customs are explored.
>
> That would lead to a dull world. All whites would be white and live only like other whites.
>
> But that's not the way it is, and it never should be. Border town residents often speak a Spanish-English hybrid, if only out of convenience for living among members of two cultures. Friends greet each other with, "Que pasa?" And Ricky Martin—like him or not—bridges musical genres with Spanglish lyrics and bilingual albums.
>
> It's a good thing. . . .
>
> Every language of the world has adopted [*sic*] and mutated because of proximity of other languages. It's a natural part of human evolution, just as every human's blood contains elements of other "races."
>
> When all lectures and studies are said and done, unless it's meant with disrespect, it really is no problemo.

While we can view the phenomenon as good, bad, or good-bad—and I prefer good-bad because it fits so well with this book and the overall noble bandit multimedia project—some of the most common forms of mock Spanish have acquired a huge pop culture cachet. This cachet is so widely dispersed in all sectors of society that Chicanos—whether native Spanish speakers, fluent nonnative speakers, or speakers who have suffered Spanish language loss at various levels—find themselves parroting "no problemo" and the like for any number of reasons, one of them being humorous self-deprecation and another a sort of polyphonic, polyvalent irony that can serve a wide number of purposes since it points to something, but the *algo* needs to be interpreted through other clues.

Another form of "good-bad Spanish," if I may be permitted the conceit to use such a term for "heuristic" purposes, is of the sort that we bilinguals use. *Dame una quebrada*, which is a "semantic transfer" or calque derived from "Give me a break," is a phrase that my Chicano buddies and I have been using for at least forty years. Apparently there is now a television show in Puerto Rico called *Dame una quebrada.* The converse phenomenon among our set of jolly language argonauts searching for a felicitous linguistic golden fleece is the phrase "you threw yourself out," which is the calque from Spanish into English of *te aventaste* (you outdid yourself). When I was a teenager, our set used to lament, "Necesito un dátile," or boast, "Ya tengo un dátile." "Dátile" (more commonly "dátil") is encrypted Spanish that can only be understood in context by a proficient bilingual since in standard Spanish it stands for a "date" strictly of the fruit kind (that comes from a tree), and not the animal kind that goes to the prom. In the bilingual lens it is transformed into a synonym for the English "date" in its social behavior meaning.

Examples like *dame una quebrada* are often used by sociolinguists to document all sorts of language mixing and sometimes to express *la voz de alarma* over the imminent apocalyptic pidginization of Spanish in English-language contact areas. There also exists the phenomenon of a nonbilingually encrypted, unselfconscious use of Spanish that is derived from English. Maybe a problem exists here, but hardly of the apocalyptic kind, when someone uses without sub rosa bilingual intent *dámelo para atrás*, which comes from English "give it back to me" but in Spanish sounds strange and suggestively sexual. However, the set of educated bilinguals with whom I am familiar use *dame una quebrada* and the like emphatically self-consciously and for novel humorous effect. Likewise, "no problemo" has caught on and can be used by a bilingual who knows what s/he is doing for a variety of humorous effects of the ironic kind.

Here is a rather famous, liminal case of Chicano Spanish that displays all sorts of interactive effects with English:

> Desde el porche de mi chante, en mi barrio de Eastlos, Aztlán, watcho a mis carnales cruzar por los cales rumbo a sus cantones después del jale, vatos cabuliando con sus jainas, pachucos fuliando afuera de la marketa de don Charlie, agüelitas con chavalios de la mano y un bonche de raza que sale de los boses que vienen del daontaon. Toda ésta es mi Raza, alegre, orgullosa y muy jaladora aunque la placa siempre los esté tisiando. (Rodríguez del Pino 129)

Just because you are a native speaker of Spanish doesn't necessarily mean you are going to decode this easily. Hence, here is a transcription into standard normal Spanish of this passage.

> Desde la varanda de mi casa, en mi barrio del este de Los Ángeles, California, contemplo a mis hermanos pasearse por las calles rumbo a sus casas después del trabajo: jóvenes plati-cando con sus novias, pachucos divirtiéndose fuera de la tienda de don Carlos, abuelitas con niños de la mano y grupos de gente chicana que sale de los autobuses que llegan del centro. Toda ésta es mi Raza (chicanos), alegre, orgullosa y muy trabajadora, aunque la policía siempre los esté provocando. (Ibid.)

Now, finally, let us note the existence of simply bad Spanish that has never caught on in the Latina/o community, but like crabgrass on the lawn has taken hold in Anglo parlance and seems to be rooted there. This sort of thing, notwithstanding the misattribution of gender in "no problemo," is based on ignorance of Spanish morphosyntax and includes the ubiquitous examples from American film and film criticism, "bandito" and "federale." Sometimes you can find these in the same sentence, as in this Web commentary on a famous film: "The mythical Sierra Madre is where the famous line in *Treasure of the Sierra Madre* was uttered by a bandito posing as a federale: 'Badges? We don't need no stinkin' badges.'"

Where do we situate the Spanish used by O. Henry in "The Caballero's Way"? From the point of view of language usage, this is no Anglocentric short story sprinkled with a few Mexicanisms or pidgin Mexicanisms like "bandito" and "federale" for local color. To begin with, he uses a considerable number and variety of Spanish words and phrases. Words include *jacal* and *jacales, mescal, chivo, lavandera, frijoles, alma, caballo, caballero, tule,* and many others. Some phrases include *quién sabe, muy mal muchacho, muy caballero, pues señor,* and *válgame Dios.*

The facsimile version of the story (see pp. 24-28) from the *Complete Writings of O. Henry* does not have the proper diacritical marks with the exception of the tilde in *señor.* Thus standard Spanish *¡Válgame Dios!, ¡Qué mal muchacho!,* and the surname Pérez are typeset in the facsimile edition respectively as *Valgame Dios!, Que mal muchacho!,* and Perez. This should not surprise us, as American publishers have been omitting Spanish diacritical marks ever since the founding of the nation with no end in sight.

In chapter 1 we reviewed the use of "lezwent" in the Cisco Kid television series and concluded that substantially more than a malaprop was involved in the phrase. We also introduced certain techniques for which Ernest Hemingway has justifiably been recognized. One of those techniques was the use of "thee," "thou," "thine," "wert," and other forms of the English second person singular. In Old and Elizabethan English these were the familiar and intimate forms in contrast to "you," "ye," and so on, which were the formal singular. Over the centuries "you" became dominant and "thou" has almost disappeared. In fact, the English omnibus pronoun "you" can be translated in this millennium into Spanish as *tú, usted, ustedes, vosotros, vosotras, ti, te, os, lo, la, le, los, las, les,* and *se.* Nevertheless, although archaic, "thou," "thee," "thine," and related forms are still generally understood in English. What needs to be recognized is that, while Hemingway is noted for the technique of using "thou" and its analogs to represent Spanish *tú* and its second person singular forms, in fact O. Henry had made use of this technique already in 1907, preceding Hemingway by decades: "But then . . . I had not beheld thee, thou great, red mountain of a man! And thou art kind and good, as well as strong. Could one choose him, knowing thee? Let him die; for then I will not be filled with fear by day and night lest he hurt thee or me" (26: 200).

CISCO'S FUNGIBLE "ESPANISH" AND THE ACADEMY AWARD

Like Don Quixote and Sancho, the Avenging Arrow (Anita Delgado), Zorro, Lasca of the Rio Grande, and many others, the Cisco Kid had more than one *salida.* Eventually the hero of this enduring cycle became a protector not only of people, but of *el pueblo* in the distinctively Hispanic sense. Whither such a seemingly counterintuitive vector over the course of one hundred years of solitude and solidarity? The film *In Old Arizona* (1929) played a major role in the establishment of that trajectory. The film won an Academy Award for Warner Baxter as Best Actor for his performance as the Cisco Kid and was also nominated for Best Picture of 1928-1929. This was the first Academy Award competition, and it coincided with the appearance of the first sound films, a key element in the phenomenon of *In Old Arizona's* garnering the popularity it did. In fact, Raoul Walsh is generally thought to have been the first director to use sound recording equipment in a full-length movie shot outdoors. *In Old Arizona,* shot in Utah, was that film. Microphones hidden in the environment captured for the first time the sound of gunshots, a stampede, the galloping of

horses, and the tour de force: sizzling eggs. The film also boasts the first Mexican song (more or less) sung in a full-length film, "My Tonia."

Throughout its history, the expression of Spanish in American film has been wholly unsatisfactory. In contrast to the standards of the American film industry, the use of Spanish in O. Henry's "The Caballero's Way" was a model of fidelity. Emilio García Riera, in his seminal six-volume *México visto por el cine extranjero,* points out the deficiencies in the rendition of Spanish by the American film industry beginning with the first fifty-two films of thirty seconds each produced by Edison Kinetoscope in 1894. One of these films, *Pedro Esquirel and Dionecio Gonzales-Mexican Duel,*

> . . . revealed simply by its transcription of the names, the inattentive spirit that would guide American film in its treatment of Mexico (and of everything exotic or strange, it should be acknowledged). . . . The first Mexicans on film, real or simulated, were called, according to the film, Pedro Esquirel and Dionecio Gonzales. Things were bad from the very beginning. What is likely is that the first character in reality was Esquivel and the second Dionisio González; but these characters were afflicted by the enduring American confusion of *zetas* and *eses* that appear in Spanish names. Sixty years later, another Mexican character in American film, Speedy Gonzales, evinced the same mistake: Gonzales instead of González. (*México visto* 1: 15; my translation)

Much of García Riera's book is dedicated to a review and analysis not only of the shortcomings in the expression of Spanish in American film, which is merely a side effect, but also of the negative stereotypes and prejudicial assumptions that suffuse the characterization, plot, choreography, props, sets, and just about everything else that goes into films. Spanish malaprops appear in *In Old Arizona* as well. Instead of the standard Spanish "Toña," the lead female is called Tonia (admittedly, just as it appears in O. Henry's story).

All that said, *In Old Arizona* benefited mightily from its use of Spanish in order to establish characters, to introduce music and song, and to support the plot, which is premised on the rivalry between a gringo and a Latino for the affections of a señorita. In chapter 4, Cisco Talks: Warner Baxter, Professor Nevins describes the sharp differences of opinion on the merit of the film between critics Jon Tuska and William K. Everson. Nevins's own view is that Warner Baxter projects a convincing demeanor of Latino stoicism and sadness and that his Latino accent is far superior to that of other Anglos who had Latino roles during the period of the early sound films.

Nuevo Mexicano author Nash Candelaria has written a short story, "The Day the Cisco Kid Shot John Wayne," that phenomenologically documents the veracity and effectiveness of Warner Baxter's Cisco not only for mainstream viewers but for Latino audiences as well. (Candelaria has generously consented to the Bold Caballeros and Noble Bandidas project's reproducing the short story in its entirety; it can be found at http://noblebandits.asu.edu/ Text/KidShotWayne.html.) In Candelaria's short story, movies mediate the protagonists' transition into biculturalism. The Spanish-dominant New Mexican kids "barely tolerated those cowboy movies with actors like Johnny Mack Brown and 'Wild Bill' Elliott and Gene Autry and even Hopalong Cassidy. ¡Gringos! we'd sniff with disdain. But we'd watch them in preference to roaming the streets, and we'd cheer for the Indians and sometimes for the bad guys if they were swarthy and Mexican" (14).

In the story, the character of Zorro was a contested one.

> Zorro drew mixed reviews and was the subject of endless argument. "Spanish dandy!" one would scoff. "¿Dónde están los mejicanos?" Over in the background hanging onto their straw sombreros and smiling fearfully as they bowed to the tax collector, I remember.
>
> "But at least Zorro speaks the right language."
>
> Then somebody would hoot, "Yeah. Hollywood inglés. Look at the actors who play Zorro. Gringos every one. John Carroll. Reed Hadley. Tyrone Power. ¡Mierda!"
>
> That was what Zorro did to us. Better than Gene Autry but still a phony Spaniard while all the indios y mestizos were bit players. (Ibid.)

It is the authenticity of his ethnicity that has the New Mexican kids rooting for Cisco.

> . . . our favorite was the Cisco Kid. Even the one gringo who played the role, Warner Baxter, could have passed for a Mexican. More than one kid said he looked like my old man, so I was one of those who accepted Warner Baxter. Somebody even thought that he was Mexican but had changed his name so he could get parts in Hollywood—you know how Hollywood is. (Ibid.)

Thus *In Old Arizona* enjoys a fundamental level of significance in the transition of the Cisco Kid from his earlier persona as bad gringo to U.S. Hispanic hero. The Cisco Kid in this film is still fundamentally treacherous, but he is the first figure in the sound period to achieve a level of Hispanic veracity,

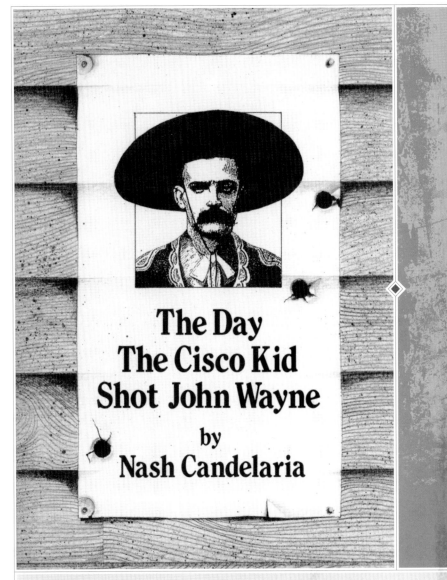

Book cover from *The Day the Cisco Kid Shot John Wayne* (Bilingual Press/Editorial Bilingüe, 1988)

psychologically and in his Spanish language use, which helped win an Academy Award for Warner Baxter. That Hispanic veracity is acknowledged, at least on the basis of Nash Candelaria's fictional, nostalgic memoir, by the U.S. Latino community as well. Even as Warner Baxter provides the platform, the Ciscos that follow Baxter are accepted even more wholeheartedly in the Candelaria story:

> . . . we conveniently leaped from that to cheering for the "real" Cisco Kids . . . Gilbert Roland, César Romero, Duncan Renaldo. With the arch-sidekick of all time, Chris-Pin Martin, who was better any day than Fuzzy Knight, Smiley Burnette, or Gabby Hayes.
>
> "Sí, Ceesco," we'd lisp to each other and laugh, trying to sound like Chris-Pin. (14-15)

The Hispanic element present in *In Old Arizona* did not emerge out of a vacuum. Quite to the

T he Cisco Kid and his sidekick were experts with their fists, their whips, and their trusty steeds. Nevertheless, guns are the staple of the Western, and Cisco and his comrade often had reason to use them.

Cisco (Duncan Renaldo) gets the drop on his adversaries in *The Daring Caballero* (1949).

Leo Carrillo peers through a window in a scene from *The Gay Amigo* (1949).

Cisco (Gilbert Roland) prepares for a duel with Smoke Kirby (Anthony Warde) in *King of the Bandits* (1947).

Cisco's aim is true in *Satan's Cradle* (1949), starring Duncan Renaldo, Leo Carrillo, and Ann Savage.

Gilbert Roland enters through a window, gun drawn, in this lobby card from *The Gay Cavalier* (1946).

Cisco (Gilbert Roland) struggles for the gun with Bennet (Harry Woods) in *South of Monterey* (1946).

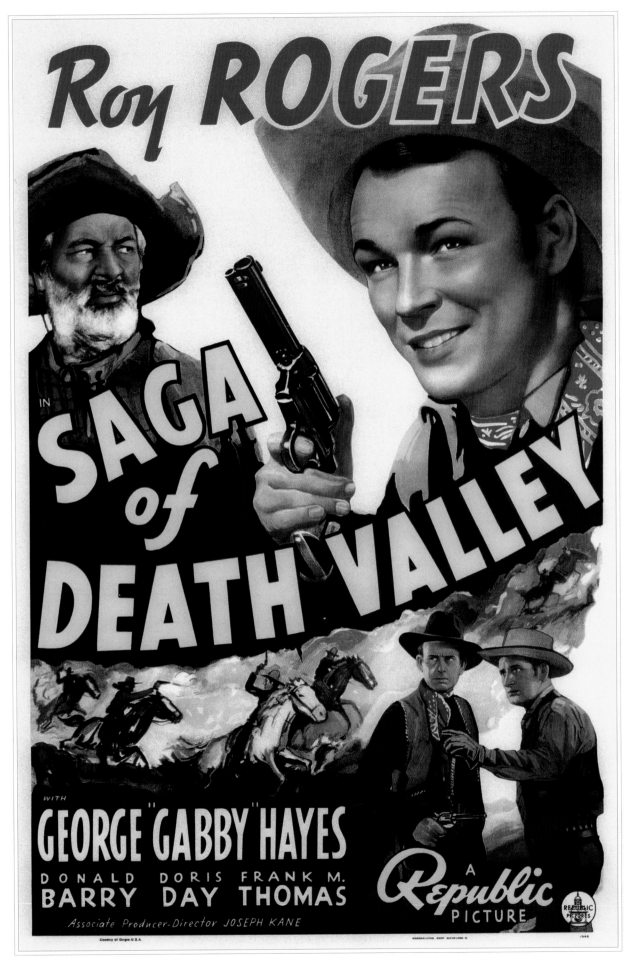

George "Gabby" Hayes was Roy Rogers's right-hand man in a number of films, including *Saga of Death Valley* (1939). The Doris Day who played the female lead is not the same woman who later costarred in romantic comedies with Rock Hudson and others.

Martín Garralaga (left) played Pancho to Duncan Renaldo's Cisco (right) in three films.

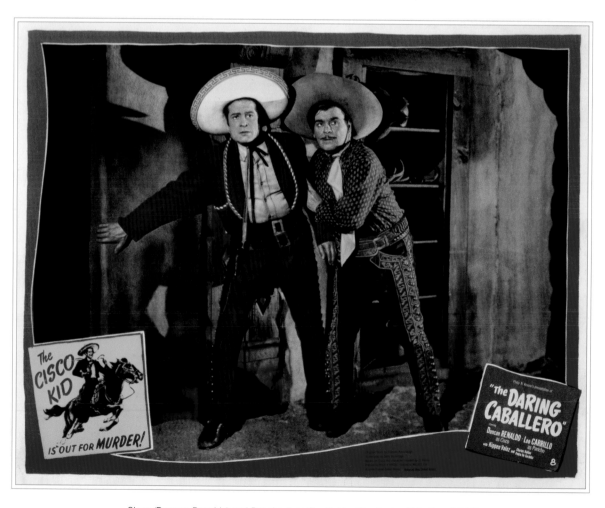

Cisco (Duncan Renaldo) and Pancho (Leo Carrillo) in *The Daring Caballero* (1949)

Claire Carleton, Leo Carrillo, Duncan Renaldo, and Douglas Fowley in a scene from *Satan's Cradle* (1949)

Gilbert Roland, Nacho Galindo, and Drew Allen in *The Gay Cavalier* (1946)

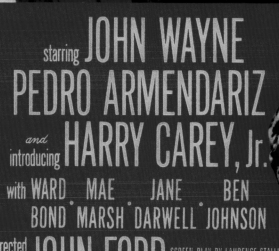

John Ford directed *3 Godfathers* (1948), featuring John Wayne, Pedro Armendáriz, and Harry Carey, Jr.

▪ ART OF BANDITRY ▪

The image of the Hispanic bandido or outlaw, both noble and base, has been a consistent theme in Mexican and Mexican American art.

Alfredo Arreguín's *Zapata's Messengers,* 1997, oil on canvas, 60" x 42"

Mexican illustrator José Guadalupe Posada (1852-1913) often expressed satire in his illustrations and prints. Commentary on revolution and violence were common in his works.

Sam Coronado's *Pancho Villa & The Cisco Kid,* 1999, serigraph, 16" x 22"

Poster showing Santiago Pérez's *El corrido de Gregorio Cortez,* 2002, oil on canvas, 48" x 72"

Joe Ray's *El Cisco Kid 2*, 2000, serigraph, 26" x 20"

contrary, it was built on a platform of numerous silent films. Similarly, numerous Hispanic-focused sound films followed the model set by the highly successful film directed by Raoul Walsh and starring Warner Baxter.

Hispanic-focused song and dance, the playing of musical instruments associated with the Latin world, and fiestas are frequent in films of the 1920s and earlier. One such film is *A California Romance* (1922, director Jerome Storm, starring John Gilbert and Estelle Taylor). John Gilbert, who was soon to achieve superstar status and make several films with Greta Garbo, plays the guitar in this film opposite Estelle Taylor, who in 1922 also was the lead in the Emmett J. Flynn-directed version of *A Fool There Was*. Gilbert Roland's professional name was created by combining John Gilbert's name with Ruth Roland's. In *Yankee Speed* (1924, director Robert N. Bradbury, starring Kenneth MacDonald and Jay Hunt), *Variety* (July 16, 1924) judged that the dances endowed the Mexican film with added local color. In *Don Q, Son of Zorro* (1925, director Donald Crisp, starring Douglas Fairbanks, Mary Astor, Donald Crisp, and Warner Oland), the character Don Q serenades his beloved with guitar in hand. *The Cowboy Cavalier* (1928, director Richard Thorpe, starring Buddy Roosevelt and Olive Hasbrouck) has an Anglo disguised as an "Aztec" who sings "Bandit's Love Song." In the 1928 version of *Ramona* (director Edwin Carewe, starring Dolores del Río and Warner Baxter) the character of Felipe, played by Roland Drew, sings in honor of his mother. *Ramona* may have been produced in both a silent version and a subsequent sound version. The most distinctive of these silent films with Hispanic musical elements is *Singer Jim McKee* (1924, director Clifford Smith), which stars William S. Hart as an Anglo who, in the intertitles, in stressful moments sings the refrain of a Mexican melody in Spanish.

The following films feature cantina girls or Latina dancers: *You Never Know* (1922, director Robert Ensminger, starring Earle Williams and Gertrude Astor), *June Madness* (1922, director Harry Beaumont, starring Viola Dana and Bryant Washburn), *The Golden Gift* (1922, director Maxwell Karger, starring Alice Lake and John Bowers), *The Girl of the Golden West* (1923, see below for further coverage), and *A Man of Quality* (1926, director Wesley Ruggles, starring George Walsh—director Raoul Walsh's brother—and Ruth Dwyer).

Fiestas were a common staple in U.S. silent film fare, and they appear prominently in the following

silent films: *The Power of Love* (1922, director Harry K. Fairall, starring Elliot Sparling, Barbara Bedford, and Noah Beery, the first and apparently only 3D film of the period, anticipating the 3D craze of the 1950s by three decades); *Yankee Madness* (1924, directed by Charles R. Seeling, starring George Larkin, Billie Dove, and Walter Long); *Hands Across the Border* (1926, director David Kirkland, starring Fred Thomson, Bess Flowers, and Tyrone Power, Sr., who died in 1931 in the arms of his more famous son, then age seventeen); and *The Yankee Señor* (1926, director Emmett J. Flynn, starring Tom Mix and Olive Borden). An interesting feature of the latter film was that while it was in black and white, the fiesta was filmed in two-strip Technicolor.

The new celebrities of the star system of the 1920s all did Mexicans/Latinos, as of course did Douglas Fairbanks, who had already achieved stardom in the preceding decade. Mae Murray starred in *Mademoiselle Midnight* (1924, director Robert Z. Leonard), set in the Mexico of Maximilian and Benito Juárez; Pola Negri starred in *Flower of Night* (1925, director Paul Bern) as a descendent of grandees forced to be a chorus girl in San Francisco before she returns to Mexico to vindicate her family; and Rudolph Valentino starred in *Moran of the Lady Letty* (1922, director George Melford) as a wealthy *hispano* from San Francisco abducted by smugglers on a Mexico-bound ship. None of these films portrayed Mexico in a particularly positive light, but a Gloria Swanson vehicle caused an international uproar. The film, *Her Husband's Trademark* (1922, director Sam Wood, starring Gloria Swanson, Richard Wayne, and Stuart Holmes) features a Mexican dance. In the film, the character played by Swanson travels to Mexico with her husband, who has obtained a concession of petroleum rights from the Mexican government. The plot includes a revolutionary general or bandit—it is hard to discern which—who attempts to abduct and ravish the woman with all possible forms of 1920s-style filmic titillation. Swanson, who wears twenty separate luxurious gowns in the film, is set in contrast to the mustachioed, cartridge-belted, and sombrero-laden "greasers."

Her Husband's Trademark caused an uproar in Mexico. Not only was it prohibited for containing scenes that were designated as "escandalosamente ofensivas," it provoked a general embargo by Mexico of all Famous Players-Lasky Corporation films, that corporation being part of Paramount at the time. The embargo extended as well to several other films considered "denigrantes" by the Mexican censors.

Wallace Beery, Lionel Barrymore, Ronald Reagan, and Chris-Pin Martin star in this 1941 Western.

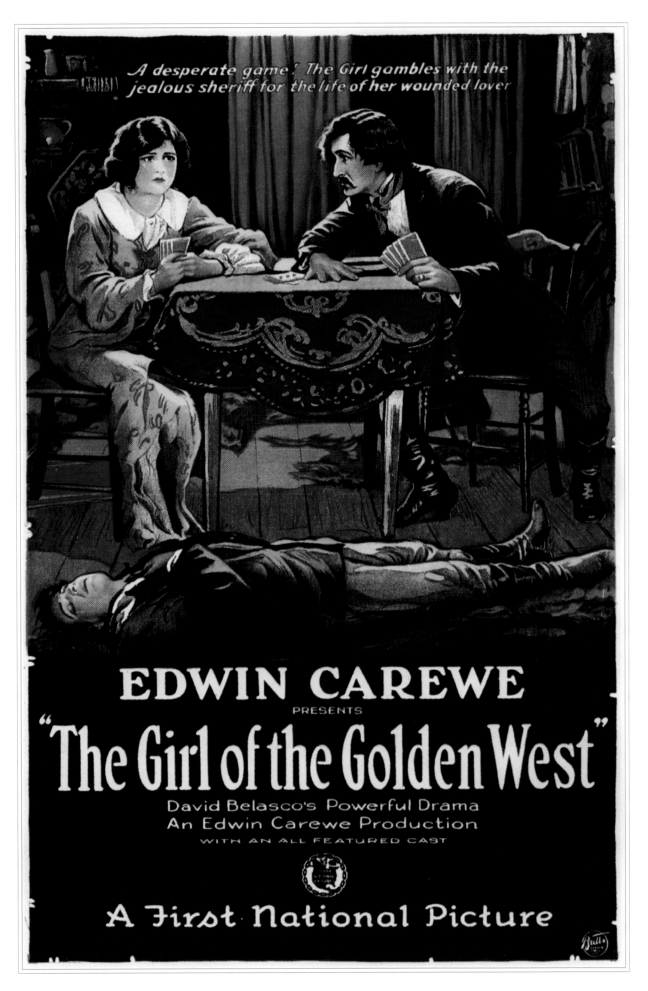

The Girl (Sylvia Breamer) gambles for the life of her wounded lover in Edwin Carewe's *The Girl of the Golden West* (1923).

The image of the good-bad hero in films has evolved in the last hundred years, and gender is no longer a boundary.

The Pride of Palomar (1922, director Frank Borzage, starring Forrest Stanley, Marjorie Daw, and Warner Oland) has been interpreted in Mexico as a film that sought to make amends. The plot revolves around the conventional threat of foreclosure on the family hacienda by an East Coast capitalist who owns the mortgage, but it adds an anti-Japanese twist to it. The foreclosure wants to sell the ranch to the evil Japanese Okada (Warner Oland) for colonization, but Don Miguel Farrell, one of numerous Irish-Mexicans that Hollywood was promoting during the 1920s (Don José O'Neil in *The Love Brand,* 1923; Juan de Dios O'Rourke in *The Fighting Edge,* 1925; Don Luis O'Flaherty in *Señor Daredevil,* 1926; Carlos Brent in *Romance Ranch,* 1924; and Pablo Wharton Cameron, in *Yankee Señor,* 1925) neutralizes both the easterner and the representative of the Yellow Peril. The film, screened in Mexico with the title *El orgullo de Palomar,* includes the re-creation of *El jarabe tapatío* (the Mexican Hat Dance), customarily identified as the Mexican national dance. The important Mexico City newspaper *El Universal* interpreted the film as a form of redress for the negative stereotypes that led to Mexico's embargo of American films:

> *El orgullo de Palomar* was a film produced to rehabilitate us in the eyes of the world and was made soon after the [Mexican] embargo was lifted on Paramount productions, about a year ago. . . . the fact that it presents a family in difficult straits, possessing a good fortune but one undermined by creditors, indicates that in the end, with a bit of effort, of dignity and of courage, the last descendent of the family is able to rehabilitate his lineage and avoid having his inheritance fall into the hands of mercenary interests. (Rafael Bermúdez Zataraín, *El Universal,* September 23, 1923; my translation)

It is useful to give some additional attention to two separate strands that precede and converge in the first sound film featuring the Cisco Kid: the endearing *bandido* and the films of the "Golden West" cycle.

The endearing *bandido* strand is well represented by *The Bad Man* (1923, director Edwin Carewe, starring Holbrook Blinn, who was the hero in the original play by Porter Emerson Browne). Browne was a playwright who in addition to his 1920 drama *The Bad Man* also did a 1909 play, *A Fool There Was,* which is an important work for the overall social bandit/noble bandit project. This play was turned into a film, but not the famous one starring Theda Bara. The origin of these vamp films, including both the Porter Emerson Browne drama/film and the Theda Bara vehicle, is Rudyard Kipling's 1897 poem "The Vampire," the first line of which begins, "A fool there was. . . ."

The 1923 *The Bad Man* was not only successful as a model of the noble bandit (see García Riera, *México visto por el cine extranjero,* vol. I, for a review of numerous other models and variations thereof), but it also incorporated elements that had an aural quality to them. The noble bandit interpreted by Blinn is called Pancho López, and he clearly harks back to Pancho Villa, who was still very much in the minds of American audiences in 1923. Pancho López, like Pancho Villa, rises from peonage to the status of head of a band of bandidos. As Arthur G. Pettit (1980) puts it, he is more of a buffoon than a bandit, but he is not ineffective both as a killer in his own right and as an avenger for a gringo to whom he is indebted for the latter having saved his life. Even more significant for us here is the melodious and sonorous quality of his persona. He boasts by means of the intertitles:

> I keel ze man sis morning,
> Heem call me dirty crook.
> I keel some more zis noontime
> And steal ess pocketbook. (Roeder 21)

The anonymous critic of *The New York Times* (October 9, 1923) recognized the endearing qualities of the Holbrook Blinn interpretation of which Warner Baxter was a genuine successor, and even more important, the critic from *Variety* (October 11, 1923) judged that at times you could hear Blinn whistle his words between his teeth and that surely they would be genuinely Mexican words despite the intertitles, which struck *Variety* as incongruously part French, part Canuck. The successful *The Bad Man* bore a sequel in *Zander the Great* (1925), with Blinn once again playing an endearing Mexican, but this time in a supporting role as sidekick to the main character (played by Harrison Ford), a bootlegger who redeems himself by defeating an evil outlaw. *The Bad Man* itself was the subject of two remakes in the sound period: in 1930, directed by Clarence G. Badger and starring Walter Huston, and in 1941, directed by Richard Thorpe and starring Wallace Beery as Pancho López, Lionel Barrymore as Uncle Henry Jones, Ronald Reagan as Gilbert 'Gil' Jones, and Chris-Pin Martin as Pedro.

The second strand, the various versions of the "Golden West," returns us to the musical and festive, but in grand form. In silent film, as we have seen previously, Mexican/Latino characters and settings had often been linked to dance, song, and fiestas, and Mexicans and Hispanics in general had assumed the role in popular culture of specialists in leisure and diversions of this sort. The orchestra, piano, violin, guitar, or other musical resources available to the movie palaces or the more modest venues were quite capable of playing Mexican/Hispanic music, and it is documented that they did. The films of the "Golden West" type are examples. This cycle of plays, operas, and what is all-important to us here, films, was initiated by David Belasco.

David Belasco (1853-1931), born in San Francisco to Sephardic parents of Portuguese heritage, was a highly important playwright, director, and theatrical producer who either wrote, directed, or produced more than 100 Broadway plays between 1884 and 1930, making him the most powerful personality on the New York city theater scene. Known for developing a new standard of naturalism, for his advanced lighting techniques, and rumored to have invented the phrase "casting couch," he is credited with having more than forty motion pictures adapted from his many plays. But Belasco is most recognized for having written *Madame Butterfly* and *The Girl of the Golden West*. He had an important relationship with Giacomo Puccini, who adapted both of these plays into operas. The relationship between *silent* (rather than sound) film and opera was significant, even though that might strike us as counterintuitive in this millennium. Geraldine Farrar, the opera diva known for her interpretation of Prosper Mérimée/Bizet's *Carmen*, was recruited to play the part in the 1915 silent film *Carmen* (directed by Cecil B. DeMille). The other 1915 *Carmen*, unfortunately now lost, was directed by none other than Raoul Walsh of *In Old Arizona*. It featured Theda Bara in the title role.

Belasco first staged *The Girl of the Golden West* in 1905 and it was a huge success, enjoying three separate Broadway productions before Puccini staged the opera. After the success of his opera *Madama Butterfly*, Puccini turned again to the source of its inspiration, David Belasco. Puccini's *La fanciulla del West* (The Girl of the Golden West), an opera in three acts, had its first performance on December 10, 1910, at the Metropolitan Opera in New York City. It was a landmark performance. The work, set in the high sierras of California in 1849-1850, is quite consistent with but also different from the original O. Henry story "The Caballero's Way," and *In Old Arizona*. Minnie is torn between two suitors/lovers, the bandit Ramerrez and Sheriff Rance, with a marked preference for *el bandido*. The key scene involves Minnie beating Rance at a "poker" duel that, if she wins, means that the sheriff must free his recently captured lover. Emmy Destinn had the role of Minnie; Enrico Caruso was Dick Johnson/Ramerrez, the bandit who sometimes played a gringo; Pasquale Amato was Sheriff Jack Rance; and, much further down the line, there were roles such as Billy Jackrabbit, "a Red Indian," Wowkle, "his squaw," and José Castro, "a greaser from Ramerrez's band."

The first film of the "Golden West" series was *The Girl of the Golden West* (1923, directed by Edwin Carewe, adapted from the David Belasco play). These films were notable, naturally, for their musical qualities. The 1927 production *Rose of the Golden West* (director George Fitzmaurice, starring Mary Astor and Gilbert Roland) featured castanets in its musical support for the film, prompting *Variety* (September 28, 1927) to applaud that for the first time a film of this Hispanic sort had not abused the guitar and there were no Spanish folkdances, implying, of course, that these features were commonplace in Hispanic-focused movies. Of course, films in the "Golden West" cycle continue into the sound period.

The phenomenal success of *In Old Arizona* only spurred the already robust incorporation of Hispanic musical elements. *The Arizona Kid* (see chapter 5), also starring Warner Baxter, has the hero wooing Lorita, a dancer, and in *Variety* (October 27, 1931) it is observed that the song "My Tonia" from *In Old Arizona* runs through the film. *Under a Texas Moon* (1930, director Michael Curtiz), a lousy film with a huge budget and a generally spectacular cast (Frank Fay, who plays Barbara Stanwyck's husband, is a stinker; otherwise, Raquel Torres, Myrna Loy, Armida, Noah Beery, and Mona Maris), has been identified as the first film completely in Technicolor, and it abounds with songs and music complete with guitar-playing mariachis as well as a character, Don Carlos, who is clearly modeled on the filmic Cisco Kid. *Rogue of the Rio Grande* (1930, director Spencer Gordon Bennet) features José Bohr as El Malo opposite Raymond Hatton and Myrna Loy. This film was the only one in the English language in which Bohr, an Argentine chansonnier in the style of Maurice Chevalier but with a South American accent, actually starred. The film confuses Mexican and Argentine music shamelessly, and it has, as *Variety* points out, Bohr playing a sort of Pancho Villa and tenor of the borderlands, singing such songs as "Song of the Bandoleros" and "Argentine Moon." Also in 1930 appeared *Beau Bandit* (director Lambert Hillyer, starring Rod La Rocque) and *Song of the Caballero* (director Harry Joe Brown, starring Ken Maynard and Francis Ford), replete with Hispanic musical elements.

The lode was rich with music-infused, flamboyant Latin *bandidos* and their love interests: Bebe Daniels in *Rio Rita* and *Love Comes Along* (both 1929); *Romance of the Rio Grande* (also 1929, featuring the likes of "My Toreador Starts to Snore"); the 1930 films *Border Romance* (with material like "Song of the Rurales," "The Girl from Topolopompo," and "Yo te adoro") and *A Devil with Women* (with "Amor Mío"); and *Girl of the Rio* (1931), with Dolores del Río as a cabaret singer accompanied by a guitar. No one has done a more extensive job than García Riera in documenting these films, all successors to the films of the silent period and to *In Old Arizona*.

THE CISCO KID WAS A FRIEND OF MINE

ar was a multiracial, multicultural funk band of the 1970s from Southern California. Formed in 1969, the band had some huge hit songs, including "Low Rider." In 1972 War came out with its hit "The Cisco Kid." The song features simple but relevant lines for this review. Outlaws have the apparently hard-drinking Cisco and Pancho pinned down at a fort, Cisco rides into the sunset with a horse made of steel, and he

Chased a gringo last night through a field
Chased a gringo last night through a field.

You can find the song on several albums, including War's *Colección Latina* (1997), which also includes songs like "Cinco de Mayo," "Salsa," "Low Rider," and "East L.A." The song "The Cisco Kid" begins Luis Valdez's Cisco film. The most telling thing is that the movie introduces from the very beginning the affiliation of the Cisco Kid with Chicanos, Mexicanos, and Latinos within the context of social awareness and political justice.

The Cisco Kid has moved the hearts of Chicanos, especially during their youth. In their adulthood, that inspiration has been cultivated in art and in literature. A few examples make this inspiration apparent. In addition to War's popular song, the Chicano/Latino appropriation of the Cisco Kid includes other examples such as Nash Candelaria's *The Day the Cisco Kid Shot John Wayne and Other Stories* (1988), which contains the title story from which we have quoted amply, and a series of serigraphs by Sam Coronado and monoprints by Joe Ray. Joe Ray's series of Cisco Kids frame the character on the television screen of his youth and capture him as if he were a portrait, not only of the Kid,

but also of the artist in his youth emulating the Latino hero. Sam Coronado displays a similar psychology, as we will see subsequently.

The most widely known Chicano/Latino appropriation of the character is the made-for-television film *The Cisco Kid* (1994), directed by Luis Valdez, starring Jimmy Smits and Cheech Marín, and including other Latino actors such as Pedro Armendáriz Jr., Phil Esparza, Joaquín Garrido, and Guillermo Ríos.

That Luis Valdez would come to direct a Cisco Kid film vehicle, and one that would have a Chicano slant to it, seems a natural occurrence, overdetermined by both Valdez's consistent interest in noble bandits and the direction of American film during the decade and more preceding his Cisco contribution.

Legitimately called the father of Chicano theater, playwright and film director Luis Valdez has given this movement a voice since 1963, when his first play was staged by the drama department at San Jose State College. The play, *The Shrunken Head of Pancho Villa*, nominally concerned a social bandit. Valdez went on in 1965 to found El Teatro Campesino, a touring farm workers' theater troupe. El Teatro Campesino produced one-act plays, often without a stage, script, or props, that dramatized the circumstances of migrant workers and ignited a national Chicano theater movement, a *teatro chicano*. Valdez has also written, cowritten, and directed many full-length plays depicting the Hispanic experience, including *Bandido! The American Melodrama of Tiburcio Vásquez, Notorious California Bandit*, which debuted in a Teatro Campesino workshop in 1981 and later appeared in revised form in the 1992 Valdez book *Zoot Suit and Other Plays*. *Bandido!* is about the California social/noble bandit Tiburcio Vásquez, who in the mid-nineteenth century was captured in Cahuenga Canyon (now Hollywood Hills). The playwright surely was moved by Tiburcio's explanation of his actions before his hanging in 1874: "A spirit of hatred and revenge took possession of me. I had numerous fights in defense of what I believed to be my rights and those of my countrymen. I believed we were unjustly deprived of the social rights that belonged to us."

Valdez's *Corridos! Tales of Passion and Revolution* (1983, adapted for television and aired on PBS in 1987) also has

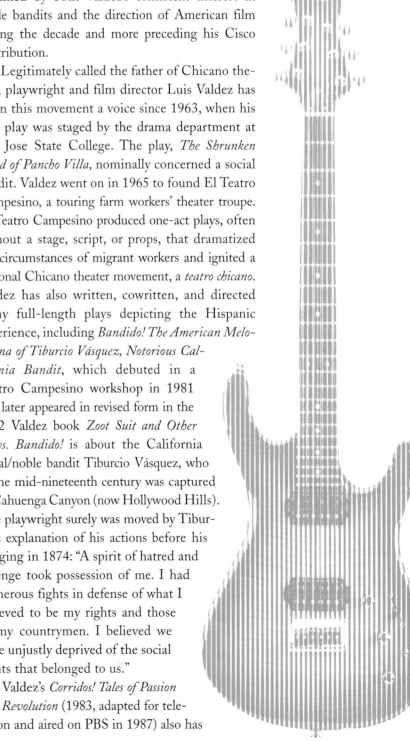

Lou Diamond Phillips (left) and Esai Morales (right) in *La Bamba* (1987)

elements of social banditry, and in fact, Tiburcio Vásquez is one of the characters portrayed. In the work's foreword, the playwright expressed his desire to recover the figure of Vásquez from the stereotypes propagated by Western conquest fiction, and he noted that he decided to concentrate on Vásquez because his story was far less well known than that of Joaquín Murrieta, whom Valdez judged a legendary icon, even among Anglo Americans. Valdez's 1986 play *I Don't Have to Show You No Stinking Badges!*, which ran successfully at the Los Angeles Theater Center, features Hollywood extra Buddy Villa, who has made a career of portraying stereotypical Mexicans in Hollywood films. It plays off the famous line uttered by Alfonso Bedoya in the role of Gold Hat, "I don't have to show you no stinking badges," in *The Treasure of the Sierra Madre* (1948, director John Huston, starring Humphrey Bogart and Walter Huston).

Valdez's greatest success came in 1987, when he directed the hit film *La Bamba*. The film depicted the brief life of Chicano singer Ritchie Valens, who helped pioneer early rock and roll. An element of high significance in this film is that Ritchie finds his soul and identity in Mexico as well as his singing style and the content for his version of "La Bamba."

A Latino Californio, the Valdez Cisco Kid has a similar moment of truth in the Mexican homeland.

As we have seen, Valdez has been fascinated for decades with noble bandidos and some less than noble ones as well. He is renowned as a writer/ director who assumes artistic control of his works, including films such as *La Bamba* (1987), and introduces emphatically Chicano/Latino content into them. There is no way he would produce a Cisco Kid that was not definitely a part of the Chicano canon. While the *New York Times* review of the Broadway production of another Valdez play, *Zoot Suit*, is unfavorable, it accurately wrote about Valdez that he "has a reputation as a cultural provocateur, thanks to his activism on behalf of the United Farm Workers of America, his authorship of works that challenge stereotypes of Hispanic Americans, and his fondness for bringing together performers of widely varying cultural backgrounds."

Those proclivities of writer/director Luis Valdez combined well with a newly awakened interest in box office vehicles that would attract both mainstream audiences and the Chicano/Latino market. As Professor Nevins points out, the TNT network was prepared to accept a Cisco Kid that they could interpret from their outsider's perspective as "politically correct."

Chicanismo had become commercially viable in the larger marketplace by 1994 and it has remained so. Robert Rodríguez's *El Mariachi* (1992) was a groundbreaker both with respect to Chicano/Latino artistic control and box office success. Moreover, it was a news sensation generally and especially so for every budding film director or wannabe with dreams but no cash. The $7,000 movie (supplemented by $1 million in post production and promotion after the film had garnered studio attention) paid for partially by Rodríguez and Peter Marquardt (who played the evil Moco) volunteering to become paid "laboratory rats" for a study of a cholesterol-reducing drug, has entered the pantheon of pop culture mythos.

El Mariachi has a few elements compatible with the Mexican American Cisco in that, through a *diabolus ex machina* involving mistaken identity, the mariachi becomes embroiled in a web of violence and deception and relies on his wits and skill in battle to defeat his corrupt adversaries. He evolves into a lone warrior who is the sole embodiment of honor and decency in a border community on the verge of implosion because of corruption and drug trafficking. He is further distinguished by being the only character in the film with a sense of identity and a reverence for Mexican traditions, as the opening of the film makes clear: "Desde que era pequeño siempre quise ser un mariachi, como mi padre, mi abuelo y mi bisabuelo . . . Mi idea era seguir sus pasos hasta el final y morir con mi guitarra en la mano." The cycle of films initiated by *El Mariachi* continues unabated. Rodríguez's *Desperado* appeared in 1995 and *Once Upon a Time in Mexico* in 2003. *The Mask of Zorro* (1998, director Martin Campbell, starring Antonio Banderas and Anthony Hopkins) is notable for including Joaquín Murrieta in the film as well as other historical or quasi-historical characters such as Three-Fingered Jack and Joaquín's fictional brother, Alejandro Murrieta, who becomes the new Zorro. *The Legend of Zorro* (2005, director Martin Campbell, starring Antonio Banderas and Catherine Zeta-Jones) continues the cycle.

In 1994 Valdez directed a remake of the 1950s television series *The Cisco Kid*. He modernized the story, transforming Cisco (played by actor Jimmy Smits) into a respectable Chicano adventurer. The *New York Times* stated, "*The Cisco Kid* is part of a larger effort to counter 90 years of omissions and distortions in the way Latino characters have been depicted in westerns." The article continued, "Film makers like . . . Valdez . . . say they are trying to provide a humanized alternative to the hot-blooded lovers, Frito banditos, drug dealers, gang leaders, and

other two-dimensional characters that [have] traditionally represented Mexican Americans on television and films." (Note the presence of the Frito "bandito," an unfortunate insertion by Frito Lay of the mock Spanish word into the commercial arena, which raised the hackles of the Latino community.)

Valdez's *The Cisco Kid* was not successful as entertainment or as art. Mike Nevins cites some of the negative critical response in chapter 11. However, as Noriega (1991, 1992) has pointed out, some of the innovations of Chicano film have been misunderstood by mainstream reviewers and misused to downgrade the film in question. This is very much the case for Valdez's *The Cisco Kid*, in which numerous cultural, historical, linguistic, musical, and subtextual elements appear that have been provided for the Chicano insider and not for the traditional monolingual Anglo viewer or critic. While Chicanas and Chicanos would not find the movie to be outstanding, they do find it to be significantly more satisfying than

Antonio Banderas in *Desperado* (1995)

SALMA HAYEK

ARE YOU A MEXICAN
...OR A MEXICAN'T?

FROM THE DIRECTOR OF DESPERADO & FROM DUSK TILL DAWN

ONCE UPON A TIME IN

MEXICO

IN CINEMAS FROM FRIDAY SEPTEMBER 26

Salma Hayek returned in *Once Upon a Time in Mexico* (2003) to play the role of Carolina. This poster references a memorable line from the film.

enduring values of a Mexico that is represented by Benito Juárez and stands for control by the people, respect as well as political and social support for the Indian population, and triumphal resistance against foreign invaders or trespassers.

In an earlier work, *Hispanics and United States Film* (Keller 1994, 207-11), I pointed to features that qualify a film as properly Chicano or other U.S. Hispanic. While this book was published in 1994, it was written more than a year prior to the release of Valdez's film. Thus the 1994 *The Cisco Kid* is not referred to in my earlier book, but it has all of the characteristics that define a Chicana/o film. One of these relates to the control of the film. Distributed by the TNT cable network, *The Cisco Kid* is nevertheless controlled by its Chicano director and other professionals, to the point that, as Nevins points out, one of the studio executives foresaw that the film would be "labeled as politically correct, [but] that's not a bad brush to be tarred with."

The second area is the content. Among the features that often appear in and help define Chicano films are the innovative use of Spanish and English (and sometimes indigenous languages); the innovative use of Chicano or other Hispanic music; the innovative use of mise-en-scène and film montage; and, very significantly, the deconstruction and subversion of Hollywood genres and formulas. Valdez's *The Cisco Kid* is redolent with each of these content features that, in addition to artistic control, place it squarely in the domain of Chicano cinema.

The Language Elements

The phenomenon of alternating use of Spanish and English and sometimes indigenous languages is called "code switching" by linguists and is incorporated as a fundamental aspect of numerous films prior to the release of the Valdez movie. Among these are *Raíces de sangre* (1979, director Jesús Salvador Treviño), *The Ballad of Gregorio Cortez* (1982, director Robert M. Young, starring Edward James Olmos), *El Norte* (1983, director Gregory Nava), *La Bamba* (1987, director Luis Valdez), and *Born in East L.A.* (1987, directed, written by, and starring Cheech Marín). In these films, the fullest appreciation of the work—the channel, as it were, at its maximum frequency—can be attained only by the bilingual, multicultural viewer. The plot of *The Ballad of Gregorio Cortez* revolves around a linguistic distinction between Spanish and English. The Anglo character thinks Cortez is lying because he denies he had traded a horse (*caballo*, which can mean either "stallion" or the

did the mainstream critics. Moreover, the film continues to be important to the U.S. Hispanic community in general and in the educational domain.

From the vantage point of Chicano-focused cultural studies, it is a significant film. In O. Henry's ethnic cornucopia, Cisco is on the bottom rung of the good-bad ladder. In Valdez's film, conflicted, hyphenated Mexican-American that he is, the Cisco Kid resides at the top along with the indigenous Mexicans who are not *vendidos* to the outside interventionists.

This heroic Mexican American Cisco may swing back and forth somewhat precariously between Hispanic and Anglo culture, but as in the case of the Ritchie Valens character in Valdez's *La Bamba*, he finds some, but not all, of his identity in Old Mexico. In Cisco's case he finds it in the traditional and

more general "horse"), saying instead the more specific *yegua*, "mare." This linguistic misunderstanding leads to a deadly shootout. Valdez's *The Cisco Kid* contains within it much code switching, and in fact, quips and double meanings apparent only to bilingual insiders appear from time to time in the film. For example, a prostitute favored by the Cisco Kid is called Libertad, a perfectly good Mexican name, but also the word for "liberty." When Cisco says together with others, "¡Viva la Libertad!" they are referring to freedom, and he is referring, somewhat cynically and removed from patriotic fervor, to a woman.

Musical Elements

IThe innovative use of music is a hallmark of Chicano film. The innovations often speak to an insider, as in certain musical numbers in *Zoot Suit* or the title song of *Born in East L.A.* (taken from Bruce Springsteen's hit "Born in the USA"). *The Ballad of Gregorio Cortez* brings the Mexican *corrido* into the title of the film itself and expresses the element of resistance to the Texas Rangers and gringo authority in general that is central to the film. *La Bamba* is another film in which music is all-important, and the music in this Luis Valdez film, as is the case of the 1994 *The Cisco Kid*, serves to introduce the main character to his Mexican heritage. As I have observed earlier in this chapter, Valdez's Cisco film makes innovative use of Chicano music as well as traditional Mexican fare, particularly in the introduction of the action and of the film credits, which feature War's notable "The Cisco Kid." This 1970s song functions effectively to situate the nominally nineteenth-century historical action film within a Chicano cultural space, one that looks at the past from a knowledgeable vantage point some 120 years in the future and that has parsed history and come to conclusions about the trajectory of the Cisco Kid over the decades. Moreover, as we will see below, that Chicano space is conflicted since it partakes of both Anglo and Mexican culture and it seeks, and ultimately is successful, to be something different and more than either of the cultures separately, or the sum of both in combination or in permutation.

Mise-en-scène and Film Montage

The use of code switching and music distinctively served up for the appreciation of a bicultural insider, together with numerous other features such as food preparation, mores and elements of folk culture, graffiti, slang, mannerisms, and other features, can be properly seen as part of the mise-en-scène of a Chicano film, and the kinetic stream of shots containing Chicano mises-en-scène makes for a Chicano film montage. All of the component elements (linguistic, musical) and numerous others make up the mise-en-scène of Valdez's 1994 *The Cisco Kid*. Moreover, the most distinctively Chicano element of the setting of Valdez's film is the filmic cultivation of the historical conflict taking place in Mexico during the French Intervention (1861-

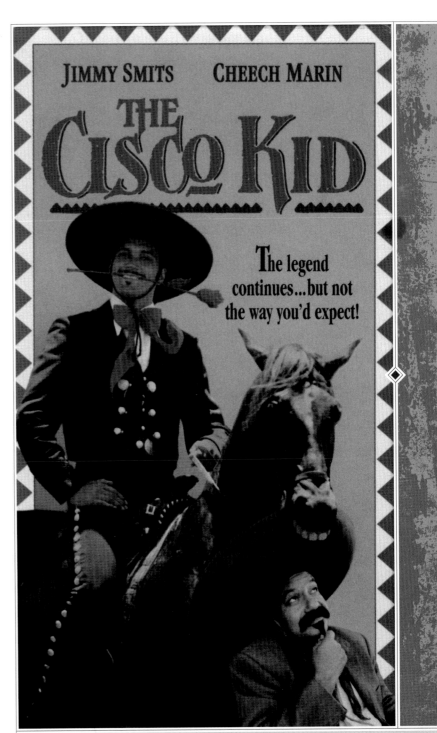

Jimmy Smits and Cheech Marín starred in Luis Valdez's 1994 film *The Cisco Kid*.

1867) interpreted in highly racial and ethnic terms, with a significant role in that ethnic exchange for the proto-Chicano persona. While the introduction of Chicanismo into a nineteenth-century Mexican setting stretches historical veracity, nevertheless it is accomplished with considerable skill, especially with respect to the framing of the conflict in terms with which a contemporary bicultural Chicano viewer might identify. The term "Chicano" is not used in the film. Nevertheless, the Cisco portrayed by Jimmy Smits is an obviously hyphenated American, and that condition of being Mexican-American is the one from which Chicanismo springs. Chicanos can be described for our purposes here as Mexican Americans with a political attitude and with a militantly and heroically earned sense of personal, political, cultural, and social self that recognizes their distinctiveness within the diverse ethnic makeups of both Mexico and the United States, neither of which, separately or in tandem, suffices to encompass the value-added quality of the Chicano identity that partakes of both cultures but that is more than their mere sum. In Valdez's *The Cisco Kid*, the Mexican American condition and the Mexican American dilemma that eventually, around the time of the Sleepy Lagoon riots of World War II, would evolve into Chicanismo, was well established during this period of the Franco-Mexican War, especially with respect to the Mexican American Cisco's allegiances to the component cultures on both sides of the border, and it is pursued to a climax that has aroused the interest of contemporary Chicanos.

At the outset of the film, the Cisco Kid, as played by Jimmy Smits, is introduced as a loner who acts as the circumstances dictate but feels no genuine allegiance or affinity to any of the specific ethnicities and social classes that are represented in the Valdez film: Anglo, Confederate, French, Mexican, Native American, and so on. These ethnic and socioeconomic groups alternately struggle or collaborate with each other as their circumstantial needs require. During the course of the film, the Cisco Kid's allegiances develop as well. In turn, he passes from a nominal partner of the Texas-based Confederate renegades, to an initially opportunistic and cynical supporter of the Juaristas, and ultimately to an enthusiastic and heroic supporter of the indigenous Mexican villagers fighting on Juárez's side, even as he maintains his love interest with Dominique, the French-born fiancée of one of the senior French officers leading the fight against Juárez. Born on "the other side," meaning the United States, initially collaborating with the renegade Texans but weaned

away from these bad guys through the influence of Pancho, and wooing the attractive French idealist Dominique, the Cisco Kid never fully integrates into either of these groups. Properly so, inasmuch as he maintains his identity as a proto-Chicano, although he finds self-realization in his adventures with the Mexican Pancho. The film ends with the prospect of a continued partnership between Cisco and Pancho that will be based on gallantry, chivalry, and considered, socially-conscious noble banditry.

Initially, Cisco is shown to be conflicted by his own ethnic identity, which does not sit well in Anglo America or even in Mexico. At one point in the film he identifies his condition as a Mexican American as the reason that he is considered a criminal in the United States. He explains that he was running guns with the Confederate renegades out of necessity.

Cisco: You want to know why I came with Washam and Lundquist? It was either run guns to Mexico or go to prison.

Pancho: Says who?

Cisco: U.S. federal agents. That's who. Hombre, you know what they call a Mexican with a good horse and money over there? A bandit. That's why I need the letter from Juárez. So I can exonerate myself and go back.

A poignant feature of the film is that Pancho does not serve as a mere sidekick. A good family man and the father of numerous children, Pancho follows Cisco's lead with respect to heroic feats and derring-do. On the other hand, Pancho assumes the role of father figure for the younger Cisco and serves as a role model who awakens the conflicted Mexican American's pride in his ethnicity and his forebears' homeland. However, while Cisco allies himself with Mexico, most especially the indigenous Mexicans and not the privileged classes, he declines to assume a Mexican ethnic identity. Cisco comments to Pancho that he has a wonderful family and a country to fight for. Rosa, Pancho's wife, tells him that Mexico is his country too, but Cisco does not share that perspective. He sees his Mexican identity as based on heritage and irrevocably set in the past as a result of the annexation of that part of Mexico that is now the Southwest of the United States.

Cisco: It used to be.

Pancho: What do you mean, used to be?

Rosa: We need men like you.

Cisco: No, I work better alone.

Ultimately Cisco needs to work out his own project. He senses that he belongs neither in the

United States, where he is looked down on because of his ethnicity, nor in Mexico, where he feels like a North American.

Pancho: I thought you were one of us.

Cisco: I wish I was, but I'm not.

Pancho: You've been living with gringos for too long, Cisco. Come back home, hombre.

Cisco: I was born on the other side of the border. Gringos or no gringos, that's my home.

Pancho is secure in his identity and devoted to his struggle to expel the French intruders. He does not realize that this goal is not entirely the focus of Cisco's life. Moreover, he cannot appreciate the difficulty faced by Cisco as a person who lives between two separate and in certain ways incompatible cultures. Ultimately, however, Cisco's bravery and inherent nobility lead to his helping the good, indigenous faction in his heritage homeland and in turn, his impulsive heroism helps him to come to terms with his own identity crisis. Moreover, by the end of the film, the Cisco Kid, in charting a course from a rather selfish, devil-may-care adventurer to a freedom fighter who is worthy of the epithet of hero, attains the attributes of the noble bandit that have been hallmarks of the previous cinematic and television Cisco Kids before him. As Nevins points out in chapter 11, the intention, not realized, was for the production of a sequel to the Valdez version of *The Cisco Kid*, and we would anticipate that any subsequent *salidas* of the Kid would have been marked by the figure's comfort with his noble bandit identity.

Deconstruction and Subversion of Hollywood Genres and Formulas

Chicano films often stand established mainstream formulas and genres on their heads. *El Norte* is not merely the alternative to the mainstream border or immigration films, it is their antithetical polar opposite. *The Ballad of Gregorio Cortez* is an emphatically Chicano Western because it subverts the classical Western as well as bandido, bad Mexican, or greaser films. *Zoot Suit* is the Chicano "answer" to gringo-controlled Latin musicals or gang films that feature the likes of blue-eyed Robby Benson with brown-tinted contact lenses (e.g., *Walk Proud*). *Seguín* is the Chicano "answer" to the Anglo glorification of the Alamo. *Stand and Deliver* creates a contradicting calculus to all of the Latino-hoodlums-rip-up-the-school films.

These are all films with a Chicano attitude, and so is *The Cisco Kid*. The subversion of the Hollywood conventions for a Western is omnipresent, but I want to take special note of this contravention in the area of race and ethnic relationships, especially as codified in racial epithets. There are an extraordinary number of racial and ethnic epithets hurled around in Valdez's *The Cisco Kid*, more by a country kilometer than in any other Cisco film. One has to go back to the original social Darwinian O. Henry story "The Caballero's Way" for a comparable count. But in Valdez's work they have the opposite valence from O. Henry's. It is hard to conceive of an Anglo filmmaker using racial epithets to the degree and with the virulence that Luis Valdez has, and these words are used with no attempt to mitigate their impact.

United States senator Ben Nighthorse Campbell once had occasion to make observations about the injurious epithets "prairie nigger" and "red nigger." From a purely linguistic perspective, these epithets, which were used often and unselfconsciously in certain sectors of white society in the nineteenth century and beyond, extend by analogy the "N-word," itself formed from the Spanish word *negro*, to American Indians, who conventionally have been identified as having skins of a reddish hue. The following dialog from the 1994 *The Cisco Kid* occurs at one extraordinary moment when the French officer, Dupré, accuses the Texans, mostly Confederate renegades, of running guns to aid Benito Juárez. A Confederate by the name of Washam responds incredulously, "That red nigger president of Mexico? Don't make me laugh." Significantly, the depiction of Juárez, who appears briefly at the end of the film played by Valdez himself, emphasizes the leader's ethnicity as the first indigenous Mexican to be elected president of his country. Moreover, Juárez emerges as a noble leader who always retains his ethnic identity and who counts on and is appreciative of the support that he receives, which comes primarily from the indigenous population that is willing to fight to the death for him. In marked contrast, to achieve their objectives, the French must rely on Mexican turncoats (who assume a Frenchified sophistication) and most especially on corrupt mercenaries drawn from the Confederacy. The mercenaries' utter disregard for the Mexican people ultimately leads to their defeat. Washam's racism is not confined to Juárez, as he taunts Pancho, played by Cheech

Marín, by telling him that "all you greasers" have the same name.

As we have seen in this book, there have been numerous versions of the Cisco Kid: the degraded, Mexicanized gringo bandido that emerged from O. Henry's bilious imagination; the early cinematic versions of the Kid that were initially anchored in "The Caballero's Way"; and a *bandido malo* who is ever more noble and generous over the course of the decades as the Mexican nature of Cisco becomes more pronounced. Eventually, during the Duncan Renaldo period, the Cisco Kid emerges as a full-form noble hero of the chivalric tradition, a man with the heart of Don Quixote and a sidekick to boot, but without the lunacy of the former, who lived atavistically the glory of a defunct age, but instead a fully-developed skill set to meet and thwart the evildoers of the nineteenth-century Southwest.

There have been numerous versions indeed of the Cisco Kid, and we surmise that there will be numerous additional ones as the archetypal character transforms himself and his *circunstancia social* according to the popular culture dictates of the time. Moreover, until Luis Valdez's 1994 version, the Cisco Kid remained primarily in heroic service to Anglo patrons, with an occasional Mexican thrown in as a secondary character. These patrons may be maidens in distress, defenseless children, or old men victimized by swindlers or other aggressors, but essentially they are Anglo patrons in need. In Valdez's 1994 *The Cisco Kid*, the character returns home in a social and cultural sense and is reborn in a dramatic one. Valdez returns to the foundational short story and does it "right" from a Chicano point of view. We first encounter the guy even before he is the Kid, just as Pancho encounters him even before the latter is Pancho the sidekick as well as father figure to this waif, this adult foundling caught in the maelstrom of Mexican and United States history. The Cisco Kid is reborn in a *bautismo de fuego* at the hands of Valdez in this film that is Chicano through and through. He takes the Kid from the condition in which he finds him as a confused, conflicted, somewhat selfish and rakish Mexican American during the post-1848 Treaty of Guadalupe period when the Southwest became part of the United States and when the Mexican American identity was just forming, to a noble bandit hero who, after his experiences in Mexico with Pancho and with the Amerindian villagers fighting on the side of Benito Juárez, assumes the character of noble bandit and freedom fighter that we conventionally identify in this figure. The Cisco Kid is transformed in this Chicano foundational version and is ready for sequels. Nevins has observed that a sequel was anticipated but never materialized after Jimmy Smits was signed up for the television series *NYPD Blue* in 1994.

By a serendipitous and overdetermined psychological convergence and from a totally different point of departure, Sam Coronado conceived and artistically executed, in a totally different medium, a Cisco Kid that shares with Valdez's cinematic version the Chicano quality of the noble *caballero*.

Like Valdez, Coronado creates a foundational Cisco Kid, but he does so by returning to his childhood, when the Kid aroused his imagination and the artist himself was a kid. In his serigraph *Pancho Villa & The Cisco Kid*, in the golden haze and halo of childhood memories of movies and revolutionary myth customized to meet a higher level of psychological and sociocultural purpose, Coronado paints the Kid as an actual kid. This is a boy who evokes the persona of the artist possibly around the time of his first encounter with noble bandits. Here the Cisco Kid rides with Pancho Villa, the most notable "Robin Hood" of the Mexican Revolution of 1910 as he has sometimes been depicted in both American and Mexican popular culture. Here the psychologic of childhood association has been substituted for the original logic of O. Henry and subsequently the filmmakers. The Kid really is one, and he looks rather like an *esquintle* on a make-believe horse as shot by one of those entrepreneurial photographers who memorialize a Chicano family outing and place the precious child on the perch of honor, right next to a majestic golden silhouette of the leader of the *dorados*, none other than Pancho Villa himself.

In Valdez's *The Cisco Kid*, the character is born again as a cultural hero in development. In Coronado's re-creation of the kid out of his childhood, the Cisco Kid is a waif, side by side with the ever-present Pancho, Mexican father of the noble and virile revolutionary bandit who confronts landed interests, social oppression, imperialism, and the United States Army. Born again out of the imagination of a Chicano film director and a Chicano painter, Cisco traverses the borderland of the two nations and fulfills the biculturalism of the Chicano vision.

 FEATURE FILMS

In Old Arizona (FOX, 1929)

PRODUCER	None Credited
CINEMATOGRAPHER	Arthur Edeson
FILM EDITOR	Louis Loeffler
MUSIC DIRECTOR	None Credited
ADAPTATION & DIALOGUE	Tom Barry
SOURCE STORY	O. Henry, "The Caballero's Way" (1907)
DIRECTORS	Raoul Walsh & Irving Cummings
The Cisco Kid	Warner Baxter
Sgt. Mickey Dunn	Edmund Lowe
Tonia María	Dorothy Burgess

These three are the only actors who receive screen credit. The rest of the cast consists of J. Farrell MacDonald (Tad), Fred Warren (Piano Player), Henry Armetta (Barber), Frank Campeau (Cowpuncher), Tom Santschi (Cowpuncher), Pat Hartigan (Cowpuncher), Roy Stewart (Commandant), James Bradbury, Jr. (Soldier), John Dillon (Soldier), Soledad Jiménez (Cook), Frank Nelson (Cowboy), Duke Martin (Cowboy), James Marcus (Blacksmith), Alphonse Ethier (Sheriff), Helen Lynch (Woman), Ivan Linow (Russian Immigrant), Joe Brown (Bartender), Lola Salvi (Italian Girl), and Edward Peil, Sr. (Man).

COPYRIGHT DATE: APRIL 4, 1929

LENGTH: 7 REELS, 8724 FEET

The Cisco Kid (FOX, 1931)

PRODUCER	Irving Cummings
ASSOCIATE PRODUCER	William Goetz
CINEMATOGRAPHER	Barney McGill
FILM EDITOR	Alex Troffey (uncredited)
MUSIC SCORE	George Lipschultz
SCREENPLAY	Alfred A. Cohn
DIRECTOR	Irving Cummings
The Cisco Kid	Warner Baxter
Sgt. Mickey Dunn	Edmund Lowe
Carmencita	Conchita Montenegro
Sally Benton	Nora Lane
Sheriff Tex Ransom	Frederick Burt
Enos Hankins	Willard Robertson
Pvt. Dixon	James Bradbury, Jr.
Pvt. Bouse	Jack Dillon
López	Charles Stevens
Gordito	Chris (Chris-Pin) Martin
Billy Benton	Douglas Haig
Ann Benton	Marilyn Knowlden

UNBILLED BIT PARTS: George Irving, Rita Flynn, Consuelo Castillo de Bonzo, Allan García

COPYRIGHT DATE: SEPTEMBER 18, 1931

RUNNING TIME: 61 MIN.

Paul Landres with *Last of the Bad Men* (1957) camera crew. Photo taken June 1956

The Cisco Kid and the Lady

(20TH CENTURY-FOX, 1939)

ASSOCIATE PRODUCER	John Stone
CINEMATOGRAPHER	Barney McGill
FILM EDITOR	Nick DeMaggio
MUSIC DIRECTOR	Samuel Kaylin
SCREENPLAY	Frances Hyland
STORY	Stanley Rauh
DIRECTOR	Herbert I. Leeds

The Cisco Kid	César Romero
Julie Lawson	Marjorie Weaver
Gordito	Chris-Pin Martin
Tommy Bates	George Montgomery
Jim Harbison	Robert Barrat
Billie Graham	Virginia Field
Teasdale	Harry Green
Baby	Gloria Ann White
Stevens	John Beach
Walton	Ward Bond
Drake	J. Anthony Hughes
Pop Saunders	James Burke
Sheriff	Harry Hayden
Sergeant	James Flavin
Ma Saunders	Ruth Warren

UNBILLED BIT PARTS: Paul Burns, Virginia Brissac, Adrian Morris, Eddie Dunn, Eddy Waller, Ivan Miller, Lester Dorr, Harry Strang, Arthur Rankin, Paul Sutton, Harold Goodwin, Gladys Blake, William Royle

COPYRIGHT DATE: DECEMBER 29, 1939

RUNNING TIME: 73 MIN.

The Return of the Cisco Kid

(20TH CENTURY-FOX, 1939)

ASSOCIATE PRODUCER	Kenneth Macgowan
CINEMATOGRAPHER	Charles Clarke
FILM EDITOR	James B. Clark
MUSIC DIRECTOR	Cyril J. Mockridge
SCREENPLAY	Milton Sperling
DIRECTOR	Herbert I. Leeds

The Cisco Kid	Warner Baxter
Ann Carver	Lynn Bari
López	César Romero
Col. Joshua Bixby	Henry Hull
Alan Davis	Kane Richmond
Mexican Captain	C. Henry Gordon
Sheriff McNally	Robert Barrat
Gordito	Chris-Pin Martin
Deputy Johnson	Adrian Morris
Mamá Soledad	Soledad Jiménez
Deputy	Harry Strang
Stagecoach Driver	Arthur Aylesworth
Hotel Clerk	Paul Burns
Bartender	Victor Kilian
Guard	Eddy Waller
Flora	Ruth Gillette
Tough	Ward Bond

UNBILLED BIT PARTS: Ralph Dunn, Gino Corrado, Herbert Heywood, Charles Tannen, Ethan Laidlaw, Max Wagner, Lee Shumway, Harry Debb

COPYRIGHT DATE: APRIL 28, 1939

RUNNING TIME: 70 MIN.

Viva Cisco Kid (20TH CENTURY-FOX, 1940)

PRODUCER	Sol M. Wurtzel
CINEMATOGRAPHER	Charles Clarke
FILM EDITOR	Norman Colbert
MUSIC DIRECTOR	Samuel Kaylin
SCREENPLAY	Samuel G. Engel & Hal Long
DIRECTOR	Norman Foster

The Cisco Kid	César Romero
Joan Allen	Jean Rogers
Gordito	Chris-Pin Martin
Jesse Allen	Minor Watson
The Boss	Stanley Fields
Moses	Nigel de Brulier
Hank Gunther	Harold Goodwin
Proprietor	Francis Ford
Don Pancho	Charles Judels

UNBILLED BIT PARTS: LeRoy Mason, Bud Osborne, Paul Sutton, Mantan Moreland, Tom London, Hank Worden, Eddy Waller, Jim Mason, Ray Teal, Paul Kruger, Willie Fung, Frank Darien, Jacqueline Dalya, Margaret Martin, Inez Palange

COPYRIGHT DATE: APRIL 12, 1940

RUNNING TIME: 70 MIN.

Lucky Cisco Kid (20TH CENTURY-FOX, 1940)

ASSOCIATE PRODUCER...... John Stone
CINEMATOGRAPHER........ Lucien Andriot
FILM EDITOR.............. Fred Allen
MUSIC DIRECTOR.......... Cyril J. Mockridge
SCREENPLAY.............. Robert Ellis & Helen Logan
STORY................... Julian Johnson
DIRECTOR................ H. Bruce Humberstone

The Cisco Kid .... César Romero
Lola .... Mary Beth Hughes
Sergeant Dunn .... Dana Andrews
Emily Lawrence .... Evelyn Venable
Gordito .... Chris-Pin Martin
Judge McQuade........... Willard Robertson
Bill Stevens .... Joseph Sawyer
Tommy Lawrence .... Johnny Sheffield
Sheriff .... William Royle
Court Clerk .... Francis Ford
Ed Stokes............... Otto Hoffman
Stagecoach Driver .... Dick Rich

UNBILLED BIT PARTS: Harry Strang, Gloria Roy, Frank Lackteen, Spencer Charters, Bob Hoffman, Boyd Morgan, Adrian Morris, Jimmie Dundee, William Pagan, Lillian Yarbo, Lew Kelly, Milton Kibbee, Sarah Edwards, Ethan Laidlaw, Thornton Edwards, James Flavin, Henry Roquemore, Syd Saylor, Charles Tannen, Pat O'Malley, Sid Jordan

COPYRIGHT DATE: JUNE 28, 1940

RUNNING TIME: 68 MIN.

The Gay Caballero (20TH CENTURY-FOX, 1940)

ASSOCIATE PRODUCERS..... Walter Morosco & Ralph Dietrich
CINEMATOGRAPHER........ Edward Cronjager
FILM EDITOR............. Harry Reynolds
MUSIC DIRECTOR.......... Emil Newman
SCREENPLAY............. Albert Duffy & John Larkin
STORY.................. Walter Bullock & Albert Duffy
DIRECTOR............... Otto Brower

The Cisco Kid .... César Romero
Susan Wetherby .... Sheila Ryan
Billy Brewster .... Robert Sterling
Gordito .... Chris-Pin Martin
Kate Brewster .... Janet Beecher
Joe Turner .... Edmund MacDonald
Carmelita .... Jacqueline Dalya
George Wetherby .... C. Montague Shaw
Sheriff McBride.......... Hooper Atchley

UNBILLED BIT PARTS: George Magrill, Jim Pierce, Ethan Laidlaw, John Byron, Tom London, Dave Morris, Jack Stoney, Lee Shumway, LeRoy Mason, Frank Lackteen

COPYRIGHT DATE: OCTOBER 4, 1940

RUNNING TIME: 57 MIN.

Lobby card for *The Gay Caballero* (1940), starring César Romero

Romance of the Rio Grande

(20TH CENTURY-FOX, 1941)

PRODUCER.............. Sol M. Wurtzel
CINEMATOGRAPHER........ Charles Clarke
FILM EDITOR............. Fred Allen
MUSIC DIRECTOR.......... Emil Newman
SCREENPLAY............. Harold Buchman & Samuel G. Engel
SOURCE NOVEL .... Katharine Fullerton Gerould, *Conquistador* (Scribner's, 1923)

Photo still for *Romance of the Rio Grande* (1940), featuring Ricardo Cortez and Patricia Morison

DIRECTOR . . . . Herbert I. Leeds

The Cisco Kid . . . . César Romero
Rosita . . . . Patricia Morison
María Córdova . . . . Lynne Roberts
Ricardo de Vega . . . . Ricardo Cortez
Gordito . . . . Chris-Pin Martin
Padre Martínez . . . . Aldrich Bowker
Carlos Hernández . . . . Joseph McDonald
Don Fernando de Vega . . . . Pedro de Córdoba
Mamá López . . . . Inez Palange
Carver . . . . Raphael Bennett
Manuel . . . . Trevor Bardette
Marshal . . . . Tom London
Marta . . . . Eva Puig
Unbilled Bit Parts . . . . Richard Lane

COPYRIGHT DATE: JANUARY 17, 1941

RUNNING TIME: 73 MIN.

Ride On Vaquero (20TH CENTURY-FOX, 1941)

PRODUCER . . . . Sol M. Wurtzel
CINEMATOGRAPHER . . . . Lucien Andriot
FILM EDITOR . . . . Louis Loeffler
MUSIC DIRECTOR . . . . Emil Newman
SCREENPLAY . . . . Samuel G. Engel
DIRECTOR . . . . Herbert I. Leeds

The Cisco Kid . . . . César Romero
Sally . . . . Mary Beth Hughes
Marguerita Martínez . . . . . . Lynne Roberts
Gordito . . . . Chris-Pin Martin
Carlos Martínez . . . . Robert Lowery
Bullfinch . . . . Ben Carter

Barney . . . . William Demarest
Cavalry Officer . . . . Robert Shaw
Dan Clark . . . . Edwin Maxwell
Sleepy . . . . Paul Sutton
Redge . . . . Don Costello
Sheriff Johnny Burge . . . . . . Arthur Hohl
Baldy . . . . Irving Bacon
Curly . . . . Dick Rich
Colonel Warren . . . . Paul Harvey
Dolores . . . . Joan Woodbury

COPYRIGHT DATE: APRIL 18, 1941

RUNNING TIME: 64 MIN.

The Cisco Kid Returns (MONOGRAM, 1945)

PRODUCER . . . . Philip N. Krasne
ASSOCIATE PRODUCER . . . . . . Dick L'Estrange
CINEMATOGRAPHER . . . . Harry Neumann
FILM EDITOR . . . . Martin G. Cohn
MUSIC SCORE . . . . Albert Glasser
MUSIC DIRECTOR . . . . David Chudnow
SCREENPLAY . . . . Betty Burbridge
DIRECTOR . . . . John P. McCarthy

The Cisco Kid . . . . Duncan Renaldo
Pancho . . . . Martín Garralaga
John Harris . . . . Roger Pryor
Rosita Gonzales . . . . Cecilia Callejo
Padre . . . . Fritz Leiber
Jeanette . . . . Jan Wiley
Nancy Page . . . . Sharon Smith
Julia . . . . Vicky Lane
Paul Conway . . . . Anthony Warde
Sheriff . . . . Bud Osborne
Tía Jiménez . . . . Eva Puig
Jennings . . . . Cy Kendall

UNBILLED BIT PARTS: Bob Duncan, Elmer Napier, Carl Mathews, Jerry Fields, Neyle Marx, Cedric Stevens, Walter Clinton

COPYRIGHT DATE: MARCH 19, 1945

RUNNING TIME: 64 MIN.

In Old New Mexico (MONOGRAM, 1945)

PRODUCER . . . . Philip N. Krasne
CINEMATOGRAPHER . . . . Arthur Martinelli
FILM EDITOR . . . . Martin G. Cohn
MUSIC SCORE . . . . Albert Glasser
MUSIC DIRECTOR . . . . David Chudnow
SCREENPLAY . . . . Betty Burbridge
DIRECTOR . . . . Phil Rosen

The Cisco Kid . . . . Duncan Renaldo
Pancho . . . . Martín Garralaga
Ellen Roth . . . . Gwen Kenyon
Padre Angelo . . . . Pedro de Córdoba
Dolores . . . . Aurora Roche

Lobby card for *In Old New Mexico* (1945), starring Duncan Renaldo

Sheriff Clem Petty	Lee "Lasses" White
Will Hastings	Norman Willis
Newspaper Editor	Edward Earle
Belle	Donna Dax
Al Brady	John Laurenz
Doc Wilson	Richard Gordon
Stagecoach Passenger	Frank Jaquet
Deputy	James Farley
Dance Troupe	The Car-Bert Dancers

UNBILLED BIT PARTS: Ken Terrell, Harry Depps, Bud Osborne, Artie Ortego

COPYRIGHT DATE: MARCH 26, 1945

RUNNING TIME: 62 MIN.

South of the Rio Grande (MONOGRAM, 1945)

PRODUCER	Philip N. Krasne
CINEMATOGRAPHER	William Sickner
FILM EDITOR	William Austin
MUSIC SCORE	Frank Sanucci (uncredited)
MUSIC DIRECTOR	Edward J. Kay
SCREENPLAY	Victor Hammond & Ralph Bettinson
STORY	Johnston McCulley
DIRECTOR	Lambert Hillyer

The Cisco Kid	Duncan Renaldo
Pancho	Martín Garralaga
Pepita	Armida
Apoderado Miguel Sánchez	George J. Lewis
Dolores Gonzales	Lillian Molieri
Torres	Francis McDonald
Sebastián	Charles Stevens
Luis	Pedro Regas
Mamá María	Soledad Jiménez
Manuel Gonzales	Tito Renaldo with the Guadalajara Trio

COPYRIGHT DATE: AUGUST 25, 1945

RUNNING TIME: 62 MIN.

The Gay Cavalier (MONOGRAM, 1946)

PRODUCER	Scott R. Dunlap
CINEMATOGRAPHER	Harry Neumann
FILM EDITOR	Earl Maguire
MUSIC DIRECTOR	Edward J. Kay
SCREENPLAY	Charles S. Belden
STORY	Charles S. Belden
DIRECTOR	William Nigh

The Cisco Kid	Gilbert Roland
Don Felipe Peralta	Martín Garralaga
Baby	Nacho Galindo
Pepita Peralta	Ramsay Ames
Ángela Peralta	Helen Gerald
Lawton	Tristram Coffin

Lobby card for *South of the Rio Grande* (1945), starring Duncan Renaldo

Juan	Drew Allen
Rosita	Iris Flores
Lewis	John Merton
Graham	Frank LaRue

UNBILLED BIT PARTS: Gabriel Peralta, Pierre Andre, Iris Becigon, Raphael Bennett, Artie Ortego, Terry Frost, Ernie Adams

COPYRIGHT DATE: MARCH 15, 1946

RUNNING TIME: 65 MIN.

South of Monterey (MONOGRAM, 1946)

PRODUCER	Scott R. Dunlap

Photo still for *South of Monterey* (1946), featuring Marjorie Riordan and Gilbert Roland

CINEMATOGRAPHER . . . . Harry Neumann
FILM EDITOR . . . . Richard Heermance
MUSIC DIRECTOR . . . . Edward J. Kay
SCREENPLAY . . . . Charles S. Belden
STORY . . . . Charles S. Belden
DIRECTOR . . . . William Nigh

The Cisco Kid . . . . Gilbert Roland
Comandante Arturo Morales . . . Martín Garralaga
Baby . . . . Frank Yaconelli
María Morales . . . . Marjorie Riordan
Carmelita . . . . Iris Flores
Carlos Madero . . . . George J. Lewis
Bennet . . . . Harry Woods
Morgan . . . . Terry Frost
Lola . . . . Rosa Turich
Unbilled Bit Part . . . . Wheaton Chambers

COPYRIGHT DATE: JUNE 29, 1946
RUNNING TIME: 63 MIN.

Beauty and the Bandit (MONOGRAM, 1946)

PRODUCER . . . . Scott R. Dunlap
CINEMATOGRAPHER . . . . Harry Neumann
FILM EDITOR . . . . Fred Maguire
MUSIC DIRECTOR . . . . Edward J. Kay
SCREENPLAY . . . . Charles S. Belden
STORY . . . . Charles S. Belden
DIRECTOR . . . . William Nigh

The Cisco Kid . . . . Gilbert Roland
Dr. Juan Federico Valegra . . . . Martín Garralaga
Baby . . . . Frank Yaconelli
Jeanne Dubois . . . . Ramsay Ames
Rosita . . . . Vida Aldana

Lobby card for *Riding the California Trail* (1947), starring Gilbert Roland

Captain . . . . George J. Lewis
Doc Walsh . . . . William Gould
Farmer . . . . Dimas Sotello
Sick Farmer . . . . Felipe Turich

UNBILLED BIT PARTS: Glenn Strange, Alex Montoya, Artie Ortego

COPYRIGHT DATE: OCTOBER 28, 1946
RUNNING TIME: 77 MIN.

Riding the California Trail (MONOGRAM, 1947)

PRODUCER . . . . Scott R. Dunlap
CINEMATOGRAPHER . . . . Harry Neumann
FILM EDITOR . . . . Fred Maguire
MUSIC DIRECTOR . . . . Edward J. Kay
SCREENPLAY . . . . Clarence Upson Young
STORY . . . . Clarence Upson Young
DIRECTOR . . . . William Nigh

The Cisco Kid . . . . Gilbert Roland
Don José Ramírez . . . . Martín Garralaga
Baby . . . . Frank Yaconelli
Raquel . . . . Teala Loring
Dolores Ramírez . . . . Inez Cooper
Raoul Reyes . . . . Ted Hecht
Mamá Rosita . . . . Marcelle Grandville

UNBILLED BIT PARTS: Eve Whitney, Frank Marlowe, Alex Montoya, Rosa Turich, Julia Kent, Gerald Echevarría

COPYRIGHT DATE: JANUARY 27, 1947
RUNNING TIME: 59 MIN.

Robin Hood of Monterey (MONOGRAM, 1947)

PRODUCER . . . . Jeffrey Bernerd
CINEMATOGRAPHER . . . . William Sickner
FILM EDITOR . . . . Roy Livingston
MUSIC DIRECTOR . . . . Edward J. Kay
SCREENPLAY . . . . Bennett Cohen
ADDITIONAL DIALOGUE . . . . Gilbert Roland
STORY . . . . Bennett Cohen
DIRECTOR . . . . Christy Cabanne

The Cisco Kid . . . . Gilbert Roland
Pancho . . . . Chris-Pin Martin
María Sánchez Belmonte . . . Evelyn Brent
Ricardo Gonzales . . . . Jack LaRue
Don Carlos Belmonte . . . . . . Pedro de Córdoba
Lolita . . . . Donna de Mario
Eduardo Belmonte . . . . Travis Kent
El Capitán . . . . Thornton Edwards
Alcalde . . . . Néstor Paiva
Pablo . . . . Ernie Adams

UNBILLED BIT PARTS: Julián Rivero, Alex Montoya, Fred Córdova, Felipe Turich

COPYRIGHT DATE: SEPTEMBER 11, 1947
RUNNING TIME: 55 MIN.

King of the Bandits (MONOGRAM, 1947)

PRODUCER	Jeffrey Bernerd
CINEMATOGRAPHER	William Sickner
FILM EDITOR	Roy Livingston
MUSIC DIRECTOR	Edward J. Kay
SCREENPLAY	Bennett Cohen
ADDITIONAL DIALOGUE	Gilbert Roland
STORY	Christy Cabanne
DIRECTOR	Christy Cabanne
The Cisco Kid	Gilbert Roland
Alice Mason	Angela Greene
Pancho	Chris-Pin Martin
Smoke Kirby	Anthony Warde
Mrs. Mason	Laura Treadwell
Capt. Frank Mason	William Bakewell
Burl	Rory Mallinson
Pedro Gómez	Pat Goldin
Connie	Cathy Carter
Colonel Wayne	Boyd Irwin
Padre	Antonio Filauri
U.S. Marshal	Jasper Palmer
Orderly	Bill Cabanne
Unbilled Bit Part	Gene Roth

COPYRIGHT DATE: NOVEMBER 8, 1947

RUNNING TIME: 66 MIN.

Valiant Hombre

(INTER-AMERICAN/UNITED ARTISTS, 1949)

PRODUCER	Philip N. Krasne
ASSOCIATE PRODUCER	Duncan Renaldo
CINEMATOGRAPHER	Ernest Miller
FILM EDITOR	Martin G. Cohn
MUSIC SCORE	Albert Glasser
MUSIC DIRECTOR	Albert Glasser
SCREENPLAY	Adele Buffington
DIRECTOR	Wallace W. Fox
The Cisco Kid	Duncan Renaldo
Pancho	Leo Carrillo
Lon Lansdell	John Litel
Linda Mason	Barbara Billingsley
Joe Haskins	Guy Beach
Sheriff George Dodge	Stanley Andrews
Whiskers	Lee "Lasses" White
Paul Mason	John James
Pete	Eugene (Gene) Roth
Deputy Clay	Ralph Peters
Outlaw	Frank Ellis
Outlaw	Herman Hack
Outlaw	George De Normand

UNBILLED BIT PARTS: Terry Frost, David Sharpe, Frank McCarroll, Hank Bell, with Daisy the Wonder Dog

COPYRIGHT DATE: JANUARY 21, 1949

RUNNING TIME: 60 MIN.

The Gay Amigo

(INTER-AMERICAN/UNITED ARTISTS, 1949)

PRODUCER	Philip N. Krasne
ASSOCIATE PRODUCER	Duncan Renaldo
CINEMATOGRAPHER	Ernest Miller
FILM EDITOR	Martin G. Cohn
MUSIC SCORE	Albert Glasser
MUSIC DIRECTOR	Albert Glasser
SCREENPLAY	Doris Schroeder
DIRECTOR	Wallace W. Fox
The Cisco Kid	Duncan Renaldo
Pancho	Leo Carrillo
Rosita	Armida
Sergeant McNulty	Joe Sawyer
Stoneham	Walter Baldwin
Bill Brack	Fred Kohler, Jr.
Captain Lewis	Kenneth MacDonald
Corporal	George De Normand
Lieutenant	Clayton Moore
Duke	Fred Crane
Old Maid	Helen Servis
Girl	Beverly Jons
Stage Driver	Bud Osborne
Ed Paulsen	Sam Flint

COPYRIGHT DATE: MAY 13, 1949

RUNNING TIME: 60 MIN.

The Daring Caballero

(INTER-AMERICAN/UNITED ARTISTS, 1949)

PRODUCER	Philip N. Krasne
ASSOCIATE PRODUCER	Duncan Renaldo
CINEMATOGRAPHER	Lester White

Lobby card for *The Daring Caballero* (1949), starring Duncan Renaldo

FILM EDITOR	Martin G. Cohn
MUSIC SCORE	Albert Glasser
MUSIC DIRECTOR	Albert Glasser
SCREENPLAY	Betty Burbridge
STORY	Frances Kavanaugh
DIRECTOR	Wallace W. Fox

The Cisco Kid	Duncan Renaldo
Pancho	Leo Carrillo
Kippee Valez	Kippee Valez
E. J. Hodges	Charles Halton
Padre Leonardo	Pedro de Córdoba
Barton/Mayor Brady	Stephen Chase
Patrick Del Río	David Leonard
Marshal Scott	Edmund Cobb
Judge Perkins	Frank Jaquet
Bobby Del Río	Mickey Little

COPYRIGHT DATE: JUNE 24, 1949
RUNNING TIME: 60 MIN.

Satan's Cradle

(INTER-AMERICAN/UNITED ARTISTS, 1949)

PRODUCER	Philip N. Krasne
ASSOCIATE PRODUCER	Duncan Renaldo
CINEMATOGRAPHER	Jack Greenhalgh
FILM EDITOR	Martin G. Cohn
MUSIC SCORE	Albert Glasser
MUSIC DIRECTOR	Albert Glasser
SCREENPLAY	Jack Benton (J. Benton Cheney)
DIRECTOR	Ford Beebe

The Cisco Kid	Duncan Renaldo
Pancho	Leo Carrillo
Lil	Ann Savage

Steve Gentry	Douglas Fowley
Rev. Henry Lane	Byron Foulger
Belle	Claire Carleton
Rocky	Buck Bailey
Idaho	George De Normand
Peters	Wes Hudman

COPYRIGHT DATE: NONE
RUNNING TIME: 60 MIN.

The Girl from San Lorenzo

(INTER-AMERICAN/UNITED ARTISTS, 1950)

PRODUCER	Philip N. Krasne
CINEMATOGRAPHER	Kenneth Peach
FILM EDITOR	Martin G. Cohn
MUSIC SCORE	Albert Glasser
MUSIC DIRECTOR	Albert Glasser
SCREENPLAY	Ford Beebe
DIRECTOR	Derwin Abrahams

The Cisco Kid	Duncan Renaldo
Pancho	Leo Carrillo
Nora Malloy	Jane Adams
Jerry Todd	Bill Lester
Cal Ross	Byron Foulger
Kansas	Don C. Harvey
Sheriff Ed Morrison	Lee Phelps
Wooly	Edmund Cobb
Tom McCarger	Leonard Penn
Blackie	David Sharpe
Rusty	Wes Hudman

COPYRIGHT DATE: FEBRUARY 21, 1950
RUNNING TIME: 59 MIN.

The Cisco Kid (TURNER PICTURES, 1994)

PRODUCERS	Gary Goodman & Barry Rosen
ASSOCIATE PRODUCERS	Moctezuma Esparza & Robert Katz
CINEMATOGRAPHER	Guillermo Navarro
FILM EDITOR	Zach Staenberg
MUSIC SCORE	Joseph Julián Gonzales
SCREENPLAY	Michael Kane & Luis Valdez
STORY	Michael Kane
DIRECTOR	Luis Valdez

Francisco Hernán Sánchez Aguilar de Solares (The Cisco Kid)	Jimmy Smits
Francisco Rivera (Pancho)	Cheech Marín
Dominique	Sadie Frost
General Achille Dupré	Bruce Payne
Lt. Col. Delacroix	Ron Perlman
Washam	Tony Amendola
Lundquist	Tim Thomerson
General Montano	Pedro Armendáriz, Jr.
Kessler	Phil Esparza

Photo still for *The Girl from San Lorenzo* (1950), starring Duncan Renaldo

Van Hoose	Clayton Landey
Haney	Charles McGaughan
Alain Vitton	Tony Pandolfo
Alcott	Roger Cudney
López	Joaquín Garrido
Hernández	Guillermo Ríos
Hidalgo	Miguel Sandoval
Treviño	Tomás Goros
Aparicio	Rufino Echegoyen
Doña Josefa	Teresa Lagunes
General Gutiérrez	Honorato Magaloni
Benito Juárez	Luis Valdez
Rosa Rivera	Yareli Arizmendi
Linda Rivera	Marisol Valdez
Antonio Rivera	Julius Jansland
Juanito Rivera	Mario Ecatl Zapata
Héctor Rivera	Mario Alberto
Eduardo Rivera	Boris Peguero
Alicia Rivera	Maya Zapata
Guerrero	Gerardo Zepeda
Libertad	Lorena Victoria
Old Cantina Lady	Valentina Ponzanneli
Prison Guard	Pedro Altamirano
Dungeon Soldier	Gerardo Martínez
Firing Squad Lieutenant	Rojo Grau
Vitton's Guard	Guido Bolanos
Farmers	Roberto Olivo, Roberto Antúnez
French Officer	Pablo Zuak
Little Boy	Lakin Valdez
San Miguel Man	Mario Valdez
Women	Luisa Coronel, Emilia Zapata, Alexandra Vicencio
Bishop	Moctezuma Esparza

Spies for the Cause: Susan Benedict, Patricia Brown, Carolyn Caldera, Corrina Durán, Claire Lewin, Herendia Silva

BROADCAST DEBUT: FEBRUARY 6, 1994

RUNNING TIME: 100 MIN.

THE CISCO KID TV SERIES

Starring Duncan Renaldo and Leo Carrillo

First Season, 1950–51

"Boomerang" 9/5/50

D: Derwin Abrahams   S: J. Benton Cheney

The Cisco Kid and his companion Pancho find themselves wanted by the law after a prominent real estate broker has two gunmen impersonate them and rob the Mesa Verde bank. With Jane Adams (Miss Harley), Byron Foulger (Mr. Harley), Stephen Chase (Jim Brent), Edmund Cobb (Martin), Lee Phelps (Sheriff), David Sharpe (Fake Cisco), and George De Normand (Deputy). Companion episode: "Chain Lightning." Note: There is considerable overlap between the cast and storyline of this debut episode and that of the last Cisco feature, *The Girl from San Lorenzo* (Inter-American/United Artists, 1950).

"Counterfeit Money" 9/12/50

D: Derwin Abrahams   S: J. Benton Cheney

Cisco and Pancho hunt a brother-sister team of counterfeiters who are using a secret room in a bank as their headquarters and forcing the banker to pass their phony money. With Peggy Stewart (Jane), Forrest Taylor (Hale), Luther Crockett (Tom Henderson), Riley Hill (Terry), Robert Livingston (Red Saunders), George De Normand (George), Art Dupuis (Marshal Ben Lane), and Fred Kohler, Jr. (Sheriff). Companion episodes: "Oil Land," "Cattle Quarantine."

"Rustling" 9/19/50

D: Derwin Abrahams   S: J. Benton Cheney

Cisco and Pancho are charged with murder when a rancher who secretly heads a rustling ring kills a suspicious neighbor and frames Cisco for the crime. With Christine Larson (Mary Austin), Raymond Hatton (Sheriff), Jonathan Hale (Barry Owens), Douglas Evans (Joe Dawson), Frank Matts (Jud Morgan), and George De Normand (Henchman). Companion episode: "Medicine Flats." Note: J. Benton Cheney recycled the rustling gimmick in this episode from his screenplay for the Hopalong Cassidy feature *Twilight on the Trail* (Paramount, 1941), starring William Boyd.

"Big Switch" 9/26/50

D: Derwin Abrahams   S: Royal Cole

Cisco and Pancho help the niece of a secretly murdered cattleman outwit a clever forger who closely resembles the woman's uncle. With Pamela Blake (Margie Murdock), Sarah Padden (Sarah), Nelson Leigh (Jim Holbrook), Fred Kohler, Jr. (Henchman), Carol Henry (Deputy), Jack Ingram (Jim Hardy/Henry Murdock), and Pierre Watkin (Sheriff). Companion episodes: "Railroad Land Rush," "Renegade Son." Note: This is the first episode to end with the familiar "Oh, Pancho!" "Oh, Cisco!" exchange between Renaldo and Carrillo.

"Convict Story" 10/3/50

D: Derwin Abrahams   S: Sherman L. Lowe

Cisco and Pancho try to help an escaped convict who stole Pancho's clothes and horse while Pancho was swimming and then tried to kill the mine owner he says framed him. With Gail Davis (Ruth Drake), Riley Hill (Bob Drake), Robert Livingston (Cantwell), Fred Kohler, Jr. (Lefty), and Forrest Taylor (Sheriff). Companion episodes: "The Will," "False Marriage." Note: This is the second episode with the "Oh, Pancho!" "Oh, Cisco!" ending.

"Oil Land" 10/10/50

D: Derwin Abrahams   S: J. Benton Cheney

When a rancher who's just discovered oil on his property is murdered by one of his hands, suspicion falls on Cisco and Pancho. With Peggy Stewart (Peggy Williams), Fred Kohler, Jr. (Hank), Forrest Taylor (listed but not in cast), Robert Livingston (Walter Stuart), Luther Crockett (Sheriff), and Earle Hodgins (Idaho). Companion episodes: "Counterfeit Money," "Cattle Quarantine." Note: This is the first of several episodes that give credit to an actor who didn't appear on screen. Usually the reason is that he did appear in a companion episode and, to save money, the production company used the same cast list for the credits of both.

"Chain Lightning" 10/14/50

D: Derwin Abrahams   S: J. Benton Cheney

After being sent to prison by Cisco and Pancho with the help of stage line owner Bill Shannon, gunfighter Jim Brent is released and sets out for revenge on all three. With Noel Neill (Rita Shannon), Don C. Harvey (Jim Brent), Edmund Cobb (Larry Martin), David Sharpe (Bill Shannon), and Lee Phelps (Sheriff). Companion episode: "Boomerang."

"Medicine Flats" 10/17/50

D: Derwin Abrahams   S: J. Benton Cheney

Suspecting a gambling-house owner of being behind the gang of rustlers that framed them for murder, Cisco and Pancho convince him that they're wanted for killing a sheriff and try to break up the gang from within. With Christine Larson (Judy Summers), Raymond Hatton (Sheriff), Jonathan Hale (Barry Owens), Douglas Evans (Curt Reynolds), Frank Matts (Parker), and George De Normand (Jack). Companion episode: "Rustling."

"Railroad Land Rush" 10/28/50

D: Derwin Abrahams   S: Sherman L. Lowe

Cisco and Pancho pursue the con man who killed a suspicious railroad detective and is using an innocent real estate dealer to foster a phony land promotion scheme. With Pamela Blake (Margie Holbrook), Pierre Watkin (Mr. Holbrook),

Nelson Leigh (James Blake), Fred Kohler, Jr. (Steve), Forrest Taylor (John Warren), George De Normand (Manning), Carol Henry (Larry), and Jack Ingram (Rocky). Companion episodes: "Big Switch," "Renegade Son." Note: This is the third episode with the "Oh, Pancho!" "Oh, Cisco!" ending, which becomes standard from this point on.

"The Will" 10/31/50

D: Derwin Abrahams   S: Royal Cole

Cisco and Pancho stop two gunmen from killing a young freight wagon driver who's just been released from prison after serving time for a strongbox robbery. Then they set out to prove that the young man was framed. With Gail Davis (Ruth Drake), Riley Hill (Bob Drake), Art Dupuis (Hanley), Fred Kohler, Jr. (Nixon), Robert Livingston (Cantwell), Eddie Parker (Barker), Forrest Taylor (Sheriff), and George De Normand (Henchman). Companion episodes: "Convict Story," "False Marriage."

"Cattle Quarantine" 11/7/50

D: Derwin Abrahams   S: J. Benton Cheney

Cisco and Pancho fight a crooked cattle buyer who's trying to gain control of a ranch by using the county livestock inspector as his tool to create a phony epidemic. With Peggy Stewart (Peggy), Earle Hodgins (Idaho), Robert Livingston (Walter Stuart), Fred Kohler, Jr. (Wiley), Forrest Taylor (Dr. Norman Slade), Art Dupuis (Utah), Luther Crockett (Sheriff Jim), and Riley Hill (Deputy). Companion episodes: "Counterfeit Money," "Oil Land."

"Renegade Son" 11/21/50

D: Derwin Abrahams   S: Betty Burbridge

Cisco and Pancho try to save a young woman who's been convicted of the poisoning murder of her wealthy uncle. With Pamela Blake (Joyce Henry), Pierre Watkin (Sheriff), Fred Kohler, Jr. (Deputy Sam), Nelson Leigh (Jeff Henry), Carol Henry (Spike), and Jack Ingram (Henchman). Companion episodes: "Big Switch," "Railroad Land Rush." Note: Betty Burbridge based her script for this episode on her screenplay for *In Old New Mexico* (Monogram, 1945), the second Cisco feature in which Renaldo starred.

"False Marriage" 11/28/50

D: Derwin Abrahams   S: Betty Burbridge

Cisco and Pancho try to help a wealthy rancher prevent his niece's marriage to a notorious gambler, but when the rancher is killed they're accused of his murder. With Gail Davis (Nancy King), Mary Gordon (Mary O'Toole), Sarah Padden (Mother Smiley), Robert Livingston (Duke Ralston), Russell Hicks (Jasper King), Fred Kohler, Jr. (Deputy), Luther Crockett (Sheriff), Forrest Taylor (Rev. William Smiley), Earle Hodgins (Gramp). Companion episodes: "Convict Story," "The Will." Note: Betty Burbridge based her script for this episode on her screenplay for *The Cisco Kid Returns* (Monogram, 1945), the first Cisco feature in which Renaldo starred.

"Wedding Blackmail"   12/5/50

D: Paul Landres   S: Sherman L. Lowe (?)

Cisco and Pancho help out a young bank cashier whose forthcoming marriage to the bank president's daughter is endangered when two gunmen who know he's an ex-convict try to blackmail him. With Phyllis Coates (Marge Lacey), Bill Kennedy (Sam Foster), Mike Ragan (Jason), David Bruce (Bill Ryan), and Tom Tyler (Sheriff). Companion episodes: "Haven for Heavies," "Phoney Sheriff," "Uncle Disinherits Niece."

"Lynching Story"   12/12/50

D: Paul Landres   S: Ande Lamb

When a mine owner is murdered by three employees who have been stealing gold from him, Cisco and Pancho stop a mob from lynching the dead man's prospective son-in-law for the crime. With Carol Forman (Pat Parker), Richard Emory (Terry), Marshall Reed (Tracy), Frank Matts (Joe), Victor Cox (Lou), Lane Chandler (Sheriff), and I. Stanford Jolley (Willard Parker). Companion episodes: "Confession for Money," "Pancho Hostage." Note: An uncredited Lyle Talbot plays the judge in this episode.

"Newspaper Crusaders"   12/19/50

D: Albert Herman   S: Betty Burbridge

Cisco and Pancho help a newspaper editor in his crusade against a crooked gambler and his cronies. With Ellen Hall (Elaine Jarrett), Dennis Moore (Henry Judd), Bill Henry (Ben Jarrett), Steve Clark (Klondike), Ted Adams (Phony Marshal), and Ferris Taylor (Mayor Carson). Companion episodes: "Freight Line Feud" (first season), "Performance Bond" (listed in second season).

"Dog Story"   12/26/50

D: Albert Herman   S: J. Benton Cheney

Cisco, Pancho, and a dead prospector's dog hunt the crooked gambler who murdered the prospector for refusing to tell the location of his secret gold mine. With Tanis Chandler (Melinda Weaver), Tristram Coffin (Dude Cottrell), Zon Murray (Omaha), Frank McCarroll (Henchman), Hank Patterson (John Weaver), and Kenne Duncan (Townsman). Companion episodes: "The Old Bum," "Water Rights."

"Confession for Money"   1/2/51

D: Paul Landres   S: Betty Burbridge

A lovely young lady asks Cisco and Pancho to help her fiancé, who has confessed to a bank robbery and murder in return for the money needed for surgery on his mother. With Carol Forman (Pat Lacey), Richard Emory (Terry Ryan), Marshall Reed (Tom Tracy), Frank Matts (Joe), Victor Cox (Lou), Lane Chandler (Sheriff), and I. Stanford Jolley (A. W. Parker). Companion episodes: "Lynching Story," "Pancho Hostage."

"The Old Bum"   1/9/51

D: Albert Herman   S: Louise Rousseau

Cisco and Pancho help out a penniless derelict who unwittingly becomes a front man for rustlers when he pretends to be a wealthy rancher so as to impress his visiting daughter. With Tanis Chandler (Paula Bonnard), Tristram Coffin (Kelly), Zon Murray (Shelby), Frank McCarroll (Henchman), Hank Patterson (Silas Bonnard), and Kenne Duncan (Sheriff). Companion episodes: "Dog Story," "Water Rights."

"Haven For Heavies"   1/13/51

D: Paul Landres   S: Warren Wilson

Cisco follows the murderer of a U.S. marshal to the haven of Twin Buttes, where outlaws enjoy immunity from the law. With Phyllis Coates (Miss Doran), Bill Kennedy (Red Kelly), Mike Ragan (Al Shelby), David Bruce (listed but not in cast), and Tom Tyler (Sheriff Jim Turner). Companion episodes: "Wedding Blackmail," "Phoney Sheriff," "Uncle Disinherits Niece."

Those Gay Caballeros in Pioneertown

Hi-Desert Magazine, a publication of Hi-Desert Publishing, featured Duncan Renaldo and Leo Carrillo on its cover in 1998. The magazine served California's Morongo Basin, including Pioneertown, a small town that began as a motion picture set where many Westerns and early television shows were filmed, including *The Cisco Kid.*

"Pancho Hostage" 1/16/51

D: Paul Landres   S: Betty Burbridge

Having jailed a bank robber, Cisco and Pancho are taken prisoners by his sister, who threatens to kill Pancho unless her brother is released. With Carol Forman (Pat Tracy), Richard Emory (Terry), Marshall Reed (Frank Tracy), Frank Matts (Joe), Victor Cox (Lou), Lane Chandler (Sheriff Sam Dawson), and I. Stanford Jolley (Parker). Companion episodes: "Lynching Story," "Confession For Money."

"Freight Line Feud" 1/27/51

D: Albert Herman   S: Elizabeth Beecher

Cisco and Pancho try to expose the outlaws who are attacking Bittercreek's freight line and putting the blame on a competing stage line owner. With Ellen Hall (Elaine Frazer), Dennis Moore (Judd), Bill Henry (Bill Jarrett), Steve Clark (Klondike), Ted Adams (Cal), and Ferris Taylor (listed but not in cast). Companion episodes: "Newspaper Crusaders" (first season), "Performance Bond" (listed in second season).

"Phoney Sheriff" 2/6/51

D: Paul Landres   S: J. Benton Cheney

Cisco and Pancho go after a cattle buyer who used a fake sheriff and deputies to trick them into turning over a friend's cattle herd. With Phyllis Coates (Miss Lacey), Bill Kennedy (Sam Kelly), Mike Ragan (Al Shelby), David Bruce (Blackie), and Tom Tyler (Sheriff). Companion episodes: "Wedding Blackmail," "Haven For Heavies," "Uncle Disinherits Niece."

"Uncle Disinherits Niece" 2/13/51

D: Paul Landres   S: Betty Burbridge

When a crooked lawyer murders a rancher who had threatened to disinherit his niece unless she stopped seeing her boyfriend, Cisco and Pancho try to clear the young man. With Phyllis Coates (Marge Lacey), Bill Kennedy (Sam Foster), Mike Ragan (Jason), David Bruce (Bill Ryan), Tom Tyler (Sheriff), and Bud Osborne (Jim Lacey). Companion episodes: "Wedding Blackmail," "Haven For Heavies," "Phoney Sheriff."

"Phoney Heiress" 2/13/51

D: Paul Landres   S: J. Benton Cheney

Cisco and Pancho try to save a young woman's inherited property from a crooked lawyer who has hired an impostor to pose as the rightful owner. With Lyn Thomas (Mary Stark), Vivian Mason (Stella Jackson), Jack Reynolds (George Holden), Robert Bice (Turk), Mauritz Hugo (Nebraska), Charles Watts (Sheriff Peabody), and Joseph Granby (Judge). Companion episodes: "Ghost Story," "Water Well Oil" (both listed in second season). Note: Quite clearly this episode, like its two companions, was filmed during the 1951–52 season. Why it was moved into the first season, and the first-season episode "Performance Bond" was released as part of the second season, is anyone's guess.

"Water Rights" 2/20/51

D: Albert Herman   S: Raymond L. Schrock

Cisco and Pancho try to expose a crooked banker and lawyer who are scheming to sabotage the ranchers' water project and then foist their own project on the valley. With Tanis Chandler (Marge Lacey), Zon Murray (Sam Foster), Tristram Coffin (Tom Barton), Frank McCarroll (Jason), Hank Patterson (Jim Lacey), and Kenne Duncan (Sheriff). Companion episodes: "Dog Story," "The Old Bum."

Second Season, 1951–52

"Performance Bond" 9/3/51

D: Albert Herman   S: Louise Rousseau

Cisco and Pancho help a freight line owner who's in danger of forfeiting a $20,000 performance bond because of "accidents" preventing him from delivering ore to a smelter. With Ellen Hall (Elaine Wilson), Bill Henry (Jarrett), Dennis Moore (Judd), Ted Adams (Caleb Wilson), Steve Clark (Klondike), and Ferris Taylor (Lem Carson). Companion episodes (both from first season): "Newspaper Crusaders," "Freight Line Feud." Note: Quite clearly this episode, like its two companions, was filmed during the 1950–51 season. Why it was moved into the second season, and the second-season episode "Phoney Heiress" was released as part of the first season, is anyone's guess.

"Stolen Bonds" 9/10/51

D: Paul Landres   S: J. Benton Cheney

While pursuing a man who stole $25,000 in bonds from their friend, Cisco and Pancho come to suspect that a young woman working as cook in a hotel is in league with the thief. With Jean Dean (Christine), Reed Howes (Dan), Pierce Lyden (Vic), Bill Holmes (Henchman), Jim Diehl (Henchman), Stanley Andrews (Sheriff), and Bud Osborne (Stage Driver). Companion episode: "Protective Association."

"Postal Inspector" 9/17/51

D: Paul Landres   S: J. Benton Cheney

When Cisco and Pancho mail a letter in the town of Baxter Center, they're arrested as part of a gang of mail robbers. With Maris Wrixon (Elaine Parker), Edward Keane (Jay Willoughby), Ilse Mader (listed but not in cast), Myron Healey (Drake), Dick Rich (Stacy), Rory Mallinson (Sheriff), and Steve Pendleton (Inspector Sam Harris). Note: Ilse Mader gets an acting credit without actually appearing in this episode because Ziv once again decided to save a few dollars by using the cast list for the companion episode in the credit crawl for this one.

"Jewelry Store Fence" 9/24/51

D: Paul Landres   S: J. Benton Cheney

While hunting for a purchaser of stolen jewelry, Cisco and Pancho encounter a crazy old man who tries to kill them with a crossbow built into an ornate clock. With Kay Morley (Martha), Michael Whalen (Pete), Michael Mark (Uncle Toby), Robert Wood (Terry), George Offerman (Ed), Steve Clark (Stage Driver), and Therese Lyon (Woman on Coach). Companion episode: "Water Toll."

"Foreign Agent" 10/1/51

D: Paul Landres   S: J. Benton Cheney

Cisco uses a coded musical score to outwit foreign spies who are trying to take over a vast deposit of tungsten. With Ann Zika (Diane), Carl Milletaire (Wharton), Paul Hogan (Henchman), Terry Frost (Dan), William M. McCormick (Panamint), John Merton (The Chief), and Garnett A. Marks (Henchman). Companion episode: "The Bates Story."

"Medicine Man Show" 10/8/51

D: Eddie Davis   S: Warren Wilson

While tracing a trunk containing guns being smuggled to the Comanches, Cisco learns that the trunk belongs to a young woman. With Wanda McKay (Sunny Benton), Stephen Chase (Dixon), Dennis Moore (Bugsy), Ray Hyke (Henchman), Cactus Mack (Henchman), George Davis (Henchman), Claudia Drake (Cheewee), Rodd Redwing (Flying Cloud), and Charles Soldani (Red Moon). Companion episode: "Ride On (Black Lightning)."

"Ghost Story" 10/15/51

D: Paul Landres   S: Elizabeth Beecher

Cisco and Pancho go after a pair of silver smugglers who killed their nervous partner, a rancher, when he tried to break with them. With Lyn Thomas (Mary Davis), Jack Reynolds (George Holden), Robert Bice (Turk), Mauritz Hugo (Nebraska), Charles Watts (Ben Larsen), and Joseph Granby (Will Harper). Companion episodes: "Phoney Heiress" (listed in first season), "Water Well Oil."

"Protective Association" 10/22/51

D: Paul Landres   S: Marjorie E. Fortin

Cisco and Pancho help a rancher and his daughter fight a gang of protection racketeers. With Jean Dean (Peggy Conlan), Reed Howes (Dan Sloan), Pierce Lyden (Vic), Bill Holmes (Henchman), Jim Diehl (Henchman), Bud Osborne (Henchman), and Stanley Andrews (Mr. Conlan). Companion episode: "Stolen Bonds."

"Kid Sister Trouble" 10/29/51

D: Paul Landres   S: Louise Rousseau

After encountering a woman gambling-house dealer doing target practice, Cisco and Pancho become involved with counterfeiters. With Maris Wrixon (Christine), Edward Keane (Conlan), Ilse Mader (Jane), Myron Healey (Sloan), Dick Rich (Martin), Rory Mallinson (Dave), and Steve Pendleton (Lefty). Companion episode: "Postal Inspector."

Publicity shot of Leo Carrillo as Pancho and Duncan Renaldo as the Cisco Kid

"Water Toll" 11/5/51

D: Paul Landres   S: J. Benton Cheney

Cisco and Pancho help a woman rancher fight a greedy cattleman who's making unsuspecting drovers pay him for watering their stock. With Kay Morley (Sondra Lindsay), Michael Whalen (Pete Sturgis), Michael Mark (Dusty), Robert Wood (Terry), George Offerman (Ed), Steve Clark (Sheriff), and Brad Johnson (Johnny). Companion episode: "Jewelry Store Fence."

"The Bates Story" 11/12/51

D: Paul Landres   S: Sherman L. Lowe

Cisco and Pancho are forced to switch clothes with two escaped convicts helped by a female accomplice and are later arrested as the fugitives themselves. With Ann Zika (Lorraine Bentley), Carl Milletaire (listed but not in cast), Paul Hogan (Slick Wofford), Terry Frost (Harry Gaines), William M. McCormick (Hayden), John Merton (Sheriff), and Anna Demetrio (Mexican Woman). Companion episode: "Foreign Agent."

"Water Well Oil" 11/13/51

D: Paul Landres   S: Ande Lamb (?)

Cisco and Pancho are shot at by a young hothead who thinks they tried to kill him because he's found oil on his ranch. With Lyn Thomas (Mary Turner), Jack Reynolds (George Holden), Robert Bice (Turk Martin), Mauritz Hugo (Henchman), Charles Watts (Sheriff), Joseph Granby (Jim Turner). Companion episodes: "Phoney Heiress" (listed in first season), "Ghost Story."

"Ride On (Black Lightning)" 11/19/51

D: Eddie Davis   S: Warren Wilson

Cisco and Pancho stop a young woman from killing the wild stallion she believes has been stealing her mares, then try to find the human thieves who framed the horse. With Wanda McKay (Sally Emerson), Stephen Chase (Frank Larsen), Dennis Moore (Duke), Ray Hyke (Steve), Cactus Mack (Utah), George Davis (Doc), and Chester Clute (Monty). Companion episode: "Medicine Man Show."

"Vigilante Story" 12/4/51

D: Paul Landres   S: J. Benton Cheney

Posing as a gambler and an organ grinder, Cisco and Pancho try to break up the band of masked vigilantes terrorizing the town of Buffalo Flats. With Lois Hall (Lois Holden), Bill George (Pike), Craig Hunter (Henchman), Hugh Prosser (Jed Haskell), James Kirkwood (Henchman), Earle Hodgins (Tom), Edmund Cobb (John Holden). Companion episodes: "Sleeping Gas," "Quicksilver Murder."

"Hidden Valley" 12/11/51

D: Eddie Davis   S: J. Benton Cheney

Cisco and Pancho get lost in the wilderness and discover a hidden valley run by a tyrannical ex-sea captain. With Virginia Herrick (Nedra Challis), Tristram Coffin (George Challis), Wee Willie Davis (Barty), I. Stanford Jolley (Jim Walker), Keith Richards (Rand), and George Eldredge (Sheriff). Companion episode: "Quarter Horse."

"Carrier Pigeon" 12/18/51

D: Paul Landres   S: J. Benton Cheney

Cisco and Pancho become involved with a woman claiming to be an insurance investigator on the trail of a stolen diamond necklace. With Sherry Moreland (Joan Bentley), Leonard Penn (Gary Mason), Milburn Morante (Tracy Parker), John Cason (Henchman), Ted Mapes (Henchman), and Garry Garrett (Henchman). Companion episode: "Jewelry Holdup."

"Hypnotist Murder" 12/25/51

D: Eddie Davis   S: J. Benton Cheney

Cisco and Pancho try to stop a former carnival hypnotist who gets tired of waiting for her wealthy father-in-law to die and mesmerizes her husband into a murder attempt. With Marsha Jones (Blanche Modell/Sue Prentiss), Riley Hill (Bill Prentiss), Joe Forte (Mr. Prentiss), Doris Merrick (Madame Lil), Denver Pyle (Jerry Roark), Zon Murray (Henchman), and Tom Holland (Henchman). Companion episode: "Ghost Town."

"Romany Caravan" 1/8/52

D: Paul Landres   S: J. Benton Cheney

Cisco visits a gypsy camp and gets involved in a knife fight over a woman while Pancho is terrified by a dancing bear.

With Dolores Castle (Marisa), Sondra Rodgers (Ilka), Craig Woods (Jay Costain), Peter Coe (Danilo), Milburn Morante (Stefan), and Jack George (Benji). Companion episode: "Buried Treasure."

"Robber Crow" 1/15/52

D: Paul Landres   S: Herbert Purdum

Cisco and Pancho intervene in a feud between the gunmen who are guarding a placer mine and the workers from town who are suspected by the guards of stealing gold. With Mary Dean Moss (Nina Loring), Michael Vallon (Scotty), Raphael Bennett (Jack Kells), Karl Davis (Gregg), Mickey Simpson (Henchman), Kermit Maynard (Albuquerque Jones), and Teddy Infuhr (Tommy Loring). Companion episode: "Spanish Dagger."

"Sleeping Gas" 1/22/52

D: Paul Landres   S: J. Benton Cheney

A bank holdup while Pancho is cashing a check involves Cisco with an outlaw family whose modus operandi includes a high-pitched fiddle and an ornamental globe full of sleeping gas. With Lois Hall (Jerry), Bill George (Joe), Hugh Prosser (Larry), James Kirkwood (Fiddlin' Sam), George Eldredge (Banker Wharton), and Franklyn Farnum (Banker Tracy). Companion episodes: "Vigilante Story," "Quarter Horse."

"Quarter Horse" 1/29/52

D: Eddie Davis   S: J. Benton Cheney

Cisco steps into a revenge-motivated plot to fix a race pitting four quarter horses against a thoroughbred. With Virginia Herrick (Helen Butler), Tristram Coffin (Joe Butler), I. Stanford Jolley (Sam Carson), Keith Richards (Terry), George Eldredge (Jackson), Stanley Blystone (Frank Wallace), and Eddie Nash (Nash). Companion episode: "Hidden Valley."

"Jewelry Holdup" 2/5/52

D: Paul Landres   S: J. Benton Cheney

Cisco and Pancho step in when jewel thieves who mailed some loot to themselves try to retrieve their package by force from an officious postal clerk. With Sherry Moreland (Judy Winters), Leonard Penn (Steve), Helene Millard (Aunt Ellen Palmer), John Cason (Jim), Milburn Morante (Jasper Peabody), and Ted Mapes (Marty). Companion episode: "Carrier Pigeon."

"Ghost Town" 2/12/52

D: Eddie Davis   S: J. Benton Cheney

In an empty town, Cisco and Pancho meet a young woman searching for proof of her identity, a crazy hotel proprietor, an eloping young couple, and some weird menaces. With Marsha Jones (Sondra Spencer), Riley Hill (George Hardy), Joe Forte (Willoughby Baxter/Napoleon Gordon), Doris

Merrick (Anita Hardy), Denver Pyle (Outlaw), and Zon Murray (Outlaw). Companion episode: "Hypnotist Murder."

"Quicksilver Murder" 2/12/52

D: Paul Landres S: J. Benton Cheney

Cisco goes after a corrupt public prosecutor who steals quicksilver shipments and uses chemical weapons to commit murder. With Lois Hall (Jennifer Hart), Bill George (Larry Scott), Hugh Prosser (Joe Wallace), James Kirkwood (Marshal Fletcher), Joe Forte (Wharton Stone), and Hunter Gardner (Sam Moore). Companion episodes: "Vigilante Story," "Sleeping Gas."

"Buried Treasure" 2/19/52

D: Paul Landres S: J. Benton Cheney

Cisco encounters an ancient witchlike hag and her sons, who resort to torture and murder while hunting the lost treasure of pirate Jean Lafitte. With Dolores Castle (Toni), Sondra Rodgers (Margot), Craig Woods (Kit), Peter Coe (Bernardo), Milburn Morante (Girardot), and Jack George (Curator). Companion episode: "Romany Caravan."

"Spanish Dagger" 2/19/52

D: Paul Landres S: J. Benton Cheney

While Cisco is rescuing a prospector from an explosion, he unearths a jeweled dagger bearing a curse that begins to work when it's stolen. With Mary Dean Moss (Shelley Drake), Michael Vallon (Uncle Pete), Raphael Bennett (Professor), Karl Davis (Smiley), Mickey Simpson (Jiggers), and Kermit Maynard (Bert). Companion episode: "Robber Crow."

Third Season, 1952–53

"Monkey Business" 8/3/52

D: Eddie Davis S: Robert A. White

Cisco and Pancho are arrested for robbery after some stolen money is planted on them by three thieves using an equestrian clown show as their cover. With Poodles Hanneford (Harry Smith), Grace Hanneford (Pat Smith), Marshall Reed (Slick), Zon Murray (Henchman), and Jack Ingram (Henchman). Companion episode: "Laughing Badman."

"The Puppeteer" 8/10/52

D: George M. Cahan S: Irwin Lieberman

Cisco and Pancho wonder why the notorious Ghost Gang has never robbed the wealthiest town in Peaceful Valley. When they find out, they use Pancho's uncle's puppet show to get word to the sheriff. With Leonard Penn (Clyde Barrows), Raymond Hatton (Uncle Gitano), Mike Ragan (Turk Evans), Joel Marston (Marcus Meeker), Ted Mapes (Sheriff Tom Enright), and Louise Manley (Townswoman). Companion episode: "Canyon City Kid."

"The Talking Dog" 8/17/52

D: Eddie Davis S: Warren Wilson

The first telephone in the West falls into the hands of bandits who use it to alert members of their gang when gold is being shipped. Without realizing it, Cisco and Pancho are the only ones who can break the gang's scheme. With Gail Davis (Miss Scott), Paul Livermore (Griff), Bruce Payne (Maddock), Allen Pinson (Rusty), Ferris Taylor (Vincent C. Emerson), and Cactus Mack (Sheriff). Companion episode: "Big Steal."

"Pancho and the Pachyderm" 10/5/52

D: George M. Cahan
S: Elizabeth Beecher & Jack Lewis

When Cisco and Pancho thwart the holdup of a one-wagon medicine show, they find themselves involved in the mystery of a stolen jade idol. With Carole Mathews (Sally Griffith), Tom London (Ben Griffith), House Peters, Jr. (Joe Shadden), Sheb Wooley (Roy Stokes), and James Parnell (Sheriff). Companion episode: "Dutchman's Flat."

"Kid Brother" 10/12/52

D: Eddie Davis S: Richard Conway

In an apparently abandoned shack, Cisco and Pancho come upon a wounded teenage boy who tells them that outlaws murdered his brother. With Edward Clark (Doc Taylor), Linda Johnson (Mrs. Hawkins), Keith Richards (Brad Torrance), Robert Wilke (Vic), Kermit Maynard (Henchman), and Teddy Infuhr (Bobby Torrance). Companion episodes: "Mad About Money," "The Commodore Goes West."

"Face of Death" 10/19/52

D: George M. Cahan S: J. Benton Cheney

Cisco and Pancho avenge an archaeologist who was murdered by his guides when on the verge of discovering the tomb of an Aztec high priest. With Gloria Saunders (Miss Spencer), Billy Griffith (Prof. John Ferris/Sam Chanfield), Robert Cabal (Tecla), Tom Monroe (Digger), William Bakewell (Rance), Wesley Hudman (Barry), Don Mahin (Henchman), Paul Marion (Henchman), and Watson Downs (Quetzal). Companion episode: "Lost City."

"Big Steal" 10/19/52

D: Eddie Davis S: J. Benton Cheney

Cisco and Pancho run into a phony U.S. land commissioner and a crooked homesteading project when they try to help their friend Don Miguel Escobar settle a dispute with a neighbor over water rights. With Gail Davis (Lucille Gordon), Paul Livermore (Barry), Bruce Payne (Don Miguel Escobar), and John Cason (Stewart). Companion episode: "The Talking Dog."

Duncan Renaldo's stunt double, Troy Melton, prepares to jump off a roof.

"Laughing Badman" 10/26/52

D: George M. Cahan   S: Elizabeth Beecher

Cisco and Pancho discover a murdered deputy sheriff whose saddlebags are stuffed with $50 bills. A strange laugh, tiny footprints, and a ventriloquist with a live dummy set them on the trail of the two counterfeiters who are responsible. With Marshall Reed (Blade Meddick), Zon Murray (Sheriff Tom Brayle), Jack Ingram (Homer Appleby), and Billy Curtis (Laughing Midget). Companion episode: "Monkey Business."

"Canyon City Kid" 11/2/52

D: George M. Cahan   S: Warren Wilson

Cisco becomes suspicious of a group staying in Canyon City. They intercept his letter of inquiry about them and then try to manipulate a local boy into challenging Cisco to a gunfight. With Leonard Penn (Curt Mathers), Raymond Hatton (Gramps), Mike Ragan (Cappy), Joel Marston (Kenny), Ted Mapes (Henchman), and Louise Manley (Lily). Companion episode: "The Puppeteer."

"Dutchman's Flat" 11/9/52

D: George M. Cahan   S: J. Benton Cheney

After being grubstaked by Cisco and Pancho, prospector Cactus Bronson strikes it rich. But he is murdered for his mine and his son thinks Cisco and Pancho are the killers. With Carole Mathews (Debby Hansen), Tom London (Dusty), House Peters, Jr. (Curt Hansen), Sheb Wooley (Bill Bronson), James Parnell (Ollie Hansen), and Guy Wilkerson (Cactus Bronson). Companion episode: "Pancho and the Pachyderm."

"Mad About Money" 11/16/52

D: Eddie Davis   S: Don Brinkley

When an eccentric old man starts giving away bags of gold coins, he's suspected of murder. Cisco and Pancho try to prove his innocence. With Edward Clark (Toby), Linda

Johnson (Nora Blake), Keith Richards (Sandy), Robert Wilke (Barney), and Kermit Maynard (Sheriff J. J. McGrew). Companion episodes: "Kid Brother," "The Commodore Goes West."

"Lost City" 11/23/52

D: George M. Cahan   S: J. Benton Cheney (?)

Cisco and Pancho try to stop three men from making off with part of the treasure from a lost Inca city. With Gloria Saunders (Princess Zenda), Billy Griffith (Prof. Winston), Robert Cabal (Mathaozin), Tom Monroe (George Hardy), and William Bakewell (Prof. Ralph Chaney). Companion episode: "Face of Death."

"Thunderhead" 11/30/52

D: Sobey Martin   S: J. Benton Cheney

Cisco and Pancho open the eyes of absentee landowner Kathy Kerrigan to the corrupt practices of her ranch manager, who then holds her captive. With Almira Sessions (Aunt Christine), Richard Barron (Winters), Rodolfo Hoyos, Jr. (listed but not in cast), Edward Colmans (José Ramón), Everett Glass (Prado), Augie W. Gómez (Manolo). Companion episode: "Bell of Santa Margarita." Note: The cast list on the credits of this episode is identical to the one on the credits of its companion episode even though the actual casts are different. The result is that the actress who played Kathy Kerrigan gets no credit at all, while Rodolfo Hoyos, Jr., is credited even though he's not in the film!

"Bell of Santa Margarita" 12/14/52

D: Sobey Martin   S: Edmond Kelso

When the good-luck bell of Santa Margarita is stolen by El Puma and his gang, Cisco and Pancho try to recover it in time for the wedding of a friend's daughter. With Almira Sessions (Michaela), Richard Barron (El Puma), Rodolfo Hoyos, Jr. (Vejar), Edward Colmans (Padre Miguel), Everett Glass (Don Fernando), and Augie W. Gómez (Santo). Companion episode: "Thunderhead."

"Lodestone" 12/21/52

D: Sobey Martin   S: J. Benton Cheney

Cisco and Pancho go after a Kansas City dude who tries to kidnap the wife and daughter of a wealthy rancher and hold them for ransom. With Peggy Stewart (Linda Blaine), Gordon Clark (Henry Duprez), Bud Osborne (Kansas), Hal K. Dawson (Charles Blaine), Henry Rowland (Rocky), and Marshall Bradford (Doc). Companion episode: "Gun Totin' Papa."

"Dead by Proxy" 12/28/52

D: Eddie Davis   S: Robert Clayton

When a gunman hired to kill the owner of a general store is himself killed instead, Cisco persuades the intended victim to play dead as part of a scheme to flush out whoever hired the killer. With Anne Kimbell (Alice Fleming), Lee Roberts (Olson), Peter Leeds (Franklin Holt), Hank Patterson (Jess Fleming), and John Hamilton (Sheriff). Companion episodes: "The Fire Engine," "Fear."

"The Devil's Deputy"   1/4/53

D: Eddie Davis   S: Richard Conway

A crooked businessman hires a gunman named López to impersonate Colonel Lucky Gonzales, who is to be the town's new marshal. Then Cisco and Pancho ride into town, and Pancho is mistaken by the townspeople for Gonzales and by the crooks for López. With Myron Healey (E. B. Johnson), Earle Hodgins (Sims), Salvador Baguez (López), Eddie Parker (Henchman). Companion episode: None.

"Church in the Town"   1/11/53

D: Eddie Davis   S: Edmond E. Kelso

Cisco and Pancho help a fighting parson build a new church, overcome the town banker's opposition, and convert a sinful community. With Tom Bernard (Danny Whitacre), Bennie Bartlett (Matt Gray), Forrest Taylor (Rev. Calvin Whitacre), Marshall Reed (Slade), Davison Clark (Luke Gray), and Lillian Albertson (Townswoman). Companion episode: None.

"Gun Totin' Papa"   1/18/53

D: Sobey Martin   S: Irwin Lieberman (?)

A meek little bookkeeper leaves home with his prize possession, a shotgun that once belonged to the notorious outlaw Shotgun Miller. When the gun is recognized, Cisco and Pancho try to help the man prove he's not Miller. With Peggy Stewart (listed but not in cast), Gordon Clark (Ace), Bud Osborne (Sheriff), Hal K. Dawson (Eric Potter), Henry Rowland (Tex), Marshall Bradford (Restaurant Owner). Companion episode: "Lodestone." Note: Peggy Stewart is listed in the credits because the identical cast list for the companion episode was recycled for this one.

"The Fire Engine"   1/25/53

D: Eddie Davis   S: Irwin Lieberman

Cisco and Pancho become involved when an old miner who's always wanted to be a fire chief buys a fire engine for his town and unwittingly interferes with the schemes of the local banker. With Ezelle Poule (Rose), Bill Henry (Todd Ritter), Lee Roberts (Matt Collins), Peter Leeds (Sheriff), Hank Patterson (Luke Higgins), and John Hamilton (John Mitchell). Companion episodes: "Dead by Proxy," "Fear."

"The Census Taker"   2/1/53

D: Sobey Martin   S: Hilda & Endre Bohem

Cisco and Pancho go after outlaws who pose as census takers to gather information on their potential victims. With Roscoe Ates (Henry Wilson), Kyle James (Floyd), Steve Wayne (Jock), Alex Sharp (Brad), William Fawcett (Zeke Tobias), and Edmund Cobb (Hobbs). Companion episode: None.

"Smuggled Silver"   2/8/53

D: Sobey Martin   S: Unknown

Cisco and Pancho set out after a band of silver smugglers who seem to know all of their pursuers' moves in advance. With John Damler (Shang Bisbee), Bill Hale (Sim Dykes), Gail Bonney (Minnie Higgins), Harvey Dunn (Cookie), and Bobby Blake (Alfredo). Companion episode: None.

"The Runaway Kid"   2/15/53

D: Sobey Martin   S: Richard Conway

Cisco and Pancho encounter an eight-year-old boy running away from home and a band of outlaws looking for the hidden loot from an old crime. With John Pickard (Layton), Harry Harvey, Jr. (Sheriff), Robert Bice (Notch), B. G. Norman (Jimmy), and James Harrison (Vic). Companion episode: None.

"Fear"   2/22/53

D: Eddie Davis   S: J. Benton Cheney

Cisco and Pancho become involved in an "old dark house" mystery in which a dead man's ghost terrorizes the heirs who are required by his will to live on his ranch. With Anne Kimbell (Jennifer Kellin), Ezelle Poule (Matilda Kellin), Bill Henry (George Bruce), Lee Roberts (Lacey), Peter Leeds (Prescott), and John Hamilton (Thomas T. Trimble). Companion episodes: "Dead by Proxy," "The Fire Engine."

"The Photo Studio"   3/1/53

D: Sobey Martin   S: J. Benton Cheney

A rancher is shot to death while posing for a photograph. Cisco and Pancho try to clear the chief suspect, an ex-convict in love with the dead man's daughter. With Rand Brooks (Clint Riley), James Seay (Harvey Price), Madeleine Burkette (Donna Burdette), Walter McGrail (Fred Appleby), Charles Williams (Stanley Burdette), Sandy Sanders (Juniper), and Frank Jenks (Marshal Sutton). Companion episode: None.

"The Commodore Goes West"   3/8/53

D: Eddie Davis   S: Robert Clayton

On their way south to attend the wedding of Pancho's cousin, Cisco and Pancho stop to help a young woman who's worried about her father, a former navy officer, and his embattled freight line. With Edward Clark (Commodore Owens), Linda Johnson (Judy Owens), Keith Richards (Frank), Robert Wilke (Judd Stone), and Kermit Maynard (Farley). Companion episodes: "Mad About Money," "Kid Brother."

Fourth Season, 1953–54

"Bodyguard"   10/1/53

D: Eddie Davis   S: Barney A. Sarecky

The wife of a cantankerous old rancher asks Cisco and Pancho to watch out for her husband while he's carrying a tote-bag full of money. With Keith Richards (Outlaw Leader), Steve Clark (Henry Williams), John Merton (Wally), Riley Hill (Larry), and Virginia Mullen (Mrs. Williams). Companion episode: "Chinese Gold."

"Pancho and the Wolf Dog" 10/8/53

D: Lambert Hillyer   S: Warren Wilson

Cisco and Pancho encounter a wild dog as they try to help an eccentric Frenchman who has built the first refrigeration plant in the West. With Gloria Talbott (Suzette Duval), John Doucette (Sandy Harris), Francis McDonald (Frenchy Duval), Robert Livingston (Miller), and Bill Catching (Sheriff). Companion episode: "The Faded General."

"Bullets and the Booby Trap" 10/15/53

D: Herbert Leeds   S: Edmond E. Kelso

Cisco and Pancho chase an outlaw gang into a ghost town inhabited only by a teenage inventor and his shotgun-toting grandmother. With Rory Mallinson (Henchman), Billy Halop (Cass Rankin), Bobby Blake (Davy), Lillian Albertson (Grandma), and Troy Melton (Winochie). Companion episode: "The Fugitive."

"The Gramophone" 10/22/53

D: Lew Landers   S: Roy Hamilton

Cisco and Pancho combat a rancher who uses a primitive record player to scare the Sioux into fighting the coming of the railroad. With William Tannen (Bix Douglas), William Boyett (Henchman), Iron Eyes Cody (Chief Big Cloud), Lyle Talbot (R. H. Wilkerson), and Rosa Turich (Rosita). Companion episode: "Indian Uprising."

"Freedom of the Press" 10/29/53

D: Paul Landres   S: Lawrence Goldman

Cisco and Pancho help out an old newspaper editor who's caught in the middle of a hotly contested election battle between a corrupt mayor and a young reformer. With Frank Wilcox (Mayor Rayburn), Paul Marion (John Vine), I. Stanford Jolley (Henry Wilcox), Richard Avonde (Murdock), Bill Catching (Jacks). Companion episode: "The Raccoon Story."

*"Battle of Red Rock Pass" 11/5/53

D: Lew Landers   S: Ben Markson

Cisco and Pancho try to help a retired Union Army artillery sergeant who spends his old age guarding a toll road with an old cannon but develops amnesia after being hit on the head by the outlaw Cisco is chasing. With Rory Mallinson (Sheriff Ed), William Fawcett (John Matlock), Red Morgan (Hank Dawson), Nan Leslie (Sue Matlock), and Troy Melton (Henchman). Companion episode: "Outlaw's Gallery." Note: This is the episode in which a rock flying the wrong way during an explosion sequence hit Duncan Renaldo and put him in the hospital for weeks. In the next several episodes filmed,

which are marked with an asterisk, Renaldo is seen only in extreme close-ups that were shot while he was recovering and most of the scripts call for him to have his face masked or bandaged so that his stunt double Troy Melton could take his place.

*"Bandaged Badman" 11/12/53

D: Eddie Davis   S: Donn Mullally

When a gunman hired to kill Cisco is blown up in an explosion, Cisco has a doctor cover his face with bandages and identify the corpse as Cisco himself. With Christine Larson (Terry Lane), Bill Henry (Gold Thief), Reed Howes (Jeff Malcolm), Forrest Taylor (Sheriff), Marshall Bradford (Dr. Shaw), Keith Richards (Winkler), and Lee Roberts (Assayer). Companion episode: "The Black Terror."

"Chinese Gold" 11/19/53

D: Eddie Davis   S: George Callahan

Cisco and Pancho try to help a community of Chinese miners who are being systematically robbed by a masked bandit. With Keith Richards (Henchman), Steve Clark (Sheriff Joe Bowers), Judy Dan (Ming Toy), and John Merton (Turner). Companion episode: "Bodyguard."

"The Faded General" 11/26/53

D: Lambert Hillyer   S: Donn Mullally

While trailing a gang of bank robbers wearing linen dusters, Cisco and Pancho are captured by a senile general and locked up in his private jail. With Gloria Talbott (Amelia Lawrence), John Doucette (Sgt. Jess Corbin), Francis McDonald (Gen. Lawrence), Robert Livingston (Col. Yancy Blake), and Bill Catching (Sheriff). Companion episode: "Pancho and the Wolf Dog." Note: Director Lambert Hillyer borrowed the stunt at the climax of this episode from a Buck Jones Western feature, *One Man Law* (Columbia, 1932), which Hillyer had both written and directed.

"The Fugitive" 12/3/53

D: Herbert Leeds   S: Donn Mullally

While hunting for a plague-stricken Mexican youth, Cisco and Pancho run into a wealthy rancher's plot to contaminate land with infected animals so he can buy it cheaply. With Rory Mallinson (Madison), Billy Halop (Dr. Jerome Alpers), Harry Strang (J. A. Kennedy), Troy Melton (Val). Companion episode: "Bullets and the Booby Trap."

"Indian Uprising" 12/10/53

D: Lew Landers   S: Larry Lund

Cisco and Pancho go after the white men who are impersonating Chief Sky Eagle and his braves and terrorizing the farmers so they'll sell out to a local realtor for a few cents on the dollar. With William Tannen (Clyde Evans), William Boyett (Henchman), Iron Eyes Cody (Chief Sky Eagle), and Lyle Talbot (Thomas). Companion episode: "The Gramophone."

"The Raccoon Story" 12/17/53

D: Paul Landres S: Warren Wilson

Cisco and Pancho are asked to deliver miner Gus Brown's death certificate to the town of Sweetwater, and soon learn that Brown's will left all his property to his dog. With Frank Wilcox (Henry Collins), Paul Marion (Henchman), I. Stanford Jolley (Gus Brown), Almira Sessions (Sarah Hotchkiss), Claudia Barrett (Sally Phillips), and Bill Catching (Henchman). Companion episode: "Freedom of the Press." Note: Despite the title, there is no raccoon in this episode. Most likely a dog was substituted when no trained raccoon could be found.

"Outlaw's Gallery" 12/24/53

D: Lew Landers S: Ben Markson

Cisco and Pancho use an express rider's hobby of painting and sketching to bait a trap for a robber gang plaguing the town of Dry River Falls. With Rory Mallinson (Will Roberts), William Fawcett (Zack Marsh), Red Morgan (Gil), Nan Leslie (Cynthia Marsh), and John Damler (Sheriff). Companion episode: "Battle of Red Rock Pass."

*"The Black Terror" 12/31/53

D: Eddie Davis S: Frank Burt

Cisco invents a masked-bandit personality for himself and uses it to join the notorious Barton Brothers gang so he can break it up from within. With Christine Larson (Molly Cantry), Bill Henry (Jed Barton), Reed Howes (Hank Barton), Forrest Taylor (Red Bell), and Lee Roberts (Link Barton). Companion episode: "Bandaged Badman."

"Sky Sign" 1/7/54

D: Eddie Davis S: George Callahan

Cisco and Pancho run out of ammunition and stop at a country store where an escaped convict and his gang are hiding. With Jan Bryant (Miss Hardin), Mort Mills (Carver), Mike Ragan (Twisty), and Steve Clark (Sheriff Cole). Companion episode: "Marriage by Mail."

"Cisco Meets the Gorilla" 1/14/54

D: Lambert Hillyer S: Edmond E. Kelso

Cisco and Pancho go after the bandits who have pulled off a series of robberies while everyone in town was out searching for an escaped carnival gorilla. With Robert Clarke (Johnny Boyle), Russ Conway (Outlaw Leader), Max Wagner (Marvin), Troy Melton (Sheriff Mike), and Bill Catching (Bevins). Companion episode: "The Ventriloquist."

"Not Guilty" 1/21/54

D: Paul Landres S: Barney A. Sarecky

Cisco and Pancho take a hand when Pancho's nephew witnesses a murder and one of the killer's pals impersonates the circuit judge in a scheme to free his friend. With José Gonzales Gonzales (José Gonzales de la Vega), Peter Coe (Joe), Tristram Coffin (Outlaw Leader), Lyle Talbot (Judge Watkins), and Troy Melton (Sheriff Brady). Companion episode: "Horseless Carriage."

*"Rodeo" 1/28/54

D: Eddie Davis S: Ed Gardner Jr. & Roy Engel

Cisco and Pancho try to protect two daredevil riding sisters from a confidence man who's promoting a phony rodeo. With Keith Richards (Jim Usher), Marshall Reed (Henchman), Shirley Lucas (Pat Lacy), John Cason (Phil Burleson), Bill Catching (Ralph London), and Sharon Lucas (Peg Lacy). Companion episode: "The Steel Plow."

"Marriage by Mail" 2/4/54

D: Eddie Davis S: Buckley Angell

Cisco wins a bride when Pancho enters his picture in a matrimonial lottery, but the lottery turns out to be an outlaw gang's ruse to empty the town. With Jan Bryant (Susan Marsh), Mort Mills (Professor), Mike Ragan (Decker), Steve Clark (Sheriff). Companion episode: "Sky Sign."

*"The Iron Mask" 2/11/54

D: Lew Landers S: Donn Mullally

Cisco and Pancho try to rescue a sheriff who's been captured by outlaws and imprisoned in an iron mask. With Dan White (Brace Hagger), John Crawford (Sheriff Al White), Michael Whalen (Cain Hagger/Matt Hagger). Companion episode: "Cisco Plays the Ghost."

Troy Melton, stunt double for Duncan Renaldo, in action

*"Double Deal" 2/18/54

D: Eddie Davis   S: Fred Leighton

Cisco finds himself a fugitive after an old enemy of his hires an actor to dress up as Cisco and commit a series of robberies. With Bill Henry (Dave Langley), Edmund Cobb (Brady), William Phipps (McNulty), Frank Hagney (Connors), Charles Watts (Clark Jones), and Bill Catching (Sheriff). Companion episode: "Powder Trail."

"Horseless Carriage" 2/25/54

D: Paul Landres   S: David Nowinson & Barry Cohon

Cisco and Pancho try to help Pancho's nephew, whose newly purchased horseless carriage is used as a getaway vehicle by bank robbers. With José Gonzales Gonzales (José), Peter Coe (Henchman), Tristram Coffin (Nick Ward), Jeanne Dean (Doris), William Fawcett (Scroggins), and Bill Catching (Sheriff). Companion episode: "Not Guilty."

*"The Steel Plow" 3/4/54

D: Eddie Davis   S: George Callahan

Cisco helps an inventive blacksmith make a steel plow to help the local farmers cultivate the stony soil. With Keith Richards (William Griff), Marshall Reed (John Sterns), Shirley Lucas (Grace Warren), John Cason (Cavvy), Bill Catching (Farmer Jarvis), and Kermit Maynard (Mr. Warren). Companion episode: "Rodeo."

"The Ventriloquist" 3/11/54

D: Lambert Hillyer   S: Roy Hamilton & Barry Cohon

Cisco uses Pancho's voice-throwing skill to expose a crooked assayer who kidnaps prospectors after they've filed their claims. With Robert Clarke (Bud Thatcher), Russ Conway (E.W. Akers), Max Wagner (Webster), and Rankin Mansfield (Hiram Thatcher). Companion episode: "Cisco Meets the Gorilla."

*"Powder Trail" 3/18/54

D: Eddie Davis   S: George Callahan

Cisco and Pancho try to find out why outlaws are stealing wagonloads of the petrified-wood curios on which the economy of the virtual ghost town of Padera depends. With Bill Henry (Blount), Edmund Cobb (Mr. Adams), William Phipps (Henchman), Frank Hagney (Lon), Shirley Tegge (Celia Adams), Patsy Moran (Townswoman). Companion episode: "Double Deal."

*"Cisco Plays the Ghost" 3/25/54

D: Lew Landers   S: Warren Wilson

Cisco uses a player piano and spook effects to convince a superstitious killer that he's being haunted by his victims. With Dan White (Alan Moxley), John Crawford (Sheriff Todd), Michael Whalen (Hank Winters), Bennie Bartlett (Jimmy Winters), Byron Foulger (Claude Bobkins, Jr.), and Troy Melton (Henchman). Companion episode: "The Iron Mask."

Fifth Season, 1954–55

"A Six-Gun for No-Pain" 9/25/54

D: Lambert Hillyer   S: Barney A. Sarecky

Cisco enlists the aid of a traveling dentist to track down a notorious killer who's set up a new identity as a cattle dealer. With Dennis Moore (Henchman), Earle Hodgins (No-Pain Norton), Henry Rowland (Steve Potter/Blackie Dawson), Joey Ray (Briggs), Mickey Simpson (Patient), and Zon Murray (Sheriff). Companion episode: "Sundown's Gun."

"The Haunted Stage Stop" 10/2/54

D: Lambert Hillyer   S: Robert Clayton

What purports to be the ghost of way station master Angus MacPherson summons Cisco and Pancho to trace the gold shipment that vanished when Angus did. With Nan Leslie (Judy MacPherson), John Cason (Henchman), Bill Kennedy (Hank Jaggett), Myron Healey (Don White), and Bob Woodward (Henchman). Companion episode: "Pot of Gold."

"Gold Strike" 10/9/54

D: Eddie Davis   S: Ande Lamb

Cisco and Pancho are escorting a safecracker to jail when their stagecoach is captured by bandits who take all the passengers to a ghost town. With Jacquelyn Park (Dolly Ferguson), Sandy Sanders (Gary Austin), James Anderson (Tap), Marshall Reed (Fred), and Ed Hinton (Outlaw). Companion episode: "Caution of Curley Thompson."

"Trouble in Tonopah" 10/16/54

D: Lambert Hillyer   S: Oliver Drake

Cisco and Pancho try to outwit a robber who has somehow learned the combination to the express office's burglar-proof safe and pulled off a series of baffling thefts. With Edwin Parker (Jeff Donovan), Kenneth MacDonald (Henry Blake), Gregg Barton (Mike Dugan), Kermit Maynard (Phil Dugan), Edward Clark (Doc), and Dan White (Sheriff). Companion episode: "Fool's Gold." Note: Oliver Drake borrowed the plot of this episode from his script for the B Western feature *Trouble in Sundown* (RKO, 1938), starring George O'Brien.

"Harry the Heir" 10/23/54

D: Lambert Hillyer   S: Robert Clayton

While trying to save an egotistical actor who's confessed to bank robbery and murder, Cisco and Pancho find that the grave of the supposed murder victim is empty. With I. Stanford Jolley (Roderick Lamoreux), Fay Morley (Antoinette Lamoreux), James Parnell (Sheriff), Leonard Penn (Jed

Proctor), and Keith Richards (London Harry Hanley). Companion episode: None.

"The Lowest Bidder" 10/30/54

D: Lambert Hillyer   S: Ande Lamb

Cisco and Pancho confront a scheming well-digger who's out to steal the funds a thirsty town has raised to secure a water supply. With Bill George (Greg Sayer), Kenneth Terrell (Paul Blackwell), Lane Bradford (Hayne), Eddy Waller (Eli Oliver), and Jack Ingram (Stableman). Companion episode: "The Hospital."

"Mining Madness" 11/6/54

D: Lambert Hillyer   S: Gerald Geraghty

When an old prospector friend of theirs is cheated by a crooked gambler, Cisco and Pancho kidnap the gambler and make him work a worthless but salted gold claim. With Raymond Hatton (Jeff Hanby), Marshall Reed (Todd Wheeler), Ted Mapes (Augie), and Lee Roberts (Sheriff). Companion episode: "Three Suspects."

"Sundown's Gun" 11/13/54

D: Lambert Hillyer   S: Wilbur S. Peacock

Cisco and Pancho try to straighten out a twelve-year-old boy who's disappointed in his father, a workmanlike sheriff, and worships his dead grandfather, who is a famous gunfighter. With Dennis Moore (Sheriff Fred), Henry Rowland (Matt Barlow), Earle Hodgins (Purdy), and B. G. Norman (Billy). Companion episode: "A Six-Gun for No-Pain."

"Pot of Gold" 11/20/54

D: Lambert Hillyer   S: Wilbur S. Peacock

When a half-crazy old man is killed by a deputy sheriff trying to make him reveal the location of a buried Civil War treasure, Cisco and Pancho and a traveling snake-oil peddler help the dead man's daughter find the fortune. With Nan Leslie (Mary Andrew), John Cason (Frank), Bill Kennedy (Deputy Cogley), Myron Healey (Jim Gault), Hank Patterson (Wind River Bill), William Vedder (Pete Andrew), and Bob Woodward (Jake). Companion episode: "The Haunted Stage Stop."

"Caution of Curley Thompson" 11/27/54

D: Eddie Davis   S: Barry Cohon

Cisco and Pancho help an ex-convict track down the leader of his old gang, who has started a new life as the owner of a general store. With Jacquelyn Park (Ruth), Sandy Sanders (Whitey Thompson), James Anderson (Jack Hanley), Marshall Reed (Wilson Ford), and Ed Hinton (Muley). Companion episode: "Gold Strike." Note: Director Eddie Davis must have changed the Thompson character's first name from Curley to Whitey after giving the part to Sandy Sanders, whose hair was light-colored and straight.

"Fool's Gold" 12/4/54

D: Lambert Hillyer   S: Gerald Geraghty

Cisco and Pancho trap some outlaws by making them believe that their hideout is the center of a major gold rush. With Edwin Parker (Outlaw Leader), Kenneth MacDonald (J. L. Webster), Gregg Barton (Grady), Kermit Maynard (Booth), and Karolee Kelly (Cindy). Companion episode: "Trouble in Tonopah."

"The Hospital" 12/11/54

D: Lambert Hillyer   S: Wilbur S. Peacock

Cisco and Pancho help a young doctor who's been framed for attempted murder by a fund-embezzling trustee of the town hospital. With Bill George (Dr. Bob Randall), Kenneth Terrell (Jason Turnbull), Lane Bradford (Blackie), Eddy Waller (Dr. Bender), and Jack Ingram (Sheriff). Companion episode: "The Lowest Bidder."

"Three Suspects" 12/18/54

D: Lambert Hillyer   S: Kenneth A. Enochs

With his only clue a bandit's hat found near the scene of a robbery, Cisco tries to figure out which of three suspects is the bandit. With Lee Roberts (Jim), Marshall Reed (Whit Jameson), Raymond Hatton (Morgan), and Ted Mapes (Burke). Companion episode: "Mining Madness."

"Pancho's Niece" 12/25/54

D: Lambert Hillyer   S: Barry Cohon

Cisco has Pancho pose as the uncle of a half-Mexican young woman whose banker father apparently killed himself after losing most of the bank's money. With J.P. O'Donnell (Dolores James), John Pickard (Riddle), Julián Rivero (Juan/Fernando Ramírez), William Tannen (Roland McCard), Roy Engel (Sheriff). Companion episode: None. Note: This episode is a remake of the B Western feature *The Fighting Code* (Columbia, 1933), which was written and directed by Lambert Hillyer and starred Buck Jones.

"Extradition Papers" 1/1/55

D: Lambert Hillyer   S: Kenneth A. Enochs

While taking a captured bandit leader to trial, Cisco and Pancho are ambushed by his gang while passing through a ghost town. With John Beradino (Jess Martin), Dayton Osmond (Tommy Martin), Mitchell Kowal (Henchman), Henry Rowland (Henchman), and Sam Flint (Sheriff). Companion episode: "Son of a Gunman."

"New Evidence" 1/8/55

D: Lambert Hillyer   S: Ande Lamb

When a rancher is murdered and his daughter's boyfriend is put on trial for the crime, Cisco uses a farmer's almanac and a full moon and the army signal system to trap the real killer.

Autographed publicity photo of Duncan Renaldo and his horse, Diablo

With Sandy Sanders (Dorsey Knudsen), Edwin Parker (Gibbs), Fay Morley (Carmel Tracy), Earle Hodgins (Judge Elias Kendall), and Edmund Cobb (Henry Tracy). Companion episode: None. Note: The plot device in this episode is lifted bodily from the classic *Young Mr. Lincoln* (20th Century-Fox, 1939), directed by John Ford and starring Henry Fonda.

"Doorway to Nowhere" 1/15/55

D: Lambert Hillyer   S: Robert Clayton

Cisco escorts a wealthy old Boston lady to her daughter-in-law's ranch but is charged with kidnapping and robbery when both women disappear. With Lillian Albertson (Mrs. Collins), Nan Leslie (Blanche), Kenneth MacDonald (Ralph Hammond), Lane Chandler (Sheriff). Companion episode: None.

"Stolen River" 1/22/55

D: Lambert Hillyer   S: Barry Cohon

Arriving at the ranch of their old friend Wayne Barbour, Cisco and Pancho find that Wayne has been murdered and that his widow is ready to sell the ranch and move back east. With Nancy Hale (Mady Barbour), I. Stanford Jolley (Slim Lennox), Zon Murray (King), Thayer Roberts (Sheriff), and Rory Mallinson (Surveyor). Companion episode: "Montezuma's Treasure."

"Son of a Gunman" 1/29/55

D: Lambert Hillyer   S: Rik Vollaerts

When the son of a famous gunfighter is run out of town, Cisco and Pancho try to help the young man outlive his father's reputation. With John Beradino (Buck Lundigan), Mitchell Kowal (Johnny Nestor), Sam Flint (Sheriff), and Henry Rowland (Will Foresby/Will Knowland). Companion episode: "Extradition Papers."

"Juggler's Silver" 2/3/55

D: Lambert Hillyer   S: Barry Cohon

Cisco and Pancho are shot at by a former circus juggler who bought what he claims is a worthless mine. With Fortune Gordien (Danny Harris), Rodd Redwing (Nimble Nick Carr), Leonard Penn (Judd), and Kenneth MacDonald (Marshal Ed Watson). Companion episode: None.

"The Kidnapped Cameraman" 2/10/55

D: Lambert Hillyer   S: Barry Cohon

When a photographer inadvertently takes a picture of a murder at the Lone Mountain mine, Cisco uses the lantern slide to trap the killer. With Tom Irish (Ted Miller), Terry Frost (Chuck Farley), Keith Richards (Red Farley), Kermit Maynard (Sheriff), and Chuck Cason (Tracy). Companion episode: "The Two-Wheeler."

"Cisco and the Giant" 2/17/55

D: Lambert Hillyer   S: Bill George

A huge dim-witted man who thinks he killed his lawman brother-in-law takes refuge with an outlaw gang. Then Cisco and Pancho join the gang in an attempt to solve a series of well-planned stagecoach robberies. With Dennis Moore (Sheriff Sam Johnson), Glenn Strange (Curly Peters), Rex Thorsen (Judd Casey), Kenneth Terrell (Lobo), and Patricia Tiernan (Ann Johnson). Companion episode: None.

"Montezuma's Treasure" 2/24/55

D: Lambert Hillyer   S: Wilbur S. Peacock

A professor, hunting for the Aztec emperor's fabulous treasure, discovers its location but is attacked by outlaws and wounded. A code message on a deck of cards leads Cisco and Pancho to the treasure. With Thayer Roberts (Prof. Bradley), I. Stanford Jolley (Prof. Danforth), Zon Murray (Bull), and Ferris Taylor (Sheriff). Companion episode: "Stolen River."

"Vendetta" 3/3/55

D: Lambert Hillyer   S: Ande Lamb

Cisco and Pancho try to settle an old family feud between neighboring ranchers that has been secretly fanned by a mercenary uncle. Based on an original story by J. Benton Cheney.

With Alan Wells (Gil Parker), Claudia Barrett (Terry Monahan), Kenneth MacDonald (Frank Guthrie), and Leonard Penn (Warren Sturgis). Companion episode: None.

"The Two-Wheeler" 3/10/55

D: Lambert Hillyer S: Barry Cohon

Cisco and Pancho help out a quick-tempered bicycle-riding young Easterner who has struck it rich with a gold claim but is being cheated by claim jumpers. With Tom Irish (Albert Taylor), Sally Fraser (Martha), Keith Richards (Frank Douglas), and Terry Frost (Webb). Companion episode: "The Kidnapped Cameraman."

"The Tumblers" 3/17/55

D: Leslie Goodwins
S: Harry S. Franklin & Otto Englander

Cisco and Pancho teach an acrobat some riding and shooting skills so he can fight the bully who runs the town of Smoky Gap. With Loren Janes (Tim Siebert), Ward James (Hearn), Harry Cody (Hank Siebert), Maureen Cassidy (Kitty Noonan), and William Fawcett (Sheriff Len Cooper). Companion episode: None.

Sixth Season, 1955–56

"A Quiet Sunday Morning" 10/6/55

D: Leslie Goodwins
S: Barney A. Sarecky & Barry Cohon

Cisco and Pancho go after three robbers—one of them a teenage boy on his first job—who killed the sheriff while making their getaway. With Frank Richards (Grant), Richard Castle (Kenny Marsh), Elsie Baker (June Sims), Margie Moran (Mrs. Sims), and Chuck Cason (Rancher). Companion episode: "Young Blood."

"Arroyo Millionaire's Castle" 10/13/55

D: Lambert Hillyer S: Barry Cohon

While hunting the gunman who murdered a young prospector, Cisco and Pancho find an eccentric millionaire living in a castle in the desert. With Wayne Mallory (Carl White), Britt Wood (Grampus White), Mort Mills (Sheriff Tom Roscoe), and Gene Covelli (Steve). Companion episode: ("Cisco and the Tappers").

"Witness" 10/20/55

D: Leslie Goodwins S: Kenneth A. Enochs

Cisco and Pancho try to persuade a teenage girl who witnessed a robbery to admit that she recognized the bandit leader as her uncle. With Tristram Coffin (Chet Morton), Terry Frost (Dorf), Russell Whitney (Mr. Cartright), and Melinda Plowman (Carol Cartright). Companion episode: "New York's Finest."

"Choctaw Justice" 10/27/55

D: Lambert Hillyer S: Robert Clayton

Cisco receives an urgent letter asking him to follow Choctaw custom and serve as the executioner of his friend Charlie Ponca, who's been convicted of murder by an Indian court. Instead he and Pancho set out to prove Charlie's innocence. With Bill Pullen (Charlie Ponca), Margaret Cahill (Molly), Paul Fierro (Fred Tofo), James Anderson (Curly), and Chief Yowlachie (Indian Judge). Companion episode: "Ambush."

"New York's Finest" 11/3/55

D: Leslie Goodwins S: John Krafft

Cisco and Pancho help a young New York policeman who has come west to search for the murderer of his former commander. With Tristram Coffin (Saunders), Terry Frost (Morgan), Charles Maxwell (Jeff Adams), and Anna Navarro (Ruth Mallory). Companion episode: "Witness."

"Cisco and the Tappers" 11/3/55

D: Lambert Hillyer S: Wilbur S. Peacock

Cisco and Pancho help an old sheriff and his young deputy capture a group of outlaws who tap telegraph wires to learn of gold shipments. With Wayne Mallory (Harry), Britt Wood (Sheriff), Mort Mills (Bart Stevens), and Bill Catching (Whitey). Companion episode: "Arroyo Millionaire's Castle." Note: This is the only episode in the entire series for which the copyright catalog does not provide a title. Therefore I've made up one of my own.

"Young Blood" 11/10/55

D: Leslie Goodwins S: Kenneth A. Enochs

Cisco and Pancho help a widow whose young hired hand is associating with a pair of teenage bandits. With Richard Castle (Dan), Elsie Baker (Mrs. Parry), Gerald Olken (Buck), and Tim Johnson (Ray). Companion episode: "A Quiet Sunday Morning."

"School Marm" 11/17/55

D: Lambert Hillyer
S: Barney A. Sarecky & Barry Cohon

Cisco and Pancho try to rescue the town of Madera's new schoolteacher, who's been kidnapped and held for ransom. With Elaine Riley (Irene Moore), Sydney Mason (Abner Craig), Marshall Reed (Dick), Joel Ashley (Mr. Bond), and Kenneth Miller (Jay Jones). Companion episode: "Gold, Death and Dynamite."

"Bounty Men" 11/24/55

D: Leslie Goodwins S: Ande Lamb

Cisco and Pancho trail a wanted killer to an army recruiting station where they encounter a corrupt military doctor who enlists outlaws in the service under dead men's names. With

Frosty Royce (Pat Pierce), Earle Hodgins (Dr. Owen Desmond), Zon Murray (Ron Copeland/Norman Castle), Mickey Simpson (Wade/Sgt. Quinn). Companion episode: "Jumping Beans."

"Quick on the Trigger" 12/1/55

D: Lambert Hillyer
S: Barney A. Sarecky & Barry Cohon

Cisco and Pancho try to help an expectant father who stole back the horse he sold to a crooked animal dealer in order to pay for medical care for his pregnant wife. With Peter Mamakos (Sheriff Carter), Robin Short (Joe Wilcox), John Compton (Barnes), and Sue England (Laura Wilcox). Companion episode: "Six Gun Cupids."

"Gold, Death and Dynamite" 12/8/55

D: Lambert Hillyer
S: Barney A. Sarecky & Barry Cohon

Cisco and Pancho become involved when the desperate owner of a stagecoach line substitutes dynamite for a gold shipment in hope of blowing up the outlaws who have been robbing his coaches. With Elaine Riley (Millie Stone), Steven Clark (Mel Baldwin), Marshall Reed (Dobie), Joel Ashley (Clem), Sydney Mason (Sheriff). Companion episode: "School Marm."

"Jumping Beans" 12/15/55

D: Leslie Goodwins   S: Jack Rock

Cisco and Pancho arrive in Rimtown too late to prevent a robbery by three escaped convicts but try to catch the trio by using a handful of Mexican jumping beans as a lie detector. With Earle Hodgins (Lang), Robert Strong (Menkin), Zon Murray (Bailey), Mickey Simpson (Judd), and Frosty Royce (Brewster). Companion episode: "Bounty Men."

"Ambush" 12/22/55

D: Lambert Hillyer   S: Stuart Jerome & Barry Cohon

Cisco encounters three rival outlaws who have joined forces to do away with him by using Pancho as bait for a clever ambush. With Paul Fierro (Ricardo Gómez), Bill Pullen (Cheyenne Jones), James Anderson (Iceberg Ike), Joe Domínguez (Uncle Alberto), Anna Navarro (Elena). Companion episode: "Choctaw Justice."

"Six Gun Cupids" 12/29/55

D: Lambert Hillyer   S: Buckley Angell

Cisco and Pancho learn that a wealthy old woman has forbidden her son to associate with the housemaid he loves, and try to help the young couple find happiness. With Robin Short (Ted Landry), Paula Houston (Isabel Landry), John Compton (Emery), Jackie Loughery (Ellen Marland), and Peter Mamakos (Leach). Companion episode: "Quick on the Trigger."

"Strangers" 1/5/56

D: Lambert Hillyer   S: Donn Mullally

Cisco and Pancho are ambushed and their horses stolen but when they try to buy fresh horses everyone drives them away. With John Cliff (Matt Pearson), Pierce Lyden (Carl Barton), John Halloran (Brace Haskell), and Don Gardner (Jerry Haskell). Companion episode: "Mr. X."

"The Joker" 1/12/56

D: Leslie Goodwins
S: Barney A. Sarecky & Barry Cohon

Cisco and Pancho go after a prankster who has made a fortune selling ranches he doesn't own. With Terry Frost (Porter), John Beradino (Crane), Lee Morgan (Muscles), and Joyce Jameson (Jill Stewart). Companion episode: "Roundup."

"Man with the Reputation" 1/19/56

D: Lambert Hillyer   S: Ande Lamb

A newspaper editor accuses Cisco and Pancho of taking bribes from a criminal in order to get them into town so he can ask their help in cleaning up local political corruption. With Steven Clark (Branch Kennedy), Marilyn Saris (Juanita Harris), Paul Hahn (Trent Wilson), Joel Smith (Constable Slate), and Lane Bradford (John Mason). Companion episode: "Kilts and Sombreros."

"The Epidemic" 1/26/56

D: Leslie Goodwins   S: Kenneth A. Enochs

Cisco and Pancho pursue the outlaws who are holding a bottle of vital smallpox vaccine for ransom. With George Meader (Doc), Leo Needham (Mackey), Jack Littlefield (Trim), Ward C. James (Ward), and John B. Duncan (Mail Rider). Companion episode: "West of the Law."

"Mr. X" 2/2/56

D: Lambert Hillyer
S: Barney A. Sarecky & Barry Cohon

Cisco rescues a mine owner who's been buried alive in a collapsed tunnel, then discovers that the apparent accident was a murder attempt and is himself trapped by the killer. With Diana Welles (Alice Blake), Gene Roth (Tom Blake), Pierce Lyden (Dana), Don Gardner (Johnny Clark). Companion episode: "Strangers."

"Roundup" 2/9/56

D: Leslie Goodwins
S: Barney A. Sarecky & Barry Cohon

Cisco and Pancho help a young woman who has come west to take control of the ranch she inherited, only to encounter trouble in the shape of a jealous foreman and some rustlers. With Joyce Jameson (Arizona Williams), John Beradino (Rick Johnson), Terry Frost (Ned), and Lee Morgan (Grubstake). Companion episode: "The Joker."

"He Couldn't Quit" 2/16/56

D: Leslie Goodwins   S: Ande Lamb

Cisco and Pancho become involved when an outlaw who's in love with a gypsy palmist returns to town to visit his now respectable former partner in crime and collect his share of the loot from their last robbery. With Lillian Molieri (Gypsy), Charles Maxwell (Sheriff Paul Jackson), James Seay (Roy Dillon), William Fawcett (Hunt). Companion episode: "The Magician of Jamesville."

"Kilts and Sombreros" 2/23/56

D: Lambert Hillyer   S: Kenneth A. Enochs

Cisco and Pancho help a Scotsman who was fired from his job as a Wells Fargo courier after being ambushed by bandits. With Ian Murray (MacDougall), Barry Froner (Billy), Sydney Mason (Sheriff), Lane Bradford (Outlaw Leader), and Joel Smith (Henchman). Companion episode: "Man with the Reputation."

"West of the Law" 3/1/56

D: Leslie Goodwins   S: Buckley Angell

Cisco and Pancho help a friendless young man who's been accused of stealing an opera singer's jewelry. With John B. Duncan (Mickey Doan), Leo Needham (Camden), Ward C. James (Durango), Fay Morley (Marla Fontaine). Companion episode: "The Epidemic."

"Dangerous Shoemaker" 3/8/56

D: Lambert Hillyer   S: Ed Gardner Jr.

Cisco and Pancho stop off at a shoemaker's shop to get Pancho's boots fixed and become entangled in a plot by the shoemaker to blackmail a man who thinks he's a murderer. With Sandy Sanders (Duke Martin), Keith Richards (Simon Telford), Bruce Payne (Tom Jordan), and Glenn Strange (Blake). Companion episode: None.

"The Magician of Jamesville" 3/15/56

D: Leslie Goodwins   S: Larry Lund

Cisco uses a boomerang from a traveling magician's kit to expose a crooked mayor and a mysterious blowgun killer. With Earle Hodgins (Orlando), Charles Maxwell (Mayor Brandon), William Fawcett (Joe/Grampaw), James Seay (Hardy), Bert Rumsey (Sheriff). Companion episode: "He Couldn't Quit."

"Tangled Trails" 3/22/56

D: Leslie Goodwins   S: J. Benton Cheney

Cisco and Pancho try to clear an old friend who has disappeared along with a shipment of money. With William Vaughan (Outlaw Leader), Ann Duncan (Trudy Banning), Don Mathers (Williams), Max Wagner (Nevada), and Lee Morgan (Henry Banning). Companion episode: None.

This index is alphabetized using the letter-by-letter system. Alphabetization of Spanish names follows standard Spanish practice (i.e., alphabetizing by the first surname). The Spanish definite articles *el* and *la* appear at the end of titles, like their English counterpart *the*. Book titles not included here may be found in the online bibliography: http://noblebandits.asu.edu/ciscobook.

Abbe, Derwin 173
Abrahams, Derwin 167, 169–70, 172–73, 176
Acord, Art 35
Across the Plains 66
Acuña y Roseta, Elisa 17
Adams, Ernie 139
Adams, Jane 168
Adams, Ted 66, 174
Adamson, Victor 63
Adelita, La 18–19
Adelita, La (1938) 16
"Adelita, La" (song) 18
Adios! 61
"Adiós El Cuchillo" 143
"Adventure of the Speckled Band, The" 180
Adventures of Champion 167
Adventures of Don Coyote, The 68
Adventures of Kit Carson, The 175
Adventures of Robin Hood, The 58, 190
After Tonight 129
Aguilar, Antonio 18
Agustina de Aragón 20
Alaskans, The 184
Alberni, Luis 63
Aldana, Vida 136
Aldrich, Robert 106, 183
Allen, Bob 69
Allen, Drew 131, 209
Allen, Irwin 181
Allende, Isabel 6
Alonso, Francisco 128
Alvarado, Don 57, 60
Amato, Pasquale 220
Ameche, Don 14, 40
Amendola, Tony 188
American Widow, An 40
Americano, The 106
Ames, Ramsay 131–32, 134–35
"Amor mío" 221
And Starring Pancho Villa as Himself 20
Anderson, G. M. 14
Andrade, Flores de 16
Andrews, Dana 97, 99–100
Andrews, Stanley 147–48, 177
Angels with Dirty Faces 58
Ankrum, Morris 165
Anthony, Stuart 66
Apache Trail 68
Apache War Smoke 68
Apfel, Oscar 59
Aragón, Agustina de 20
Archainbaud, George 129
"Argentine Moon" 220
Arizmendi, Yareli 188
Arizona 33
Arizona Ames 66
Arizona Cyclone 174

Arizona Kid xi, 19
Arizona Kid, The 54, 56, 59, 85, 220
Arizona Wildcat 146
Arlen, Richard 139, 174
Armendáriz, Pedro 17–18, 210
Armendáriz, Pedro, Jr. 188, 221
Armetta, Henry 51
Armida (Armida Vendrell) 58, 115, 124, 149–50, 157, 220
Army Bound xiv
Arness, James 180
Around the World in 80 Days 106
Arreguín, Alfredo 211
Arthur, Jean 33, 173
Astor, Gertrude 215
Astor, Mary 61, 215, 220
Atchley, Hooper 101–2
Ates, Roscoe 180
Atkins, Tommy 64
Augustine, St. 1, 20
Autry, Gene 66, 69, 101, 108, 139, 162, 167, 181, 201
Avenger, The 61–64, 67, 74
Avenging Arrow, The (Anita Delgado) xi, 3, 6, 19, 200
Avenging Arrow, The (1921) 19
Azuela, Mariano 17
Baca, Elfego 19–20
Back in the Saddle 181
Back Trail 143
Bad and the Beautiful, The 143
Badger, Clarence G. 219
Bad Man, The 219
Bad Man from Red Butte, The 174
Bad Men of Thunder Gap 174
Bailey, Buck 167
Baker, Bob 69
Bakewell, William 142
Baldwin, Walter 150
Ballad of Gregorio Cortez, The 224–25, 227
Bamba, La (film) 187, 222, 224–25
"Bamba, La" (song) 222
"Bandaged Badman" 182
Banderas, Antonio 6, 20, 223
Bandidas 20
"Bandido, El" (Valdez sketch) 186–87
"Bandido, El" (*Zorro* TV episode) 143
Bandido! The American Melodrama of Tiburcio Vásquez, Notorious California Bandit 221
Bandit Queen 19
Bandit Queen, The (1950) 6, 19, 68
"Bandit's Love Song" 215
Bara, Theda 34, 219–20
Barbara Frietchie 51
Barbarosa 144
Bardette, Trevor 102
Bari, Lynn 91–92, 116, 121

Barnes, Binnie 70
Barnes, Rayford 2
Barrat, Robert 91–95
Barry, Don 167
Barry, Tom 39
Barrymore, Ethel 40, 130
Barrymore, Lionel 130, 216, 219
Barthelmess, Richard 19, 57, 61
Bartlett, Lanier 61
Bartlett, Virginia Stivers 61
Barton, Buzz 35, 58, 86
Barton, Charles 66
Bass, Sam 22
Batman 106, 190
"Battle of Red Rock Pass" 182
Baur, Esperanza 16
Bautista, Aurora 20
Baxter, Warner ii, x, 2–3, 19, 33–34, 38–41, 49–57 passim, 59, 63–64, 67, 70–71, 74–75, 79, 91–92, 94–95, 102, 116, 121, 130, 146, 181, 185, 192, 195, 200–201, 215, 219–20
Beach, Guy 148
Beach, John 95
Beatles, The 198
Beaton, Kenneth C. 59–60
Beau Bandit 58, 63–64, 114, 220
Beaumont, Harry 215
Beauty and the Bandit 131, 134–35
Beck, Jackson 107
Bedford, Barbara 215
Bedoya, Alfonso 3–4, 222
Beebe, Ford 146, 163, 167
Beecher, Janet 102
Beery, Noah 66–67, 146, 152, 215, 220
Beery, Wallace 54, 80, 216, 219
Belasco, David 220
Belden, Charles S. 131, 133
Belén Gutiérrez de Mendoza, Juana 17
Bell, Hank 148
Bell, Rex 65, 69, 86, 109
Bellamy, Madge 41
"Bell of Santa Margarita" 180
Bells of San Fernando 68, 145
Bendix, William 72
Bennet, Spencer Gordon 60, 66, 133, 174, 220
Bennett, Constance 129
Bennett, Raphael 102, 119, 133, 177
Benson, Robby 227
Benton, Jack 163
Beresford, Bruce 20
Berke, William 68
Bermúdez Zataraín, Rafael 219
Bern, Paul 215
Bernerd, Jeffrey 139
Bernstein, Isadore 65

Betrayed xiii, 34, 39
Bettinson, Ralph 114
Bickford, Charles 3, 66, 68, 128
Big Trail, The 61, 73
Billingsley, Barbara 148–49, 154
Billy the Kid 19, 24, 193
Billy the Kid 59, 61, 80
Binney, Constance 41
Birell, Tala 147
Birth of a Nation, The 11, 34
Bizet, Georges 220
Black Cat, The 68
Black Gold 139
"Black Terror, The" 182
Blake, Bobby (Robert) 180, 182
Blane, Sally 96
Blinn, Holbrook 219
Block, Ralph 59
Blue, Monte 34
Bluebeard 68
Blystone, John 51
Boehm, Sydney 68
Boetticher, Budd 51, 143
Bogart, Humphrey 4, 70, 86, 222
Bogdanovich, Peter 38, 68
Bohr, José 60, 220
Bolaños, José 18
Bold Caballero, The 65
Bonanza 144, 175–76
Bonaparte, Napoleon 20
Bond, Ward 91–92, 95
"Boomerang" 170, 173
Booth, Adrian 19
Booth, Edwin 33
Booth, Edwina 44, 108, 148
Booth, John Wilkes 34
Borden, Olive 215
Border Romance 221
Border Terror, The 34
Border Vigilantes 167
Borgnine, Ernest 2–4
Born in East L.A. 224–25
"Born in the USA" 225
Born to the West 66
Borzage, Frank 173, 219
Boston Blackie 169, 171, 175–77, 179
Bosworth, Hobart 34
Bow, Clara 128
Bowers, John 215
Boyd, William xiii, 69, 165
Boyer, Charles 173
Bradbury, James, Jr. 53, 55
Bradbury, Robert N. 66, 215
Bradford, Lane 183
Brady Bunch, The 180
Brand, Max 68
Branded 68
Brando, Marlon 13
Brave Eagle 175
Breamer, Sylvia 217
Brenon, Herbert 41, 146
Brent, Evelyn 3, 19, 139–40, 165
Bridge of San Luis Rey, The (1929) 108
Bridge of San Luis Rey, The (1944) 116
Bridge of San Luis Rey, The (novel) 116
Britton, Barbara 19, 68
Broken Arrow 72
Broncho Billy 14, 20
Broncho Billy and the Greaser 14

Bronco 175, 184
Brooks, Rand 180
Brooks, Richard 143
Brower, Otto 101
Brown, Harry Joe 59, 220
Brown, John (Johnny) Mack 51, 59, 62, 66, 69, 80, 109, 112, 114–15, 128, 136, 143, 146, 148, 162–63, 165, 167, 174, 183, 201
Browne, Porter Emerson 219
Bruce, Nigel 62
Brulier, Nigel de 97
Bryson, Winifred 50
Buchman, Harold 102
Buck, Pearl S. 20
Buffalo Bill, Jr. 35
Buffington, Adele 64, 148
"Bullets and the Booby Trap" 182
Bullets for Bandits 148
Bullfighter and the Lady 143
Bullock, Walter 101
Burbridge, Betty 109, 112, 151, 173
Burgess, Dorothy 39, 51–52, 62, 146, 152, 195
"Buried Treasure" 177, 179
Burkett, James S. 107, 145
Burnette, Smiley 201
Burns, Walter Noble 64
Burt, Frederick 55
Busey, Gary 144
Busquets, Narciso 18
Byrd, Ralph 148
Caballero's Way, The (1914) xi, 12, 29–30, 32–33
"Caballero's Way, The" (O. Henry story) xiii, 2, 12, 23–24, 34, 191–95, 197, 199–200, 220, 227–28
Cabanne, Bill 141
Cabanne, W. Christy 33, 35, 139, 141, 143, 146
Cabiria 11
Cactus Kid, The 84
Cagney, James 70, 86
Cahan, George M. 180–81
Calderón de la Barca, Pedro 195
Calhoun, Alice 41
California I Love, The 184
California Romance, A 215
California Trail, The 63, 76
Calleia, Joseph 64, 68
Callejo, Cecilia 110
Call of the Coyote 63–64, 68
Camille 129
"Campaña de los Bilitos" 193
Campbell, Ben Nighthorse 227
Campbell, Martin 6, 223
Campeau, Frank 53
Candelaria, Nash 201, 221
Cansino, Rita 64
Cantrell, Don 29, 32–33
Captain Blood 58
Captain from Castile 106
Captain Kidd 129
Captain Thunder 60
Carewe, Edwin 215, 217, 219–20
Carey, Harry 35, 47, 101, 108, 127, 130, 139, 148, 164
Carey, Harry, Jr. 210
Carleton, Claire 209
Carlo, Val 68
Carlos V 20
Carlyle, Patrick 63–64, 68
Carmen (1915 film by Cecil B. DeMille) 220

Carmen (1915 film by Raoul Walsh) 220
Carmen (novel) 196, 220
Carmen (opera) 23, 220
Carpenter, Horace B. 63
Carr, Thomas 177
Carradine, David 20
Carranza, Venustiano 15, 31
Carrillo, Carlos Antonio 145
Carrillo, Edith 184
Carrillo, Leo viii, 2–3, 7, 15, 21, 31, 41, 51, 62, 64, 67–68, 70, 78, 90, 124, 139, 145–47, 149, 152, 154–55, 157, 163, 165, 169–70, 173–74, 176, 179–85 passim, 198, 202–3, 206, 209
Carrillo, Marie Antoinette 184
Carrillo, Ottie 184
Carroll, John 65, 108, 201
Carson City Kid, The 88
Carter, Ben 104, 106
Carter, Cathy 142
Caruso, David 190
Caruso, Enrico 220
Casablanca 58
Cason, John 177, 179, 183
Cassidy, Butch 20
Catching, Bill xiv, 15, 170–74, 176, 178–79, 180–83
"Cattle Quarantine" 173
"Celebrated Jumping Frog of Calaveras County, The" 180
Cervantes, Miguel de 8, 14
Chandler, Lane 176
Chaney, Lon 130
Chaplin, Charlie 14, 96
Charge of the Light Brigade, The 58
Chase, Stephen 162, 179
Cheney, J. Benton 163, 165, 170, 173, 177–78, 180, 184
Cherkose, Eddie 130
Chevalier, Maurice 220
Cheyenne xiv, 175, 184
Chicken Wagon Family 146
"Cinco de Mayo" 221
Cisco Kid, The (1931) ii, 51, 54–56, 70, 94, 99–100, 114
Cisco Kid, The (1942 radio series) 107
Cisco Kid, The (1946 radio series) 127
Cisco Kid, The (1994) 187, 190, 221, 223–24, 226–28
"Cisco Kid, The" (song by music group War) 221, 225
Cisco Kid, The (TV series) 91, 169–71, 176–77, 179, 181, 183–84
Cisco Kid and the Lady, The 92–95
Cisco Kid Returns, The 109, 111, 125, 147, 173, 185
Cisco Kid 2, El 214
Citizen Kane 130
Clansman, The 33
Clark, Steve 84, 174, 177
Clayton, Ethel 41
Clayton, Jane 66
Clements, Stanley xiv
Clooney, George 20
Close-Up: The Contract Director 98
Coates, Phyllis 176
Cobb, Edmund 162, 168, 177, 183
Coby, Fred 67
Cock-Eyed World, The 51

Cody, Bill 69, 174
Coffin, Tristram 130–31, 165, 174, 179
Cohen, Bennett 59, 139, 141
Cohn, Alfred A. 55
Cohn, Martin G. 109
Cohon, Barry 183
Colbert, Claudette 96, 146
Colección Latina 221
Coleman, Sara 22
Conan Doyle, Sir Arthur 180
Connery, Sean 1
Connors, Barry 63
Connors, Chuck 176
Conquistador 57, 102
Coogan, Jackie 180
Cooper, Gary 54, 59, 106
Cooper, Inez 126, 137
Cooper, Miriam 34
Copeland, Bobby 14
Corazón bandolero 9
Córdoba, Pedro de 102, 113, 140, 151
Corey, Wendell 143
Coronado, Sam 213, 221, 228
Corrado, Gino 60
Corrido de Gregorio Cortez, El 213
Corridos! Tales of Passion and Revolution 221
Cortés, Hernán 20
Cortez, Gregorio xi, 10, 20
Cortez, Ricardo 102–3, 119
Cortina, Juan 20
Costello, Don 104–5
Cotten, Joseph 96
Couderc, Pierre 60
Covered Wagon, The 35–36
Cowboy Cavalier, The 215
Cowboy G-Men 175–76, 180
Craig, James 66
Crawford, Joan 54, 130
Cregar, Laird 99
Crime, Inc. 146
Crisis 143
Crisp, Donald 215
Cromwell, John 59
Crosby, Bob 184
Crosland, Alan 60
Cross Fire 101
Cruz, Joe de la 3, 84
Cruz, Penélope 20
Cruz diablo 9
Cruze, James 35
Cry in the Dark, A 144
Cucaracha, La 16, 18
Cukor, George 51, 129
Cullison, Webster xi, 29, 33
Cummings, Irving 39–40, 51, 55, 70, 146
Cummings, Irving, Jr. 40
"Curse of Capistrano, The" 13
Curtis, Sandra R. 6
Curtiz, Michael 58, 129, 220
Custer's Last Fight 11
Dalton Gang, The 167
Dalya, Jacqueline 101–2
Dámaso Alonso, Luis Antonio 128
Damita, Lily 108
Dana, Viola 215
Danchak, Gary 190
Dangerously Yours 70
Daniels, Bebe 221
Darcel, Denise 106

Daring Adventurer, The 3, 185
Daring Caballero, The 151, 155, 185, 202, 206
Daring Rogue, The 185
Dark Hazard 71
Darvi, Bella 106
Darwin, Charles 192
Daughter of Don Q xi, 19
Daughter of Don Q (1946) 19
Davis, Bette 129
Davis, Eddie 109, 170–72, 177–79, 181–83
Davis, Gail 173, 179
Davis, Jerry 68
Davitt, Hal 60
Daw, Marjorie 219
Dawn Trail, The 139
Dax, Donna 113
Day, Doris 205
Day the Cisco Kid Shot John Wayne, The 201, 221
Dean, Eddie 127
DeCamp, Rosemary 72
Dekker, Albert 67
Del Río, Dolores 18, 34, 50, 67, 96, 146, 215, 221
Demarest, William 104
DeMario, Donna 140
DeMille, Cecil B. 11, 146, 220
DeMille, Katherine 139
De Normand, George 166
Depp, Johnny 20
Desert Hawk, The 129
Desperado 20, 223
Desprez, Frank 62
Destinn, Emmy 220
DeSylva, Brown & Henderson 53
Detour 68, 165
Devil Horse, The 101
Devil Is a Woman, The 70–71
Devil's Den, The 185
Devil with Women, A 221
Devine, Andy 67, 139
DeWitt, Jack 67–68, 145
Diamond from the Sky, The 39
"Diamond Necklace, The" 180
Díaz, Cameron 6
Díaz, Juan Martín (El Empecinado) 20
Díaz, Porfirio 15–17
Dickens, Charles 180
Dickey, Basil 65
Dieterle, William 129
Dietrich, Marlene 70–71
Dillon, Jack 53, 55
Dimples 71
Dinner at Eight 70
Diplomatic Courier 72
Disneyland 96
Dix, Richard 35, 54, 148
Dixon, Denver 63
Dixon, Thomas 33–34
Dodge City 58
Dolly Sisters, The 40
Don Amigo 185
Don Daredevil xi, 19
Don Daredevil Rides Again 14, 19
Donlevy, Brian 145
Don Q xi, 19
Don Q, Son of Zorro 19, 215
Don Quixote 1–3, 8, 191, 200, 228
Don Quixote de La Mancha 8, 14, 109
Don Ricardo Returns 67, 145

Dooley, Gerry 6
Doré, Gustave 8
"Double-Dyed Deceiver, A" 59, 66
Double Dynamite 40
Doucette, John 181
Douglas, Kirk 106, 143
Dove, Billie 215
Dove, The (1925 stage play) 67
Dove, The (1928) 67, 146, 152
Dracula's Daughter 114
Drake, Claudia 165
Drake, Oliver 60, 183
Dressed to Kill 51
Drew, Roland 215
Driftin' Kid, The 84
Dru, Joanne 143
Drums of the Desert 41
Duffy, Albert 101
Dumas, Alexandre 50
Duna, Steffi 64, 67, 146
Duncan, Kenne 174
Duncan, Renault 67–68, 145
Dunlap, Scott R. 127–30, 133, 138–39
Dunn, Bertha 30
Dunn, Eddie 29
Dunn, Emma 59, 66
Dunn, Herbert Stanley (also known as Stan Dunn, Arthur Dunn, or Herbert Stanley) 29–33
Dunn, Ralph 67
Dunning, John 127
Durango Kid, The 89
Duryea, George 58
Dwan, Allan 3
D. W. Griffith: An American Life 57
Dwyer, Ruth 215
Each Man in His Time 139
Earle, Edward 113
Eason, B. Reeves 35, 98–99, 101, 129, 139, 163
"East L.A." 221
East of Suez 51
Eastwood, Clint 180
Eddy, Nelson 31
Edeson, Robert 57
Elfego Baca: Six Gun Law 19
Elliott, Bill 67, 69, 148, 183, 201
Elliott, Robert 60
Ellis, Robert 99
Ellison, Jimmy 70, 129
Empecinado, El, *see* Díaz, Juan Martín
Enamorada 17–19
Engel, Samuel G. 97, 102, 104
English, John 65, 67, 108, 130
Ensminger, Robert 215
"Epidemic, The" 184
Errol, Leon 183–84
Escape From Hong Kong 146
Escobar, Pablo 20
Esparza, Phil 221
Espinosa Barrera, María de la Luz xi, 15
Estes, Athol 22
Evans, Evan 68
Everson, William K. 53, 56–57, 59–60, 62, 63–66 passim, 95, 107, 130–31, 133, 135, 139, 200
"Extradition Papers" 183
"Face of Death" 180
"Faded General, The" 181
Fads and Fancies 146

Fairall, Harry K. 215
Fairbanks, Douglas 3, 13, 19, 57, 60, 90, 139, 160, 215
Falcon Crest 106
"False Marriage" 173
Fanciulla del West, La 220
Farfan, Bob 171
Farnum, William 64
Farrar, Geraldine 220
Farrow, John 145
Fay, Frank 58, 220
Faye, Alice 40
Faye, Randall 62
"Fear" 179
Félix, María i, 17–19, 45, 48
Fernández, Emilio "El Indio" 3–4, 17–18, 143
Ferrer, José 143
Ferrero, Martín 186
Field, Virginia 95
Fields, Stanley 97–98
Fighting Code, The 183
Fighting Edge, The 219
Fighting Thru 130
Figueroa, Gabriel 17–18, 48
Filming of the West, The 62, 107, 130, 184
Fitzgerald, Michael G. 15
Fitzmaurice, George 220
Five of a Kind 71
Fix, Paul 61, 63, 74
Fleming, Eric 180
Fleming, Victor 41
Flint, Sam 150, 183
Flores, Iris 132–33
Flothow, Rudolph C. 163
Flower of Night 215
Flowers, Bess 215
Flynn, Emmett J. 215
Flynn, Errol 58, 70, 129, 190
Foelker, Adam 173
Fonda, Henry 146
Fontaine, Joan 96
Fool There Was, A 215, 219
Foran, Dick 67
Ford, Francis 11, 60, 98–99, 220
Ford, Glenn 106
Ford, Harrison 219
Ford, John 11, 14, 34–35, 38–39, 50, 52, 70, 98, 139, 146, 183, 210
"Foreign Agent" 177
Foster, Norman 67, 96–97, 146
Foster, Preston 139
Foulger, Byron 165, 168
Four Frightened People 146
Four Walls 130
Fowley, Douglas 165, 209
Fox, Wallace W. 147–48, 151, 162
Franco-Mexican War, *see* French Intervention
Frazer, Robert 63
Freeman, Mona 68
French Intervention 225–26
From Dusk till Dawn 20
Frontier Badmen 146
Front Page Detective 51
Frost, Sadie 188
Frost, Terry 131, 148, 177, 183
F Troop 184
Fugitive, The 146
Fung, Willie 97
Furies, The 143

Gable, Clark 31, 57
Galindo, Nacho 131, 133, 209
Galindo de Topete, Hermila 17
Gallian, Ketti 64
Galloping Kid, The 82
Garbo, Greta 215
García Riera, Emilio 9, 200, 219, 221
Garfield, John 143
Garner, James 184
Garnett, Tay 167
Garralaga, Martín 109, 111–12, 131–33, 135, 137, 145, 157–59, 185, 206
Garrett, Oliver H. P. 59
Garrett, Pat 193
Garrido, Joaquín 221
Gaucho Serenade 108
Gay Amigo, The 49, 124, 149–50, 185, 202
Gay Bandit of the Border, The 63
Gay Caballero, The (1932) 63, 76
Gay Caballero, The (1940) 101, 122, 156, 165
"Gay Caballero, The" (original story by Hal Davitt) 60
Gay Cavalier, The 131, 135, 161, 204, 209
Gay Desperado, The 64–65, 124
Gaynor, Janet 40
Gene Autry Show, The 162
Gentleman from Texas, The 115, 165
Gentlemen of the Press 96
Geraghty, Carmelita 60, 65
Gerald, Helen 131
Germonprez, Louis 171
Geronimo 55
Gerould, Katharine Fullerton 57, 102
Ghost Rider, The 148
"Ghost Town" 179
Gibson, Hoot 35, 82, 87, 98, 101, 109–110, 112, 139, 148
"Gift of the Magi, The" 21
Gilbert, John 128, 130, 215
Gill, Tom 63
Gilligan's Island 180, 184
Girl and the Gambler, The 67, 146
Girl from San Lorenzo, The 90, 157, 166–67, 170, 173, 185
"Girl from Topolopompo, The" 221
Girl of the Golden West 215, 217, 220
Girl of the Rio 67, 146, 221
Girls in Chains 51
Gish, Lillian 139
Giuliano, Salvatore 20
Glasser, Albert 21, 109, 147, 170, 172, 177
Gleason, Jackie 72, 184
"Gold, Death and Dynamite" 183
Golden Boy 94
Golden Gift, The 215
Golden Trail, The 174
Goldin, Pat 141
Gonzales Gonzales, José 183
González Ortega, Beatriz xi, 15
Good Bad Man, The 3
Goodwin, Harold 97
Goodwins, Leslie 72, 183–84
Gordon, C. Henry 63, 91–92
Gordon, Richard 113
Gortari, Rosaura 16
Gould, William 134–35
Grable, Betty 40, 99
Grand Canyon 174–75
Grandville, Marcelle 138

Grant, Cary 20, 31, 143
Grant, Kirby 148
Great Dictator, The 96
Great Gatsby, The 41
Greene, Angela 141
Green Hornet, The 96
Greppi, Michelle 190
Grey, Zane 35, 66, 69, 101
Griffith, D. W. 11, 19, 34, 43, 57, 139
Gross, Jack 171
Guízar, Tito 64, 66
Gun Packer 148
Guns and Fury 185
Gunsmoke 180–81, 183
Gunsmoke Trail 66
Hadley, Reed 65, 201
Hadley-García, George 10
Haig, Douglas 55
Hale, Alan 36
Half Angel 71
Hall, Jon 163
Hall, Lee "Red" 22, 24
Halton, Charles 155, 162
Hamilton, George 20
Hammett, Dashiell 51
Hammond, Victor 114
Hands Across the Border 108, 215
Hardy, Oliver 54
Harlow, Jean 31
Harrison, June 165
Hart, John 148, 179
Hart, William S. 35, 58, 114, 123, 183, 215
Hartigan, Pat 53
Harvey, Don C. 168
Harvey, Harry 34
Harvey, Paul 104
Hasbrouck, Olive 215
Hathaway, Henry 106
Hatton, Frederic and Fanny 41
Hatton, Raymond 3, 60, 67, 108, 127–28, 173, 180, 183, 220
Hawaiian Eye 176
Hawkey, Rock 65
Haycox, Ernest 68
Hayden, Russell 180
Hayek, Salma 20, 224
Hayes, George "Gabby" 164, 201, 205
Hayworth, Rita 64, 77
Healey, Myron 177, 179, 183
Hearn, Edward 62
Hecht, Ted 137
Heflin, Van 139
Heller in Pink Tights 51
Hell's Heroes 3, 14
Hemingway, Ernest 144, 192, 200
Henry, Bill 174, 179
Henry, O. (William Sydney Porter) xi, xiii, 2, 6, 9, 12, 21–24, 29, 33–34, 39, 53–55, 59, 130, 185, 191–97 passim, 199–200, 220, 224, 227–28
Henry, Orrin 22
"Here's Adventure! Here's Romance!" 186
Her Husband's Trademark 215
Herman, Albert 173–74, 176
Heyburn, Weldon 63
Hi, Gaucho! 64
"Hidden Valley" 179
High Chaparral, The 144
Hill, Doris 60

Hill, Jane 198
Hill, Riley 179
Hill, Robert F. 65
Hill Street Blues 186
Hillyer, Lambert 35, 41, 51, 58, 63, 67,
    114–15, 123, 165, 181–83, 220
History Is Made at Night 173
Hitchcock, Alfred 144
Hitler, Adolf 96
Hobsbawm, Eric 4–5
Hodgins, Earle 173, 177, 179, 183
Hoeffer, Norman 96
Hoffman, Otto 100
Hohl, Arthur 105
Holden, Gloria 114
Holden, William 2–3, 33, 94
Hollywood Corral 101, 107, 129, 131, 133,
    139, 151
Hollywood Western, The 60, 62–66 passim, 95,
    107, 130–31, 139
Holmes, Stuart 215
Holt, Jack 35
Holt, Tim 67–68, 146, 181
Hopalong Cassidy 173
Hopalong Cassidy Returns 165, 167
Hopkins, Anthony 6, 223
"Horseless Carriage" 183
Horton, Robert 68
Hot Pepper 51
Hough, Emerson 36
Howes, Reed 177, 182
Hoxie, Al 35
Hoxie, Jack 35, 101
Hubbard, Elbert 72
Hudman, Wes 168
Hudson, Rock 205
Huerta, Victoriano 15, 17
Hughes, Howard 33
Hughes, J. Anthony 95
Hughes, Mary Beth 99–100, 104–5, 174–75
Hull, Henry 91–92
Humberstone, H. Bruce 98–99
Humbert, George 63
Hume, Cyril 68
Humes, Fred 35
Hunt, Jay 215
Hunt, Marsha 66, 128
Hunter, Jeffrey 19
Huston, John 3, 143, 222
Huston, Walter 96, 143, 219, 222
Hutchins, Will 184
Hyland, Frances 95
*I Don't Have to Show You No Stinking
    Badges!* 222
Iglesias, Eugene 68
Iglesias, Norma 9
I Led Three Lives 169, 181
Ingram, Jack 173, 179–80, 183
In Old Arizona xi, 2–3, 14, 29, 33–34, 38–40,
    42, 49–51, 53–59 passim, 61–63, 70,
    92–93, 99–100, 114, 130, 146, 152, 192,
    195, 197, 200–201, 220–21
In Old Mexico 66
In Old New Mexico 112–13, 119, 147, 173
Inspector Morse 189
*Intolerance: Love's Struggle Throughout the
    Ages* 11
Invisible Ray, The 114
Irish Gringo, The 14, 64, 68

Iron Horse, The 11, 35
"Iron Mask, The" 182
Irwin, Boyd 142
Island in the Sky 71
Islands in the Stream 144
Isunza, Agustín 18
I Wake Up Screaming 99
Jaccard, Jacques 64
Jack Armstrong 148
Jackson, Helen Hunt 50
Jacobs, Harrison 165
James, Alan 65
James, Jesse 5
James, John 149
Janney, William 164
Jaquet, Frank 112, 162
Jarabe tapatío, El 219
Jefferson, L. V. 63
Jennings, Al 22
"Jewelry Store Fence" 177
Jiménez, Soledad xii, 52, 93
Jiménez y Muro, Dolores 17
Joaquín Murrieta xi
Johnny Rocco 138
Johnson, Ben 2
Johnson, Henry 64
Johnson, Julian 99
Johnston, J. W. 29
Johnstown Flood, The 40
Jolley, I. Stanford 176, 179, 183
Jones, Buck 35, 61–64, 67, 69, 74, 76, 114,
    118, 120, 127–28, 139, 148, 182–83
Jones, Jennifer 143
Jory, Victor 165
Journey into Fear 96
Juana Gallo 48
Juárez 129
Juárez, Benito 9, 187–88, 215, 224, 226–28
Judels, Charles 60, 97
Judge Roy Bean 173
"Juggler's Silver" 183
Julius Caesar 180
June Madness 215
Jungle Flight 145
Kane, Joseph 66
Kane, Michael 186
Karger, Maxwell 215
Karloff, Boris 19, 127, 130
Karlson, Phil 139
Kavanaugh, Frances 151
Kay, Edward J. 114, 130, 136–37
Kazan, Elia 13
Keene, Tom 58, 64, 69, 84, 101, 127
Keitel, Harvey 20
Keith, Donald 128
Kelly, Paul 71
Kendall, Cy 110
Kennedy, Arthur 68
Kennedy, Bill 176, 183
Kent, Travis 139
Kenyon, Doris 58
Kenyon, Gwen 112–13
Kerrigan, J. Warren 36
Kerry, Norman 65
Kid from Kansas, The 146
Kid from Texas, The 81
Kill Bill Volume I 20
Kill Bill Volume II 20
King, Bradley 61, 64

King, Henry 14, 106
King of the Bandits 141, 158, 203, 208
Kipling, Rudyard 219
Kipness, Sid 179
Kirkland, David 215
Kiss of Hate, The 130
Kiss the Blood off My Hands 96
Klein, Philip 63
Knight, Fuzzy 201
Knott, Lydia 114
Knowlden, Marilyn 55
Kohler, Fred 3, 61
Kohler, Fred, Jr. 150
Korngold, Erich Wolfgang 147
Kramer, Stanley 20
Krasne, Philip N. 8, 107, 109, 114, 145,
    147–48, 163, 169–71, 175
Kress, Harold 68
Krims, Milton 63
Kristofferson, Kris 192
Kruger, Otto 114
Lackteen, Frank 99–100
Ladd, Alan 68, 145
Lady Robinhood xi, 3, 19
Lady Robinhood (1925) 19
Laemmle, Edward 62–63
Lafitte, Jean 177
Lagunes, Teresa 188
Lake, Alice 215
L.A. Law 187
Lamb, Ande 183
Lamont, Charles 67
Lancaster, Burt 96, 106
Landers, Lew 50, 67, 146, 181–82
Landeta, Matilde 18
Landey, Clayton 189
Land of the Giants 181
Land of the Lawless 115, 165
Landres, Paul xiv, 139, 174–79 passim,
    181–83
Lane, Allan 108
Lane, Nora 54–55
Lane, Vicky 110
Lang, Harry 127
Langellier, John 29
Larkin, George 215
Larkin, John 101
La Rocque, Rod 58, 64, 220
LaRue, Frank 132
LaRue, Jack 139–40
LaRue, Lash 127, 188
Lasca of the Rio Grande xi, 19
Lasca of the Rio Grande (1931) 51, 62–63, 146,
    152
Lash, The 60
Last of the Mohicans, The 163
Last Outlaw, The 139
"Laughing Badman" 179–80
Laughton, Charles 129
Laurel, Stan 54
Laurenz, John 113
Law and Lead 65
Law of the Plainsman 175
Law of the Range, The 130
Lease, Rex 174
LeBorg, Reginald 68
Leeds, Herbert I. 70–72, 91–92, 95, 102, 104,
    146, 181–82, 184
Leen, Catherine 6

Legend of Zorro, The 6, 223
Leiber, Fritz 110
Leonard, David 151
Leonard, Robert Z. 215
Leslie, Nan 182–83
Lesser, Budd 68
Lester, Bill 168
Levine, Nat 58, 163
Levy, Herbert 71
Levy, Melvin 64
Lewis, George J. 63, 114–15, 125, 131, 133, 136
Lewis, Joseph H. 136
Lewis, Mitchell 58
Life and Legend of Wyatt Earp, The 175, 183
Life of General Villa, The 33–34
Life of Riley, The 72, 184
Lightning Carson Rides Again 65
Lillian Russell 146
Lindbergh, Charles 104, 192
Lindsay, Vachel 22
List, Christine 10
Litel, John 147–48
Little, Mickey 151
Liu, Lucy 20
Livingston, Robert 65, 67, 70, 108–9, 173, 181
Llano Kid, The 64, 66
Lloyd, Frank 61
Lloyd, Harold 173
Logan, Helen 99
Lombard, Carole 59
Lombardi, Ltd. 41, 146
London, Tom 97, 102, 104, 180
Lone Defender, The 58
"Lonely Runner, The" 144
Loner, The 96
Lone Ranger, The 7
Lone Ranger, The 175, 177, 179, 183
Lone Ranger Rides Again, The 67, 108, 117
Lone Star Vigilantes, The 148
Long, Hal 97
Long, Walter 58, 215
López Tarso, Ignacio 18
Loren, Sophia 20, 51
Loring, Teala 137, 159
Lorre, Peter 71
Los de abajo (book, 1915) 16–17
Los de abajo (1940) 17
"Lost City" 180
Lost in Space 181
Love Brand, The 219
Love Comes Along 221
Lovejoy, Frank 106
Lowe, Edmund ii, 50–51, 55, 59, 70, 99
Lowery, Robert 104
"Low Rider" 221
Loy, Myrna 58, 60, 220
Lubitsch, Ernst 106
Lucky Cisco Kid 98–99, 105, 150
Luden, Jack 69
Lugosi, Bela 130
Lupino, Ida 64, 124
Lyden, Pierce 177
MacDonald, Edmund 102
MacDonald, Kenneth 150, 183, 215
MacGregor, Jock 107
Maciel, David 9
Mack, Willard 67
MacLane, Barton 68

MacMurray, Fred 67
Madame Butterfly 220
Mademoiselle Midnight 215
Madero, Francisco I. 15–17
Magaloni, Honorato 188
Magers, Boyd 14
Mahoney, Jock 162
Malaya 143
Mallinson, Rory 143, 183
Maloney, Leo 163
Maltese Falcon, The 12
Malverde, Jesús 20
Mamoulian, Rouben 64–65
Man from God's Country 138
Man from Hell's River, The 40
Man from Texas, The 174
Mann, Anthony 143
Man of Quality, A 215
Mapes, Ted 180
Marcus, James 52, 59
Margo 64
Mariachi, El 20, 223
María Félix with Rifle i
Marín, Cheech 20, 187–88, 190, 221, 224–25, 227–28
Marín, Gloria 19
Maris, Mona 58–59, 63, 118, 220
Mark, Mel 175
Marked Trails 109
Mark of the Renegade 144
Mark of Zorro, The (1920) 14, 57, 61, 90
Mark of Zorro, The (1940) 9
Marquardt, Peter 223
Marqués, María Elena 18
Marshall, Herbert 146
Martí, José 70
Martin, Chris-Pin (Ysabel Ponciana Chris-Pin Martín Píaz) 55, 64, 70, 91–94 passim, 109, 139, 141, 145–46, 158–59, 201, 207–8, 216, 219
Martin, Richard 68
Martin, Ricky 198
Martin, Sobey 180–81
Martínez, Al 129
Martini, Nino 64, 124
Marx, Groucho 40
Mask of Zorro, The 6, 223
Mason, Leroy 97
Mason, Lesley 59
Maté, Rudolph 68
Mather, Jack 127
Matts, Frank 170
Mature, Victor 99
Maupassant, Guy de 180
Maverick 51, 175, 184
Maximilian, Emperor 9, 187, 215
Maxwell, Edwin 105
Maynard, Ken 35, 59–60, 69, 101, 112, 130, 220
Maynard, Kermit 177, 179, 183
Mayo, Frank 65
McCarthy, John P. 109–110
McCaughan, Charles 189
McCoy, Tim 35, 65, 69, 83, 101, 127, 130
McCulley, Johnston 13, 68, 114
McCullough, Philo 63
McDonald, Francis 114, 181
McDonald, Joseph 102
McKim, Robert 57

McLaglen, Victor 51, 63
Médico de su honra, El 195
Melford, George 215
Melton, Troy 170–73 passim, 178, 181–82
Men Are Such Fools 146
Men of the North 129
Merchant of Venice, The 70
Mérimée, Prosper 196, 220
Merton, John 65, 131, 177
Message to Garcia, A 71–72
Mexicali Kid, The 148
Mexicali Rose 66
Mexican Revolution of 1910 228
Mexican's Faith, The 14
Mexican War, The 196
Miami Vice 187
Middleton, Charles 58
Mildred Pierce 58
Miles, Betty 84
Milestone, Lewis 129
Miller, Don 56, 101, 107, 129, 131, 133, 139, 151
Miller, Walter 58, 60
Millionaire, The 181
Million Dollar Mystery, The 39
Minnelli, Vincente 143
Miranda, Carmen 113
Mister Antonio 146
Mister Dynamite 51
Mitchell, Yvette 34
Mix, Art 63
Mix, Ruth 86
Mix, Tom 35, 39, 49, 63, 69, 114, 215
Molieri, Lillian 115, 125
"Monkey Business" 179
Monroes, The 96
Monster Maker, The 147
Montalbán, Ricardo 144
Montana Rides! 68
Montenegro, Conchita 55, 63
Montgomery, George 95
Moore, Clayton 150, 174, 179
Moore, Colleen 41
Moore, Dennis 174, 179, 183
Moore, Pauline 88
Mora, Carl J. 9
Morales, Esai 222
Moran of the Lady Letty 215
Morante, Milburn 177
Moreland, Mantan 98
Moreno, Antonio 57–58
Morgan, Gene 60
Morgan, George 61
Morgan, Ralph 147
Morgan, Red 182
Morison, Patricia 102–3
Morris, Gordon 64
Morris, Stephen 165
Morris, William 176
Morrison, Chick 14
Morse, Terry 67–68
Mr. and Mrs. North 175
Mr. Wu 130
"Muerte del afamado Bilito" 193
Muir, Jean 139
Mulford, Clarence E. xiii
Muni, Paul 129
Muñoz, Rafael F. 7
Murieta 19

Murphy, Audie   81
Murray, Mae   215
Murray, Zon   174, 179–80, 183
Murrieta, Joaquín   xi–xii, 5–6, 9–10, 19–20, 43, 49–50, 60, 62, 64, 67, 74, 222–23
My Favorite Martian   184
Mysterious Mr. Wong, The   130
Mystery Mountain   101
Myton, Fred   65
"My Tonia"   220
"My Toreador Starts to Snore"   221
Nadel, William   24
Naish, J. Carrol   129, 147
Naked Dawn, The   68
Napier, Alan   180
Napoleon's Barber   38–39, 52
Napoleon III   190
Nareau, Bob   14
Natteford, Jack   63
Nava, Gregory   224
Negra Angustias, La (1950)   16
Negra Angustias, La (novella)   18
Negrete, Jorge   16, 19
Negri, Pola   215
Neill, Noel   173
Neill, Roy William   61–62
Nelson, Jack   63–64
Nelson, Willie   144
Neri, Margarita   xi, 15
Neumann, Harry   130
Neville, John Thomas   64
"New Evidence"   183
Newfield, Sam   65
Newill, James   107, 174
"New Lion of Sonora, The"   144
New York Nights   129
Niblo, Fred   57, 129
Nigh, William   130–31, 133, 136, 138–39, 143, 146
Nine Lives of Elfego Baca, The   19
Nixon, Marian   61
Nolan, Lloyd   68, 72
Norte, El   224, 227
"Not Guilty"   183
Novarro, Ramón   57
Nyby, Christian I.   186
NYPD Blue   190, 228
Oakley, Annie   179
Oakman, Wheeler   34
Oates, Warren   2
Obregón, Álvaro   15, 17
O'Brien, Dave   174
O'Brien, George   14, 40, 63, 69–70, 76–77, 183
O'Brien, Jack   14
O'Dasi, E. R.   65
Oklahoma Kid, The   86
Oland, Warner   215, 219
"Old Bum, The"   174
Olmos, Edward James   186–87, 197, 224
O'Malley of the Mounted   114
Once upon a Time in Mexico   20, 223–24
One Man Law   114–15, 120, 182–83
Orduña, Juan de   20
Orgullo de Palomar, El   219
Orozco, Pascual   15
Ortega, Margarita   xi, 16
Orth, Marion   57
Osborne, Bud   97, 110, 112, 177, 180
Our Betters   129

Outcasts of Poker Flat, The   139
Outlaw   68
Outlaw, The   33
Painted Stallion, The   108
"Paiute War, The"   176
Paiva, Néstor   140
Palange, Inez   102
Pals of the Silver Sage   174
"Pancho and the Pachyderm"   179
"Pancho and the Wolf Dog"   181
"Pancho Hostage"   176
"Pancho's Niece"   183
Pancho Villa & The Cisco Kid   213, 228
Pancho Villa Returns   78
Pandolfo, Tony   188
Panza, Sancho   3, 8, 200
Parker, Willard   68
Pascal, Ernest   64
Pat Garrett and Billy the Kid   192–93
Patterson, Hank   174, 179, 183
Patton   13
Patton, George S., Jr.   13
Payne, Bruce   188, 190
Payne, Edna   29
Peach, Kenneth   170, 172
Peckinpah, Sam   3
Pecos Dandy, The   63, 68
Pedro Esquirel and Dionecio Gonzales—Mexican Duel   200
Pegg, Vester   34
Penn, Leonard   167, 180, 183
Percival, Walter   61, 74
Pérez, Santiago   213
Perlman, Ron   188
Perrin, Jack   84
Pershing, John J. "Black Jack"   13
Peters, House, Jr.   180
Peters, Ralph   148
Petersalia, Patrick   64
Pettit, Arthur G.   219
Phantom Empire, The   101
Phantom of Santa Fe, The   64
Phelps, Lee   168
Phillips, Alex   18
Phillips, Lou Diamond   187, 222
"Phoney Heiress"   177
Pickard, John   180
Pickford, Lottie   39
Pickford, Mary   13
Pidgeon, Walter   143
Pinal, Silvia   18
Pirates of Monterey   142
Pitts, ZaSu   51
Plastic Age, The   128
Pony Post   174
Ponzanneli, Valentina   188
Porter, William Sydney, *see* Henry, O.
Posada, José Guadalupe   212
Powdersmoke Range   148
Powell, Dick   143
Power, Tyrone   9, 65, 72, 201
Power, Tyrone, Sr.   215
Power of Love, The   215
Prairie Gunsmoke   114
Prescott Kid, The   83
Pride and the Passion, The   20
Pride of Palomar   219
Prisoner of Shark Island, The   50
"Protective Association"   177–78, 182

Pryor, Roger   110
Puccini, Giacomo   220
Puig, Eva   103, 110
"Puppeteer, The"   179
Pyle, Denver   179
Quartaro, Nena   65
Queen Elizabeth   11
Quinn, Anthony   51, 139
Quo Vadis?   11
Racers, The   106
Rafferty, Frances   68
Ragan, Mike   176, 180
Raíces de sangre   224
Raiders of the Border   109
Raiders of the Lost Ark   188
Ramar of the Jungle   163, 175
Ramírez, Sara Estela   17
Ramírez Berg, Charles   9
Ramona   34
Ramona (1928)   50, 215
Ramona (1936)   14
Randall, Jack   66, 69, 127, 148
Range Rider, The   162, 182
Rangers of Fortune   67, 129
Rangers Take Over, The   174
"Ransom of Red Chief, The"   21
Rathbone, Basil   58, 62, 190
Rauh, Stanley   95
Rawhide   180–81
Ray, Joe   214, 221
Reagan, Ronald   216, 219
Realm of Unknowing   71
Rebellion   64
Red Desert   167
Reed, Donald   65
Reed, Marshall   176, 179, 183
Reed, Philip   68
Reed, Rod   185
Reed, Tom   62
Renaldo, Duncan   vii–viii, 2–3, 8, 21, 47, 49, 63–64, 67–68, 70, 90, 108, 111–12, 115, 117, 124–25, 128–30, 145–49 passim, 154–55, 157, 163, 165–66, 169–71, 173, 176, 181–86 passim, 201–3, 206, 209, 228
Renaldo, Tito   115
Renegade Ranger   77
"Renegade Son"   173
Renfrew of the Royal Mounted   174
Renfrew on the Great White Trail   174
Rennie, James   61
Return of the Cisco Kid, The   x, 66, 70, 79, 91, 94–95, 116, 121, 156
Return of the Durango Kid, The   89
Revere, Paul   189
Revier, Dorothy   61
Reward, The   143
Rey, Fernando   20
Rey, Florián   20
Reyes, Luis   10
Reynolds, Burt   190
Rich, Dick   99
Richards, Keith   179, 183
Richmond, Kane   91–92
"Ride Amigos Ride"   133
Ride On Vaquero   104–6, 207
"Ride On Vaquero" (song)   103
Riders of Death Valley   146
Riding the California Trail   126, 136–38, 159, 161

Rifleman, The 175–76
Rigby, Gordon 58, 60
Rin-Tin-Tin 58
Riordan, Marjorie 126, 132–33
Río Rita 221
Ríos, Guillermo 221
Rising Voices 129
Ritter, Tex 69, 114, 148, 174
Rivera, José Eustasio 197
Rivero, Julián 66
Roach, Hal 129
Road Agent 67
Roads of Destiny 59
Roberts, Lynne 102, 104
Robertson, Willard 55, 99–100
Robin and Marian 1
Robin Hood 1, 3, 5–6, 20–21, 24, 29, 106,
    131, 228
Robin Hood of El Dorado, The (1936) 19, 50,
    64, 74
Robinhood of El Dorado, The (novel) 64
Robin Hood of Monterey 139–41, 159, 208
Robinson, Edward G. 31, 54
Roche, Aurora 113
Rodríguez, Clara E. 9
Rodríguez, Ismael 18
Rodríguez, Robert 20, 44, 223
Roenning, Joachim 20
Rogers, Ginger 96
Rogers, Jean 97, 122
Rogers, Roy 66, 69, 85, 88, 171, 205
Rogers, Will 146
Rogue of the Rio Grande 60, 220
Rojas González, Francisco 18
Roland, Gilbert 2–3, 55, 63, 66–68, 106, 126,
    128–32 passim, 134–47 passim, 149,
    152–53, 158–59, 161, 185–86, 201, 203–4,
    208–9, 215, 220
Roland, Ruth 3, 19, 128, 215
Rollin' Home to Texas 174
Rollins, Hyder E. 22
Romance of the Rio Grande (1929) 54, 57, 102,
    221
Romance of the Rio Grande (1941) 103, 119,
    207
Romance Ranch 219
"Romany Caravan" 179
Romero, César 2, 8, 52, 70–72, 91–97 passim,
    99, 101–2, 105–6, 119, 121–22, 130, 144,
    181, 185, 201, 207
Rooney, Mickey 174
Roosevelt, Buddy 35, 215
Root, Wells 65
Rosen, Phil 112
Rose of the Golden West 220
Rose of the Rio Grande 109
Roth, Gene 143, 148
Roy, Rob (Robert Roy MacGregor) 5
Royal, Charles Francis 65
Rubie, Peter 10
Rubin, Daniel Nathan 59
Rudman, Marjorie 72
Rudman, Mark 71–72, 91
Ruggles, Wesley 33, 128, 215
Russell, Jane 40
Russell, Lillian 39
Russia House, The 144
"Rustling" 172
Rustling for Cupid 40

Ryan, Sheila 101–2, 122
Saga of Death Valley 66, 205
Sainpolis, John 60
Salinas, José Luis 185
"Salsa" 221
San Antonio Kid, The 108
Sánchez, Jaime 2–3
Sandberg, Espen 20
Santell, Alfred 57, 59
Santschi, Tom 53
Sanucci, Frank 114
Satan's Cradle 155, 163, 165, 167, 185, 203, 209
Savage, Ann 163, 165, 203
Sawyer, Joe 97, 99–101, 150
Scarlet Days 19, 43, 57
Scarlet River 101
Schaffner, Franklin J. 144
Schepisi, Fred 144
Schickel, Richard 57
Schneider, Nina & Herman 68
Schroeder, Doris 150
Schwarzenegger, Arnold 198
Scott, Fred 139
Scott, George C. 144
Scott, Randolph 129
Sea Hawk, The 58, 129
Secret of the Wastelands 167
Secret Service in Darkest Africa 108
Seeling, Charles R. 215
Seguín 227
Selander, Lesley 165
Señor Daredevil 219
77 Sunset Strip 176
Shadow of the Eagle 163
Shakespeare, William 70, 129
Sharpe, David 90, 148, 166, 168, 170, 173
Shaw, C. Montague 101–2
Sheehan, Winfield 38–39
Sheffield, Johnny 100, 167
Sheriff of Sundown 108
Sherman, George 66
Sherman, Harry 66, 171
Shores, Lynn 64
Shrek the Third 6
Shrek 2 6
Shrunken Head of Pancho Villa, The 221
Shumate, Harold 63
Si Adelita se fuera con otro 19
Sickner, William 114
Side Streets 71
Silva, Héctor i
Silverheels, Jay 174
Silver Raiders 162
Silver Trails 143
Silvera, Frank 144
Sinatra, Frank 20, 40
Singer Jim McKee 215
Singing Sheriff, The 184
Sky King 175
"Sleeping Gas" 177
Smith, Clifford 215
Smith, Sharon 110
Smith, Wallace 58
Smits, Jimmy 187, 190, 221, 223, 225–26, 228
Soldadera, La 16, 18
Soldiers of Fortune 175
Sondergaard, Gale 66
"Song of the Bandoleros" 220
Song of the Caballero 59–60, 220

"Song of the Rurales" 221
Son of His Father, A 41
Sons of the Pioneers 171
Sorin, Louis 107
South of Monterey 126, 132–33, 158, 204
South of the Border 108–9
South of the Rio Grande (1932) 63, 114, 118
South of the Rio Grande (1945) 114–15, 123,
    125, 157, 181
Sparling, Elliot 215
Sper, Norman 60
Sperling, Milton 91
Sports Album 169
Sports Illustrated 128
Springsteen, Bruce 225
Square Deal Sanderson 114
Squaw Man, The 11
Stack, Robert 143
"Stage Station" 68
Stand and Deliver 227
Stanley, Forrest 219
Stanwyck, Barbara 143, 220
Starrett, Charles 69, 89, 167
Star Wars 188
State Penitentiary 50
Steck, H. Tipton 34
Steele, Bob 35, 66, 69, 87, 109–110, 148
Steinbeck, John 13
Steiner, Max 147
Sterling, Robert 101–2, 122
Stevens, Charles 55, 63, 114
Stevenson, Robert Louis 180
Stewart, James 72, 143
Stewart, Peggy 173, 180
Stewart, Roy 51
Stirling, Linda 20, 48
St. John, Betta 68
Stoddard, Lothrop 192
"Stolen Bonds" 182
Stolen Jools, The 54
Stoneking, Marion 33
Storm, Jerome 215
Story Theater 180
Strange, Glenn 84, 135, 183
"Strictly Business" 58
Stuart, Gloria 71
Suez 101
Sugarfoot 184
Sundance Kid 20
Sundown on the Prairie 174
Sundown Rider, The 114
Surfside 6 184
Sutton, Paul 104–5
Swanson, Gloria 215
Sword of the Avenger 145
Take Me Back to Oklahoma 174
Talmadge, Norma 67, 129, 146, 152
"Tangled Trails" 184
Tarantino, Quentin 20
Tarshis, Harold 68
Tashman, Lilyan 51
Taylor, Estelle 215
Taylor, Forrest 173, 179
Taylor, Kent 175
Teatro Campesino, El 186, 221
Temple, Shirley 40, 70
Terry, Robert 65
Texan, The 59, 66
Texas Bad Man, The 49, 63

Texas Rangers 225
That Lady in Ermine 106
Thin Man, The 70
Thomerson, Tim 188
Thompson, William C. 64
Thomson, Fred 215
Thomson, Kenneth 63
Thorpe, Richard 58, 68, 143, 215, 219
Those Who Dance 41
Three Bad Men 14
3 Godfathers 210
Three Mesquiteers, The 173, 181
Three Musketeers, The 160
Three Word Brand 114
Thunder 130
Thunder Bay 143
Thundercloud, Chief 67, 108
Thunder Trail 66, 128–29, 153
Thurman, Uma 20
Tia Juana Kid, The 64, 68
Tiger Woman, The 108
Tigre de Yautepec, El 9
Timber 146
Time Tunnel, The 181
Tinling, James 64
Tiomkin, Dmitri 147
Toler, Sidney 71
Toll Gate, The 114, 123
Tonto Kid, The 86
Topper 175
Top Sergeant 146
Torrence, Ernest 108
Torres, Raquel 58, 220
Townley, Jack 61
Tracy, Spencer 143
Trader Horn 47, 108
Trapped in Tia Juana 148
Treadwell, Laura 141
Treasure of the Sierra Madre, The 3, 199, 222
Treviño, Jesús Salvador 224
Trouble in Sundown 183
"Trouble in Tonopah" 183
Tuchock, Wanda 66
Turich, Felipe 136
Turner, Lana 143
Turner, Ted 186
Tuska, Jon 8, 53, 60, 62, 98, 107, 109, 130, 133, 145–47, 184, 200
Twain, Mark 180
Twilight on the Trail 172
Twist, John 38
Two Gun Caballero 63–64
Two Gun Justice 65
"Two-Gun Man" 58
Two Years Before the Mast 145
Tyler, Tom 35, 69, 109, 176
Ulmer, Edgar G. 51, 68, 165
Uncle Tom's Cabin 39
Under a Texas Moon 58, 220
Under the Pampas Moon 64, 75
Under the Tonto Rim 181
Under Two Flags 101
Unger, Maurice 171–72, 176–79, 181
United States Marshal 181
Up in Smoke 187
Urrea, Teresita xi, 20
Urueta, Chano 3, 17, 19
Utah Kid, The 87
Valdez, Daniel 186–88

Valdez, Luis 186, 190–91, 197, 221–28 passim
Valdez, Marisol 188
Valens, Ritchie 187, 222
Valentina, La 16
Valentino, Rudolph 57, 60, 70, 112, 215
Valez, Kippee 162
Valiant Hombre, The 147–48, 154
Vámonos con Pancho Villa 7, 9
"Vampire, The" 219
Vanishing Frontier, The 112
Varconi, Victor 60–61
Variable Harvest, A 60
Vásquez, Tiburcio xi, 20, 221–22
Vélez, Lupe 184
Venable, Evelyn 99–100
Vengeance of the West 67
Venturini, Edward D. 66
Vera Cruz 106
Vidor, King 59, 80
Vigilante, The 148
"Vigilante Story" 179
Villa, Buddy 222
Villa, Francisco "Pancho" xi, 5, 7, 10, 12–16 passim, 19, 31–34 passim, 128, 228
Viva Cisco Kid 96
Viva Zapata! 13
von Eltz, Theodor 59
von Sternberg, Josef 70
Voyage to the Bottom of the Sea 181
Wagon Tracks 114
Wakely, Jimmy 107, 114, 143, 167
Walker, Alexander 38–39
Walker, Clint xiv
Walk Proud 227
Waller, Eddy 91, 97, 183
Walsh, George 34, 215
Walsh, Raoul 14, 29, 33–34, 38–40, 50–52, 54, 70, 73, 139, 163, 200, 215, 220
Walt Disney Presents 143
War (rock group) 185–87, 221, 225
Warde, Anthony 111, 142, 203
Warner, Jack 71
"War of the Silver Kings" 51
Warren, Earl 146
Washburn, Bryant 215
Waterfront 175
"Water Rights" 174
Waters, John 41
"Water Toll" 177, 183
Watson, Minor 97
Watt, Nate 165
Wayne, John 66, 69, 73, 163, 210
Wayne, Richard 215
Weaver, Marjorie 95
Week-End Marriage 71
Wee Willie Winkie 70
Welles, Orson 96
Wellman, William A. 35, 50, 64
Wells, William K. 60
Werker, Alfred 63
West, Victor 68
Western Justice 66
Westward Ho 66
We Were Strangers 143
Whalen, Michael 71, 177, 182
What Price Glory 51
Whitaker, Slim 84
White, Gloria Ann 95
White, Lee "Lasses" 113, 148–49, 154

White, Stewart Edward 58
Wide Open Town 165
Wife, Husband, and Friend 70
Wild Bunch, The 2–3
Wilde, Oscar 180
Wilder, Thornton 116
Wildfire 39
Wiley, Jan 110, 125
Wilke, Bob 179
Wilkerson, Guy 174, 180
Williams, Big Boy 174
Williams, Bob 68
Williams, Earle 215
Williams, Guy 143
Williams, John 188
Willis, Norman 113
Wilson, Lois 36
Wilson, Whip 114, 162
Wind in the Willows, The 109
Window, The 39
Withers, Jane 71, 91
Witney, William 65, 67, 108, 130, 133, 144
Women of All Nations 51
Wood, Sam 67, 215
Woodbury, Joan 104
Woods, Donald 68
Woods, Harry 131–33, 158, 204
Wooley, Sheb 180
Woolrich, Cornell 99
Worden, Hank 97
Wray, Fay 59–61
Wyler, William 3, 14
Wyman, Jane 106
Yaconelli, Frank 67, 131, 133, 136, 138–39, 158–59
Yankee Madness 215
Yankee Señor, The 215, 219
Yankee Speed 215
Yellow Dust 148
Yellow Streak, A 130
Yepes, George 44
Yesterday's Newsreel 169
Yost, Robert 66
"Yo te adoro" 221
You Never Know 215
Young, Clarence Upson 67, 136
Young, Loretta 14, 70
Young, Robert M. 224
Young Man of Manhattan 96
Young Mr. Lincoln 183
Young Rajah, The 112
Your Show Time 180
Yule, Joseph, Jr. 174
Zander the Great 219
Zapata, Emiliano xi, 10, 13–17 passim, 19
Zapata, Eufemio 14
Zapata's Messengers 211
Zeta-Jones, Catherine 6, 223
Ziv, Frederick 169, 171–72, 176–77, 179–81
Zoot Suit (1978 play) 186, 197, 222
Zoot Suit (1981 film) 187, 197, 225, 227
Zorro xi, 3, 6, 9–10, 13–15, 19–20, 74, 89, 96, 129, 144, 160, 200–201, 223
Zorro (novel) 6
Zorro, the Gay Blade 20
Zorro de Jalisco, El 9
Zorro Rides Again 65, 90, 108
Zorro's Black Whip 20, 48
Zorro's Fighting Legion 65, 130, 133, 188–89